STATE OF ISRAEL
DS132 .G65

D0883505

THE STATE OF ISRAEL IN JEWISH
PUBLIC THOUGHT

Also by Yosef Gorny

ZIONISM AND THE ARABS, 1882–1948: A Study of Ideology

FROM ROSH PINA AND DEGANIA TO DEMONA: A History of Constructive Zionism

THE BRITISH LABOUR MOVEMENT AND ZIONISM, 1917–1948

The State of Israel in Jewish Public Thought

The Quest for Collective Identity

Yosef Gorny
Professor
Tel Aviv University, Israel

Foreword by
Professor Michael A. Meyer

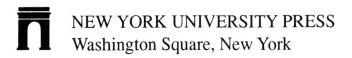 NEW YORK UNIVERSITY PRESS
Washington Square, New York

Riverside Community College
Library
4800 Magnolia Avenue
Riverside, California 92506

OCT '94

© Yosef Gorny 1994

DS132 .G6513 1994
Gorni, Yosef.
The state of Israel in
Jewish public thought : the
quest for collective
identity

assistance
from Tel Aviv University in the publication of this book.

Library of Congress Cataloging-in-Publication Data
Gorny, Yosef.
[Hipus ahar ha–zehut ha–le umit.   English]
The state of Israel in Jewish public thought : the quest for
collective identity / Yosef Gorny.
p.   cm.
Includes bibliographical references and index.
ISBN 0–8147–3055–8
1. Israel and the diaspora.   2. Jews—Identity.   3. Zionism.
I. Title.
DS132.G6513   1994
956.94—dc20   93–27378
                                                      CIP

Printed in Great Britain

With the memory of my parents,
Hanna and Raphael

Contents

Foreword

Michael A. Meyer

The establishment of the State of Israel in 1948 was at once the Zionist movement's greatest triumph and the beginning of an ongoing crisis of self-doubt. Its
principal goal achieved, Zionism could have ceased to exist, as did the movement
for women's suffrage in the United States with the passage of the Nineteenth
Amendment. Indeed, some Jewish leaders quickly argued that its historical mission was complete; its continued existence served no useful purpose. For American Jewry as a whole, which had emerged after the Holocaust as the largest
Jewish community and chief representative of the Jewish Diaspora, the transformation of Palestinian Jewry into an independent political entity immediately
made their relationship highly problematic.

The initial questions were political ones. Would Israeli leadership be entitled to
interfere in American Jewish affairs and vice versa? Was American Jewish support
of a sovereign state to be construed as dual loyalty? But the more basic issue,
which struck at the heart of Diaspora Jewish identity, concerned the role that Israel
would now play in defining American Judaism. Would American Jews, at least in
part, henceforth necessarily identify themselves as Jews in terms of their relationship to the Jewish state? And could this new relationship be termed a new Zionism, one hereafter no longer directed toward a well-defined political goal, but
descriptive of an Israel-centered Jewish orientation?

The Jewish citizens of the state, now called 'Israelis', began to wonder whether
their new self-designation did not supplant the old one of 'Jew', at least for those
among them who no longer practiced the Jewish faith. A small fraction sought to
return to the autochthonous culture of ancient times, disowned Diaspora Jewish
history, and purposefully set Israelis wholly apart from Jews living outside the
land. Others recognized Diaspora Jewry only as a valuable reservoir of immigration, negating its actual and potential cultural significance. They argued that Jews
could preserve themselves as a distinct cultural entity only in their own land,
where they were free of assimilatory pressures. If Jews continued to live elsewhere, that was because they had made the conscious or unconscious choice to
prefer the comforts of a familiar landscape over the anxiety-laden prospect of
becoming Israelis, and they were prepared to pay the inevitable price in terms of
their Jewishness.

To be sure, most Israelis have been far more uncertain and ambivalent about
their relation to Diaspora Jewry. The migration of hundreds of thousands of
Israelis to the United States has dwarfed the few thousand American Jews who
have made *aliyah* (migrated to Israel). In no small measure, it has been their need

to resist this temptation that has led Israelis to widespread negation of Diaspora Jewish existence as beset by the twin forces of anti-Semitism and assimilation. Only in their own state, Israelis have argued in self-justification, could Jews live 'normal' lives as Jews. They have understood their community, consisting of about four million Jews today, to stand at the center of contemporary Jewish history. Unlike the five and a half million Jews of the United States, their Jewishness, because embedded in an independent national culture, could not be peripheral or residual, as it was for the Diaspora, where identity was necessary shaped by non-Jewish influences.

Yet Israel has not, in fact, produced an integral Jewish culture. Observant Jews who live there place religion at the center and argue for its rightful influence on national life and even government. Secularists either fall back on historically continuous, but selectively chosen and secularized ethical and literary traditions (following the turn-of-the-century Zionist cultural thinker Ahad ha-Am), or they make do with more shallow cultural roots sunk into the Hebrew revival of the last century. Whereas religious Israeli Jews have the bond of their faith to unite them with similarly religious Jews in the Diaspora, secular Israelis have progressively less in common with Jews who do not share their national Israeli experience. The unifying memories of common origin in Eastern Europe have dimmed and the large numbers of Israelis of Near Eastern and African origin do not possess these memories at all. Not surprisingly, the two Jewries seem to be drifting apart.

For American Jews, the establishment of the Israeli state fundamentally altered their self-perception as Jews. They had witnessed the return of their people to its land and the re-creation of Jewish sovereignty after two millenia. Yet they chose not to participate in that return themselves. Working for the establishment of the state in the years after the Holocaust had been justified as procuring a secure refuge for its survivors and for Jewish communities suffering persecution in Arab lands. But once that state came into existence, its presence raised the unavoidable question of how it was related to a Jewry that needed no refuge either then or in the foreseeable future. As Israel still required the material and political support of American Jews, it remained possible to see the relationship as continuing to be principally philanthropic. Zionism became 'pro-Israelism', defined as concern for the welfare of fellow Jews in Israel and for their geographically distant enterprise. Such support, indeed, became the minimal litmus test of Jewish identification. One could be a religious believer or unbeliever, affiliated or unaffiliated with Jewish organizations, but one could not reject concern for Israel's well-being and still claim recognition from the community as a positive Jew. Most American Jews thus chose to let it go at accepting responsibility for Israel's security and economic success. But the more thoughtful among them sought to analyze the relationship and formulate its ideology. They have tried to define the role Israel plays, not only in organized American Jewish life, but in the individual Jewish identities of American Jews.

Just as among Israelis the Jewishness factor in their personal identities varies greatly, so among American Jews does the Israeli factor differ. Some have shown disinterest in the task of creating cultural bridges and restricted the relationship to the political sphere. For them the Israeli component of their Jewishness has consisted of trying to strengthen Israel against its enemies. For Orthodox Jews, it has been less the secular state and its essentially secular culture that has mattered than Israeli religious institutions and, for some, the possibility that Jewish sovereignty may represent the beginning of a messianic redemption that will lead from democracy on to theocracy.

The relationship of most American Jews to Israel, however, is not purely political or confined to religious concerns. For them the state is the flagship of the people to which they belong. Their Jewish identity is as much ethnic as religious, and their religious expression of that identity as much as affirmation of their peoplehood and the importance they attribute to preserving it as it is an expression of religious faith. American Jews visit Israel, teach their children about it, and celebrate its Independence Day because these acts express their own inner Jewishness. Yet they also recognize that Jewishness grounded in identification with Israel is a vicarious identity, emanating from a Middle Eastern country where they do not live.

For close to fifty years now, American Jews have been debating what the State of Israel means for their collective and individual identities as Jews. A few have retained the traditional notion of exile (*galut*) or reinterpreted it; most have discarded it in favour of a less oppressive term like 'dispersion' (*golah* or *tefutzah*). Given the profound importance of the relationship with Israel, an ongoing debate has raged over its shape. Is Israel the center and the Diaspora the periphery? Or are American and Israeli Jewry best understood as the two foci of an ellipse that constitutes the Jewish people? And how is world Jewry to express its collective will? Should it be through an international body representative of the people as a super-territorial entity or within the framework of world Zionism, and hence centered on the State of Israel? These definitional and organizational issues raise others about the right of American Jews to influence the religious and social structure of Israel, and even its foreign policy – and of Israel to regard itself as the custodian of Jewish interests everywhere.

Such questions have stood at the center of all dialogue between American and Israeli Jews. They have created an ongoing, variegated, and sometimes acrimonious conversation. It is the merit and novelty of Yosef Gorny's book that he allows us to listen in on that discussion as it is conducted in the public sphere by the two sides. Nearly all of the important intellectuals, writers, scholars and politicians who have dealt with his subject appear on these pages, their views set against the historical events which have helped to shape them. The author, as analytic historian, provides us with a framework for understanding what we hear, setting out categories for differentiating fundamental differences in ideology. Only at the end does he speak for himself, becoming an independent participant who has his own views to present. Yosef Gorny has not despaired of the Zionist enterprise despite the problems of which he is so well aware. Zionism – seen as a rebellion against the easier path of assimilation and normality – can, to his mind, still play a vital role in Jewish life. Whether or not they agree with his views, Jewish readers, after listening to the discussion, have no choice but to ask themselves where they now stand and whether Zionism can, in fact, hold together a very divided people.

Acknowledgments

This book is not a historical research in the usual and the strict sense. It does not analyze a process which has come to an end, or describe a past event. Its concern is the continuous developing process of the Jewish collective consciousness since the Holocaust and the rise of the State of Israel until the present time. Hence, a historical perspective and an evaluation of this process is still demanded. Moreover, the closer the research approached our decade the more significant became my own personal involvement with the subject. In that sense, this book is an intellectual discourse of two generations with whom and among whom I have lived and still live.

Since the concern is with the collective mind of my generation, many personalities, including friends and colleagues, fill this book with their presence. If I did not always understand them correctly or missed some of their important writings, it was because of the plenitude of material and not from lack of appreciation.

In the years I spent on this research and while writing the book I was fortunate to be supported by institutions and friends. First of all, the TelAviv University and its faculty of Humanities; the Institute for Research in Zionism; the Israel Democracy Institute in Jerusalem.

On the personal level, I am indebted to Professor Itamar Rabinowitz, former Rector of TelAviv University; to Professor Anita Shapira, Dean of Humanities; to Professor Daniel Carpi and Dr Ronald Zweig, heads of the Institute for Research in Zionism. I wish to thank as well Dr Arye Carmon, Head of the Israel Democracy Institute; Professor Aryeh Kasher of the School of Jewish Studies; Mr Simha Diniz, President of the World Zionist Organization; and Mr Amos Yovel.

I owe special gratitude to Professor Paul Ritterband and Professor Michael Meyer for their concern and help. I am also thankful to Mr Niko Pfund of New York University Press, and Mr Tim Farmiloe of Macmillan, for their active support; to Ms Giovanna Davitti for the valuable assistance that she provided, and Ms Anne Rafique for the accurate copy-editing. Lastly I have to thank Mrs Chaya Galai for her gifted work with the translation.

Finally, this book would not have come to completion without the devoted help of my wife Geulah, who never lost patience and always gave plenty of encouragement.

The work is not upon thee to finish
nor art thou free to desist from it.

Rabbi Tarfon, Mishna Avot

Introduction

Over the last hundred years the historical destiny of the Jewish people has been determined by three processes. The first was the steady rise of European anti-Semitism which led inexorably to the horrors of the Holocaust; the second was the Jewish part in the general immigration to the United States, which has created the largest community in the Diaspora; the third process was the constructive and political efforts of the Zionist movement which brought about the birth of the Jewish state. The Holocaust spelled the end of a major epoch in Jewish history. Ever since, everything that European Jewry had been as a national entity and a cultural and intellectual phenomenon has influenced Jewish history only by its absence; whereas the new Jewish centers which arose in the United States and in Palestine were to shape Jewish life and its future through the social and cultural forces operating within each of them and through the relationship between them. The separate development in each of them, and the ties binding them, differences and even conflicts notwithstanding, constitute a unique historical phenomenon.

This phenomenon, unparalleled in history, has fascinated Jewish intellectuals in both countries, who have tried to shape it as well as interpreting it. To what extent intellectuals can influence the course of history is a question that we may well ask with regard to the *philosophes* of the eighteenth century, the Russian intelligentsia of the nineteenth, the ideologues of the socialist movements right up to the liberal and neo-conservative philosophers of our day. What is clear, however, is that whatever the impact of intellectuals in world history, in modern Jewish history they have undoubtedly enjoyed a special status. Just because of the absence of political sovereignty and the institutions of statehood and because of the unique social structure of Jewish society with its amorphous class divisions Jewish intellectuals often had a significant influence on social developments. They formulated the various patterns of integration in their countries, they accelerated the modernization of the Jewish society and it was they who founded the Jewish labour movement and endowed the Zionist interpretation of the Jewish national movement with its main thrust – the return to Zion. In the past two generations, intellectuals have played an important role in crystallizing a suitable conceptual approach which could afford an explanation and ideological formulae to explain and consolidate the relations between the two sectors of the Jewish people.

The theme of this book is Jewish public thought concerning the identity and essence of the Jewish people from the Holocaust and the establishment of the State of Israel up to the present day. As regards the singularity of Jewish history this issue is yet another link in the chain of Jewish thought which extends from its origins in the Bible through the Mishnah and the Talmud, through medieval theology right up to the new religious and secular trends in the Jewish thought of the last two centuries. In this period, as a result of the internal and external processes which had transformed traditional Jewish society the question of identity became the subject of controversy. It was raised in the National Convention at the outset of the French Revolution; Napoleon presented it bluntly to the Assembly of Jewish Notables in Paris; it was the focus of the struggle of the Maskilim for emancipation in Central and Eastern Europe and was part and parcel of the religious outlook of the Reform movement. It was an integral part of the ideology of Jewish socialism, and the core of Jewish national thought, particularly of Zionism, finally becoming the overriding cardinal concern in the wake of the catastrophic massacre of European Jewry and the Zionist movement's astounding feat of establishing a Jewish state.

The number and variety of public bodies and schools of thought which have concerned themselves with the question of Jewish self-identity, indicate that the problem goes beyond that of national self-determination, which has been the goal of a number of European peoples ever since the French Revolution. It pinpoints the problematics of modern Jewry compared to other peoples. The latter based their demand for rights on their identity while the Jews had first to clarify their identity in order to know which rights to demand.

Jewish public thought in the past two generations is thus different in several ways from that of the period extending from the Emancipation to the Second World War. The two periods are separated by the yawning chasm of the Holocaust and the watershed of the establishment of a Jewish state. The earlier witnessed accelerated modernization processes which undermined and gradually eroded the all-encompassing nature of traditional Jewish society, based as it was on religious law, while the present age has confronted Jews with an almost totally new reality, born out of national tragedy and revolution. The Jews are no longer a European nation, since their two largest concentrations are in Israel and the United States. The masses no longer suffer from economic hardship and political pressures. And above all, and this is the crux of the change, the Jews, for the first time since they went to exile, have become free individuals, with the right and the possibility of choosing between remaining in their countries of birth and returning to their homeland in Israel.

Certain problems, previously academic, have been made concrete for contemporary intellectuals by these drastic changes. Whether the Jews are a religious community dispersed among other nations, a community of equal citizens of various countries with their own cultural and historical identity, or a nation with its own homeland are questions that have acquired political, socio-economic and cultural significance since the founding of the State of Israel. Moreover, since world Jewry is now crisscrossed by divisions between religious and secular Jews, between various religious streams, between groups of different cultural background, between those living in a sovereign Jewish state and those who are equal citizens of other countries, it is the link between Israel and the Diaspora which confers collective identity on this multiform entity. The Jews as a group have no other real identity. Identity, however, is not the same as essence and it is the question of the essence of contemporary Jewish identity that divides the various intellectual streams in Israel and the United States.

Our discussion is confined to these two Jewish centers for several reasons. Let us start by noting that this choice is not intended to imply that the two are of equal national status, this being one of the substantive issues in the debate between them. These are the largest, most dynamic and influential concentrations of Jews in the world. They represent two different and even polar manifestations of the revolution which the Jewish people has undergone in the past century. Jewish society in Israel is the greatest collective achievement in the annals of modern Jewry and perhaps throughout Jewish history. The standing of US Jewry is an expression of the greatest individualized success in the history of the Diaspora. The national collectivity in Israel has evolved and endured as a revolt against and a rebuttal of the hopes of the Emancipation, while the flourishing of Jewish individuality in the United States attests to its success. The success of Israel as a collective has transformed the existence of a unique Jewish entity into a natural phenomenon, whereas individual Jewish success in the United States is endangering the continued existence of the same Jewish entity and calls for extraordinary effort for preservation of its distinctiveness. The two communities enjoy power status in the Jewish domain and in the international arena, but the power of the Israeli concentration stems from its political sovereignty, while that of US Jews is related to their rights as citizens of their country, and the essential difference between these two sources of power will be discussed at greater length in the concluding section of this book. Apart from this the Jewish individual in the sovereign state of Israel exists in a world of collective needs, while the Jewish individual in the United States is free to accept this yoke or to reject it.

Yet, despite, and even because of this difference, close ties of mutual dependence have evolved between these two centers. Israeli Jewish sovereignty has need of the constant political and economic support of US Jewry, whereas American Jewish freedom with its concomitant threat to the continued existence of Judaism, which even the most optimistic of observers cannot ignore, needs the lifeline of this tie with Israel.

The relationship is not simple and one-dimensional. It generates mutual tension, and ebbs and flows under the influence of historical events, social developments and ideological trends in each of the countries. The way in which public thought in both countries has given expression to this relationship and its problems, and how it has tried to mold it is the subject of this book.

Discussing public thought means first and foremost defining its character. What it includes and what it doesn't. 'Public thought' is not theological speculation nor a philosophical system, though it includes elements of both. Nor are we dealing with ideological doctrine, although the debate is influenced by ideological concepts. In short, it is pluralistic literary and cultural phenomenon, an attempt to elucidate reality and to guide the course of its development on the basis of historical tradition, moral principles and religious faith. The instruments it employs to influence the public are mainly the press, to some degree the popular but mainly intellectual journals, as well as literature aimed at a wider public. It should also be emphasized that the participants in these debates are not only intellectuals and academics, but also public figures: leaders of religious movements and national organizations, party activists and Israeli cabinet ministers. In all these respects the ongoing debate is closely connected to shifting realities and constantly changing political considerations. Hence, it primarily reflects the public moods and trends among intellectual and political elites.

Therefore, 'public thought' is a pluralistic multiply-created phenomenon. It may be defined as the collective creation of individuals, and, in this particular case, Jewish individuals from different countries and cultures: America and Israel. It is very difficult to define to what extent 'public thought' influences 'public opinion', or how they interact. But there is no doubt that 'public thought' shapes the patterns of thought, principal concepts and spiritual symbols of the public mood which explain the political or social action, and provide their moral justification.

The book covers the period from the early forties to the second half of the eighties. The beginning is clearly demarcated since it is contemporaneous with the onset of the Holocaust and the commencement of the struggle for statehood. The end point, on the other hand, has been chosen more arbitrarily. I have assumed that the protest of American Jews against President Reagan's visit to the German military cemetery at Bitburg; the campaign of the World Jewish Congress against the election of Kurt Waldheim as President of Austria; and the shock experienced by both American and Israeli Jews following the exposure of the Pollard affair, are evidence of both the scope and the limits of Jewish power, and of the complexity of the relations between the two communities.

I have chosen to divide the forty-year period into four sections:

1942–50 – the major issue was whether the establishment of Israel had normalized Jewish existence.

1951–66 – the debate centered around the problem of whether, in the face of Israel's existence, the Jewish communities of the free countries could still be regarded as exiled.

1967–82 – the period commencing with the Six Day War, which was marked by a national renaissance in the Diaspora. The ensuing debate focused on the question of the essence of Jewish ethnicity in the pluralistic-democratic societies of the Diaspora.

1982–87 and onward – the debate has addressed itself to the question of whether Israel occupies a central position in the religious-ethnic experience of the Jewish people, or whether historical developments have created two centers, one in the United States and one in Israel. This raises the further question of whether

Diaspora Jewry enjoys equal status with the Jews of Israel in all that pertains to Jewish existence.

All four issues have been relevant in each period in varying intensity, influenced by such events as Israel's wars and social developments among Diaspora Jews. The issue of normalization is, perhaps, the most pervasive and intense of the four.

Since the book is constructed both chronologically and by theme, I have tried to go beyond the confines of the various movements and ideological frameworks of organized Jewish community life. Hence, I do not deal separately with the Reform, Conservative and Orthodox movements. This rule does not apply, however, to the Zionist movement in the second part of the book, since attitudes towards Zionism were the crux of the debate in that period. Above all, I have been careful not to draw too sharp a line between the perplexities of American Jews and Israelis, since the issue concerns them all. This common preoccupation stems from the subjective will of the Jews, which often runs counter to objective processes occurring in the two countries. In the course of the century-long historical process, since the First Aliyah to Palestine and the mass migration to the United States, these two societies have moved in different directions. Palestine was marked by a continuous process of intensification of Jewish national consciousness determined by the ideological and political decision to found a sovereign Jewish society; the protracted Jewish–Arab confrontation; the ethos and reality of the ingathering of the exiles; and the strengthening of the Orthodox movement after the Six Day War. At the same time, US Jewry was undergoing a three-stage process of social integration. First they joined enthusiastically in the trend towards an Anglo-Saxon oriented 'melting-pot'; a generation later, they adopted the ideology of pluralism, seeking to create an American culture which would maintain the traditional cultural heterogeneity of the immigrants. Since the sixties, there has emerged an ethnic outlook which sees American society as a federation of groups with singular historical and cultural traditions. According to this theory, the ethnic fabric is the expression of authentic Americanism. Whatever the differences between the three positions, they all advocate integration.

Consequently, the Jews of the United States and of Israel have experienced contrasting processes: crystallization of identity and national separatism versus intensified integration, in the ethnic sense.

This cultural process has been accompanied by a demographic development which, in the course of the next two generations, could change the numerical ratio between these two concentrations of Jews. In the past four decades the US Jewish population has grown by 15 per cent, from 5 000 000 in 1948 to 5 814 000 in 1986. In the same period the Jewish community in Israel has grown more than fivefold, from 630 000 in 1948 to close to three and a half million. This rate of expansion, extraordinary by any standards, is attributable, of course, to the mass immigration of the 1950s. There is however no explanation for the overall phenomenon. An examination of the 1966–86 period shows that the growth in Israel's population does not stem solely from mass immigration. In a period in which immigration decreased and emigration rose to the point of average balance between them, the number of Jews in Israel rose by 50 per cent from 2 334 000 in 1966 to approximately 3.5 million in 1989. In the same period US Jewry registered almost zero growth, from 5 720 000 in 1966 to 5 814 000 in 1986. At the end of the decade this tendency of zero growth population among the American Jews has continued. In 1990 their estimated number was 5 535 000, compared with which the Jewish population in Israel mounted to 3 946 700. In 1992 the Jewish population in Israel is 4 200 000. The demographic forecast for the year 2001 is 5 000 000 Jews in each of the two countries.

This zero population growth in the US, resulting from very low birthrates and a high rate of intermarriage, is reducing the proportion of Jews within the general population. In 1930, the percentage of Jews was 3.6 per cent, while fifty years later, in 1986, it was only 2.5 per cent. Without entering into the public debate between the pessimists who foresee a gloomy future for US Jewry and the optimists who discern positive phenomena which are injecting vitality into this community, one cannot totally dismiss the fear that the decrease in their relative weight and the numerical decline could undermine the ability of US Jews to withstand sweeping integrative processes.[1]

I have dwelt on the ideological-cultural and sociological-demographic processes in order to emphasize that the public debate on the search for group identity, which is the theme of this book, attests not only to the perplexities of intellectuals in the face of prevailing conditions but also to the desire to rebel against these very conditions.

Part I
The Jewish People
at the Historical Crossroads

1 The Tangle of Normalization, 1942–50

The debate on the question of Jewish group identity, which ensued in the United States after the tragic dimensions of the Holocaust had become known and the political struggle for a state commenced, was marked by paradox. Ostensibly, it could be argued that the destruction of the Jewish national center in Eastern and Central Europe and the renewal of territorial political independence in Palestine restored normality to Jewish existence. Now, the Jews like other nations had a sovereign country, while groups of their brethren enjoyed equal rights as citizens of free countries. On the other hand, this recognition of the possibility of achieving normalization, for the first time since the Jews had gone into exile, occurred at a time when they had undergone two unique national experiences which highlighted the abnormality of their existence. The tragedy of the Holocaust differed in scope and aim from the tragedy of other European peoples during the Second World War. Nor did the struggle for statehood resemble the wars of independence of other nations. In this context it should be pointed out that, in the period under discussion in this chapter, the Holocaust and the establishment of the state were accorded different weights in public thinking and discussion. The tragedy of the Holocaust stunned the Jewish people, leading many to conduct a national stock-taking. The lesson impelled Jewish leaders and organizations to harness themselves to aid activities and to the political struggle for their fellow Jews, but they were not drawn to tackle the ideological implications. Among the people with whom we are concerned in this work, its historical significance lay more in the realm of memory than in the national implications. In contrast, Zionism's political struggle and the establishment of Israel confronted this public with a constant challenge, irrespective of whether they rejected it or identified with it. In other words, the Jewish state transformed the problem of essence of Jewish existence into an existential question, in the national sense. The dilemmas raised at the beginning of the nineteenth century – whether Jewish self-identity was based on religion or nationality, whether their country of birth was a homeland or merely a place of residence, whether non-Jews were their compatriots or foreigners – questions which had once been of solely theoretical interest to the majority of Jews, now became pressing problems demanding an answer. The dividing line between the various outlooks was the attitude towards Zionism and the Jewish state rather than the evaluation of the historical significance of the Holocaust, although the debate on new Jewish identity was inseparably linked to both these events.

The central hypothesis of this book is that, due to these historical changes, Jewish intellectuals, both as individuals and as leaders of religious or political organizations, began to yearn for normalization and to believe in the possibility of achieving it, whether through clearcut ideological and political decisions or as the result of a lengthy and gradual process. There were three main schools of thought. The first advocated *general normalization*, as in non-Jewish society, and its proponents included secular intellectuals whose basic premise was denial of the existence of the Jewish problem, as well as thinkers, mostly rabbis, who saw Jewish existence exclusively in the religious non-national sense. The second approach can be defined as *singular normalization* – its advocates chose to replace exile by diaspora, and believed that the simultaneous existence of Jewish life in Israel and in the Diaspora was a repetition of the historic situation in the Second Temple period, and that the situation of US Jews resembled that of other ethnic minorities in American society. Ideologically speaking, most advocates of this approach were affiliated to modern religious movements, and included Zionist leaders whose non-Jewish intellectual world was closely linked to Anglo-Saxon culture.

The third school of thought, which may be denoted *Jewish normalization*, encompassed such diverse elements as the remnants of the Polish Bund, Yiddishist intellectuals and Zionists whose cultural outlook had been shaped in Eastern Europe. They shared the assumption that Jewish existence was primarily national and mainly secular, and a profound esteem for Yiddish culture as the expression of the national ethos of the Jewish people. Despite their disparate views on the historical standing of the Exile in the past and future, they perceived the Exile, after the establishment of Israel, as a normal Jewish phenomenon.

Though the differences between them were not always sufficiently clearly defined and internal alliances sometimes appeared paradoxical, these three schools of thought were alike in their attempt to confront the historical changes and to endow Jewish existence with significance appropriate to the new reality. This lent importance to the public character of the debate conducted within the Hebrew- and Yiddish-language Jewish press, which was undoubtedly followed by hundreds of thousands of readers.

GENERAL NORMALIZATION

In 1944, at the height of the tragic events which befell European Jewry, the editors of the *Contemporary Jewish Record* (published by the American Jewish Committee), initiated a discussion on the role of the young Jewish writer in contemporary American literature. The participants were eleven writers, poets, critics and academics, all under forty.[1] According to their own autobiographical sketches, it seems that by origin they covered the whole spectrum of Jewish experience in the United States. Their backgrounds ranged from assimilated, radically secular, socialist and reform to orthodox.

The editors posed two main questions: one concerned the link between Jewish origins and creativity; the other, more relevant to our study, was aimed at clarifying whether the resurgence of anti-Semitism had affected them as citizens of the United States and, if so, in what way. Underlying this question may have been the hope that the catastrophe of the Holocaust would bring these young people back into the Jewish fold, and arouse in them not only compassion for their fellow Jews but also a sense of responsibility towards them. The basis for this hope was the historical experience of the previous century, when anti-Semitic outbursts had generated renewed Jewish identification among many of those who had grown away from their religious and national heritage.

If this was in fact the secret hope of the editors, they must have been bitterly disappointed. Only one of the participants, the writer Albert Halper, declared unequivocally and emphatically that the tragedy of the Jews of Europe had affected his outlook and way of writing. He confessed that for the past fifteen years his only wish had been to become an American writer, and that he had not been concerned in the slightest with his Jewish origins. But since Hitler's rise to power, his views had changed. The cry of five million fellow Jews, suffering in ghettoes and concentration camps, haunted him and gave him no rest as he wrote. Halper felt it necessary to explain, almost apologetically, that he had not been affected by national hysteria and was not one of those Zionists who were occupied in convening meetings. Nor did he move among his non-Jewish friends as a peddler of Jewish woes. He had no doubt, however, that the catastrophe of his fellow Jews was his own personal tragedy as well, and had rendered him, as a Jew, more sensitive to the sufferings and plight of others. Only one other of the participants in the discussion asserted that the Holocaust had restored him to his Jewish origins, but he did not elaborate on this statement. As for the others, the Jewish tragedy did not appear to play a sufficiently important part in their lives to influence their attitudes towards their origins or their artistic efforts. Moreover, indigenous manifestations of anti-Semitism, which for many of them were part of childhood or adolescent experiences, were but suppressed or vague recollections.

Their alienation from Jewish suffering emanated not from denial of their origins, but from total lack of identification with the Jewishness with which they were familiar. Most of them denounced Jewish society as bourgeois, materialistic and superficial. Although some nursed warm childhood memories of home and of their Jewish milieu, they regarded secular Jewish life as lacking significance, and saw nothing singular in the suffering of Jews. For the poet Muriel Rukeyser, the Warsaw ghetto uprising recalled the struggle of the Spanish loyalists in Madrid. Howard Fast declared bluntly that, for him, there was no difference between a Jew and any other human being. Jewish suffering was the outcome of the rule of reactionary forces in society, and only its overthrow could end their plight as human beings.

The critic Alfred Kazin, declared that he had long since learned to accept the fact that he was a Jew, without participating in Jewish life and without playing a part in Jewish culture. Both he and others admired the figure of the historic Jew which emerged from biblical tales, and felt warmly towards the poor Jewish

masses of Eastern Europe. Jewish pioneering endeavors in Palestine aroused some
sympathy, not for Zionist reasons but out of admiration for social achievements.
Those who referred to Zionism usually condemned it as a nationalist and reactionary movement.

Because of this alienation from Jewish life and intellectual and ideological
detachment from the Jewish past, they were unmoved by assimilation, neither
advocating nor condemning it. As far as they were concerned, it was a natural
phenomenon, stemming from the social conditions under which Jews lived.

The attitudes which emerged from these statements, did not cause a furor,[2] possibly because the participants in the discussion, although their views were indubitably
shared by many others, were not part of the Jewish national and religious establishment. Hence, their opinions were of no public political significance. They were
merely more outspoken representatives of general information, in that they stressed
the insignificance of the Jewish problem. Another extreme example of the general
normalization school of thought was the outlook of the American Council for Judaism, whose members had seceded from the Reform movement due to the controversy on the latter's stand on the Zionist demand that post-war Palestine become a
Jewish political commonwealth. The majority of the Reform leaders and rabbis
tended to support this demand, while the minority vehemently opposed it. At the
beginning of 1942, the spiritual leader of the group, Rabbi Elmer Berger, delivered a
programmatic speech to the Jewish community of Flint.[3] In his address, which may
be considered as the ideological platform of the group, he sought to formulate a new
yet old approach to the nature of Judaism and its future in modern society.

He depicted the political controversy between the American Council for Judaism and the Zionist movement and its reform supporters as a historical confrontation between two Jewish outlooks: the religious view of Jewish life and the
political interpretation. There was a yawning gap between them, he held, related to
the question of whether Judaism, for its survival, required its own sovereign state.
Berger replied in the negative and cited two arguments to support his assertion.
First, he argued, Judaism, by nature, was anti-nationalist, and had won status and
influence throughout history only because of its universalist principles. The
second argument was historically based. The Jews, he said, had no reason to be
proud of those periods in their history when they had been a sovereign nation. The
reigns of David and Solomon were eras of moral turpitude. He was careful to
explain that his philosophy of history did not deny the historic and religious significance of Palestine for the Jews, but claimed that this served only to reinforce
his main hypothesis, namely that the unique character of Judaism lay not in
nationality but in the nature of the Jewish faith. Unlike most Reform rabbis,
Berger clung to the traditional view that the singularity of Judaism derived from
its universal religious values. These were not linked to a specific time or place and
could be transmitted from country to country and from era to era. It was for precisely this reason that the Jews had survived as a separate religious community,
while larger and stronger nations had vanished from the stage of history.

Consequently, Zionism, being a secular, political and separatist movement and seeking to nullify the singular nature of Jewish existence as a scattered religious community, was liable to bring about the final eradication of Judaism. It was for this reason, argued Berger, that even ultra-orthodox Judaism condemned Zionism, although he hastened to add that he could not accept its separatist religious reasons. Zionism, he asserted, expressed a pessimistic view of life stemming from loss of faith in the possibility of the progress of human society. This led him to one of the most paradoxical and distorted definitions of Zionism. He claimed that the Zionist conviction that there was no place for Jewish existence in the Diaspora constituted, in effect, a sanctioning and perpetuation of the barbaric theories of the fascists. Nor did he shrink from claiming that there was a certain similarity between the Nazi plan to separate the Jews from their surroundings by concentrating them in Madagascar and the separatist aspirations of the Zionists, who advocated territorial concentration in Palestine.

On the basis of these arguments, and the additional observation that Zionism was essentially anti-democratic, as witness its stand towards the Arab majority in Palestine, Berger concluded that the movement was disqualified from taking its place among the democratic powers fighting fascism.

This anti-nationalist outlook also determined the stand of the Council for Judaism on the Palestine question. Towards the end of the Second World War the Council proposed that Palestine be transformed into a democratic state in which all religions would enjoy equal rights. Since its leaders did not wish to ignore the plight of the Jewish refugees, and were aware that their immigration to the US would not be permitted, they demanded the abrogation of the 1939 White Paper and the opening of the gates of Palestine in accordance with its economic absorptive capacity.[4] It should be clarified here that the heads of the Council rejected the idea of a binational state as proposed by Judah Magnes because of their fear that this would constitute recognition in principle of Jewish nationalism and because they considered the proposal to be anti-democratic since it ran counter to the wishes of the Arab majority in Palestine. After the establishment of the Jewish state had, inter alia, also represented the political failure of the Council, Berger attempted to highlight the differences between the American Jewish community and the Jews of Israel. In an article published in 1948,[5] he demanded of US Jews that they choose between two irreconcilable alternatives: fallacious Jewish unity on a national basis, as advocated by the Zionists, and the true unity of the American people, of which the Jews were an organic part, living within it as a different religious group but not as a separate nation. Berger was not certain that the clash between these two outlooks was inevitable, but he was convinced that wherever they existed side by side, the individual could not achieve total identification with either. In other words, the anomalous Jewish situation would endure. Hence, separation was required in order to expedite the process of integration of the Jews, members of a different religious group, within pluralistic American society, where 'the Judaism of American Jews would then become as it should be: American

Judaism'. In a spirit of political realism, and because of his familiarity with the prevailing moods within the American Jewish community, which had greeted the establishment of Israel with enthusiasm, Berger did not object to US support for Israel. He claimed, however, that it should be proffered on the political rather than the Jewish plane. He was also ready to accept ties between the Jews of the two countries, but on an exclusively religious rather than a national basis.

Paradoxically enough, Elmer Berger might have been expected to welcome the Jewish state, since henceforth, so he believed, there was an increasing prospect that the normalization process of American Jews would be expedited. They would come to resemble American citizens of other faiths who extended assistance to their co-religionists in other countries. He did, in fact, accept the existence of the state, but at the same time stepped up his opposition to any attempt to perceive the Jews as a national minority in the United States. He stressed the difference between his own outlook and that which advocated parallel Jewish existence in two 'civilizations': the international Jewish and the American national realms.

Concurrently with the secular universal approach of the radical writers and the religious-universal approach of the Reform thinkers, a universalist-territorial theory was evolved in Palestine. Its main spokesmen were two charismatic figures: the poet Yonathan Ratosh and the Revisionist leader Hillel Kook, who had spent the war years in the United States on a mission for the Irgun Zvai Leumi. Due to the marginal political and public significance of this approach, I shall devote only a brief discussion to the relevant theories.

Ratosh, the intellectual progenitor and political leader of the Canaanites, drew a sharp dividing line between Judaism, grounded on religious faith unconnected to any particular country, and Hebraism, the expression of the process of consolidation of a new territorial nationalism in Palestine, encompassing all the inhabitants of the country irrespective of origin. As he wrote in his ideological essay 'Masa Pticha' in 1944, the future Palestinian state would be neither Jewish nor even Hebraic-Jewish, since '... Judaism has no need of a state and a state is not essential to its life, and it has several arguments to cite against any state or independence, for its homeland is the diaspora, and its life is the diaspora and its strength is the diaspora. This has been true since it came into being and will be until the end of time, and it has proved this clearly and explicitly for thousands of years, all its days'. In other words, the establishment of a Hebrew state in Palestine, totally detached from the Jewish past, is the expression of a normal situation, and any other attempt to create a synthesis between Judaism and sovereignty is doomed to failure and to swift ruination of the state. Ostensibly, Ratosh agreed with the radical outlook of the Zionists who rejected the Diaspora. But, in fact, there is a fundamental difference between the two viewpoints. They rejected the Diaspora in the name of the renaissance of Jewish nationalism in Palestine. For Zionist radicals of this type, the role of the state was to save Judaism. Ratosh, on the other hand, did not negate the Diaspora, but rather annulled it. The essence of Judaism, he argued, is exile and dispersal, and only thence does its vitality stem. He is not even ready to agree that it is exile which differentiates the Jews from all other nations. 'Jews and Judaism are not an extraordinary phenomenon in human history,' he says. '... Nor is the capacity for survival of a community in exile a uniquely Jewish phenomenon.'[6] And he cites, in support of his assertion, the Greeks in the Hellenistic era and the Persians in India or the contemporary German emigrants. In contrast to the Zionist outlook, therefore, Ratosh was not willing to acknowledge the special rights of the Jews, despite their dispersal throughout the world for two millenia and more, as a national phenomenon. Herein lies the profound dissimilarity between him and Zionist radicalism, although it too was marked by Canaanite undertones.

Ratosh's theories can be defined by the paradoxical phrase 'national universalism'. The logic of this phrase derives from the realities of the United States where a new nation was created out of immigrants from various countries, whose children assimilated into the common culture, and ceased to belong to the nationality of their parents. In this new nation the Jews, anxious to preserve their American-Jewish identity, were the exception. Ratosh was a proponent of the 'melting pot' concept, which he hoped to adapt to the future Hebrew state. One thing, however, is unclear in his rejection of the term 'American Jew'. If the term Jew represents nationalist feeling, he is correct according to his own logic. But if it merely represents religious faith, why should the combination be considered less feasible than American Protestant or American Catholic? After all, he himself argued that Judaism was only a religious community. In any event, in his territorial national outlook, his adherence to the national civil principles of the American constitution and his denial of the concept of exile with regard to the Jewish Diaspora, Ratosh was a proponent of universalist-national views.

Another example of national-political normalization is the views of Hillel Kook. The statement he published on behalf of the Hebrew Committee for Liberation of the People which he headed, was an example of how far radical political Zionism could go. Unlike Ratosh, Kook was not contemptuous and dismissive of the Jewish Diaspora. The reverse was true. He stressed the noble character of the cultural and moral concepts which went to make up the identity of the Jewish people in the religious sense. But, in accordance with the accepted criteria of the progressive world, he sought to distinguish between the 'Hebrew nation' as a political-territorial entity and 'the Jewish people' as a historical-cultural and religious phenomenon. Furthermore, he regarded the existence of the Jewish people, both in the physical and the spiritual sense. Thus, according to Kook and unlike Ratosh, those Jews who had survived and who wished to join the Hebrew nation were *a priori* – even before immigrating to Palestine – Hebrews. Those whom Ratosh perceived as immigrants joining a new society, are for Kook *olim*, an integral part of one nation. Thus, Ratosh's normalization was primarily ideological and only then political, while Kook's is first and foremost political and only afterwards, to a minor degree, ideological. And it developed within the intellectual Jewish circles of his supporters, who were remote from any religious or national interest in the Jews of the Diaspora. They considered it vital to base the new state on liberal democratic tenets like those of the United States, which had separated religion and state and granted equal rights to all its citizens.[7]

The common denominator of the radical writers, the Reform thinkers, Elmer Berger, the Hebrew national poet Ratosh, and the Hebrew Zionist Hillel Kook, was the separation of religion and nationality and the perception of nationality as a territorial phenomenon. They differed in that the writers and Berger rejected the nationalist ideology on principle while Ratosh and Kook advocated it. As to their attitude to Jewish existence, for most of the writers the Jewish problem had dwindled into insignificance while Berger and Kook believed that it was undergoing gradual nullification or disappearance as a result of the post-war normalization of Jewish life.

SINGULAR NORMALIZATION

The mainstream approach to Jewish existence in American public thinking sought to understand it in two dimensions: equal civil rights in democratic society and integration in the culture of the pluralistic society, together with the preservation of Jewish singularity both historically and on the international plane, beyond religious difference. Its centrality derived primarily from its social and political scope. This point of view was shared by the Conservative and Reform movements. Ranged with them were the Reconstructionist Society and a large section of the Zionist movement. Added to these were certain individuals who were not identified organizationally with any of these bodies. Thus, this outlook embraced a wide spectrum of views.

Our discussion commences with two individuals who provided a gradual transition between the various approaches: the historian Solomon Zeitlin and Rabbi Jacob Agus.

Solomon Zeitlin pondered the historical significance of the concepts of 'nation' and 'exile' in the annals of the Jewish people. With regard to the former, he argued that it had been attributed to the Jews by the fathers of the Christian church, with the negative intention of indicating that their religion was of particularist rather than universal significance, the faith of a small and exceptional group. Since the Jews had not regarded themselves as a separate nation in the past, the term 'exile' was also of theological rather than territorial significance. Zeitlin cited proof that the Jews generally felt at home in their countries of residence.[8] Hence, his conclusion was that the phenomenon of 'international Jewry' had never existed and was the invention of anti-Semites. It is strange that a historian such as Zeitlin did not note the semantic differences between the concept of 'nation' referring to a certain group, and the modern concept with its spiritual, cultural and political content.

Zeitlin also levelled criticism against Mordecai Kaplan. He took issue with his theory of Judaism as a 'religious civilization', arguing that the existence of a national civilization depended on a national territory and language. His own view was that a Jewish civilization was in fact evolving, but that it would have no impact on Jews living outside this territory and speaking other languages. Most of the Jews of the world were affiliated, both theoretically and in practice, to other cultures and nations. So far the views of Berger and Zeitlin are identical. The latter went even further than did Berger in stressing the link between Jews and their countries of residence. The two thinkers were divided, however, on one concept. For Berger, Judaism was solely a religion. He even objected to attempts to define the Jews as a people since, to his mind, this term was indistinguishable from 'nation', both terms denoting political entities.[9] Zeitlin was of a different opinion. In his eyes, the total identification of Jewish essence with religion implied disregard for history. The Jews, he stated, were a 'historic people'. Despite geographical distance, cultural variation, differences in political and economic status, and even differences stemming from patriotic considerations, the Jews of the world still constituted a single 'folksorganism', which responded to injury to any of its parts.

This historiosophical biological theory led Zeitlin to admit, thereby contradicting his own anti-national outlook, that Jewish history offered manifestations of national identification and commitment, for example in the time of Bar Cochba or in the wake of the recent tragic events in Europe. Consequently, unlike Berger, he favoured the establishment of a Jewish national state in Palestine, which could offer a just solution for Jewish refugees from Europe. This new state and nation, however, could not demand the loyalties of the Jews of the rest of the world, who were integrated in their homelands. This meant that 'Jewish peoplehood', a wider concept than affiliation to the Jewish religion, would in future encompass the territorial Jewish nation in Palestine and the Jewish people affiliated to other nations in their countries of birth. This, then, was normalization in both the American and the international sense. National identification of the Jews with their countries of residence did not imply assimilation. Just as Berger wanted to preserve religious differences in Anglo-Saxon society, Zeitlin aspired to maintain the Jewish cultural heritage.

Agus's approach was more complex and even convoluted than that of Zeitlin, and his views had wider impact. His theories on the nature of Jewish existence underwent a striking change after the establishment of the State of Israel. In 1946 he published an article in the bulletin of the Reconstructionist Society in which he voiced the view that Zionism was the precondition for the continued survival of Judaism.[10] In the past, he argued, Jewish existence had been grounded on two principles: readiness for sacrifice for the sake of the faith and the hope of returning to Zion. In the modern world, the concept of *Kidush ha-Shem* (Sanctification of the Name) had forfeited much of its validity, but the principle of the return to Zion had gained force. Zionism, he believed, had bestowed new content and significance on the struggle of the Jews for survival. It had bestowed on the individual Jew a sense of pride, taught him to understand the conduct of his persecutors from a rational and normal viewpoint, and persuaded him that he was an equal among equals in this world. The article in general was directed against the inferiority

complex of those Jewish intellectuals who favoured assimilation, such as Franz
Werfel, or those who advanced the theory of the eternal nature of Jewish suffering,
like Herman Cohen. Agus, on the other hand, argued, in typical Zionist phraseol-
ogy, that the possibility of the existence of Jews of healthy spirit, upright stature
and proud aspect was dependent on belief in the Jewish religion and total identification with the Zionist venture.

Two years later, immediately after the establishment of Israel, Agus underwent
a metamorphosis.[11] The balanced point of view, which perceived Jewish survival
as contingent on religious faith and Zionist ideology now yielded place to the one-
sided view that religion alone could ensure the continued existence of Judaism.
Zionism, according to his revised theory, had ceased to be a factor maintaining
Judaism, because once Israel came into being it had become a political entity and
thereby forfeited its spiritual essence. In addition, Zionism's national message on
the territorial concentration of the Jewish people in Palestine had lost its validity.
Since the area of the Jewish state had been reduced, only a small proportion of the
Jewish people would be able to settle there. Hence, paradoxically enough, Zionism would be forced to acknowledge that the Jewish Diaspora was the 'normal'
way of life of the Jewish people.

With the aim of grounding Jewish existence on religion alone, Agus set out to
refute the views of his predecessors. He declared the Reform movement's idea of
the 'mission' of the Jewish people to be outdated, and claimed that it had never
taken hold of the masses. He rejected Ahad ha-Am's theories on the grounds that
the national 'will to live' in the secular sense was non-existent. He also took issue
with Mordecai Kaplan's views on an international Jewish civilization with Jewish
Palestine at its center. This was because he did not believe in the possibility of a
'normal' Jewish center in Palestine, with Jewish concentrations around it in the
Diaspora. This reconstructionist theory, he considered, was the American version
of Ahad ha-Am's theories.

Agus was particularly concerned with the question of the continued existence of
US Jewry. In this context he declared that, in order to survive, the American
Jewish community required a purpose, namely a way of life guided by a Jewish
religion of functional essence. Just as the liberal state existed in order to serve its
citizens, and not vice versa, the role of a religion was to fulfill the spiritual aspirations of the individual Jew, and not to transform that individual into the means of
ensuring the existence of Judaism or Jewishness. The religious content of Jewish
life in the United States was influenced, he thought, by the character of American
society, which was culturally monolithic but religiously pluralistic. Through full
integration in Anglo-Saxon culture, while exploiting the possibilities of pursuing
their own religion which would serve their special needs, the Jews would become
an integral part of American society.

He believed that, paradoxically enough, where Zionism was concerned, the
establishment of the Jewish state would speed up the process of integration in
American society. The foundation of Israel symbolized the end of the process of

emancipation which had commenced with the French Revolution. The free choice open to the Jews of the world between Israeli nationality and the nationality of any country where Jews lived had rendered their existence normal.

Agus's article sparked off controversy among Jewish intellectuals. *Menorah* published some of the responses in the form of a symposium. Among those who responded were young academics, veteran rabbis, journalists and community leaders.[12] Most of them rejected Agus's opinions in full or in part. The arguments against him related to three areas. Agus was accused of emptying the Jewish religion of its national content, and thereby deliberately obscuring the differences between Judaism and other religions, thereby inadvertently encouraging assimilation. The second charge was that he had erred in defining the American Jewish community as a religious community, since it was largely secular. Thus, he was excluding the majority of American Jews from the fold. The third critique took a grave view of his denial of the importance of Zionism for the continued survival of US Jewry. Several of the respondents hinted that Agus and Elmer Berger were in agreement.

In his response, published a year later, Agus tried to justify his views. Firstly, he attempted to elucidate his central argument. The separation of religion and nationality was not an essential part of Judaism, or even of Christianity, which blended the two, he declared. In this respect, he was refuting Zeitlin's historical outlook. The distinction between nationality and religion was the outcome of the birth of the modern state, which had separated religion and state and identified citizenship with nationality. Hence, the desire to preserve this ancient identity whose day had passed was but a reactionary attempt, which could eventually endanger the survival of Judaism. He based this view on the historical evidence of the past century, which, he insisted, had demonstrated how romantic messianism, which preached the 'singularity' and 'differences' of groups of human beings, had eventually led to the moral deterioration of national movements, thereby bringing down catastrophe on society and a holocaust on the Jews.[13]

In order to emphasize the differences between his own views and Berger's, Agus tried to formulate a new synthesis between religion and Jewish nationality. He spurned the two conflicting alternatives – that of the Reform movement which removed nationalism from religion, and that of Herzlian Zionism, which held that the new Jewish nationalism had no need of religion. His synthesis was based on acceptance of Ahad ha-Am's pattern of thought but in reverse order. Whereas the latter had perceived religion as the attire of the national spirit and a vital component in the struggle against assimilation, Agus took the opposite view – namely that nationalism was the raiment of religious sentiment and a means of bolstering religious faith. All the constructive forces and trends in Jewish social and cultural life, apart from extreme militarist nationalism, he said, serve the noble and moral objectives of the Jewish religion, bringing the secular masses closer to it through strengthening Jewish unity within the various communities and bolstering the ties among them.

Agus went on to declare that after the triumph of Zionism, it was clear beyond the shadow of a doubt that nationality and religion could not each separately express the essence of Jewish existence. The combination of the two could perhaps explain it, but could not provide a satisfactory answer to the question of how to consolidate it. The way to achieve this, he argued paradoxically, was liberation from the tradition of separation of Jews and non-Jews. This tradition, deriving from the Jewish sense of apartness and awareness of how different they were from other nations, is the last expression of Jewish anomaly. Agus defined the mutual relations between Jews and others as alienism and hoped that after the establishment of the State of Israel, this separation and alienism would disappear, because the Jews, by winning national sovereignty, had proved themselves to be a nation like all others. The new reality had conferred on Jews as individuals the freedom of self-determination as members of the Jewish nation living in Palestine, or members of the Jewish religion, bringing an end to the Jewish sense of exile both in the ideological and the psychological sense. Henceforth Jewish existence would be normal, with its own distinct qualities, based on religious faith not only as ritual but also as a way of life, and on special ties with the Jewish state adapted to the circumstances of the times.

As a result of this change in outlook, Agus was now more in tune with the religious-national views of the Conservative leaders than with those of Elmer Berger. The formers' approach can be defined as post-Shechterian. Solomon Shechter had laid the foundations for Conservative Zionism at the beginning of the century and considered its political aspirations to be a means of reinforcing religious belief, while his spiritual heirs sought to establish a mainly religious base for Jewish existence, depreciating the value of the political element in Zionism. Louis Finkelstein, the most important religious thinker in this movement, stated after the 1942 Biltmore Conference that the Jewish renaissance in Palestine could be of both national and universal significance only if its content were religious. In October 1943, in an address to the Political Committee of the American Jewish Committee, he announced that he opposed the establishment of a Jewish state in Palestine. He believed it necessary to distinguish between the right of Jews to return to Palestine, which was sacred to them, and the national demand for political sovereignty over that country. This demand was inadmissible, he said, on fundamental universal grounds. Just as the United States was not a country of Christians or Anglo-Saxons, Palestine could not be the state of the Jews alone. Ideally, states would exist on a geo-economic and not an ethnic basis.[14] In this respect, namely the basic conflict between the religious outlook and the nationalist viewpoint, Finkelstein was not far removed from Berger. The differences between them arose in the course of the political developments around the question of Jewish statehood. Whereas Berger and his group differed from the consensus on the question of relations with the State of Israel, Finkelstein and his movement accepted it and advocated close and strong ties. Notwithstanding, they were not able to reconcile themselves to Zionism as the embodiment of Jewish nationality. After the establishment of the state, Finkelstein's disciple Robert Gordis declared emphatically that Zionism had terminated its constructive role in modern Jewish history.[15] Its main historical value had been rooted in the utopian yearnings for national sovereignty which it aroused among Jews who were on the verge of total assimilation. Now that that utopia had become a political and national entity, it no longer had any contribution to make to the Jews of the Diaspora. Their lives would henceforth be founded on religious belief and a traditional way of life within the organized Jewish community. What emerges from Gordis's remarks is that although he favored Jewish unity, he distinguished clearly between the nature of Jewish existence in Israel and in the Diaspora. Rabbi Louis Katzoff honed this distinction. In this critique of Mordecai Kaplan's philosophy (to be discussed below), he offered, in place of Kaplan's vision of Judaism as a 'religious civilization' his own vision of Judaism as a 'civilizational religion'.[16] Katazof explained his objections by saying that Kaplan assumed *a priori* the existence of a Jewish entity whose unity was determined from outside and lay beyond the realm of religious belief. Since inherent in this view was the danger of dual cultural and political loyalty, it was preferable to relate to Judaism as a religion with certain features of a civilization. According to this definition, the singular normalization of the Jews would consist from now on of the national entity in Palestine, a civilization in every sense of the word, and the Diaspora, which was essentially religious in character, with certain features of a unique civilization. Such existence, he believed, would rely considerably on the mutual ties between the Jews of the Diaspora and the State of Israel.

Unlike Gordis and Katzoff, the editor of the movement organ, Leon S. Lang, attempted to expand the concept of Jewish existence beyond the religious significance with which his colleagues had endowed it. He defined the unity among Jews as a form of kinship, including within it the concepts of civilization, religion, denomination and peoplehood. Underlying Jewish unity, he stated, was the sense of overall responsibility stemming from this kinship and encompassing Jewish existence in both Israel and the Diaspora. This viewpoint did not differ greatly from the prevalent view in the Reform movement in the 1940s.[17]

The profound change in the outlook of the Reform movement which occurred at the end of the 1930s and the beginning of the forties, created a new understanding of the essence of Jewish existence. The shift from universal religious principles to recognition of the Jewish entity as a people; replacement of vehement opposition to Zionism by acceptance of its national-cultural objectives in the Ahad ha-Amite sense, and finally the discarding of fears of the political character of Zionism and the decision to support the establishment of a Jewish state in Palestine – all these related to the question of the normal or abnormal existence of the Jewish people throughout the world.

The process of 'nationalization' or reversion to several nationalist principles which the Reform movement underwent led it to abandon its views on the normal existence of the Jews as a religion and as equal citizens in various countries, and to accept a more balanced definition – which may be called singular normalization

– namely a synthesis of universal and particularist elements, which derived its legitimization, so they held, from the pluralistic and liberal character of American society.

This change, which was initially inspired by the rise of Nazism and the plight of the Jews of Europe, and whose catalyst was the struggle for the establishment of a Jewish state, also generated a new historical evaluation of the reasons for the previous anti-nationalist stand of the Reform movement.

This new self-evaluation found systematic expression in an article by Solomon B. Freehof, President of the Central Conference of American Rabbis/(CCAR), entitled 'Reform Judaism and Zionism – a Clarification', published in 1944. Underlying the article, which was almost certainly intended to counterbalance Berger's anti-Zionist arguments, was historical methodology. In other words, Freehof tried to understand the principles of Reform Jewry's outlook against the background of the period in which it had developed. His claim was that the traditional anti-nationalist ideology of his movement derived from the spiritual world of the European Enlightenment and was influenced by the rationalist-universal belief in the prospect of the disappearance of the particularist differences characterizing the old world, and dividing man from man. In this context, Freehof drew an analogy between the attitude of Marxist socialism towards religion and the attitude of the Reform movement towards nationalism. In both cases, the opposition was not an integral part of the *weltanschauung*, but was colored by contemporary moods. Thus, the passage of time changed the Reform stand on Jewish nationalism in general and Zionism in particular.[18]

This historical approach enabled Freehof to take a balanced view of Zionism and anti-Zionism in the past. He asserted that the leaders of the Reform movement who had perceived the Jews as a religious denomination were correct as regards Western Jews, while the Zionists who had defined them as a nation were right as regards the Jews of the rest of the world. This, he wrote, was valid in the present as well, since Jews in various parts of the world defined themselves in different ways in accordance with their political conditions and civil status. Although he rejected the uniform definition of Judaism, he perceived a historical uniformity in Jewish existence.

Freehof's approach to Jewish history, based on historical unity, and taking into consideration geographical and historical disparities in civil status and a variety of approaches to self-comprehension, sought a solution to the dilemma of the Reform movement, by acknowledging the present and future heterogeneity of Jewish existence. It would henceforth consist of three dimensions: Jews defining themselves as a people in their historic homeland; the Jews of Eastern Europe, enjoying the status of national minorities; and the Jews of the West and the United States, perceiving themselves primarily as a religious denomination.

Freehof was convinced that Zionism and Reform Judaism had a common ideological base. Just as the working class in Palestine had found a constructive synthesis between Zionism and socialism, the Zionist middle class could reinforce itself by means of a synthesis with the universal ideals of the Reform movement. All this would come to pass when Reform Judaism ceased to define itself exclusively as a religion and Zionism liberated itself from its pessimistic view of the surrounding world and reverted to faith in human progress.[19] The bestowing of mutual historic legitimization by Zionism and Reform Judaism which Freehof sought held out implications for the future as well. Unlike his opponent, Elmer Berger, who regarded Zionism as a reactionary movement like fascism, Freehof considered it to be the bearer of universal liberal values identical with those of his own movement. He also emphasized the importance of Palestine in contemporary Jewish experience, not as the sole home but as a unique place for Jews. This approach, which emphasized Jewish singularity in the national and not only the religious sense without offering it as the sole solution for the entire Jewish people, was borne out by American conditions.

After the establishment of Israel, the heads of the movement argued that henceforth Jewish existence in the United States would be normalized, like that of the Italians or the Irish. And just as those two groups identified with the national problems of their compatriots, it was only natural for Jews to identify with the aspirations of the Zionist movement and to aid the new state in its struggles.[20] Thus they had devised a formula with two components: normalization and singularity. The former related to the pluralistic American experience and the latter to the experience of a people scattered all over the world, maintaining historical cohesion and bound to their homeland by fortifying spiritual ties. In other words, even in relation to other ethnic minorities in the United States, the Jewish status was unique. The others had no links with a national diaspora and their attitude towards their homeland was expressed mainly through economic and political aid, while in the case of the Jews, in addition to these types of assistance, there was a spiritual link. Thus, whereas for other ethnic groups the connection was unilateral, among the Jews it was reciprocal.

This approach, based in the philosophy of history, was endowed by the charismatic leader of the Reform movement, Abba Hillel Silver.[21] The basic tenet of his outlook was that, upon the establishment of the Jewish state, a new era had been launched in Jewish history: the annals of the Jewish people would henceforth be totally different to their history since the destruction of the Second Temple and the loss of their sovereignty. This difference was expressed primarily in the fact that the freedom of choice open to the Jews to return to their homeland or to continue to reside in other countries had, to all intents and purposes, invalidated the Diaspora. This could only have a beneficial effect on the psychological status of Jews everywhere, granting them security, self-esteem and 'a normal tone long wanting in Jewish experience'. He envisaged this new normality as a kind of return to the conditions prevailing during the Second Temple era, when most Jews lived outside the borders of the Land of Israel. They considered themselves citizens of their countries of residence in every way, but unlike other emigrants, continued to maintain very close ties with their religious-spiritual center in Jerusalem, and in times of distress were expected to extend material and even political succor to their brethren in Palestine.

In the historical sense, the survival of the Jews as a people was made possible by these two phenomena: their dispersal among other nations and their religious, spiritual and practical links with Palestine. This meant that as regards the view of Jewish existence in the past and future, Silver allotted equal value to the periphery and to the center – the Diaspora and Palestine. The future existence of the Jewish people, therefore, was conditional on the existence of this link, but it should not be a solely national connection, because of the risk that Judaism might disintegrate or be distorted as a result. Nationalism, he argued, could not be a substitute for religion in either the moral-historic sense or in the modern context of the increasing tendency in both Jewish and non-Jewish circles to return to the religious fold. Hence, again in an attempt to achieve equilibrium, Silver argued that the urgent historical mission of world Jewry was to build up the State of Israel, but that the renaissance of Jewish religious life in the United States and elsewhere, including Israel, was a no less important goal. Consequently, the maintenance of a singular Jewish normalization required a synthesis between political nationalism in Israel and religious culture in the Diaspora.

Silver's predecessor in consolidating the concept of singular normalization and providing its ideological basis in his historical studies, was the doyen of Jewish historians, Professor Salo Baron. He was not affiliated to the Reform movement, but his views, which influenced intellectual circles, were in harmony with those described above. In 1944, at the height of the Second World War, Baron remained optimistic as to the prospect of reviving and restoring Jewish life in Europe.[22] He believed that American Jewry would play a central role in this endeavor, in both the material and the spiritual sense. Baron was convinced that the synthesis between American culture and Jewish tradition contained the promise of the renaissance of Jewish culture in the spirit of that of the Hellenistic world and of medieval Spain. He wanted to base the links among the Jews of the world on religious culture, and preferred to denote his fellow Jews as 'co-religionists'.

Two years later, under the impact of horrifying revelations of the Holocaust, he changed his views. In an article published in 1946 in a Zionist journal, he stressed the historic importance of Zionism in the past and its tasks in the present and future. Before the Holocaust, he wrote, the theory of 'denial of the Diaspora' was of positive value because it spurred the Jews to maintain their national culture and to create within it. After the war, with the disappearance of Eastern European Jewry, which had suffered from political and economic distress, this demand was no longer practical and could even be considered harmful. Henceforth, pioneering Jewish youth should be exhorted to contribute to the constructive endeavours in Palestine. The next national task should be to rehabilitate the Diaspora for the sake of the Land of Israel and to strengthen the Jewish community in Israel for the sake of the Diaspora.[23] The transition from the view of the United States as the focus of Jewish renaissance to advocacy of a balance between Palestine and the United

States, emphasizing the principle of national unity, is the crux of the change in Baron's outlook.

The clearest expression of singular normalization is the philosophy of Mordecai Kaplan and his followers. The term 'religious civilization', which Kaplan coined in the 1930s, reflected an attempt to encompass the spectrum of Jewish secular and religious life and to contain them in a world-wide communal organization. In his acceptance of normalization, and acknowledgment of its value and importance for Jews, Kaplan did not differ from Conservative and Reform theoreticians. Like them, he considered the Jews of the United States and other countries of the free world to be equal citizens, involved in the culture of their countries of residence while maintaining their religious differences. He differed from them in his accentuation of the unique element in Jewish existence, above and beyond religious belief. By postulating that the Jews constituted a homogeneous historical entity in the ethnic sense, with its own unique civilization, he came closer than the others to the Zionist conception of national unity. Furthermore, Kaplan based his hopes for reconstruction of Jewish life on the precedent provided by the Zionist movement. Zionism, he believed, had brought to the surface the latent activist forces of the Jewish people and given them both the goal and the means of action. Thanks to its activist character, Zionism had won international acknowledgment and had demonstrated to the people that the reconstruction of national life, on a worldwide basis, was feasible.[24]

Kaplan recognized the fact that Zionism was the sole path to construction of a complete Jewish life. He was also aware, however, that it could not offer a solution to the majority of the Jewish people, who would not be ready to abandon the countries in which they enjoyed freedom. In his view, these Jews were liable to suffer from the internal rift between their normal political existence on the one hand and their abnormal self-image as members of a religious denomination distinct from others. The solution he proposed was the revival of Jewish civilization, adapted to the spirit of pluralistic democracy and reflecting the essence of Jewish existence in both the religious and the secular sense.

The man who consolidated and refined the theory of the special link between Reconstructionism and Zionism was Kaplan's disciple and heir, Ira Eisenstein. In a leaflet he published during the war,[25] he developed a historical-philosophical theory aimed at defining various stages in the life of the Jewish people. He held that the history of the Jewish people could be divided into two periods: the first, normal, millennium when the people had lived in their own land, and the following two millennia, the period of abnormality when they had lived outside it. He claimed that the war had brought Jewish history to a new watershed. Now that the Zionist movement had good prospects of founding a Jewish national commonwealth in Palestine, a new era had been launched in Jewish history. Henceforth the Jews would be required to learn to exist simultaneously as a territorial and extraterritorial nation. In this way their singular normalization would find expression. Eisenstein's views were not dissimilar from the theory of the eternity of the Jewish

Diaspora, but, more than others, he emphasized the fact that Palestine was the homeland of the Jewish people and the center of their national experience. On this question of the centrality of Palestine, his views were close to those of Ahad ha-Am, though not identical. He perceived Jewish life as consisting, not of the center – Palestine – and the periphery – the Diaspora – but of two poles: the Jews of the world and the Jews of Palestine. Eisenstein did not consider them equal and recognized that the Diaspora would always require the assistance of Israel in three spheres: national–religious community organization, the revival of Jewish culture and the reinforcement of religious belief. Again, unlike Ahad ha-Am, he saw Palestine not as a model for emulation, but rather as a center of guidance. The Jews of the Diaspora, particularly those of the United States, should not confine themselves to emulating the lives of the Jews of Palestine as regards culture and community organization, but should adapt the latter's achievements to their own conditions. It was his opinion that the Jewish community of Palestine served as living proof of the possibility of reconciling individual yearnings with general aspirations, the change of lifestyle with preservation of ancient tradition. The Jewish community in Palestine – the Yishuv – he asserted, had demonstrated the ability to fashion the life of the community in accordance with idealistic or pioneering principles, and similar principles should also be inculcated in the Jews of the Diaspora.

The second principle which distinguished this outlook from the theories of Ahad ha-Am was the reciprocity between the Diaspora and Palestine, in other words material and economic aid in return for spiritual help. In short, Eisenstein wanted to reconstruct US Jewry in the spirit of Zionism, implying national activism aiming at auto-emancipation; faith in the Jewish people as a creative people; manifestation of initiative and courage; and readiness to make sacrifices for the sake of the common good. All these were components of the pioneering spirit, by means of which he hoped to instill a new spirit into the dispersed communities in order to rouse them to cultural and organizational effort so as to enhance their existence as a religious civilization.

Despite the central role he assigned to the Palestinian Zionist model in reconstructing Jewish community life in the United States, one may deduce from his remarks that the process of development of the relationship between the two, dialectically speaking, leads from the theory of Palestine as center towards the concept of two poles of equal status. As the Palestinian spirit was diffused and took root among US Jewry, the status of the two communities would become increasingly balanced.

The man who explicitly linked Zionism to the singular normalization of Diaspora Jewry was the young rabbi Milton Steinberg (1903–50). In 1945 he published a book which was intended as a guide to the Jewish problem,[26] in which he clarified that the implementation of Zionism could render the Jews normal in the eyes of the rest of the world. In their present situation, the Jews were anomalous, a religious denomination but at the same time something more than this. They were a group with its own culture but this culture was not exclusive to them. In short, they were a group without a homeland. When a Jewish commonwealth was established in Palestine, in accordance with the definition formulated in the 1942 Biltmore Declaration, the Jewish people would attain normality again. The Jews of Palestine would gain political and territorial normality, while the Jews of the Diaspora would enjoy a normal status similar to that of the Swedes, the Irish or the Italians in the United States. At the same time, theirs could not be perceived as the usual 'American normality' since Jewish existence in the United States, in the spiritual sense, was dependent on close ties with Palestine.

Steinberg also concurred with Ahad ha-Am in the view that the entire spectrum of life in Palestine must constitute a qualitative center, exerting influence over the Jews of the Diaspora. Other minorities in the United States had no need of links of this kind with their former homelands. Their connections with the 'old country' were more sentimental and emotional in nature, and not constructive, as envisaged by Steinberg and his reconstructionist associates.

Interestingly enough, articles by the leaders of the Reconstructionist movement, written during and immediately after the war, do not refer to a Jewish state in Palestine. The terms they use are: a territorial national entity, a Jewish homeland, a community or a commonwealth. The Yishuv in Palestine had been allotted a role in Jewish civilization on a community basis, as a Jewish social organization. This did not apply to a sovereign national state. Immediately after the establishment of Israel, in 1949, Mordecai Kaplan declared that the establishment of the state had created more problems for Jews than it had solved.[27] Firstly, it had created understandable confusion, stemming from the need to tackle a new phenomenon with such profound national implications. The change was expressed primarily in the fact that from now on there would be two kinds of Jews in the world: the minority living in their sovereign state, and the majority who had chosen to remain in their countries of residence in the Diaspora. The truth was, Kaplan asserted, that although the Jews had established the state, no Jewish nation would arise in Palestine, just as the establishment of the United States by the British had not created a British nation there. Thus, according to the territorialist approach that a nation came into being in a territory and in accordance with democratic principles, the nation which would come into being in Israel would be Israeli and not Jewish. Such a nation would be unable to serve as the center of world Jewry and would not be part of Jewish religious communal civilization. Not the state but the Jewish community in Palestine would become the center. Kaplan explained that Jewish existence could not be defined by the term 'religion', which was too narrow, nor by the term 'nation' which was too wide and imprecise. He claimed that the term 'people' implied acknowledgement of historical continuity and unity, identification with a common culture linked to Palestine, and faith in a unique religion. It was highly suited to the new post-statehood Jewish entity. Kaplan identified the term 'people' with the concept of *Kelal Yisrael*, meaning Judaism as a religious civilization uniting the Jews in their state and in the Diaspora and safeguarding their separate existence.

It should be noted that the term 'people' as used by Kaplan was much wider and more comprehensive than the expression 'folksorganism', by means of which S. Zeitlin tried to understand Jewish existence. The latter referred to a sense of mutual commitment evident throughout Jewish history, while Kaplan demanded a common Jewish lifestyle for religious and secular Jews in both the cultural and the organizational sense. Kaplan, it would seem, more than others, sought to emphasize the unique nature of normal Jewish existence in the free world following the establishment of the Jewish state.

JEWISH NORMALIZATION

There is something ironic in the term 'Jewish normalization' since the adjective appears to contradict the noun. We are deliberately employing this seemingly paradoxical term, in order to stress the uniqueness of the Jewish condition, as reflected in contemporary reactions.

The nature of the term suggests that it can encompass traditional rivals, such as the Bund, Poalei Zion and non-Zionist intellectuals. The affinity between them is based on their practical evaluation of Diaspora existence, particularly relating to Jewish national identity which was not characterized solely by religious beliefs. The Bund's ideological heritage should have aligned it to those who advocated 'general normalization'. After all, despite the ideological, spirtual and cultural distance between the pre-war Bund and the American Council for Judaism or the Hebrew Committee for National Liberation, there were similarities in their outlook. All three bodies took a one-dimensional view of Jewish existence: basing it on religion, nationality or class alone. Because of this approach, all three preached total separation of religion and nationalism because they recognized the existence of the nation solely within the territorial framework. Hence their shared conviction that no extraterritorial and universal Jewish national entity could exist. Above and beyond these shared patterns of thinking, the traditional negative attitude of the Bund towards Zionism was identical to that of the Council.

All this was true of the pre-war period. The Holocaust, and in particular the destruction of the Jewish center in Poland, which had been the stronghold of the Bund in the inter-war period, wrought far-reaching changes in the views of its members concerning the essence of Jewish existence.

In February 1947, Bund delegates convened in Brussels for their first international conference. This outstanding event in the history of the movement was preceded by a protracted debate between two opposing camps. For the opponents of the conference, the very idea of holding such a gathering threatened to undermine the ideological basis of a movement which had never acknowledge the national unity of the Jewish people even on a class basis, and, unlike Poalci Zion, had never maintained a worldwide organization. The advocates of the conference, on the other hand, argued that the movement must re-examine itself in the light of the changes which had taken place. With great circumspection they promised that their sole intention was to set up a coordinating committee between the Bundist bodies scattered all over the world, rather than a centralized and binding organization.[28]

Emmanuel Scherer, formerly one of the leaders of the Polish Bund, and now one of the heads of the Bund in the United States, spoke of the modification of the movement's outlook.[29] In his opinion, for as long as the Jewish center in Poland had existed, there had been no need for deliberate action aimed at safeguarding national existence, since the Jewish national entity in Poland had been a natural and objectively indisputable fact. In light of the tragic annihilation of this community, concerted effort was now required in order to rescue the people from the danger of assimilation. He stated emphatically that the conference should not be perceived as a kind of Bund International since it represented not workers of different nationalities but workers of the same nationality living in different countries. Since this was a revolutionary shift in the Bund outlook, his remarks deserve to be quoted in full: 'The International includes parties from different countries and different nations. We belong to different countries but to one people'. In other words, from now on the basis of the reconstruction of the Jewish people was Jewish national affiliation above and beyond the territorial framework.

Scherer also fostered the hope that the great Jewish territorial center in the United States would now replace the vanished Polish center. Yet, the change in the conception of Jewish nationality did not bring with it an altered attitude towards Zionism. Scherer remained strongly antagonistic towards that movement, was particularly opposed to its aspirations to national hegemony, and did not shrink from hinting at a resemblance between its Palestinocentrist aims and the ideology of Nazism. Whereas Nazism claimed that Germany stood above everything else, he said, Zionism preached '*Eretz Yisrael, Eretz Yisrael, uber alles*'. He himself believed that the future of the people would be decided not in Palestine but through the struggle for national survival in the Diaspora, and particularly in the United States.

At its Brussels meeting, the coordinating committee of the Bund's international organization condemned the resolution establishing a Jewish state. It acknowledged the right of the Jews of Palestine to exist as a national community, but opposed its claim to the title of national center for world Jewry. The committee argued that it was not possible to change two thousand years of history during which the Jews had been an international people (a *velt-folk*).[30] They objected to the establishment of Israel on socialist political grounds as well, because of the struggle with the Arab world and the involvement in the imperialist interests of the Western powers. The statement of the committee sparked off a bitter debate in Bundist circles in the United States. The critics, headed by the veteran leader, Jacob Pat, sought to differentiate between their negative attitude towards Zionism and their positive view of the Jewish state. Their statements reflect a clear distinction between aggressive Zionism, as they defined it, which denied the Diaspora and thereby expedited the process of national fragmentation, and that Zionism which accepted its existence. In the wake of their readiness to accept moderate Zionism, they expressed approval of the Jewish state, perceiving its establishment as the objective and necessary outcome of post-Holocaust developments, and its mission as the strengthening of international Jewish unity. Their remarks are redolent of yearning for an alliance between the new Bund and the newly founded Jewish state, for the consolidation and preservation of Jewish nationalism.[31]

In contrast, Scherer argued that Zionism and the Jewish state could not be separated. To accept the state as a vital and positive national phenomenon, even while rejecting aggressive Zionism, implied acceptance of the principles of Zionism and spelled the end of Bundist ideology.[32] Politically speaking, Scherer proposed that Palestine be transformed into a bi-national state, and he demanded institutionalization of the links between the Yishuv and the Diaspora, on a national basis.

The controversy between the two sections of the Bund in the United States was continued at the second world conference, held in New York in the fall of 1948.[33] Thirty-six speakers took part in the debate on the stand towards Zionism and the State of Israel. Twelve to fourteen of them supported Pat, while the remainder identified with Scherer's standpoint. The conference's resolution, therefore, was based on the convictions of the majority of participants, but the trend towards a changed attitude to Zionism was not checked and continued to gather momentum.

Six months after the conference, Y. Trunk published an article on the historical roots of the Bund and Zionism, which constituted a definite rejection of the anti-Zionist tradition of his movement.[34] According to his historiosophical view, two distinct conflicting trends could be discerned in Jewish history which were dialectically linked: concentration versus expansion, as he termed them, or particularism versus universalism, to use modern terminology. These two trends, he wrote, were already evident in the Bible. In the Diaspora, the integration of Jews into their surroundings, on the one hand, and the yearning for Zion, on the other, were evidence of their existence, and in recent decades the Bund and Zionism were their heirs. Since both movements represented historical continuity, it would be a mistake to assume that at some time in the future one could cancel out the other. After having granted Zionism historical sanction, Trunk turned to his own movement, claiming that the Bund had erred in the past in its belief that it could gain hegemony over the future of Judaism. The spiritual trends and messianic yearnings represented by Zionism were rooted deep within the Jewish people, and could not easily be eradicated. Moreover, they had contributed greatly to the molding of the nation.

The revised outlook was expressed succinctly by P.L. Hersch, who believed that the main difference between Zionism and Bundism lay in Palestinocentrism alone, namely the demand of the former that the Golah support the Zionist endeavor in Israel until it was finally eradicated. Thus, Trunk and Hersch restored the debate between the Bund and Zionism to the framework of the Jewish national consensus, in both the historical and the ideological sense. Their articles were clear indications of the decisive shift in the outlook of the Bund, or important sections of it, in the United States, namely the change from advocacy of 'general normalization' to belief in 'Jewish normalization'.

This change brought them ideologically closer to the group of American Yiddishist intellectuals who clung to the conviction that Yiddish culture could be revived in that country. More than any other group, they were convinced of the positive significance of Jewish existence in the Diaspora, as a cultural and social experience. For them, the essence of Jewish normality was life in exile. The writer and satirist Shmuel Niger went further than his colleagues, in asserting that even the Yishuv, and later the State of Israel, could not escape the *galut* character of the Jewish people.[35] Mass immigration to Israel, he said, would cause that country to be conquered by the Diaspora, because the historical and cultural continuity of each community would eventually prove stronger than the innovations provided by Zionism. Even if it was agreed, Niger continued, that Zionism had wrought the greatest revolution in Jewish history, it could not be doubted that, like the revolutions of other nations, it could change the external lifestyle of the people but not the inner content. The lesson of history, he declared, was that nations create revolutions in their countries, countries do not change nations. Even though it aimed at becoming the antithesis of the Diaspora, in the final analysis, *nolens volens*, it would be its continuation. Similar views were expressed by the poet H. Leivick.[36] He attacked the Zionist-Canaanite view of the creation of a new Jewish nation in Palestine. This theory, he said, stemmed from the ideology of 'negation of the Diaspora' which could lead its proponents to negation of the Jewish people. On the other hand, Leivick advocated parallel existence of the two national cultures, Yiddish and Hebrew, in the Diaspora and in the State of Israel, and hoped for fruitful collaboration between them. Another participant in the debates conducted by the journal *Zukunft*, was Simon Rawidowicz, who reiterated the views he had expressed twenty years before the Holocaust and the establishment of Israel. Among the Yiddishists who were not affiliated to the Bund or the Zionist movement, his theory of Jewish normalization was the most comprehensive and systematic. He defined the relations between the state and the Jews of the Diaspora as 'two that are one', based on total equality.[37] Rawidowicz acknowledged the historical uniqueness of Palestine and its importance to the Jewish national entity, which was greater than that of any other country, but he regarded the various Jewish communities as full and equal partners in the effort to maintain Jewish life. For him, this partnership was a substitute for the Ahad-ha-Amite Zionist theory of the dependence of the Diaspora on the Palestinian center. This led him to demand that autonomous status be bestowed on each Diaspora community in its efforts to contribute to Jewish existence. In other words, he did not consider the impact of the evolving Israeli culture on the Diaspora to be inevitable. Such influence was possible and even desirable, but only if it was accepted voluntarily: he believed in the complete and balanced unity of Jewish existence. The Diaspora should be perceived, not as a negative or a positive essence, but as an eternal historical phenomenon, accepted as such with all its permutations. The Diaspora had become an inseparable part of 'normal' Jewish existence, which now included life within it and in Palestine. Rawidowicz refused to define the situation between these two components as a connection, since a connection can only exist between two separate parts, while the Jews of the Diaspora and Israel are one.

In the period under discussion, Zionist thinking in the United States was divided on the question of Jewish existence, between the proponents of 'singular normalization' and of 'Jewish normalization'. It should be noted that the former, whose outstanding spokesman was Abba Hillel Silver, continued the tradition of American Zionists of the school of thought represented by Richard Gottheil, Solomon Schechter and Louis Brandeis. The latter, particularly the leaders of Poalei Zion, were influenced by the Eastern European Zionist tradition. The common denominator of these two approaches was grounded on the following assumptions: the conviction that Zionism was a vital condition for the continued existence of the Jewish people as regards communal cohesion, bolstering of individual confidence and pride, and the revival of national culture; the awareness that the standing of US Jewry within the surrounding society differed fundamentally from the situation in Eastern Europe or in most places in the world where Jews were concentrated in significant numbers; and finally, acceptance of national responsibility as expressed in political and economic aid to the Yishuv and to the Jews of other communities, and unqualified support for the pioneering efforts of the Zionist movement.

The difference between the two approaches stemmed from the fact that the former considered US Jewry to be a unique and positive community, while the latter perceived it as a particular manifestation of the Golah. The concept of exile was a problematic one in the context of the American Jewish experience, because of the open, democratic and pluralistic nature of American non-Jewish society. In the absence of a collective plight, some of these thinkers perceived exile as an individual problem. Joachim Prinz stated that the manifestations of anti-Semitism in a free society attested to the existence of the condition of exile, and believed that each and every individual should be aware that 'despite total freedom, we should arrive within ourselves at the personal decision of being a people on its way home in order to build a homeland for the Jews'.[38]

Ben Halpern, who was one of the leaders of the Habonim youth movement at the end of the 1930s, interpreted recognition of the condition of exile as an individual moral feeling.[39] He criticized the proponents of 'singular normalization' who saw the Diaspora as their home and believed that national culture could flourish there. He himself argued that a national culture should not aspire to be at home everywhere in the world. The reverse was true. The sense of alienation was the guarantee and even the precondition for its survival outside the homeland, and this was particularly true of secular nationalists, who were already integrated in the general culture. He took a positive view of general culture and acknowledged its attractions, and it was precisely for this reason that the sense of alienation or exile was important to him as a bulwark against total assimilation. Its importance also derived from a moral obligation towards those Jews who were being annihilated by the Nazis. As he wrote:

> One people – the whole and single people, in America and abroad – is in exile. It can be rescued, collectively and – the tragic necessity of our very days – individually, only in its own land. Until *the people* is firmly and safely planted at home, we Jews in America cannot allow ourselves the dear luxuries of being at home. Collectively we cannot be at home here, individually we must not, until our people has a home to itself and to all its suffering sons. For American Jewry exile is not a fact only, it is a duty.[40]

Among Poalei Zion Yiddishists the issue of the Diaspora Jewish anomaly should have been clearer. However, as has been hinted, here too attitudes were not so simple. Having spent most of their lives in the United States, while drawing on memories of life in Eastern Europe, they could not draw analogies between these two experiences of exile. And as lovers of Yiddish culture, they were unwilling to forgo this cultural treasure. Thus, while agreeing that exile as a form of national existence was a negative phenomenon, they still found many positive factors in the Diaspora.

Hayim Greenberg, one of the most important Zionist Yiddishist thinkers in the United States, formulated this dilemma in paradoxical fashion. In a debate on the future of the Jewish people, conducted by the weekly *Zukunft*, he argued that 'our catastrophe is reflected less in the fact that we are in exile than in the fact that in several respects, we have freed ourselves of exile, of its existential tensions, creativity, way of life and mystery'.[41] For contemporary Jews, the implication of this liberation (which meant the transformation of Exile into Diaspora) was directionless and aimless Jewish existence. The distinction between exile and diaspora led him to a positive evaluation of the Diaspora Jew, whom he considered to be the greatest rebel and adventurer in history, who for centuries had borne his faith and culture with him from country to country, despite pressures exerted against him and the temptations placed in his path. Exile, he said, was indeed a tragedy, but in no way a disgrace.[42] Greenberg agreed with the Yiddishists that Palestine could not offer a territorial solution for the majority of the Jewish people. Unlike them, however, he regarded Zionism, as an ideal and a movement, as the sole national force capable of uniting the Jewish people in the joint effort to build their own future. He defined this task as the 'primordial deed' and hoped that it would free Jewish individuals and Jews as a group from concern for their continued national survival.[43]

At the same time, Greenberg did not believe that in the Diaspora, Jews could develop their culture in absolute freedom. This was possibly because the Jew could never totally free himself from his sense of insecurity as to his future and the unease of one who is forced to adopt 'dual loyalties'. It was because of this 'Jewish normality' that Hayim Greenberg counted himself among the 'deniers of the Diaspora'.[44]

His denial of the Diaspora led him to defend the right of the Zionist movement to appeal to American Jews to immigrate to Palestine, unlike those who perceived this demand as an attempt to persuade Jews to become conditional citizens. Greenberg argued that American society granted both individuals and groups the right to be different. In their case, this difference, 'andershkeit',[45] consisted of the yearning for Zion which they had brought with them from their scattered communities to the shores of America. Immigration out of free choice, as the expression of objective freedom and not the outcome of collective coercion, is commensurate with the spirit of American culture, and is the distinct sign of 'normal difference' in the Jewish world.

Shlomo Grodzensky, critic and writer, held similar views to Greenberg, but his ideas on Jewish existence underwent a change during this period. During the war, Grodzensky was skeptical as to the possibility of reviving Jewish culture in the United States. He perceived exile as the root of all the evils afflicting the Jewish people.[46] After the establishment of Israel, he changed his mind. Henceforth he accepted the Diaspora as a part of Jewish normality. In order for it to continue to exist, he reverted to Herzl's exhortation that before a Jew returned to his Palestinian homeland he should first return to Judaism. The main task of Zionism from now on would be to instruct Jews in the Jewish-Zionist culture which would be linked to religious tradition, with all its symbols and values.[47] As for immigration, it would be the choice of few in the foreseeable future.

The Jewish sociologist, Jacob Lestschinsky, expressed similar views,[48] hoping that his territorialist theories would be implemented in Palestine, as did the Poalei Zion leader, Baruch Zuckerman,[49] who considered the Ingathering of the Exiles to be a protracted process, which would unite the entire people and lead to normal national existence. On this issue he proposed a formula: until the ratio between the Jews living in their homeland and those residing in other countries came to resemble that prevailing among Italians or Greeks in their home country and abroad, the Diaspora would endure.

Finally, let us conclude this survey of the views of the proponents of 'Jewish normalization' with the remarks of the Transylvanian-born Zionist rabbi, Eliezer Berkovits. He stressed that the links of world Jewry to Palestine existed not because they sought to become a nation, but because they were already a nation, and this was the basis of their right to exist as a sovereign people in its own land and as a national minority in all the countries in which they resided.[50]

This discussion of the essence of Jewish existence, marked by the desire for normalization, was conducted in a period of abnormality for the Jewish people. The generation which witnessed the Holocaust and the establishment of the State of Israel sensed that these were not ordinary times. This awareness intensified their historical consciousness and their sensitivity *vis à vis* the problem of Jewish survival. The perplexities of the Jewish community in these years related less to the means of action than to their definition. The question was not 'What is to be done?' but 'What shall we become?' After a period of almost total inertia (the reasons for which will not be discussed here) as regards the wartime rescue of European Jewry, this community rallied to the national effort to establish a Jewish state and aid Holocaust survivors. It appears that it was precisely the achievements in these two spheres which caused them to ponder the future essence of Jewishness.

Within the three schools of thought that evolved in response to this dilemma, different patterns of thinking are discernible. In the first case, the conception was essentially rational and universal; in the second, the historical and religious outlook predominated, while the third was based mainly on nationalist emotion. Close perusal of the development and crystallization of these approaches leads to conclusion that there is a connection between the degree of acknowledgment of the singularity of Jewish existence and the intensity of the hesitation, in other words, the more the differences were stressed, the greater the quandary.

Proponents of the first approach solved their dilemma through the concept of general or total normalization. And it was possibly in the absence of the dilemma that these views could be shared by people of totally conflicting outlook: assimilated radicals, members of the American Council for Judaism, the Canaanites and supporters of the Committee for Liberation of the Hebrew Nation.

Advocates of the second school of thought, who regarded the Diaspora as a historical and universal phenomenon, wrestled with the question of the link between religion and nationalism, which they were unable or unwilling to separate, and particularly Jewish nationalism which took political form. In contrast to the first school of thought, they had a common ideological denominator, namely religious belief (of various shades). In addition, they agreed that the political and cultural reality in the United States provided legitimization for the special existential status they sought, without undermining their normal integration in the society in which they considered themselves to be full partners.

The representatives of the third school of thought experienced the greatest hesitations and doubts, because their comprehensive national conception was without parallel; it was entirely and exclusively Jewish. Its most important component was the grounding of Jewish existence on nationalist theory. This created an ostensibly paradoxical common denominator between traditional rivals – the Bund and the Poalei Zion; this was due to the fact that the Bund changed its views on nationalism, although it did not go as far as Zionism, while Poalei Zion rejected the 'denial of the Diaspora' theory although they continued to believe in the Ingathering of the Exiles.

The following chapters trace the ideological development and historical fate of these three schools of thought. At this stage in our discussion, it is already possible to assert that after the establishment of Israel, the two main approaches – singular and Jewish – were at odds within the Zionist Organization.

Part II
Singular Normalization
1951–66

Introduction

The years 1948–52 marked the end of a tragic and heroic period in Jewish history: the Nazi rise to power, the Holocaust, the struggle for statehood and the first great wave of immigration to Israel. The years which followed, up to the Six Day War, were characterized by an easing of tension and by quest for answers to troubling questions.

Two parallel and conflicting processes of integration took place within the Jewish communities of Israel and the United States in this period. In Israel, it was marked by relative success in the absorption of immigrants; the dissemination of the Hebrew language among the newcomers; and the resounding military victory of 1956. A society made up of numerous, highly varied cultures underwent a rapid and sometimes painful process of consolidation. In the United States, on the other hand, Jews made rapid progress towards integration in general society, infiltrating economic spheres which had previously been almost totally barred to them and entering universities in ever-increasing numbers, both as students and faculty. The marked success of individual Jews speeded up the overall process of cultural and psychological integration, thereby undermining the cohesion of Jewish society. This weakening was manifested not only in the increase in the ratio of mixed marriages, which by the sixties accounted for 17 per cent of all marriages among American Jews, but also in the growing indifference of educated young Jews towards all Jewish matters.

Many young Jews were deeply involved in the various protest movements against the Vietnam War in the mid-sixties. The large proportion of Jewish students in these movements and among its leadership proclaimed clearly the fact that the young generation of Jews considered themselves as integral part of American society. Unlike the Jewish radicals of the 1940s, who perceived themselves to some extent as outsiders in American capitalist society, the young Jews of the sixties were ardent spokesmen for the other non-materialistic, freedom-living America. There was little common ground between US social radicalism and Israeli national radicalism.

Concomitantly, both of the Jewish societies were undergoing normalization processes which highlighted the economic and social disparities between them. American Jews exploited the trend towards technological advancement and modernization in order to ascend the social ladder. In Israel, on the other hand, normalization took a different form as immigrants went into industry and the working class. The country boasted a higher proportion of Jewish farmers and blue-collar workers, in industry and services, than any Diaspora community at any time. While the social standing and educational levels of American Jewish society were rising, Israeli society – as a result of mass immigration – was gradually losing its elitist-pioneering image.

39

Both societies were moving away from their Eastern European heritage. In the United States, the Jews were enthusiastic consumers of English language culture, to which they made a valuable contribution through the introduction of Eastern European Yiddish cultural elements. But by so doing, they forfeited their own distinctive cultural identity. In the same period, Israel was undergoing 'creeping' integration (only recognized a generation later) of the Hebrew culture of the Yishuv with Middle Eastern culture. Palestinian Hebrew culture had tried to sever its connections with the Eastern European heritage, but without success, since its roots were deeply imbedded there. Mass immigration put into motion a unique process of synthesis of two Jewish cultures: Eastern European and African-Asian.

2 Confusion Follows Triumph
The Zionist Organization in Search of a National Role

The explanation for the decline of the World Zionist Organization lies primarily in the fact that it was routed by its own success in Israel and among the Jewish people.

Zalman Aranne, 1952

Once the Jewish state had come into being, Zionism was forced to re-evaluate its role and its tasks. In the course of its history, it has passed through three stages: the spiritual era of Hibbat Zion, the Lovers of Zion; the essentially political and organizational stage, dominated by the personality of Theodore Herzl; and the stage of political constructivism, headed by Chaim Weizmann and the labor movement. Now Zionism was in its fourth era, focusing endeavors on reviving Jewish sovereignty. After decades in which political effort and strength had been invested solely in the existential national struggle, it was only natural for political triumph to be followed by ideological confusion. Because of the urgent need for economic aid to the young state, which faced the gargantuan task of absorbing floods of immigrants, the question of 'what to do next' was not yet relevant. But the question of 'what to become' was being raised in intellectual circles, and was particularly pertinent for American Zionists.

American Zionists had always considered themselves partners in the Zionist dream, but had not contemplated putting the dream into practice. Led in turn by Solomon Schechter, Louis Brandeis, Stephen Wise and Abba Hillel Silver, the movement had evolved a twofold attitude to Zionism. Through helping to consolidate the Zionist project in Palestine, it could bolster its own Jewish image, without coming into conflict with its American identity. Thus, the main contribution of American Jews lay in the financial and the political spheres, particularly during the years of political constructivism. This was reflected in the mass mobilization of US Jews on behalf of Zionism towards the end of the First World War under Brandeis's leadership, and towards the end of the Second World War led by Silver. Ironically enough, it was the political gains and triumphs of Zionism, transforming it into a leading force, which left the movement without purpose and hence without distinctiveness.

The dilemma facing Zionism in the Diaspora and in Israel stemmed not only from its own successes, but also from the fact that, by the very fact of its existence, Israel posed a challenge to Jews. It bestowed on them the freedom to choose between their countries of birth and their ancient homeland, and, because of its pressing needs, demanded self-actualization through immigration. The questions which now surfaced were simple yet profound, and challenging in their plan logic. They centered on three issues: the distinction between Zionists and non-Zionists; the role of the Zionist movement alongside the state; and the status of the Zionist Organization among other Jewish organizations in the Diaspora. These issues were hotly debated between 1948 and 1952 among the American Zionists (ZOA), in the World Zionist Organization, and between that movement and the Israeli government. They also generated fierce polemics within the Israeli political establishment between coalition and opposition parties, and passionate debate between David Ben-Gurion and some of the veteran Zionist leaders.

In June 1948, less than a month after the new state had been proclaimed, a ceremonial gathering of US Zionists was convened, at which the central address was delivered by Emmanuel Neumann, second-ranking leader of the ZOA after Abba Hillel Silver.[1] His basic premise was that the establishment of Israel had redressed the central abnormality of Jewish life. This political normalization, however, affected only the Jews of Palestine and those Jews who chose to immigrate there, and not the Jews of the Diaspora, who remained subject to the sovereignty of the countries whose nationalities they bore. In order to spare Diaspora Jews problems of dual political loyalties, he advocated unconditional and total separation between Diaspora Jewry and Israel. To this end, he deemed it necessary to reorganize the Zionist Organization so as to preclude attempts by either side to intervene in the internal affairs of the other. This organization, it was implied, should become an autonomous body, consisting exclusively of Diaspora Jews. Its ties with the State of Israel should be regulated by an agreement, granting Israeli representatives solely advisory status. The Zionist Organization, as perceived by Neumann, would be not only an instrument for recruiting aid for the new state, but also a means of promoting a Jewish renaissance in the Diaspora, Like his mentor Abba Hillel Silver, Neumann was a 'Zionist-Dubnowist', believing that the historic conditions of the Second Temple and Mishnaic eras were being repeated, and that the United States could become the 'new Babylon' or 'new Spain'. Underlying this belief was a desire to establish political equilibrium between the Jewish state headed by Mapai and its leader, Ben-Gurion, and a Diaspora body to be led by the General Zionists, with Silver at the helm. This trend (and its reverse, as we shall see below) reflected certain fundamental problems which had arisen in the wake of the establishment of Israel. Neumann's basic tenets – total separation between Israel and the Zionist Organization; clear distinction between the role of the Zionist Executive, to be relocated in New York, and the functions of the Israeli government; and recognition of the need for an independent cultural revival in the Diaspora – were radically opposed to the Palestinocentric conceptions which had been predominant in the Zionist movement since the Balfour Declaration. Palestinocentrism, prescribing dedication of all means to the end of constructing a Jewish society in Eretz Israel, was primarily an ideology, and only then, in the methods it employed, a political system.

Neumann's remarks attracted considerable attention in Israel. At a meeting of the Zionist Executive in Jerusalem in June, Moshe Shertok (Sharett) and Eliyahu Dobkin advised that the issue of division of authority between the Israel government and the Jewish Agency, and the abolition of duplication of functions, be considered cautiously and without haste.[2] Two months later, the Executive held a meeting, attended by representatives from the United States,[3] at which Ben-Gurion was present. As was his wont, he tried to go straight to the root of the problem, and proposed four guiding hypotheses. First, he argued that the state was a sovereign body and could not be restricted or controlled by any extraneous entity, whether the Zionist Organization or any other Jewish body. Second, he said that if Zionism was to achieve its aims, it needed the aid of the Jewish people. Consequently, the Jewish Agency should be granted legal standing in Israel, as representative of the Jewish people. Third, the Jewish Agency should be open to all Jews, or organized Jewish bodies, who wanted to take part in its activities. Fourth, he said, it was essential to distinguish between the Zionist Organization and the Jewish Agency. The former should be alloted the task of Zionist implementation – through immigration, settlement and education, while the latter should be a popular organization extending aid to Israel. Ben-Gurion was reviving an old idea which he had broached during the Second Aliyah and again in the twenties, namely, the establishment of two separate organizations, one of 'donors' and one of 'doers'.[4]

Silver and Neumann concurred with Ben-Gurion on two questions: the absolute sovereignty of the state, and the need for a popular Jewish organization – but on nothing else. The two American Zionist leaders proposed abolishing the Jewish Agency and transforming the Zionist Organization into a widely based body. They also envisaged the Zionist Organization as acting mainly on behalf of the Diaspora rather than for Israel, and consequently recommended the transfer of most Zionist Executive offices to New York. They were backed in this demand by Nahum Goldmann and Rose Halprin, opponents of the Silver–Neumann leadership. Ben-Gurion vehemently attacked this proposal, declaring that the proper place for a Zionist center was neither London nor New York but Israel. A center located in the Diaspora could exert no influence, even if it had ten Herzls at its head, he said. How could pioneering propaganda be disseminated from outside Israel? There was indeed considerable scope for Zionist activity abroad: education, pioneering training, political activity, 'but the center must be Israel. Your proposal is founded on good intentions, but it will not strengthen Zionism. No movement can tolerate two centers, and we have no center except Israel'. The General Zionist leader, Fritz Bernstein, supported this argument.

The individual who was most adamantly opposed to the idea of territorial and organizational separation was the charismatic veteran leader of Polish Jewry, Yitzhak Greenbaum.[5] Unlike most of the other speakers, including members of Mapai, he considered it a matter of principle for cabinet ministers to hold joint appointments as Jewish Agency Executive members, this serving to symbolize the organic links between the Zionist movement and the State of Israel. Unlike the American Zionists, who spoke in political-civil terms, Greenbaum, who had been one of the founders of the 'Association of National Minorities' in the Polish Sejm, saw no basic contradiction between the two functions.[6]

Neither Neumann's demand for total separation, nor Greenbaum's insistence on complete amalgamation, was realistic in light of historical traditions and current needs. At this zenith-point in Zionist history, when the new state was still at risk and the heavy task of absorbing hundreds of thousands of immigrants lay ahead, it was not feasible to consider shifting the center of gravity of the Zionist leadership from Jerusalem to New York. The opposition to such a move was based both on the desire to continue controlling the distribution of Israel Appeal Funds and the fear that the Palestinocentric principle might be eroded. Pinhas Lubianiker (Lavon) of Mapai asserted that at this unprecedented moment in Zionist history, what was required was an Executive willing and able to work in full harmony and in concert with the Jewish state. It was unthinkable for such a body to be located outside Israel. In other words, the Palestinocentrists insisted on the identity of Zionist movement and state, Zionist Executive and Israel government, as the ideological and political expression of 'Jewish normalization'. It was no coincidence that its advocates were the products of Eastern European political culture, where the Jew, in his own eyes and in the view of the world around him, was not considered an organic part of the country where he resided.

This viewpoint was challenged by the American proponents of 'distinctive normalization', with Emmanuel Neumann as their main spokesman. 'We are not only Zionists and Zionist leaders, but also Jewish leaders', he emphasized. As such, they bore a heavy responsibility for both the existence of the state and that of Jews living outside it. After all, he said, the Jews did not exist for the sake of Israel; the reverse was true. He expressed disapproval of Diaspora Zionists who called the Israel government and flag 'ours'. Despite being a Zionist 'from birth', he declared, and despite his own intention to live in Israel, he was apprehensive about such statements.

It appears, therefore, that what distinguished the proponents of the 'Jewish' approach from supporters of the 'distinctive' approach was not only their conception of the Diaspora as exile, but also the civil and political issue of dual loyalty. If we assume that this was a fundamental problem, and that the political apprehension which accompanied it was of marginal importance, we may observe a correlation between the attitude to *galut* and the problem of dual loyalty. The more a Jew felt himself an exile, the less intense would be his preoccupation with the problem of loyalty to his country of birth.

Ben-Gurion, who understood the political fears of Diaspora Jews, but was unwilling to betray his Zionist convictions, emphasized the distinction between the concepts of state and national home. He argued that statehood did not mean that all the aims of Zionism had been achieved; something was missing, which he defined as 'a Jewish national home'. 'The Jewish state,' he said, 'is a state for all the Jews living in it; what we want is a national home for the entire Jewish people ... Herein lies the true partnership between the state and the Jewish people, raising no questions of dual loyalty.' Ben-Gurion had first broached this idea in his testimony before the Peel Commission in 1937, declaring then that a national home was to be preferred to a state, since a state belonged only to its citizens, who could, if they saw fit, bar their brethren from entering it. By reviving this idea, Ben-Gurion added an important dimension to the concept of 'Jewish normalization'. Henceforth, Jews could be simultaneously citizens of their own countries of residence and part and parcel of the Jewish national home in Israel. Even the US Senate, he pointed out, had expressed its support for the establishment of a national home for the Jewish people in Palestine, affirming thereby that loyalty to a national home did not run counter to the American constitution. This theory of a joint framework for the Jewish state and the Jewish people was later to develop into a theory that was 'anti-Zionist' as Zionism was perceived at the time by the leaders of the World Zionist Organization.

As was customary in the pluralistic Zionist Organization, the debate ended in compromise.[7] The Zionist Executive remained in Jerusalem, but members of the Israeli government no longer served on the Zionist Executive (with the exception of Eliezer Kaplan, Minister of Finance, and Treasurer of the Jewish Agency, an indication of the degree to which control of the budget was important to the Mapai leaders). It should be noted that the separation of functions had personal and formal rather than political implications, since the composition of the Executive was determined on a party basis. The compromise was devised due both to American Zionist pressure, and because the opposition parties, for reasons to be discussed below, gave it their backing.[8]

Although Silver and Neumann appeared to have won this round, their gain was in fact illusory. The indirect political outcome of the controversy was their deposal from leadership of the Zionist movement at the beginning of 1949, through a coup engineered by the United Palestine Appeal. The background to this move was the ever-stormy relationship between the two leaders and other Zionist leaders, who charged them with dictatorial conduct, compounded by the personal rift between Silver and his friend and associate, Henry Montor, Chairman of the United Palestine Appeal (UPA). A clear motive was the desire of the non-Zionist community leaders to control and supervise all community fund-raising bodies. The chief spokesman of this group was the President of the United Jewish Appeal, Henry Morgenthau, scion of one of the most aristocratic Jewish families in the United States, who joined forces with Silver's long-time political rival, Nahum Goldmann. After initial reluctance, Ben-Gurion and his party joined the 'revolt', thus turning the scales against Silver. The latter was forced to resign from the Jewish Agency Executive, and to retire permanently from Zionist public life.[9]

Ben-Gurion's conduct indicated his desire to establish links with the non-Zionist Jewish leadership at the expense of his alliance with the Zionists. His next move was to draw up an agreement in 1960 with Jacob Blaustein, President of the

American Jewish Committee. In it, they affirmed that the prime loyalty of Jews as US citizens was to the United States, and stressed that, as such, they had no political commitment towards the State of Israel, which represented only its own citizens. Ben-Gurion also gave his pledge, on behalf of Israel, that the Jewish state would not intervene in the internal affairs of Jewish communities abroad and would respect their autonomous standing and their right to conduct their own affairs according to their own wishes. The agreement was grounded on mutual awareness that any attenuation of the status of American Jewish organizations would prove detrimental both to US Jewry and to the State of Israel. Ben-Gurion reaffirmed his pledge in his correspondence with Blaustein in 1956 and 1961.[10] It should be pointed out that the erroneous impression was created by the agreement that Blaustein was representing US Jewry as a whole. This was somewhat embarrassing for Ben-Gurion, who declared that he would be willing to sign a similar agreement with any other American Jewish leader (a statement which affronted Blaustein, who considered himself BG's close personal friend). Essentially, this act was an expression of Ben-Gurion's disillusionment with the American Zionist leadership and desire to gain direct access to the Jewish community without the mediation of its leaders. This was a source of controversy between the Israeli government and the Zionist movement, and within the Israeli political scene, and much attention was focused on the problem of the standing of the Zionist Organization in Israel.

The debate on the movement's legal status in Israel was conducted in three forums: the Zionist Executive, the 23rd Zionist Congress (held in Jerusalem for the first time in 1951) and the Knesset. Since the cast of characters was the same in all three, I have chosen to analyze their views by party rather than by forum.

In May 1949, the Zionist Executive convened in Jerusalem.[11] In his address to that body, Ben-Gurion did not diverge from his basic stand regarding the Zionist Organization. Although the state was now the main driving-force in Zionist implementation, he said, 'the Zionist movement's hour has not yet passed'; the Zionist Organization, just as it had been since the first Zionist Congress, was still the representative of the common historic affairs of the Jewish people. He did not elaborate on his meaning, but examination of the tasks he proposed assigning to the Zionist movement after the establishment of the state suggests that he was referring to the recruitment of pioneering forces for the building of Israeli society. In this context, he distinguished between 'a touch of pioneering spirit', required of Jews who supported Israel, donated money to the state, bought Israeli products, studied a little Hebrew and visited Israel periodically, and the pioneering spirit and self-imposed deeds of the chosen few. He exhorted Zionists to educate and inspire young people to immigrate to Israel and take part in the constructive revolution 'which will become the pride and joy of Jews everywhere'. One gains the impression that Ben-Gurion was, as yet, reluctant to enter into discussion of the status of the Zionist movement. In light of his conversations with representatives of non-Zionist American Jewish organizations, he preferred to leave the question open at this stage, and to reserve discussions for the next Congress, two years later.

Nahum Goldmann, then Chairman of the US Executive of the Jewish Agency, on the other hand, was anxious to establish certain basic premises regarding the standing of the Zionist movement under new conditions. Unlike Ben-Gurion, who had referred to the role played by the Jewish people as a whole in establishing the state, Goldmann emphasized the role of the Zionist movement which had undertaken certain great tasks that could not have been assigned to the Jewish masses, however strong their support for the Jewish state. To make his point even clearer, he added that the more he thought about the matter, the more convinced he was that the time had not yet come for Zionism to hand over its historic mission 'to the anonymous masses'. What counted for him was ideological and organizational affiliation and commitment rather than emotional identification which, however generous and ardent, could evanesce. Furthermore, he added, Diaspora Zionists did not fear the specter of dual loyalty as did non-Zionists. It is feasible to assume that Goldmann's arguments were inspired by fear that the deposal of Silver and Neumann might have undesirable repercussions for him since those who had recruited the aid of non-Zionist leaders in order to depose their Zionist rivals, might themselves, in turn, fall victim. But, beyond this consideration, Goldmann was drawing attention to a fundamental problem relating to the problem of dual loyalty. Those who feared facing the test claimed that the issue was non-existent and that their sole loyalty was to the country which had granted them equal rights. Zionists like Goldmann, on the other hand, although they never fully clarified the problem, believed in the existence of dual loyalty. At the time this was considered a theoretical issue but the Jewish community was forced to come to grips with it forty years later (see the final section of this book).

A year later,[12] Goldmann defined the Zionist Organization as 'the natural link between the Jewish people and the State of Israel', which should be accorded powers of mediation in internal disputes in the Diaspora. He envisaged a three-level structure: the State of Israel, the Zionist movement and the Jewish masses. Of necessity, there should be an intermediate level, which could carry out tasks which were neither popular nor easy and which Israel could not undertake itself. Having spent decades studying the Jewish people, he knew that the ingathering of the exiles was a long-term, perhaps unending, project. Hence, he declared that the organization of immigration was the 'lifeblood' of the Zionist movement. He also hinted at even more important tasks, probably referring to maintenance of the cohesion and Jewish character of Diaspora communities. The State of Israel must acknowledge the World Zionist Organization's role as representative of the Jewish people, and grant it a 'certain exclusivity' in relation to other Jewish organizations. In the absence of such exclusive status, it would be unclear why most of the funds collected by the United Jewish Appeal (UJA) should be allotted to the Jewish Agency rather than to other organizations. Thus, without discouraging the eagerness of other bodies to work for and within the state, it was essential, he claimed, to proclaim the Zionist movement the representative of the 'organized Jewish people' in working for Israel. Cooperation with other institutions should be regulated through Zionist channels. As a pragmatic politician, Goldmann did not want, at this stage, to determine the formality of ratifying this status (through charter, agreement or legislation). He merely argued that, if the Zionist movement was considered Israel's partner, it must be granted status and prestige.

A total reversal of roles had occurred. The movement which had established the state now needed to receive powers from the state in order to survive. This immediately raised the dialectical question of whether the bestowal of special status by the state would not weaken Israel's own sovereignty. Goldmann representing himself as a Zionist who had aspired to create a Jewish state and did not believe that Zionism could be realized without a state, dismissed this problem. The question of sovereignty was totally unimportant, he said, since the body which bestowed powers could also revoke them. The state reigned supreme in the sphere of foreign affairs but, where the Jewish people was concerned, what harm was there in partnership with the Zionist movement? Goldmann asked. There was a political undertone to this debate. And, in fact, at two sessions of the Zionist Actions Committee in 1949–50,[13] the two radical wings of the movement, Mapam (or MPM, the United Workers' Party) and the Revisionists, found themselves political bedfellows. Each, according to its own views and style, went beyond Goldmann in demanding unique and independent status for the Zionist movement within Israel. Yaakov Hazan of Mapam said that its task should not be confined to fund-raising and dealing with immigration, and demanded on its behalf equal status and a role in constructing Israeli society. It had a moral right to exist and to call on Diaspora Jews for funds only if it was engaged in constructive work in Israel, he argued. Thus, the left-wing opposition found itself advocating the sovereignty of the movement as a counterbalance to the Mapai-dominated sovereignty of the state.

Whereas Mapam sought special status for Zionism in nation-building efforts, the Revisionist movement demanded that it be allotted political sovereignty and the right to intervene in basic political issues affecting the State. Isaac Remba declared that the existence of a Zionist movement with authoritative political standing was sometimes in the interest of the Israeli government. He thought that the movement should be granted the prerogative of voicing its views on such political matters as peace treaties with neighboring countries, which might call for territorial concessions. Joseph Schechtman formulated the Revisionist outlook slightly differently. The state had the right to sovereignty over its own internal and external affairs, he said, but the Zionist Organization should enjoy sovereignty over organized expression of opinion on matters concerning the interests of the entire Jewish people. The veteran Revisionist Meir Grossman, went even further, and in a statement echoing Jabotinsky's declaration to the British Government during the Mandate, he asserted that the Jewish people, though scattered throughout the world, had sovereign rights within the State of Israel. As a consequence, the Zionist Organization, as their representative body, should be accorded special status in Israel. All these Revisionist spokesmen were anxious to impose the political supervision of the Jewish people over the Mapai-led government of Israel.

The General Zionists concurred with both the left- and right-wing radical opposition. Elimelech Rimalt said that just as Zionism could not survive or prove its relevance without political standing and without becoming a partner in the building of the state, the Zionists of Israel could not act on behalf of the state without being able to express their opinions on internal Israeli political matters.[14] Rimalt envisaged a structure reflecting the dynamic growth of the state, based on three concentric circles: the inner nucleus of the state, surround by the Zionist movement, with an outer peripheral circle consisting of the entire Jewish people. 'The state will draw sustenance from the movement, and the movement will derive strength from the periphery'. Whereas Goldmann demanded a mediating role for the Zionist Organization, Rimalt sought organic unity between the three components of state, movement and people.

The views of Silver and Neumann are of particular interest in light of the dramatic events which had preceded these deliberations. Having won a partial victory in 1948 in the debate on the separation of the functions of the Jewish Agency Executive and the Israeli government, and having suffered defeat a year later on the UJA leadership question, Neumann and Silver adopted a moderate and conciliatory approach at the 23rd Congress in Jerusalem. They still insisted, however, on the absolute right of Diaspora Jewry to determine the extent of their support for Israel. Nahum Goldmann, attuned to Mapai's anxieties on this matter, with its strong financial and political implications, and desirous of arriving at a compromise with Ben-Gurion, stated that the Zionist movement should commit itself to unconditional support for the state. Neumann concurred but demanded, in return, that Israel grant the movement the status of 'partner and ally', authorized representative of the Jewish people and instrument for the organization and management of activities on behalf of Israel.[15] In the absence of a consensus, not only was unconditional support not feasible, but there was no point in defining the legal status of the Zionist Organization within Israel, he said. This was a change of direction for Neumann, who had previously attributed great significance to the formal, independent status of the Zionist movement in Israel. Now he preferred mutual consent to any legal charter and argued the need for achieving this consent before any legal status was determined.

Abba Hillel Silver continued this conciliatory trend, seeking to establish an atmosphere of mutual trust as the precondition for formal arrangements. The remarks of this forceful and authoritative man, who had slighted many in his time and roused much animosity, were now tinged with the tragic melancholy of a great leader in decline. Silver explained that Israel was now being called on to recognize the status of the Zionist movement in the Diaspora not as a monopolistic movement but as a leading force. This, he said, was more a matter of attitude than of legal definition. The granting of a charter would fulfill its central function if it symbolized a new approach and willingness to regard the Zionist movement as the representative of the Jewish people. The question of sovereignty would then no longer be relevant. 'It should not arise at all between the State of Israel and the

Jewish people, which is so deeply involved in the building of the state, and whose efforts are the essential condition for the wellbeing of Israel.' It followed that the demand for unconditional support was also not feasible, since this was not a reasonable demand to make of a partner. And, he continued, thereby arousing the ire of the Mapai leaders, 'the support which world Jewry extends and will continue to extend to Israel is, of course, conditional on their satisfaction with what occurs here. If the Jews of the world are not satisfied, if they come to feel that Israel is belittling or disregarding that which is dear to them, their support will automatically and rapidly decrease.'[16] His somewhat paternalistic tone may have resulted from the fact that he hoped to be elected Chairman of the Zionist Executive, a mainly honorary position. He was disappointed, however, as his enemies attacked him on the grounds that he refused to advocate unconditional support for Israel on the part of the Zionist movement.[17]

Unlike the opposition, which unequivocally demanded autonomous status for the Zionist movement in Israel, as representative of the interests of the Jewish people, the coalition parties, and in particular Mapai, had no emphatic views. Zalman Aharonovitch (Aran) spoke of threefold dependence: the building of the state depended on the efforts of the Jewish people; the Jewish people could only be mobilized through the Zionist movement; and the activities of the movement were dependent on aid extended by the state.[18] Eliezer Livneh preferred to deal with facts rather than legal status. The rights of the Zionist movement, he said, were only the expression of its obligations, which were two: to maintain the unity of the Jewish people in a period of threatening disintegration, and to assist in building the state, a task which could not be completed without the extensive aid of the Jews of the West.[19] Thus, according to Livneh, then closely associated with Ben-Gurion, the criterion for determining the status of the Zionist movement was the unity and potential for action of the Jewish people.

Mapai's loyal coalition partner, the National-Religious movement, consisting of the Mizrahi and Hapoel-Hamizrahi parties, had no clear opinions on this subject, and fluctuated between the Mapai view and the moderate General Zionist approach. Up until the 23rd Congress, Ben-Gurion had confined himself to voicing his own emphatic views on the Israeli stand *vis à vis* the Zionist Organization. In his response to the radical opposition's statements at the 1950 Executive meeting, he tried to turn their own weapons against them. Addressing the Revisionists, he cited political legalism, and brandished the banner of constructive pioneering at the left-wing parties. 'That public which has devoted its life to the Zionist endeavor has no need of outside supervision,' he declared. 'Nor does the state require supervision. If the state were to deny its Zionist character supervision would be useless. I take issue with the argument that any Zionist force could possibly be more loyal to Zionism than the self-realizing pioneering Zionist movement, which has linked its destiny to Zionist goals.'[20] Consequently, the binding tie between Diaspora Jews and the State of Israel was morally grounded and could not be defined legally. Two months later, Ben-Gurion convened a meeting of col-

leagues in his office, at which he revealed his thoughts and intentions with regard
to the American Zionist Organization.[21] He maintained that the Zionist ideal, as
espoused by American Jews, was of no further value and that the Zionist Organization now constituted a barrier between the Jewish people and the State of Israel.
Zionist leaders who did not practice what they preached acted as negative role-
models, he said. Ben-Gurion proposed that the Zionist movement be sidestepped
and that a direct appeal be launched at Jewish youth in the United States through a
new organization, which should be established initially by Mapai and then taken
over by the state.

At the 23rd Congress, Ben-Gurion avoided the issue of legal status, reserving
his statement for a future occasion. Since he had resolved, for ideological and
political reasons, to shift the focus of discussion to the Knesset, a wide consensus
was established at the Congress, based on compromise. Nahum Goldmann, one of
the architects of the compromise, emphatically criticized both the radical Revisionist demand that the Zionist movement be granted 'supervisory' powers, and
the Mapam demand for autonomous status for the movement. Goldmann also took
issue with Silver, insisting that Zionists were obligated to extend unconditional
support to Israel, irrespective of the ideological orientation of the Israeli government. He did, however, concede the movement's right to question the government,
and to become an exclusive partner in the building of Israeli society. While
opposed to imposing Zionist authority on Jewish organizations, he thought the
Zionist movement should enjoy preferential status in contacts with Diaspora
Jewish communities.

The following resolution was passed unanimously:

(a) The Congress declares that the practical actions of the World Zionist Organization and its member bodies, aimed at fulfilling its historic tasks in Eretz
Israel, call for full cooperation and coordination with the State of Israel and its
government in accordance with Israeli law.
(b) The Congress deems it necessary that the State of Israel, through appropriate legislation, confer recognized status on the World Zionist Organization, as
the representative of the Jewish people in all matters pertaining to organized
participation of the Jews of the Diaspora in the development and building of the
country, and in the rapid absorption of immigrants.
(c) Regarding all activities carried out for the benefit of Israel within Jewish
communities in the Diaspora, Israel should act only after consultation and coordination with the World Zionist Organization.[22]

The resolution had been phrased carefully to satisfy all those involved. The
emphasis placed on the historic task of the movement in Eretz Israel (rather than
the State of Israel) was intended to placate religious and Revisionist circles. The
clause on determination of the movement's status on the basis of Israeli law was a
bow to the Ben-Gurionist advocacy of state sovereignty, while the mention of
Zionism's role in building the country was aimed at appeasing Mapam. The term

'representative status on all matters pertaining to organized participation' was acceptable to all parties, while the term 'consultation and coordination' was intended to reassure non-Zionist bodies.

A year later, in May 1952, the Israeli government submitted to the Knesset the first draft of the 'Law on the Status of the Zionist Organization and the Jewish Agency'.[23] In his opening statement, Ben-Gurion attempted to clarify the difference between the state's power to confer legal status on the Zionist Organization within the borders of Israel, and its inability to determine the movement's standing outside Israel and among Diaspora communities. Thus, he declared, the question of which body represented the Jewish people in Israel could not be discussed by the Knesset. The draft law, as submitted, contained the following clause: 'The State of Israel recognizes the World Zionist Organization as the authorized agency for continuing to operate within Israel for the development and settlement of the country, absorption of immigrants and coordination, within Israel, of the activities of Jewish institutions and associations active in this sphere.' This clause, which diminished the importance of the Zionist Organization by transforming it from the formal representative of the Jewish people into an authorized agency, aroused controversy during its second and third readings in the Knesset. Although the government was ready to accept the Zionist Organization as a coordinator of activities, most of the opposition and coalition speakers considered the use of the term 'agency' to be a historical injustice and a grave error, and reiterated the views voiced in the executive and the Zionist Congress. The Mapai speakers tried to obscure the true intention by claiming that this was merely a question of semantics. They argued that the law, as written, conferred on the Zionist Organization the status it had requested. It was pointed out that the Zionist movement had been defined as an agency in the mandate over Palestine as drawn up by the League of Nations. (Not mentioned, however, was the fact that the Mandate had referred to a 'Jewish' agency, namely a body representing in Palestine the interests of the entire Jewish people.)

In the course of the acrimonious debate, Ben-Gurion did not mince words and made it abundantly clear that two elements of the Congress resolution could not be included in the final law. Firstly, the state could not decide to award the Zionist Organization the status of representative of the dispersed Jewish people, since 'the state has no authority and control outside its own borders. I personally, as a Jew, have the right to state who represents the Jewish people, and if I am asked by what right I do so, I am not obliged to reply. My own conviction will suffice. But a state is a state, and can act outside its own borders only within the framework of international relations'. Secondly, he said, it was not feasible for the State of Israel to consult and coordinate with the Zionist movement in its activities within Jewish communities abroad. 'Congress has the right to express this wish, and we should not disregard it, nor have we done so in practice, but this practice cannot be made law.'[24] Were it not for our knowledge, in hindsight, of Ben-Gurion's true views, as expressed at his confidential meeting with his colleagues two years previously, this argument would be convincing in its inherent logic. But the formalistic reasoning concealed Ben-Gurion's desire to establish strong ties with the Jewish people and the wide spectrum of their community organizations to replace his reliance on the Zionist movement. This was yet another example of his great skill in employing formal argument, valid in itself, to justify his intentions.

At the conclusion of the debate, Ben-Gurion's wishes notwithstanding, the clause on the status of the Zionist Organization was amended. It was recognized as 'the organized representation of the Jewish people'.[25] Israel Bar-Yehuda explained that this amendment was a compromise between the standpoints of the government and the Congress. The term 'organized representation', he said, did not imply that the Zionist Organization was the sole representative of the people, but that it was the sole organized representative.

The debate was not over, however: Ben-Gurion refused to admit defeat on the fourth clause. The coalition, through a subtle parliamentary tactic, claimed that there was a procedural irregularity in the resolution and returned the draft law to the government. It was retabled in November 1952, in its original form.[26] This time the coalition of Mapai, the religious parties and the Progressives succeeded in pushing it through by a majority of 52, with 21 abstentions. The opposition, aware that it had no prospect of foiling the passage of the law, preferred to abstain. Two years later, in July 1954, when Moshe Sharett was premier, a charter was signed between the government and the Zionist Organization, detailing the latter's sphere of action and authority within Israel.

3 The Zionist Movement in Quest of its Ideological Essence

Galut (exile) is, in a way, an algebraic concept. If exile can be compared to night, then there are pitch-black nights and moonlit nights.

Hayim Greenberg

The political struggle over the status of the Zionist Organization in Israel was accompanied from the outset by ideological self-scrutiny and self-questioning on the meaning of Zionism in a drastically-changed situation. The debate was conducted on two interconnected planes, the political and the ideological. However, ideological clarification continued after the political struggle had been completed, and it became increasingly complex as the realities of the new situation in Israel and in the Diaspora became clearer. The fundamental gap between the 'singular normalization' and the 'Jewish-normalization' approaches grew wider. The debate was conducted mainly on ideological issues, since there was no profound disagreement on practical matters. None of those taking part believed in the prospect of mass immigration from the west, while all of them advocated pioneering immigration. Moreover, nobody demanded that the Zionists of the Diaspora become citizens of Israel, but all agreed on a limited degree of 'dual loyalty', based on the special links between world Jewry and the State of Israel. Even Ben-Gurion, who opposed the Zionist Organization in its existing form, thought that it should be given unique, if not totally representative, status; and when the polemics died down his opponents assented. The ideological debate, in contrast, was profound and rancorous, because it touched on the fundamental elements of national existence. It revolved around two central axes: the relations between the Zionist movement and the Jewish people, and the tension between the concepts of diaspora (*tefutzah*) and exile (*golah*). Participants in the debate included political leaders and activists, headed by Ben-Gurion, and scholars and thinkers, the most prominent among them being Mordecai Kaplan.

Ben-Gurion's attitude towards the Zionist Organization from the beginning of this political career, reflected one of the fascinating aspects of his personality as leader, namely the ability to change direction while maintaining ideological continuity. Initially, it should be pointed out that, since the Second Aliyah, Ben-Gurion had been one of the policy-makers of the Palestinian Jewish labor movement, which called for achievement of the Zionist ideal through pioneering activism. This

demand exacerbated the tension between the pioneering segment, which put ideals
into practice, on the one hand, and the Zionist establishment, bogged down in political routine and the traditionally-minded Jewish masses, on the other. The more
intense the demands that the labor movement made of itself and of others, the more
difficult and protracted the process of changing the values of the Jewish people as a
whole. Ben-Gurion, though a partner to these demands, sought to accelerate the
process of change by political means. In the course of more than half a century of
political activity, he amended his views on this issue several times.

Up to the eve of the First World War, he tried to persuade his comrades of the
need for a 'short cut' in organizing the Jewish masses outside the Zionist Organization with the aim of building a Jewish society in Palestine. In 1909, he proposed the
establishment of a general association of Palestinian Jews, including the 'Old
Yishuv', to represent their political interests before the Ottoman authorities and, in
this sphere, to replace the Zionist Organization. He hoped thereby to introduce
reforms in the community organization, economy and educational network of the
Old Yishuv. A decade later, after the Balfour Declaration, a time of messianic aspirations, he broached a different version of the same idea. Together with Yitzhak
Tabenkin, he proposed the establishment of a popular national association for constructive labor in Palestine, to be initiated by the labor movement. This association,
to be wider-based than the Zionist Organization, would serve as the institutional
foundation for the future Jewish state. Finally, in 1937, during the deliberations on
the partition of Palestine and the establishment of a Jewish state, Ben-Gurion met
with Waldek, one of the prominent American Jewish labor leaders, in order to persuade him to bring his organization into the Zionist fold. His argument was that the
social image of the Jewish state would be determined within the Zionist Organization and that, this being so, it was vital for the labor movement to constitute the
majority of that body. Only if American Jewish workers joined it *en masse* could
this aim be achieved.[1] Nothing came of any of these schemes, but Ben-Gurion did
not forget them, and reverted to them after statehood.

Between 1948 and 1953, after the life-and-death struggle of the War of Independence, when Israel was struggling to absorb mass immigration and to give
shape to national institutions, Ben-Gurion showed himself willing to coexist with
the Zionist Organization. In the following decade, marked by his first resignation,
return to power and final retirement, he declared war on the Zionist movement.

The equilibrium of the first period was based on his assumption that, once the
state had come into existence, it was the main force and lever for the implementation of Zionism. This revolutionary change of direction was not inspired by a
desire to abolish the Zionist movement, since he conceded that 'as long as the central objective of Zionism, and the main mission of the State of Israel have not been
achieved, these two bodies must act in concert'.[2] The transformation of the Zionist
movement into a partner and helper in the Israeli endeavor was compatible with
his traditional outlook, and it enhanced his understanding of the Diaspora and his
forbearance towards those Zionists who chose to remain there. In 1950, speaking

of Zionists living outside Israel, he declared in an address to the Zionist Actions Committee: 'I do not deny their Zionism, and do not consider them to be worse or of lesser standing in the Zionist kingdom. The moral grandeur of the Zionist movement lies in the fact that all are equal: those who have joined the movement only yesterday...each according to his abilities and his path...and each kind of Zionism is acceptable.'[3] At the same time, he hastened to clarify that he was referring to equal partnership in Zionist action, but not in the day to day life of the Jewish state. Israel, though it was the supreme instrument for the realization of Zionism, was to be run solely by its own citizens.[4]

In the same speech, Ben-Gurion reiterated one of his old theories on the role of the Jewish people in the realization of Zionism. 'The state as a whole is a Zionist endeavor and belongs to the Zionist movement and the Jewish people', he asserted. In other words, a kind of national triumvirate had now come into existence, composed of the state, the movement and the people. This conviction that the Jewish people were of equal status to the state and the movement was to grow stronger as time passed, but even at that time was not mere theorizing. Inspired to some degree by his controversy with Silver on the question of the independence of the ZOA, it was to be applied in later years to the World Zionist Organization.

Ben-Gurion believed that the Jewish people had changed since the Holocaust. In Eastern Europe, Zionism had been in the 'egotistic' national interest of the Jewish community in its struggle for improved political and economic status. Among the Jews of the free world, however, Zionism was essentially the expression of altruistic national identification. This being so, he was willing to accept the distinction that American Jews drew between *golah* (exile) and *tefutzah* (diaspora), and agreed with those who claimed that, in Jewish history, *tefutzah* had always preceded *golah*. Although he qualified his agreement, arguing that a diaspora could become a place of exile if conditions worsened, he did, in practice, accept the standpoint represented by the American Jewish Committee, namely that Jewish life in the United States had no parallel in Jewish history.[5] In 1951, during a visit to the United States, he declared that he considered the ingathering of the exiles to be possible, but doubted if it was a historical necessity.[6] All he asked of American Jewry was that they be an active factor in the new national triumvirate: through personal contacts with Israel, through studying Hebrew and through pioneering immigration. At the same time, he hastened to emphasize that, at this time, 'the Zionist mission depends on two elements – the state and the entire Jewish people'.[7] This accentuation of the importance of the Jewish people implied the diminished importance of the Zionist movement, and Ben-Gurion's critics immediately took note of this trend.

In 1952, in submitting the draft law on the status of the Zionist Organization to the Knesset, Ben-Gurion emphasized the historic importance of the organization, its achievements in the present and its role in the future.[8] He did not forget to praise the contribution of the Jewish people to the establishment of the state. In the ensuing debate, his opponents claimed that he was placing excessive emphasis on the contribution of the people and playing down the role of the Zionist movement. In reply, he said: 'I admit to an even weightier sin: my Zionism is but part of and expression of my Jewishness, rather than the reverse. I am a Zionist only because I am a Jew, and not because there is antisemitism in the world.' He acknowledged that another form of Zionism, like Herzl's, was possible and should not be rejected outright. 'But those of us who come of Russian-Jewish stock, and I am one of many – were born Zionists because we were born Jews. We inherited our Zionist aspirations, and our ties to our ancient homeland from our Jewish past.'⁹

These remarks are indicative of a new change of direction in Ben-Gurion's Zionist outlook. At the beginning of the thirties, he had sought to implement the transition from a working class to a working people; now he wanted to extend activities beyond the Zionist Organization and go out to the Jewish people. In the first case, the practical measures had consisted of the transfer of the center of gravity of national activity from the labor movement to the Zionist Organization, whereas now, he intended to shift emphasis from that organization to the Jewish people. Once he had believed it possible to mold the people through inculcating class values; now he hoped to win the people over to the Zionist ideal. Again, in the thirties he had known full well that the cost of going out to the people was temporary suspension of all social and political activism within the pioneering younger generation and within the party. Now, in the fifties, he rapidly decided that the price to be paid for appealing to Western Jews was limiting realization of the Zionist vision to small groups of pioneering idealists. Thus, at the same time that he was working to ratify the law defining the status of the Zionist movement, he was already convinced that that movement's time had passed and that it had become superfluous. In a private letter in 1953, he wrote: 'Zionism means living in the Land of Israel, and not just belonging to the Zionist Organization...According to my beliefs, a man is a Zionist if he lives in Israel and raises his children here, and devotes his life to the Israeli cause and to the fostering of Hebrew culture and the absorption of new immigrants.'¹⁰

There is a clear ideological progression from this private statement to the blunt and provocative public declaration in late 1953, in a letter to the Executive of the WZO, that Zionism meant only one thing – immigration, and that he had nothing in common with anyone who thought otherwise. But, in the political context, was there any connection between his retirement to Sede Boker and his secession from the Zionist Organization? Ben-Gurion resigned because he was weary after six years of emotional tension, and disillusioned with political developments in the young state.¹¹ In addition, as the absorption of mass immigration reached its end, he appears to have become concerned at the outcome. The man who had rejected outright the argument that a war-battered state with a limited budget could not absorb hundreds of thousands of immigrants was now deeply anxious as to the future character and image of Israeli society. As his concern increased, he appealed, as on previous occasions, to the sole group in which he had always invested his trust – the younger generation. He asked them to function as the 'serving elite' of Zionism in the task of realizing Zionist pioneering ideals, and as role-models. But he demanded this first and foremost of himself, as well as from the leaders of the Zionist movement.

The greater the importance he attributed to the younger generation as the idealistic vanguard, the fiercer were his attacks on the Zionist Organization, which he perceived as a barrier between these young people and the realization of national goals. The more he pinned his hope on the young, the more evident was the utopian dimension in his personality and outlook. His utopia was based on four elements: the vision of messianic redemption, belief in the Eternity of Israel (Netzah Yisrael), the yearning for the ideal state, and the need for individual self-realization. Since becoming more openly critical of the character of Zionism, he had begun to contemplate the role of the messianic ideal in Jewish history and its influence on Zionist ideology. Without going into the details of Ben-Gurion's messianic historiosophy, its down-to-earth nature should be emphasized. The most unambivalent interpretation of his views can be found in his correspondence with Nathan Rotenstreich in 1957. Rotenstreich argued that Zionism could not be identified with messianism which meant the end of history, since it was a historical movement, which grew out of specific conditions with the aim of creating a new historical reality for the Jewish people. To this Ben-Gurion replied: 'I do not grasp the messianic mission and vision in metaphysical terms, but as a socio-cultural and moral conception. The messianic ideal does not mark the end of history – but the process of its redemption.' And in order to stress the real implications of his views, he added: 'This conviction is based on my acquaintance with the Jewish people, and not on any mystic faith. Any "holy radiance" is within us, within our souls and not outside us.'[12]

The same is true of his own interpretation of his belief in the Eternity of Israel. From his point of view, this belief is valid only when the existence of the people and its historic continuity are guaranteed, and it cannot be confined to 'some abstract, anonymous, non-binding affinity'. Only a 'personal commitment to the Eternity of Israel, even if only by a few, has any value, and its historic and constructive force is greater than the fictitious affinity which many profess to a name which has been emptied of content. And even this individual commitment to the Eternity of Israel has no validity without Hebrew education and self-realizing pioneering effort'.[13] His faith in the messianic mission of the Jew and activist conception of the Eternity of Israel led him to the concept of the ideal state, which he perceived as the sole security for the continued existence of the Jewish people and the noblest expression of its national character as a chosen people. In 1957, in the aftermath of the Sinai Campaign victory, exhilarated by his release from the existential dread of the anxious days before the war, he declared:

> We have sufficient reason to believe that we are capable of being a chosen people. And one can already discern three forces at work in the State of Israel, which indicate clearly the moral and intellectual ability which lie in our midst.

They are: the labor settlement movement, the Israel Defence Forces and our men of science, literature and art.[14]

Thus, he envisaged the 'serving elite' as containing within them a yearning for the utopian vision, for the endless path which has no final objective. In answer to his critics, and particularly to Martin Buber, who voiced the fear that political messianism on the one hand, and the messianic state on the other, would not bring about achievement of the end through the means, Ben-Gurion replied that he did not believe in the existence of the final objective, but in the practical path leading towards it. At the same time,

man's aspirations have no final destination...either in reality or in vision. Man's nobility lies in a constant striving for a goal, and as we approach it – it grows distant or, to be more exact, we see that the goal lies beyond us. And it is a good thing that we never reach our goal. Our lives would be empty and would dwindle if the vision were checked and we clung to the goal we had attained.[15]

This explains his paradoxical idea that it is necessary to believe in the Messiah in order for Him not to come.[16] Ben-Gurion was a utopist for whom the eternal path was a goal in itself, and hence his constantly reiterated appeal to the young, the sole group in society which had not yet achieved its goal and was still en route to it. Hence, the young could be exhorted to realize the fourth principle – individual realization of the pioneering mission. After the Sinai War, Ben-Gurion became even more convinced that it was possible to hand down to the young generation in Israel and in the Diaspora the vision of messianic redemption, with all its Jewish and universal implications. 'Our young people', he said, 'are worthy of this vision ... more perhaps than young people in any previous time they are capable of bearing it not only on their lips but in their hearts and through their actions.'[17]

As the messianic mood took hold of him, and as his thoughts turned increasingly towards the younger generation, Ben-Gurion's attitude to institutionalized Zionism became hostile. His conciliatory attitude towards the Jews of the Diaspora also underwent a change. In 1954 he could still ask the Zionist Organization whether Zionism was taking note of actual assimilation, integration into non-Jewish culture.[18] He was inferring that his demand that Zionists immigrate to Israel was aimed primarily at combatting the process of assimilation in the Diaspora. In 1957, however, addressing the Zionist ideological convention in Jerusalem, he did not hesitate to declare: 'The title of Jew not only preceded the title of Zionist, but says much more than does "Zionist". Judaism is more than Zionism and the existence of Judaism cannot be reconciled with assimilation, which is the fate of most of those in the Diaspora who call themselves Zionists.'[19] He hastened to stress that assimilation was not a deliberate and conscious act but a spontaneous process, but was no less dangerous because of this and perhaps even more so. He went on to state explicitly that 'the State of Israel is now the Zionist movement, and bears the vision of redemption to those who dwell within it and to the people in the Diaspora'.[20]

Ben-Gurion had also adopted a new tone with regard the Diaspora. Here he was torn between his recognition of the process of constant change in history in general and Jewish history in particular, which demanded constant re-evaluation of reality, and his adherence to durable and unchanging values. It may safely be asserted that, in practice, Ben-Gurion accepted the existence of the Diaspora (*golah*), but, in theory, he rejected exile (*galut*). Although he distinguished between Soviet Jewry, still living in the *golah*, and the Jews of the United States, in the Diaspora (*tefutzah*), he perceived a common factor in both situations, based on the link to the Land of Israel, minority status and the state of tension peculiar to Jews living between two cultural entities and maintaining their own unique economic structure. In short, he asserted that Jews outside Israel were 'human debris, trying to adhere to one another perhaps more than other human beings under the same conditions'.[21] This discordant term, (*avak adam*, literally human dust) was not used negatively, in this context. It was, rather, his objective view of any group trying to preserve its national consciousness in the absence of a political framework. Ben-Gurion advised this group, if they wished to maintain their national identity, to guard the messianic vision in their hearts, to learn Hebrew, and to maintain personal ties with the State of Israel.[22]

As for his views on exile (*galut*) as a historic phenomenon, in 1957 he launched a vehement attack, reminiscent of the fervor of his early years, against those, headed by Nahum Goldmann, whom he perceived as 'glorifiers' of *galut*. 'Every one of us', he said,

> bows his head in awe and profound admiration before the great moral force displayed by the Jews in their wanderings and tribulations in the Diaspora, their ability to withstand enemies and despoilers, oppressors and murderers, without renouncing their Judaism. But as to the *galut* in which Jews lived and still live, I regard it as a sorry, miserable, pathetic and dubious experience, nothing to be proud of. The reverse is true – it should be utterly rejected. I admire any sickly and suffering individual who struggles for survival, and does not submit to his bitter fate, but I do not regard his condition as ideal...I do not despise Shylock for making a living at usury. He had no alternative in his place of exile, and his moral attributes outweighed those of the elegant nobles who humiliated him; but I cannot make Shylock my ideal and strive to resemble him. The Jews of the Diaspora are not Shylocks, but it is hard to reconcile the glorification of *galut* life with the ideal...of Zionism. As one who rejects *galut*, I must reject glorification of *galut*.[23]

At the 1961 Zionist Congress, Ben-Gurion quoted the talmudic saying: 'He who resides outside the Land of Israel is as one who has no God'[24] (Ketubbot 110b). When this quotation roused a storm of protest, particularly from the American Jewish leaders, Ben-Gurion replied that this was not his own opinion; he was merely quoting the sages. He had been trying to illustrate the dilemma of religious Jews in the Diaspora; he himself was convinced that 'a Jew is a Jew – wherever he may be'.[25] However, in light of his basic outlook in these years, it seems that he was referring not only to observant Jews, but implying that any Jew living in the Diaspora was excluded from sharing in the constant striving for the messianic ideal on earth.[26] These beliefs were linked to his profound concern for the future of the Jewish people in the West, faced with the threat of assimilation, and for the social and moral image of the Jewish state, as he envisaged it. This concern continued to haunt him when he retired from the premiership for the last time, shortly afterwards.[27]

It was the very point on which Ben-Gurion condemned contemporary Zionism, which Mordecai Kaplan considered to be a positive feature. The fundamental difference between the two men lay in their view of the focal point of the Zionist ideal and deed: Ben-Gurion was a pure 'Palestinocentrist' in every sense of the term, while Kaplan was a consistent 'Diasporacentrist'. It is more than a symbolic coincidence that in 1909, when Ben-Gurion issued a call for the overall organization of the Yishuv in Palestine as a political-territorial body led by Zionist activist forces, Mordecai Kaplan delivered an address in which he expounded the basic tenets of his Zionist outlook, primarily the spiritual, national and religious renaissance of Judaism in the Diaspora in general and the United States in particular through Zionist activist means. He repeated this view in 1925, in a speech at the foundation-laying ceremony of the Hebrew University on Mount Scopus in Jerusalem, and a decade later, in his important book *Judaism as a Civilization*,[28] and in articles he wrote on the eve of the establishment of Israel and immediately after statehood was proclaimed (see early chapters of the present book). At all these stages of Zionist development, when Ben-Gurion put his Zionist beliefs into practice, Kaplan continued to be a spiritual Zionist in American-religious Ahad ha-Amite style. According to his convictions, Zionism as a national concept and Jewish Palestine as a religious and historical center should be the inspiration for Jewish civilization, finding organizational expression on a universal basis. Precisely because of the significance he attributed to Zionism, and because he was never a political Zionist, he was obliged to conduct an ideological reckoning when Israel came into being, and transformed the reality of Diaspora life. In 1955, he published a book entitled *The New Zionism*, consisting of a collection of his speeches in New York.[29]

The speeches addressed the problem of the ongoing crisis in Zionism, which was also the crisis of Judaism, threatening to introduce disarray into the Zionist movement, to affect the State of Israel and to undermine the unity of the Jewish people. This crisis, he said, stemmed from the dispute between the deniers and the advocates of the Diaspora, which was even more acute than the controversy which had once divided Herzl and Ahad ha-Am. Its settlement was now even more important than in the past because of the existence of the Jewish state. He cautioned that if Zionism was not capable of creating a basis for close collaboration between the

Jewish community in Israel and Jewish communities in the Diaspora, the outcome would be totally different from the intentions of Herzl and Ahad ha-Am.[30] This warning followed on Ben-Gurion's onslaught on the Zionist movement abroad, launched in 1953/4, which was warmly approved by various writers, prominent among them Eliezer Livneh. Kaplan's central contention was that Zionism existed for the sake of the Jews, and not the reverse. Hence, it should adapt itself to what could and might, logically, be expected of the Jewish people. Otherwise, the Jews of the United States would become alienated from events in Israel and might reduce their support for the building of the Jewish society in the new state.[31]

Similarly to Ben-Gurion, Kaplan was a pragmatist and a man of values, who attributed importance to morals and to ideals in their practical manifestation. As long as collective Jewish existence in the world was an enigma, he argued, the attempt to determine whether Jews lived in an exile or a diaspora was impossible and superfluous. What was necessary was to seek ways of safeguarding and strengthening Jewish existence. And, since, according to his axiomatic assumption, Zionism was 'active present-day Judaism'. The crisis of Zionism was also the crisis of Judaism and the search for a solution would continue as long as the collective existence of Judaism was not secure. His inevitable conclusion was that the establishment of the state had been only the first essential step towards the redemption and spiritual rebirth of the Jewish people. This historic move could be completed only if Zionism refused to confine itself to the role of a cultural and political movement, and became a religious movement in tune with the spirit of the times.[32]

Why was the religious dimension of Zionism so important to Kaplan, who rejected the traditional Jewish theories on divine revelation and the Chosen People?[33] The answer lies in his perception of Zionism as a unique civilization, existing above the historic time-span outside a particular territory, and beyond any single culture. The sole model suited to this type of existence was monotheistic religion, the only form of supranational society.[34] Beyond this, Kaplan believed that modern society had particular need of religion, which preached moral values. Even greater was the need of Zionist Judaism as a civilization, since the demand for the right to return to Palestine and the desire for continued Jewish existence in the Diaspora could be realized only through the moral tenets of the Jewish faith and way of life. Moreover, for the Jews, the building of the Land of Israel was more than an act of political liberation – it was 'religion in action'. This, therefore, was the new Zionism which, alone, had the power to inspire the pioneering spirit in Israel and in the Diaspora. Kaplan was seeking to create a new tri-dimensional Zionist synthesis: Ahad ha-Am's spiritual outlook; Herzl's political approach; and his own religious-moral-pragmatic ideas. This ideology led him to espouse a new and original theory on Jewish existence in the future. Following on Dubnow's theory of the changing centers, Ahad ha-Am's qualitative spiritual center, and Rawidowicz's elliptic structure, Kaplan evolved his own theory, borrowing from all the above, yet uniquely his own.

At the 1957 ideological convention where he clashed indirectly with Ben-Gurion, Kaplan delivered a speech outlining his theories and proposals for action in the near future.[35] He offered his own interpretation of Ahad ha-Am. Those who claimed that Ahad ha-Am had viewed Diaspora Jewry as the perimeter with Israel as the center were in error, he said. Ahad ha-Am had merely stressed that the main objective in building Eretz Israel should be the renaissance of the Jewish people. To this end the Jews in the Diaspora should be re-educated in the spirit of the nationalism which they had lost in the course of their wanderings. Ahad ha-Am hoped that the impetus for this education would come from Palestine, as it grew and developed. It was in this sense that he perceived Palestine as the center. Regardless of whether this was the true interpretation of Ahad ha-Am's intentions, it is clear that Kaplan perceived Eretz Israel as a source of temporary inspiration for Jewish culture, until the Diaspora became its match. Only then would there be true unity between them. This meant, he claimed, that, as regards social structure and ideology, it was necessary to redefine the term 'Jewish people'. Socially speaking, it was a hub with spokes radiating from it. The Jewish community in Israel was the hub, and the communities in the Diaspora were the spokes.[36] In this respect, and ideologically as well, Jewish tradition should be seen as the rim holding together all the spokes. In other words, where Ahad ha-Am had believed that the national center would maintain the perimeter, namely the Diaspora, Kaplan argued that it was pluralistic faith which would bind the two together.

On the basis of this theory, he hoped that it was possible to create Judaism of varying degrees of intensity. At the core, in Palestine, Judaism would be realized in every sphere, from politics and culture to religion and everyday life. Judaism outside Israel would forgo various spheres of life without forfeiting its right to identify with historic Judaism.[37] He envisaged communities in Israel and abroad which though not identical in essence would be equal in standing. It should be noted that Kaplan was careful, in referring to the Jews of Palestine, to use the term 'Jewish community' and not 'Jewish state', for several reasons: firstly because he had never been a political Zionist; secondly because, as far as he was concerned, religion, and not the Jewish state, was the central element; and thirdly, as an ardent advocate of American democracy and a great believer in its liberal-pluralistic spirit, he refused to identify the State of Israel, which also encompassed non-Jewish citizens, with Judaism. None of these arguments was original and unique to him, but together they created a singular outlook, which explains his clash with Ben-Gurion. The latter, at this time, had arrived at the conclusion that the Jewish state blended Zionism as idea and as deed, and that the links of Diaspora Jews to Israel, in various ways, were the guarantee of the continued existence of Judaism.

If we pursue the logic of this thought, it implies that Judaism can survive without the state, on condition that Zionism exists, with the socially and culturally activist Jewish community in Palestine as its core. This theory does not deny the importance of the State of Israel in Jewish experience, but diminishes it. A year later, Kaplan published a plan entitled 'A Proposed Platform for the Greater Zionism'.[38]

In it he distinguished between the State of Israel, the Jewish community in Israel and the land of Israel. In the first clause he argued that recognition of the centrality of the state in Jewish experience was vital for the continued existence of the Jewish people. In the fourth clause he wrote of the establishment of unity between the community in Israel and Diaspora communities on the basis of mutual responsibility and partnership so as to maintain world Jewry as a vital element in universal civilization. In enumerating the functions of Zionism he declared that it should bolster and guarantee the rights of the Jews in the land of Israel as the spiritual homeland of the Jewish people. The Poalei Zion historian Bezallel Sherman was roused to respond. He commented that to employ such terms as 'state' and 'spiritual homeland', which belonged to the realm of theoretical concept, could harm the Zionist movement, which still faced political challenges and obstacles.[39]

Kaplan replied that, in using the term 'Greater Zionism' he was implying not only political support for Israel but concern for the existence of Judaism as a whole throughout the world. As for the distinction itself, he made it abundantly clear that the state of Israel was not the Jewish state. It was a state established by the Jewish Agency to enable the Jews of the world who chose to do so out of free choice or were forced by external circumstances, to settle there, and to maintain a national majority there. Until the political and economic problems of the state were solved, and as long as it required the assistance of Diaspora Jews, the existence of the Zionist movement, operating through the Jewish Agency, was essential. In other words, the state was central to Jewish existence but was not a Jewish state; on the other hand, the country traditionally belonged to all the Jews of the world and the community was Jewish in essence. One of the first principles of the 'Greater Zionism', therefore, was that it should be distinguished from the existing Zionist Organization. The latter was intended to be an instrument and means for recruiting aid for Israel as long as that country needed it, while 'Greater Zionism' was to be the organizing ideology of a worldwide based 'Jewish civilization'. Since the future of Judaism depended on the organization and institutionalization of Judeo-Zionist civilization, the question of the Ingathering of the Exiles was marginal to this approach to the point that Kaplan did not even refer to it. When Sherman commented on this, Kaplan replied that the fundamental element of Greater Zionism was the renunciation of the dream of the Ingathering of the Exiles not only because of its unrealistic nature, but also because it was dangerous. He went on to explain that to concentrate on bringing all the Jews of the world to Israel, an unattainable objective even if one believed that most Jews wanted to come, could lead to neglect of efforts to develop and maintain Jewish life in the Diaspora. This, paradoxically enough, even tragically, meant that Zionism might be a contributing factor in the assimilation of Jews into the cultures surrounding them. In place of the impractical idea of ingathering all Jews, Kaplan envisaged an international Jewish framework in which the Jewish community in Israel and the communities in the Diaspora would resemble the sun and the planets, or the nucleus and the electrons clustered around it.

At this point, one notices a certain similarity between Kaplan's Greater Zionism and Ben-Gurion's 'ideal state', despite the undeniable differences between them. Ben-Gurion too doubted the possibility of bringing all the Jews of the world to Israel, and hence issued his call for pioneering immigration. Kaplan, in contrast, viewed with disfavor the desire to ingather all the Jews of the Diaspora, but did not reject pioneering immigration, which he considered to be part and parcel of national activism aimed at ensuring the survival of the Jewish people.

Ben-Gurion considered that the process of building the ideal Jewish state was the realization of the messianic vision without goal or end. Kaplan's Greater Zionism was a modern form of messianism, directed at all Jews who were concerned for the future of the Jewish people and its place among the nations.[40] The messianic character of Zionism stemmed from the fact that it had transformed modern Jews from a 'ghost people' to a living international community; it has bestowed significance on Jewish life, and given it definition, and it offered hope of revelation of the new moral, idealistic and religious mission of the Jewish people. According to Kaplan, this ideal had often undergone change of form in classic Zionism. For Kalisher it was the renaissance of the Jewish religion in its homeland, Palestine. For Ahad ha-Am it meant the building of a society perfectly attuned to the moral teachings of the prophets. For Gordon it was grounded on the concept of the sanctity of labor and the return to nature. Kaplan's modern version was based on the creation of a transnational Jewish people in the territorial sense of the term, with Eretz Israel at its heart or core. Herein lies the great difference between the two men. Both postulated a link between the existence of the Jewish people and the messianic vision and thought that it was conditional on the existence of an organizational framework, but whereas, for Ben-Gurion, this framework was the ideal state of Israel, for Kaplan it was the worldwide pluralistic Zionist movement.

The third area in which there was both a certain similarity and a profound contrast between the two men was in their attitude to the existing Zionist organization. Ben-Gurion objected to its existence and consequently decided to leave its ranks. Kaplan was not reconciled to its prevailing image but regarded it as a means or a lever for the establishment of the framework of Jewish civilization. To Zionism, he declared, should be entrusted the task of granting the Jewish people 'de facto existence' through convening a constituent assembly to compose a constitution, 'a new type of social organism' for the people.[41] The constitution would be enforced not by a government but by a managing committee to be democratically elected by the Jews of the world. Its task would be to conduct all activities in the cultural, spiritual and organizational spheres of Jewish life. This, he felt, was the only way of maintaining constant and organic ties between the State of Israel and the Jews of the Diaspora.

In the interim stage, until the new international structure came into being, Kaplan proposed that all Jewish organizations join the Zionist movement on the basis of the guidelines he had proposed. In this fashion, he believed, the Zionist organization would become a movement for Zionist Judaism.

To sum up, Ben-Gurion's Jewish approach placed the state at the center of Jewish life, while Kaplan's distinctive approach perceived the Zionist movement as the focus. Ben-Gurion perceived Jewish life only as linked in various ways to Israel, while Kaplan thought that Jewish existence in the Diaspora was distinctive in its inclusion in a single framework of Zionist Jewish civilization. Consequently, they were also divided on the idea of the messianic mission. For Ben-Gurion, the ideal state was the instrument realizing this mission through never-ending endeavor, while for Kaplan, Greater Zionism was the precondition for fulfilment of the mission on a universalist basis.

History has shown that both approaches, despite their inherent logic, was utopian; yet they found ardent supporters who accepted them in part or in full. Ben-Gurion enjoyed the backing of the activists within his party, headed by Eliezer Livneh.[42] He also won hearts within the constructivist pioneering left-wing. The Mapam leaders Tabenkin and Hazan and others shared his Israelocentric views.[43] In the United States, some Zionist intellectuals supported him, foremost among them the Zionist essayist and editor of the *Jewish Spectator*, Trude Weiss-Rosmarin. She totally rejected the view popular among American Jewish intellectuals, that the United States was a kind of new Babylon. At the most it was Alexandria, she wrote, and thus its fate would be assimilation, as in that ancient city and in modern Germany. She propounded a historical-philosophical theory of two types of Jewish centers, on the one hand Alexandria, Germany and the United States and on the other Babylon, Spain and Eastern Europe. The yardstick for distinguishing between them was the attitude of the Jews who lived in them. In the first type, the Jews saw themselves as belonging both culturally and spiritually to the society into which they had been born, while in the second type they felt alienated. The Jews of the latter countries were on their guard and preserved and fought for their national and religious distinctiveness, while the former renounced it of their own volition. Her unequivocal conclusion was that US Jewry was wholly American, while Babylonian Jewry had never been Babylonian. Therein, she wrote, lay the difference, which would determine the future of US Jews.[44]

Weiss-Rosmarin challenged Kaplan's belief that Jews could live simultaneously in two civilizations, American and universal-Jewish.[45] She demanded instead a return to Herzl's classic Zionism, which had highlighted the plight of Jews, and that of Ahad ha-Am, which had focused on the plight of Judaism. American Jews, she asserted, were threatened by 'the plight of Judaism', meaning the threat of assimilation. But at the same time they were not indifferent to 'the Jewish plight', because they were the sole minority in the country fighting for their distinctive existence. This being so, the 'Jewish plight' was not confined to the Jewish communities of the persecuted diasporas, as most American Zionist leaders argued, but was a universal Jewish problem. Both aspects of this classic Zionist ideology were in need of revitalization within the American Jewish situation.[46] Zionism was not an exercise in intellectual nit-picking, but 'the march onwards to Zion to aid in building the State of Israel', so that the largest possible number of Jews could live there and realize their Jewishness to the full. Weiss-Rosmarin composed a new Basle proclamation in Israelocentric spirit, declaring that all political, economic and organizational activity should be directed towards the building of the Jewish society in Israel. She wrote with profound admiration of Ben-Gurion, who had offered an example to all American Zionists through his retirement to Sede Boker. This act would disturb them as long as they lived. 'We will certainly not follow in his footsteps,' she wrote, 'but we will think of him and of his life there, with a sense of shame.'[47]

Kaplan was, of course, championed by those of his followers who had founded the Reconstructionist movement with him, but not by them alone.[48] His non-etatist and neo-religious interpretation of Zionism was shared by other Zionist thinkers. The writer and philosopher Ludwig Lewisohn considered Zionism to be the continuation and modern interpretation of the traditional yearning for redemption, and identified the struggle of Zionism with Judaism's struggle for survival. He believed that, for every Jew, Israel was a 'religious achievement'.[49]

Particularly close in views to Kaplan was the veteran Zionist writer, Maurice Samuel. In early 1953, before Ben-Gurion's famous attack on the Zionist movement, Samuel cautioned against the statist-Canaanite mood which threatened to dominate Israeli thinking, describing it as an anti-Jewish and even anti-Zionist phenomenon.[50] Rejection of Jewish tradition meant detachment from the roots of the Jewish survival ability. Hence, the demand for pioneering immigration alone was dangerous, since it indicated detachment from the Diaspora and from tradition, as advocated by the Israeli labor movement, and greatly reduced the dimensions of the Jewish problem.

For Samuel, as for Kaplan, the state was never the supreme objective of Zionism, but a means of strengthening the Jewish people. Hence the necessity for ties between the state and the Jews of the Diaspora, to be founded on equilibrium. Just as Israel reinforced the spirit of Judaism in the Diaspora, American Jews would contribute to the implanting of the liberal-democratic spirit, which was also a Jewish value. Moreover, Samuel explained, just as the United States was the leading power of the free world, US Jewry should become the leading force among the Jews of the world.[51]

So far, Samuel's views were identical with those of Kaplan, but in overall view there were differences between them. In a series of articles published in 1954, in which he also took issue with Ben-Gurion, then at the height of his assault on the Zionist Organization and its leaders, Samuel laid down four principles for contemporary Zionism.[52] The first was bolstering of the Jewish consciousness of Diaspora Jews, which could be achieved only through close collaboration with and assistance from Israel. Secondly, the pioneering movement was, primarily, the concern of American Jewry. Kaplan, of course, did not regard pioneering in this light, although he was not opposed to it on principle. It was the fourth principle, however, which separated the two men. Samuel argued that the Ingathering of the Exiles had not been completed, and should encompass the Jews of the free countries as well. Finally, again unlike Kaplan, Samuel believed in a spiritual center as envisaged by Ahad ha-Am, a place with a Jewish majority, maintaining a healthy society. It would influence Diaspora Jewry by the very fact of its existence, enhance their national self-awareness, bolster their unity and bestow meaning on their lives as Jews. From this it transpires that, unlike Kaplan, Samuel did not believe that the Diaspora could ever achieve equal status with the center in Israel in the Jewish sense. American Jewry should become the leading force in world Jewry as regards the democratization of Jewish society, while the State of Israel should become the consolidating center in the national sense.

Reuben (Robert) Gordis, one of the important thinkers of the conservative movement, was not far behind Mordecai Kaplan in placing religion at the center of Jewish experience. He asserted that Jews could not be defined in the accepted terms such as 'race', 'national entity' or even 'cultural community'. The most suitable definition for them was 'people', a word whose traditional meaning was 'religious-cultural-ethnic entity'. To replace this unique combination by the concepts and contents of modern nationalism, would lead to assimilation, not only in the Diaspora but also in Israel. The danger of emergence of a generation of 'Hebrew-speaking goyim' was not unimaginable. He went on to point out the unique and outstanding elements in Jewish existence. Like Kaplan, he concluded that Jewish dispersal was not only possible but also essential, so that it was incumbent on the spiritual leadership to promote the Diaspora and to enrich the content of its life in the spirit of the prophets. They were divided only on the question of the role of the State of Israel in Jewish life. Gordis allotted the state a central role, 'not only as a place of refuge for our oppressed brethren, but as the essential background for complete Jewish life and for the creation of enduring values for the people and for all of mankind'.[53] Therefore, 'it is incumbent on all Jews of the world to take part in building Israel and defending it'. This unique partnership between the state and the Diaspora would mitigate the impact of particularist nationalism, provide anomalous Jewish existence with its universalist element and enable the Jewish people to fulfil its messianic mission and continue to struggle 'to re-form the world in the divine spirit'.

The American-Zionist political leadership also essentially accepted Kaplan's views on the essence and role of Zionism after the establishment of Israel. It should be noted that, from the beginning of the debate in 1948, when Abba Hillel Silver and Emmanuel Neumann proposed separating the Zionist Organization from the state, they used Kaplan's definitions of the role of Zionism in the Diaspora. Even if they did not borrow from him, and had no intention of creating a general framework for 'Jewish civilization', as he did, they identified with his idea of organizing world Jewry within an overall Zionist framework. On the second issue as well, the definition of Jewish existence outside Israel, exile or diaspora, they concurred. They too considered the debate on definitions to be unimportant and irrelevant. The Hadassah leader, Rose Halprin, defined exile (*galut*) as pertaining to political pressure and economic distress, and hence unrelated to Western

Jews, particularly those of the United States.[54] Silver argued that there was no precise definition for the terms *galut* and *tefutzah*, and that they were interchangeable as a result of historical development. Consequently 'we have no need of definitions'. On the other hand, 'the aim of Zionism, as defined in the Basle program, is to express, even if insufficiently, the will of the Jewish people, to put an end to life in alien countries and to rise up again as a free nation in the land of their fathers'.[55] This objective had already been attained. As for the question of *galut* or *tefutzah*, it would be decided by history. At the 23rd Zionist Congress, under pressure from American Zionists, the '*heh*' of the definite article was omitted from the word *galuyot* (diasporas) in the first clause of the definition of Zionism. It read: 'The task of Zionism is the consolidation of the State of Israel, the ingathering of exiles (*galuyot*) in Eretz Israel and the guaranteeing of the unity of the Jewish people.'[56] The original version contained the word *ha-galuyot* (the exiles), i.e. all Jewish communities abroad, including the United States.

The debate between the two schools of thought was endowed with profound theoretical significance by two important thinkers: Nathan Rotenstreich in Israel and Ben Halpern in the United States. They began to ponder these subjects towards the end of the Second World War, and contributed to clarification of the concept of *galut* in a time of change. In 1944–5 Rotenstreich pointed to the growing 'distinctive-normalism' trend among American Zionists and non-Zionists. He wrote that the Zionists were ignoring the functional ties between the ingathering of the people in their own land and their sovereignty over that land. According to Rotenstreich, 'the crux of the Jewish problem, according to this approach, focuses on the formal political sphere rather than the social one'.[57] In other words, Zionists believed that by winning sovereignty, they had rendered *galut* null and void, although the majority of the Jewish people were still living outside their national state. Non-Zionist Jews *a priori* excluded the United States, which had granted them full emancipation, from the roster of countries which could be defined as *golah*. These were 'two different attempts to prove that a political regime can solve and eliminate the Jewish problem, and that *galut* can disappear spontaneously rather than through the auto-emancipatory efforts of the Jewish people'.[58] Dismissing these two ways of thinking, Rotenstreich dwells on the auto-emancipatory approach, entailing liberation from political subjugation through the restoration of national sovereignty; liberation from the threat of division and dispersion through assembling large parts of the Jewish people in their historic homeland; and liberation from the threat of assimilation in the surrounding cultures. As long as this situation remained fundamentally unchanged, the Jews outside Israel were living in *galut*, he said, and it was immaterial if it was defined as diaspora by the Jews of enlightened countries, or exile by Jews suffering oppression. Rotenstreich did not view the ingathering of the exiles and the abolition of *galut* as a realistic possibility. He did, however, demand of the Jews auto-emancipatory effort out of awareness of the existence of galut with all that this implied in the political, social and cultural spheres.

Rotenstreich's distinction between the emancipatory and auto-emancipatory approaches clarified the differences between the Jewish normalistic and distinctive normalistic outlooks, and led him to a practical conclusion. In 1949, at a time when the waves of mass immigration were flooding in to the new state, Rotenstreich spoke of the future of Zionism as a minority movement of educators.[59] He proposed that the Zionist education of the chosen few be based on four premises. He wanted to abolish the unidimensional catastrophic theory of Zionism, and to base it, instead, on a variety of arguments, adapted to changing historic conditions and the unifying link between them. In the moral sphere, he challenged the distinction drawn between suffering Jews who were in need of Zionism and those living comfortable and peaceful lives who were required only to aid in realizing the Zionist vision. This division, he asserted, was harmful to the concept of national unity and morally abhorrent since it provided justification for evasion of national obligations. He also adopted an activist-pioneering approach, aimed at endowing the lives of the pioneers, as individual Jews, with special meaning. His fourth theory related to the cultural and psychological spheres. Unlike many Zionists, Rotenstreich acknowledged the success of Jewish emancipation in the Western countries, but wanted to direct Zionist education precisely at the problem created by this very success, namely the threat of the eradication of Judaism through cultural assimilation. Only disproval of the conviction that emancipation had solved the Jewish problem in the Diaspora could create a dialogue between the two parts of the Jewish people, he wrote. This should be based on recognition of the existence of parallel Jewish life in the United States and in Israel as a historical phenomenon, but not as national content.[60] Educational activity, guided by this spirit and aimed at a minority, was appropriate for the interim stage in Zionist development, until all Jews had been brought home to Israel, he declared. These views are reminiscent of those of Ben-Gurion and the left-wing and activist sections of the kibbutz movement. Understandable in this context is the criticism he levelled against Ahad ha-Am's advocacy of the spiritual center, and particularly against those who hoped to achieve it.[61] His starting point was the confrontation between two concepts, 'mission' and 'pioneering'. He defines the idea of the spiritual center as the mission of a minority living under ideal national conditions *vis à vis* the Jews of the Diaspora, who could never achieve this status. He defined pioneering as the deeds of the select few directed towards the larger group in the hope that some day, after a protracted process of education, they too would play an active part in the deed. The theory of pioneering endeavour implied the equal value of all sectors of the people and hence contributed to unity, while the mission theory did not, since it would create dependence of the majority in the Diaspora on the minority in the Israeli center. 'In this situation, the Jews of the Diaspora will remain eternal clients.' This assertion, which was to be cited three decades later by the advocates of the Jewish center in the Diaspora, was aimed at spurring the Jews of the free diasporas to auto-emancipatory action, which would link them to Israel not as clients but as equal partners, thereby removing the threat of assimilation, and eventually guiding them towards the State of Israel.

His views on pioneering as a unifying force led Rotenstreich to adopt a stand in the debate on the status of the Zionist Organization in Israel.[62] He took up cudgels against the desire of some American Zionists to win autonomous status for the Zionist Organization, because he felt that this trend stemmed from and was nurtured by the *galut* ideology which accepted the division and dispersion of the Jewish people. At the same time, the state could not replace the Zionist Organization, because its sphere of sovereignty did not encompass most of the Jewish people.

As regards Israel–Diaspora relations, Rotenstreich distinguished between two kinds of sovereign state powers: the power to decide and the power to act. The former was fundamental and absolute, while the second was practical and relative.

It is clear that as regards the power to decide, the state will always have the greater right and there is no escaping this advantage, since it depends on the status of the state. But, where the power to act is concerned, there is partnership between the Jews of the Diaspora and the Jews of Israel.

Precisely because of its greater right to decide, the state should display 'generosity' towards Diaspora Jews. He proposed the establishment of an 'upper chamber' with representation for the Diaspora. Even if the Diaspora Jews rejected this proposal, for fear of being accused of dual loyalties, it was incumbent on the state to make the offer.

In line with his aim of merging diverse forms of Jewish life within one framework, he also proposed changing the structure of the Zionist Organization.

It should be an alliance between the state of Israel and the Jews of the Diaspora, in which the state is represented not directly by its citizens but by its legislative institutions. This will express the basic difference between Israeli Zionists, who are Zionists within a political unit, and other Zionists.

This combination of state and Zionist institutions would highlight the Zionist character of the state. Rotenstreich was well aware that such an alliance was no simple matter and would be cumbersome in several respects, because it reflected a complex situation. He stressed that the constitution should 'mirror Jewish sociology rather than ignoring it'.

Although a member of Mapai, he was at odds with the party and with Ben-Gurion on this issue. The upper chamber which he proposed, even with powers limited to the sphere of Diaspora–state relations, would, by its very existence, have appropriated some of the sovereign authority of the state. Ben-Gurion objected to this on political grounds, while Rotenstreich advocated it on grounds of Jewish unity. For the same reason he disagreed with Ben-Gurion, who was willing to grant the body restricted official status within the state. Rotenstreich sought a formula for creating a framework organically uniting the state and the Zionist Organization. Hence his proposal to link the Knesset, representing the collective Jewish will, with the Zionist Organization, representing the will of Jews as individuals within the unifying framework of the Zionist Organization. This proposal recalled, to a certain extent, Ben-Gurion's statements immediately after the establishment of the state, on the ideological and political identity between the state and the Zionist movement, and in particular its leadership. In Rotenstreich's case, the idea stemmed not from belief in this identity but from respect for diversity. He did not aspire to impose the will of the state on the movement, but to create conditions for cooperation within a single framework. His desire for unification of the two organizations led him to make similar demands of the Zionist organization and of the state. The former, he said, should be awarded unifying status within the state and the Jewish people only if it acknowledged 'that the Jewish question has not been solved and is the problem of all Jews, and there is no discrimination between Jew and Jew'. The refusal to distinguish between oppressed Diasporas and free Diasporas would be the touchstone of Zionism, and would separate Zionists from non-Zionists. 'An ordinary Jew supports the state as the central project of the Jewish people, while a Zionist supports it because it is the instrument for solving the Jewish question.' The fundamental difference therefore, lies in acknowledgement of the universal existence of the Jewish question and of the connection between the existence of the Jewish state and solution of this question. Only a Zionist Organization which advocated this ideology was entitled to special standing, otherwise 'by its own doing, it will devalue its demand and destroy the force sustaining it'.

Rotenstreich's Zionist outlook led him to criticize Rawidowicz's views, but the two were of one mind on several basic matters. They agreed that dispersal endangered Jewish national existence and that this was the implication of the *galut*. The Jewish problem was the same everywhere, and there could be no meaningful distinction between various categories of Jewish existence. Believing that all sections of the Jewish people were of equal value, they expressed qualified objections with regard to Ahad-ha-Am's theory of the spiritual center. They differed on two major, related issues; the distinction between the Jewish state as a central factor in Jewish life, and the state as an instrument for solving the Jewish problem. Rotenstreich agreed with Rawidowicz that 'no part of the Jewish people is by itself of intrinsic value', so that consequently all parts were of equal value, but, where the Jewish state was concerned, 'the part of the Jewish people concentrated in the State of Israel, has greater value that other parts because of its overall national status, and the fact that the destiny of the whole Jewish people hangs on the achievements and success of the endeavour being carried out by this section'. This led him to the important dialectical assumption that 'the unity of the Jewish people is not only compatible with the idea of giving precedence to the State of Israel over any other Jewish issue, but actually demands such precedence'. And he continued: 'As long as our prevailing consideration is the overall national significance of Israeli life, we can take the Diaspora into account, but cannot give it equal status from the national standpoint.' In other words, he was rejecting utterly Rawidowicz's argument that acknowledgement of the equality of all parts of the Jewish people would solve the Jewish existential problems. 'It is equality itself which is the most problematic issue in this framework', he said. This was because, while Rawidowicz believed that Jewish life in Israel and the Diaspora were of equal value, he refused to concede that the Jewish normalistic approach, based as it was on acceptance of the Exile, also advocated a protracted process of ingathering of the large part of the Jewish people into their historic homeland.

Rotenstreich, on the other hand, predicted the dwindling of the diasporas through constant immigration to Israel. 'To avoid exaggeration,' he wrote,'let us speak of dwindling rather than eradication – that is to say, their inner creative force will be strengthened rather than undermined.' This being so, he could not accept Rawidowicz's proposal for the abolition of the existing Zionist organization and its replacement by a pan-Jewish organization. Instead, it should be reinforced as the organization of the Jewish minority, cognisant of its mission, and incessantly striving to attain it. It should be recognized as a revolutionary minority which did not sanction the existing situation, as Rawidowicz would have wished, but was constantly seeking to change it.

This is not to suggest that Rotenstreich considered Jewish existence in the Diaspora to be morally inferior to Israeli life. The reverse is true. In the mid-fifties he declared that 'there can be no doubt that the will of the Jews of the West to survive as Jews is strong and determined, impelling them to various actions and enabling them to face various trials'. Objectively speaking, however, this desire was all that was left to the Jews, while the other dimensions of national existence – such as language, territorial concentration, a network of governing institutions and even a uniform religious pattern – were lost to them. He had no doubt that in the confrontation between Jewish subjective will and objective reality the latter would prevail. On the other hand, 'the Jewish concentration in the State of Israel requires the Jews of Israel to locate themselves objectively within the domain of Jewish history and to live within the Jewish historic horizons', while the situation of Diaspora Jews had no such binding force, and their historic consciousness was abating. Their ties to Israel were now confined to the political, economic and emotional spheres 'and are not complemented and bolstered by ideological coordination'. The Jews of the free world feared ideological definition, since it could create a barrier between them and their surroundings, whereas their everyday ambition was to gain a foothold in this milieu.[63] Therefore, he reasoned, 'this desire of Diaspora Jewry is fortified and supported by the standing of the state of Israel which represents the dimension of Jewish life, without its history becoming a real part of Diaspora life and consciousness'.[64] The state, thereby, (paradoxically enough), gains prestige among Jews, but the underlying trend is not beneficial for the national cause. The ideal situation would be espousal of the view which acknowledged the preferential status of the state, admitted the existence of the Jewish problem wherever there was a Jewish minority and perceived the state as the instrument for solution; sought to establish an institutional framework for implementation through concerted action; and endeavored to educate the people in the spirit of a historical consciousness linking past to present and both to the future.

Rotenstreich's views embroiled him in a public debate with Ben-Gurion on the place of the state in the continuum of Jewish history. The polemics began on the eve of the Sinai campaign and continued, in an exchange of letters, throughout the political crisis of late 1956 and early 1957. Ben-Gurion reiterated, concisely and rather bluntly, the views he had been voicing publicly since leaving the Zionist Organization in 1957. His basic hypothesis was that Zionism, as an ideology born in Eastern Europe in a particular time and under specific conditions, was no longer valid, and did not appeal to the Jewish masses – particularly the younger generation. Instead, he felt, it was necessary to inculcate in Jewish youth 'Jewish consciousness, drawing sustenance from the great spiritual heritage of the Jewish people, from the common destiny which, whether they are aware of this or not, binds all Jews, and from the messianic vision, the vision of the redemption of Jews and all mankind, which the prophets handed down to us.'[65] 'It is this vision, drawn from the Bible, which moved the bearers of Zionism and its first implementors, and only through this vision can we understand fully the miracle of the establishment of the state and the ingathering of the exiles.... The climate of the Bible is the climate of our lives.'[66] Here we observe Ben-Gurion's advocacy of the historic leap, the sharp transition, entailing disruption of a certain historical continuity and adherence to a new historical reality. He insisted that this leap was possible, but wanted to move forward inspired by the biblical heritage.

'If we attempt to liberate young people in the homeland from the objective yoke of "Zionist" perception, namely the view that their obligations are part of some Jewish whole', replied Rotenstreich, 'we will be weakening their roots in their natural homeland instead of reinforcing them.' In the absence of Zionist consciousness, 'discarding of the yoke could mean that the native Israeli will be cut off from the historical and emotional justification for the very existence of his homeland'.[67] This historic justification, according to Rotenstreich, stemmed not from messianic awareness but from 'realistic awareness', based on the realities of the Jewish condition and the Zionist interpretation given them in the past few generations. The messianic ideal had indeed played a role in renewing the ties of the people to their historic homeland, but not the decisive role, as Ben-Gurion thought. According to Rotenstreich, the messianic idea alone could not create a link with the Jewish people, because ties to the past were impossible without ties to present day Jewry. 'The absence of this bond is one of the main flaws in our education – and any connection to modern-day Jewry is meaningless without perception of the significance of the Jewish question and all its manifestations.'[68] This was a universal Jewish issue, as relevant for the Jews of North Africa and the United States as it had been for the Jews of Eastern Europe. Rotenstreich was hinting here at Canaanite tendencies among the younger generation, which he discerned even in Ben-Gurion himself. It was his fear of this latent Canaanism which led him to attack Ben-Gurion's 'biblical ideology'. He distinguished between reviving a bygone era and making the leap from one era to another; between renewal of the distant past and denial of the recent past, which could lead to alienation from the common Jewish destiny.[69] Ben-Gurion's 'historic leap' contained within it the threat of 'Karaism, the suspension of development and disregard for changes wrought by time, and the threat of Canaanism with its excessive respect for change and consequent detachment from the past'.

Rotenstreich did not dismiss the possibility of a historical leap but believed that it should not necessarily entail rejection of the past.[70] It was quite possible, he wrote, that the younger generation in Israel would some day revert, for reasons of their own, to the popular culture of the Diaspora. Young Israelis tended 'to believe that we are already normal and with a certain degree of justification...but the changes we have undergone call for reformulation of our core issues and not for spiritual and ideological iconoclasticism...'[71]

While Rotenstreich abhorred Ben-Gurion's 'historical leap', Ben Halpern argued against the historical leap advocated by Mordecai Kaplan, which he denoted 'new Zionism'.[72] Halpern concurred with some of Kaplan's views in theory, but rejected them on practical grounds. He agreed that Jewish life in the United States was meaningless beyond its religious content, and as a secular Zionist admitted that his brand of Zionism was losing its foothold in that country in every sense. It was not putting into practice the ideal of ingathering the exiles, had nothing unique to offer in its view of the historical unity of the Jewish people and its support for Israel, and was incapable of transforming Hebrew education into a significant factor in shaping the image of the Jewish community. Consequently, it clung to religious tradition as the sole means of preserving Jewish distinctiveness. Precisely because of the blurring of the dividing lines between Zionists and non-Zionists and because Kaplan's Greater Zionism (which Halpern called neo-Zionism) was completely synonymous with Americanism – it had no hope of realization, even though its ideas had some basis in reality. There were several reasons why this was so. The idea of living in two civilizations according to 'two constitutions', as advocated by Kaplan, raised the question of 'dual loyalties' to which American Jews were highly sensitive. Therefore, they would flatly reject this theory, even though it was applied solely to the realm of culture and faith. But even if it were possible to ignore the political implications of the 'two constitutions' and to limit it to the religious aspect of 'Jewish civilization', the problem would not find its solution. In the face of the pluralism, dissent and conflicts in Jewish religious life, Halpern was in no doubt that the attempt to provide an exclusively religious definition of Jewish nationalism and culture would have a drastic outcome. Precisely because it was generally agreed that Jewishness as a religious tradition was the tie binding Jews into one nation, it would be very dangerous to seek to establish binding formulae. According to Halpern, American Jews wanted to believe but did not want too precise a definition of their belief. 'Jewish civilization' implied pluralism of faith, and thus there could never be a consensus of this issue. Any attempt to impose uniformity would cause further strife.

Halpern recognized an additional paradox relating to the links between American Jewry and Israel. He agreed with Kaplan that Israel was the center or core of world Jewry, but for this very reason he exhorted Kaplan to recall that the secular majority in Israel identified with every form of belief that denoted itself Jewish. The religious Jewish community in the United States – which was tenuously bound together – could establish religious and cultural ties with Israel only on condition that Israel rejected any definition and canonization of its own culture as a religious culture. Only thus could American Jewry maintain religious unity with Israel, each sect and group in its own way.

Halpern also criticized Kaplan's conception of *galut*, and his denial of its philosophical validity. In the forties Halpern had proposed a moral interpretation of *galut*, arguing that as long as the majority of the Jewish people lacked a home, American Jews, as an integral part of the Jewish people, were obliged to feel themselves in exile. Now, after the establishment of Israel, in light of the intensified trend towards normalization which seemed liable to foster discord, he made this concept the cornerstone of his national-Zionist outlook.

'In the system of Jewish ideas,' he said, '"Exile" is the inalienably Jewish idea, the most intimate creation of the Jewish people, the symbol in which our whole historic experience is sublimated and summed up.'[73] This was a religious rather than a political concept and hence the debate on whether the United States was a *galut* was irrelevant, since its existence and national significance did not depend on a given political and economic situation. The intellectual principle underlying Zionism was rejection of exile and not its denial, because Zionist faith was grounded on recognition of the phenomenon of exile. It objected to two conceptions of *galut* – the Reform view which perceived it as a mission and the Orthodox view which was reconciled to its existence until the coming of the Messiah. In their stead, Zionism offered its own historical-activist interpretation of the ideal of redemption. Those who ignored the historical significance of the term were depriving the people of its memory and its consciousness. Writing in 1954, Halpern could only express the hope that the way out of the 'strange limbo' would be reinterpretation of the term *galut*, providing the Jews with the reason for their existence, based on memory of the past, the desire to exist in the present and the yearning for redemption in the future.[74]

He continued to argue that *galut*, beyond its religious meaning, symbolized the wondrous historical deed of ingathering of the exiles and the knowledge that the process would not end in the forseeable future. Only a sense of exile could evoke desire for return to the homeland, and this was what distinguished the Zionists from other Diaspora Jews. By identifying with the idea of ingathering of the exiles, the Zionist, even if he himself did not immigrate, was taking a part, however small, in the common experience that would determine the destiny of the Jewish people. Eight years later, speaking at a symposium on the meaning of the Diaspora, Halpern postulated the connection between the sense of *galut* and the hopes of redemption.[75] Addressing those Jewish intellectuals who preferred the term 'alienation' to 'exile', Halpern argued that the Jewish sense of exile or alienness was not identical with the universal state of man, even though Jews are part of general society. The *galut* of Jews is shared by all Jews wherever they may be, and it is this that sets them apart from other human beings. The yearning for redemption is universal, while Jewish yearning is unique. There was a metaphysical tinge to these convictions, particularly when Halpern asserted that the Jews of Israel were also in a condition of exile, though only partial. As a sociologist and historian and a secular Jew, however, he tried to place the concepts of exile and redemption in their proper historical and socio-cultural perspective. He emphasized the inescapable duty of every Jew, as an individual, to shape his world outlook and to maintain public institutions based on moral values. Among other nations, this task was undertaken by churches or political ideologies. Christianity and Islam were religious ideologies which aimed at uniting diverse groups within one faith. Judaism, in contrast, having transmitted its beliefs to the world, remained apart, and its separateness continued to the present day. In this respect, the Jew, whether religious or secular, who regarded his religion as an integral inseparable historical heritage, was in exile. Thus, exile and redemption are almost the sole principles underlying continued Jewish existence. Ben Halpern, like Rotenstreich, was inclined to Zionism without extreme conclusion, namely the ending of Diaspora.

Cognizant of the fact that the ideal of ingathering of the exiles was not pertinent for the large part of American Jewry, including himself, Halpern focused on those few young pioneers for whom exile was a personal problem which required solution, and who were incapable of basing their lives on compromise as most American Jews were forced to do.[76] He was in agreement with Ben-Gurion on this and in his view of the limited importance of American Zionism as a leading force in Jewish public life. Unlike Ben-Gurion, however, he considered this state of helplessness to represent not hypocrisy but resigned acceptance of the impossibility of solving the problem. Halpern agreed with Mordecai Kaplan on the central role of religion in American Jewish life but thought the latter's Zionist program unrealistic and even dangerous. While he was drawn to consider the questions of exile and redemption, as was Ben-Gurion, he refused to perceive the Jewish state as the instrument of the Messiah. He was sceptical as to Israel's ability to influence Jewish educational and cultural life, or to extend political succor, apart from opening her gates to immigration.[77] Halpern also objected to Ben-Gurion's scheme to replace the Zionist Organization by another Jewish body. It was his conviction that wherever the state, for internal Jewish reasons, was unable to act (as for example on the question of Jewish education), the Zionist Organization should carry out this task. That body, more than any other, was suited to such tasks, because Zionism, in its outlook and organization, was the truest representative of the Jewish people.

To sum up, Halpern identified conflicting trends within the sociological and ideological diversity of Jewish life. The Jewish people, he argued, were in no immediate danger of decline and assimilation, even in the Diaspora, but were likely to undergo changes in the future as in the past. He foresaw, paradoxically, that Israel, in the near future, would undergo a centrifugal process of separation. 'Those who immigrate to Israel will be separated from those who remain in the Diaspora, the assimilationists will be set apart from those who hold fast, etc.' But above and beyond these periodic separatist trends he perceived a trend to unity. The desire for unity should be nurtured and encouraged by the few 'and by those who are willing to undertake the task and to swim against the current in certain areas, and yet whose activity will be aimed at the internal trend of Judaism...and will find suitable forms of expression and action if we grant them a voice outside the ideological framework of the era'.[78] To the extent that he was referring to the Zionist movement, these remarks indicate that Halpern shared Ben-Gurion's opinions. In this respect, he differed from Rotenstreich who, attributing importance to historical continuity, believed that the chosen few could be roused to action within the framework of the Zionist movement on condition that the movement observed the basic tenets of its ideology. Halpern doubted Zionism's ability to do this and pinned his hope on groups of young activists. Both men devised ways of defining Jewish identity: Rotenstreich, the philosopher, from a socio-cultural viewpoint, and Halpern from the psychological-philosophical aspect. Both saw *galut* as the central experience of post-Emancipation Jews, and thus revitalized the Jewish normalistic approach.

Their views were further elaborated by Arthur Hertzberg, who pointed out that since the emancipation the Jews have lived in a contradictory situation. They did not choose to assimilate themselves, nor did they want to be themselves. The only way, in his opinion, to heal themselves and to dissolve this unique tension is to admit honestly that they are still in exile (*galut*). Meaning, by accepting their abnormal human condition they will become normal as Jews.[79]

In conclusion, the 'interim approach' consisted of a basic admission of the existence of *galut*/exile and indecisiveness on the question of its historical fate. This approach was elucidated succinctly by Hayim Greenberg at the 23rd Zionist Congress in 1951. He compared *galut* to an algebraic formula, the letters existing wherever and whenever Jews lived as a minority, but the figures changing from country to country and time to time. 'If exile can be compared to night, then there are pitch-black nights and moonlit nights.'[80]

As the last two chapters show, Zionism was vainly seeking the solution to its dilemma. Its relations with the State of Israel had been formally regulated and its organizational framework had not disintegrated despite internal conflicts, but it had not succeeded in meeting the challenge of the partial normalization of the Jewish people, and had created not one but two Zionist formulae with which to confront the non-Zionist Jewish world: singular normalization and Jewish normalization. The debate between them was not confined to the framework of the Zionist movement but extended to circles of intellectual non-Zionists or Zionist sympathizers, who were often remote from organized Jewish life and institutions. In the dialogue, fraught with tension, between the two camps, the question of self-identity shifted from the sphere of Zionism to Judaism in general.

4 The Intellectuals in Search of Jewish Identity

...New York...an exile whose existence is denied by those who dwell there. They ignore it, as it ignores them...the very concealment is hidden from them, and perhaps the Hassidic preacher was right in saying that this is the cruellest kind of concealment.

Gershom Scholem

For two centuries the processes of modernization, emancipation and auto-emancipation in Jewish society had been accompanied by the quest of Jewish intellectuals for collective identity.[1] The quest which began in the United States in the 1950s did not accompany a process but rather followed in its wake. It was accelerated by the rapid erosion of external Jewish identity in that country between the two world wars. In the twenties this was still mainly an Eastern European immigrant society. In the thirties it was influenced by the rising tide of anti-Semitism, and in the forties by the impact of the Holocaust and the struggle for Jewish statehood. By the fifties, the Jews were speedily becoming integrated in American society in almost all spheres, while the infant Jewish state had 'settled down' after its victory in the War of Independence and its successful absorption of mass immigration, and was no longer the source of collective concern to US Jewry.

As the problem of existence eased, the question of identity gained urgency and won increasing attention. The discussions focused on the cultural, religious and existential aspects of the issue.

The cultural approach to Jewish identity was based on the view of the Zionist philosopher, Horace Kallen (1883–1974), father of the cultural-pluralistic approach to American culture in general, and Jewish culture in particular. Kallen, whose Zionist beliefs and pluralistic outlook were interwoven, was an admirer of Louis Brandeis, although he never failed to point out that it was he who had helped to bring Brandeis to Zionism, and not vice versa. Like Brandeis, he asserted that Zionism was necessary in order to bolster Jewish existence in a pluralistic American society, and thereby to reinforce pluralism itself. For him, Zionism replaced religion and confirmed his right, as a US citizen, to be different, as proclaimed in the Declaration of Independence and the constitution.[2]

In 1959, when the debate on 'Who is a Jew?' was raging in Israel, Kallen referred to the problem at a symposium he edited in *Judaism*. Loyal to his convictions, he defined Jewish identity as a many-sided phenomenon – ethnic, religious, ideological, historical and cultural – and as such, not open to unequivocal definition. Jewish diversity, nurtured by the very fact of its existence in a free society, could not endure. The Jewish individual was encouraged to adopt a positive approach to the whole spectrum of his heritage, since only thus could he comprehend his identity. Otherwise, Judaism was doomed to fragmentation and division into numerous different heritages. Consequently, he considered the new tendency in Israel of defining Jewish identity to be highly dangerous, since its immediate consequences could be the onset of a process of disintegration of the Jewish entity.[3] Due to his constant awareness of this threat, his Zionism was influenced by Ahad ha-Am, with a 'touch' of Dubnowism. At one time he even considered the need of establishing an autonomous cultural community organization of US Jewry, to be closely linked to Israel.

The sociologist Milton Konvitz offered an extreme, not to say paradoxical interpretation of Kallen's views.[4] American Jews had chosen freely to live in the United States, he declared, and so instead of accepting the Haggada injunction that every generation should regard itself as having come out of Egypt, American Jews should regard themselves as having come out of Jerusalem. Despite the free choice, a Jew, wherever he lived – in the United States or in Israel – was still in exile, outside his true home, and Zionism, in his eyes, meant the universally-Jewish feeling. Paradoxically, Konvitz considered himself a disciple of Herzl as regards the unity of the Jewish people, without accepting Herzl's political conclusion that the Jewish people must be concentrated in Palestine. Like Kallen, he conceived of Zionism as the return to Judaism rather than to the Land of Israel. In the post-Herzlian era, Zionism was richer and more profound, more Jewish and more humanistic, the meeting-point between the normal and the abnormal, binding every Jew with all the Jews of the world in a unity of religion, history, etc. Only this type of Zionism could overcome the two evils which Herzl believed to be threatening the Jews: assimilation and division. The one fundamental difference was that Herzl advocated the Zionism of return, while Konvitz believed in a Zionism of homelessness.

Pluralism as a method for understanding Judaism as a belief and culture and as a way of life for the Jews belittled the role of Israel as a main component of the new Jewish identity after the Holocaust and the founding of a Jewish state. In the symposium on 'Who Is a Jew?' held in New York in 1959 all twenty-one participants agreed that there could be no single definition of Judaism. The majority perceived religion as the foundation of Judaism and only few allotted an important role to Israel in Jewish life.[5]

More significant in this aspect was a conference on 'Jewish Identity Here and Now', held by the American Jewish Committee in 1964.[6] All the participants agreed that in the last hundred years, as a consequence of a cultural and social process, there is no longer a single Jewish identity. When asked about this, only one delegate included the State of Israel among the components of Jewish identity. Even devoted Zionists such as Arthur Hertzberg and Ben Halpern, dealing with problems of 'Here and Now', were not exceptional in understanding the existential components of Jewish identity.[7]

In the early sixties, these outlooks entered into direct confrontation with the two Zionist approaches discussed in the previous chapters. The framework was the series of dialogues (16 in all) initiated by the American Jewish Congress in 1962, between American Jewish and Israeli intellectuals, which extended over a period of twenty years. Whereas the participants in the symposia in the United States were mainly religious leaders and scholars, the dialogues were also attended by leaders of American Jewish organizations and leading Israeli politicians. The dialogues also differed from the symposia in that they were conducted not within the pages of journals but on platforms, with the active participation of the audience, and dealt with a wide range of issues: Israel–Diaspora relations; the Jewish identity of Jewish intellectuals; Judaism and creativity; religion and democracy, etc. All the dialogues were held in Israel, with the locale moving in the first five years between Jerusalem, Haifa, Tel Aviv, Rehovot and kibbutz Givat Brenner. The 120 speakers included politicians, academics and writers; a noticeably high percentage of young people took part in the discussions, and efforts were made to bring in intellectuals of Asian and African origin.

In the first five dialogues, held before the Six Day War, certain issues surfaced again and again: Israel–Diaspora relations; the dangers of assimilation; Jewish identity and immigration.[8] The series was launched against the background of the awareness of the participants that the differences between the Jews of Israel and the Diaspora were growing, and this was reiterated at each subsequent meeting. Speaking at the first dialogue, Joachim Prinz, President of the American Jewish Congress, declared that the objective was to destroy each side's erroneous image of the other. Abba Eban said that the motive behind the gathering was general concern that US Jewry and Israel were growing apart. The organizers believed that this was due to the objective process of evolvement of singular characteristic features in each society. Whereas a normal political society was developing in Israel, American Jews increasingly felt a sense of Jewish isolationism. The young generation, in particular, was becoming aware that the independent Jewish religious community in their country had no need of special identification with Jews in Israel or anywhere else in the world.

The foreword to the minutes of the fifth dialogue, in 1966, stressed that the two centers were discernibly drifting further and further apart and that this was perhaps inevitable.[9] They were becoming increasingly estranged as the percentage of Oriental Jews and native-born Israelis grew in the Israeli population, since these two groups, like the second and third generation American Jews, lacked the common cultural and sociological background shared by the older generation. The editors noted with concern the shift from faith to commitment and then to nostalgia and sentimentalism, which would lead to confusion and eventually indifference, unless steps were taken to reverse the situation.

In summing up the fifth dialogue, the journalist Max Frankel, one of the youngest participants, noted that there was a distance between the two sides, particularly wide on the question of identity. The sociologist, Nathan Glazer, pointed to the different sociological structures of the two societies: American Jewish society was based on a middle class, consisting largely of the liberal professions, while Israeli society was almost normal in socio-economic structure and political needs. Attempts at rapprochement were doomed to failure because of the fundamental differences between social structures, interests and historical consciousness, the common heritage and partial ideological identity notwithstanding.[10]

Yehoshua Arieli, Hebrew University expert in American history, said that Jewish life in Israel was grounded on ideological choice, based on intellect and will, at least of the pioneering groups which had built the society. Israel had developed out of total historical awareness, revolutionizing the private and public lives of all those who had chosen to live there. Hence the constant need of Israeli society to seek ideological justification for its very existence and continuation. The American Jew, on the other hand, had no need to create an ideology to justify his existence. It was a fact to him, like Jewish existence in any other diaspora. These were different responses to the crisis which had befallen Jewish society in the nineteenth century: the collective response, aspiring to shape Jewish destiny and focusing on statehood as the solution, and the individual response (of the majority) who had immigrated to the 'citizen nation', whose foundation was universal principles. The dialogue between them was fraught with tension because of their polar reactions.[11] The tension which did, in fact, exist between the participants is illustrated by Golda Meir's emotional question to the US interlocutors: 'Tell us where we went wrong? What should we have done in order for you to come here to us?' to which Joachim Prinz replied that for him, the great tragedy of his life was that he had not immigrated to Israel.[12] The traditional tension between leaders of the two camps was compounded by the dispute on the obligation to make *aliyah*, which erupted among the younger participants.[13] Also discussed was the future of American Jewry in light of the trend among educated young Jews to distance themselves from their heritage.[14]

The twofold concern for the continuity of the ties between the two centers and for the essence of American Jewish life brought to the fore the vital issue of Jewish identity. The very first dialogue was marked by a debate between Abba Eban and the Vice-President of the American-Jewish Congress, Stanley Lowell. The latter understood Eban to consider Judaism synonymous with Israeli nationalism and the existence of Israel, while Lowell chose to define Judaism as a religion.[15] The Jews of America should practice their religion as they saw fit, while Israelis should nurture their Israeli nationality as they saw fit, and both should cooperate to preserve Jewish culture. Abba Eban protested at this interpretation of his views. In his own words, 'Judaism is religion, it is culture, it is nationalism, it is memory, it is hope, it is a dream, it is civilization. Any one word to describe Judaism is bound to lead you into a false definition'.

In other words, Eban accepted the Anglo-Saxon definition of the nation as a territorial entity, and for him, the Israeli nation as a territorial entity and the Jewish people as a universal phenomenon were interwoven. Beyond questions of definition, there were basic divisions of opinion at the dialogue, inter alia on the question of the centrality of Israel. Lowell's view that there were two separate Jewish essences, religious in the United States, and national in Israel, refuted the existence of the center, even though he advocated collaboration. Joachim Prinz grasped the dangers inherent in this view, arguing that Judaism was not a religion in the sense that Christianity was. As a religion, Judaism did not involve only faith, but also self-determination through a unique lifestyle, which implied identifying with the Jewish people as a whole, and sharing the collective Jewish memory. Every Jew was part of this process in the emotional and intellectual sense, and life in the United States alone, as everywhere else in the world, could not give expression to historic Judaism. There could be no Jewish identity without identification with the Jewish people and with the State of Israel. Being part of the organized religious community meant being part of the Jewish people, and life around the synagogue was, in effect, 'national life'. It should be pointed out that despite the agreement between Abba Eban and Prinz on the essence of Jewish identity as a unified-pluralistic phenomenon, there was a striking divergence of views on the role of Israel in Jewish life, Eban perceiving it as the center, and Prinz as an inseparable part.

Moshe Sharett, Chairman of the Zionist Executive, joined in this debate, elaborating on the distinction between 'nation' and 'people'. A nation, he said, was a people with political and territorial existence, and consequently, the Jews were one people if not one nation. The Jews of Israel are a nation, constituting only part of the Jewish people, but are also a people, enjoying sovereign political standing. A people is an organic phenomenon, while a nation can be a mechanical entity. A people entails a history, tradition and shared values, a collective consciousness which develops naturally and binds the individual to the group.

In response to Eban and Prinz, Lowell retracted his distinction between Jewish religion and Israeli nationality, but continued to argue that the question of the essence of Jewish existence was insoluble. Rotenstreich attacked Lowell's viewpoint as untenable. Israel, he said, was created by spiritual aspiration, and any other form of Jewish life, however important and influential, was a mere fact. Israel, he asserted, was the sole form of Jewish life that was formulated by the Jewish collective as such. US Jewry, in contrast, was a collection of Jewish individuals, joined together in order to maintain collective life. He went on to distinguish between the objective of Diaspora Jewry, Jewish survival and the aim of Jewish society in Israel to maintain creative Jewish life. These remarks aroused resentment among the US delegates who believed that he was underestimating the importance of US Jewry, and they protested that, if these were the views of the Israeli delegation, there was no room for dialogue between the two sides. Furthermore, they could not accept Sharett's theories on the definition of people as an organic phenomenon, since this would have implied admission that their affiliation to the American people was mechanical. They preferred the formula of political separation on the one hand, and spiritual and cultural collaboration on the other, which they believed to hold out the promise of solution to the problem of the bond of religious and secular Jews to Israel.

The second dialogue, devoted to 'Jewish intellectuals and Jewish identity', was attended by academics and writers from both countries, and was a stimulating event. Max Lerner of Brandeis, who opened the discussion, offered a new definition of Jewish identity, on the basis of the accepted view that the Jews of Israel constituted a nation in itself, while American Jews were part of the American nation. He postulated the existence of a superstructure, linking the Jews of the two countries and nations, Jewish Israelis and Jewish Americans, as members of the Jewish historical community. This, he said, was neither a nation, nor a people as defined by Sharett, but an association for the sake of preserving Jewish distinctiveness while constantly adapting to the changes wrought by the historical process. Lerner acknowledged that it was easier and simpler for Israeli Jews both to exist within the process of social change and to belong to the Jewish historical community, with its own distinctive nature. The Jews of the United States had chosen to be part of the American nation, not only for reasons of convenience and security, but also because they had themselves made a more considerable contribution to the spiritual content of this national entity than had been customary in the case of Jewish communities in the past in other countries.

As a scholar of American civilization, Lerner emphasized the role of Jews in the American revolutionary heritage, which encouraged social and cultural change and confronted America's conservative traditions. Jews felt at home in the United States because many of the bricks from which their home had been built were essentially Jewish in origin. Yet American Jews could not cease being Jews, however slight their knowledge of Jewish history or of the Hebrew language, because of the inner need which demanded that they be part of the Jewish historical community and contribute to its existence. Lerner's views are reminiscent of Kaplan's, though with variations. The terms 'Jewish civilization' and 'historical community' are similar in that both postulated the existence of supranational civilizations, religious according to Kaplan and regional according to Lerner. Kaplan, however, sought to shape a historical-religious civilization, while Lerner referred to a secular-historical one. Both believed that their ideas would win the hearts of the young Jewish generation, which rejected particularist national principles and advocated universal ideals. Thus, for Lerner, who defined himself not as a Jewish intellectual but as a man who wished to be a Jew, Jewish identity was embodied in social and moral action. He did not, unlike many of his contemporaries, speak of a mission and a goal, but for him the struggle for equal rights of the blacks, for example, was a Jewish value. It was because of the identity of Jewish and American values, that he felt at home in America. Lerner was, in essence, trying to cling to two identities: the prevailing, unambiguous American Jewish identity, and the ideal, though vague historical Jewish identity. Because of the imbalance between them, his theory was no less at odds with the Zionist ideas than were those of his colleagues, to be discussed below. If Lerner was levelling his theories against the consensual Zionist outlook, he was wide of the mark, since it did not exist. The Israeli intellectuals were also divided on the essence of Jewish identity.

The Egyptian-born writer Jacqueline Cahanoff, who had settled in Israel after living for several years in the United States, agreed that Israelis were marked by a strong sense of national affiliation, but doubted if an Israeli national identity had as yet evolved. In so diverse a society as Israel, it could not be assumed that a single national tradition, like that of the Eastern European immigrants, could serve as a cohesive factor for immigrants from different countries and cultures. The hundreds of thousands of immigrants from Asia and North Africa were not acquainted with the Eastern European Zionist tradition which had shaped the Yishuv, and their spiritual roots were imbedded deep in their traditional Jewish consciousness and identity. She tended to agree with Lerner that the Jews were a historical community, which included Israel. Within it was occurring a process of constant self-discovery and self-definition.[16]

Professor Shalom Kahn, an immigrant from the United States, stressed that in modern times identity in the Diaspora was a question of choice, and said he had chosen his identity by the act of immigration. But he too argued that *aliyah* in itself could not totally solve the problem of Jewish identity. In Israel as well, there was constant and insoluble tension between intellectual pursuit, universal in essence, and particular Jewish identity. The writer and diplomat Yehuda Yaari, echoed the view that Israeli Jewish identity had not yet been defined.

As against this intellectual incertitude, Professor Lev, physicist and immigrant from the United States, represented the view that identity was a natural phenomenon. As an observant Jew, he said, he believed that the identity handed down to him by his forefathers was a sense of exile in both the negative and positive senses. Positively speaking, it meant that, although the Jew was taking part in the culture of the society in which he lived, basically he did not feel at home there and yearned to settle in Israel and help to build the society there.[17] The two young Israeli writers Moshe Shamir and Aharon Meged were equally certain of their Jewish identity. What was self-evident to Professor Lev through his Jewish faith was natural to them because of their presence in their homeland. Shamir defended the 'superficiality' of the assumption that 'we are Jews because we are Israelis and Israelis because we are Jews'. This simplicity of outlook was the foundation of Jewish life in Israel. Meged was more forceful in explaining the existential meaning of his Judaism. 'I am not a Jew in order to carry out a spiritual mission in the world; I am not a Jew in order to fulfil the wishes of other Jews in the world; I am not a Jew in order to bestow on American Jews the good feeling that I am the manifestation of their hidden yearnings; I am not a Jew in order to be different from other nations. I am a Jew because I am a Jew'. He acknowledged that he was deviating from Jewish tradition and limiting the definition of Judaism, and dismissed the traditional perplexities of secular Jewish intellectuals, because for him, being an Israeli Jew 'is life itself'.

In these discussions, framework and content became identical. The content of Horace Kallen's 'cultural pluralism' and Lerner's 'historical community' was mainly secular. In contrast, Israeli Jewish identity was ideological-Zionist in content. The monistic Zionist conception of Jewish identity was counterbalanced by a different monistic conception, which sought social and moral expression. At the fifth dialogue, Arthur Lelyveld, the new president of the American Jewish Congress, expounded the idea of moral monism.[18] It was 1966, and the American civil rights movement was at its height. Lelyveld asserted that the high percentage of young Jews among the movement's activists was an expression of the continuity of Jewish tradition. Judaism's distinctiveness lay in its moral values, he said, and proclaimed his belief that it was the task of building a world in the Divine spirit which lent significance and honor to continued Jewish existence. The moral element was the common denominator of all the religious, cultural and ideological trends of Judaism, the overall Jewish experience, which went beyond religious faith. He did not intend, he declared, to attempt to restrict Judaism to its religious dimension. Morality was what rendered Jews 'a discernible group personality'. Hesitant to grant this group personality a monopoly over morality, he stressed that these principles were universal, but said that their distinctive guise over the centuries had been mainly religious. In modern times, when religion had become the domain of the individual, it should be accepted that Jewish morality was not synonymous solely with Jewish religion and had other forms of expression. This combination of distinctive religion and moral mission, which was but a modern and updated version of the traditional Reform theory of the 'covenant', made the Jews the 'covenant people'. Lelyveld's views were supported by two Israeli speakers representing the traditionalist and secular viewpoints respectively – Zvi Kurtzweil and Amnon Rubinstein.

On the other hand, Rabbi Irving Greenberg, a pro-Zionist member of the Orthodox movement, while concurring with many of Lelyveld's statements, refused to accept his views on the religious morality which was the core of Jewish identity. Like Eliezer Berkovits, he accepted Judaism with all its shades of opinion, and perceived Eretz Israel as the center of its life and experience. He interpreted the moral mission as the exertion of American Jewish influence on Jewish identity, encouraging religious definition, however incomplete. Greenberg rejected any attempt to cram Judaism into a religious framework, even though, personally, he would have preferred to see it within this framework. His acceptance of pluralism was not a matter of principle, but a practical decision, taken in a spirit of profound respect for all trends and spiritual phenomena in Judaism, whether religious or secular. Greenberg won the commendation of the young secular activist, Shulamit Aloni, for his open and tolerant outlook. She stressed the paradox of the fact that it was an Orthodox rabbi who displayed the most pluralistic outlook on Jewish identity.

In all discussions of the subject, speakers representing the entire spectrum of views emphasized the importance of the religious element and the historical component, but not all agreed on the decisive weight of religion in preserving the Jewish people. At the third dialogue, a debate took place between historians on this question.[19] Zvi Ankori of the Hebrew University tried to shatter two 'myths' current among Jewish intellectuals and public figures, namely that throughout history religion had been a unifying force which had enabled the Jews to continue to exist as a separate entity. He surveyed Jewish history in an attempt to demonstrate that the separate existence of the Jews depended not on their religion but on their special historical status, while religion was a kind of ideological expression of this status. By order of importance, the unifying factors were: the sense of shared destiny, borne out by historical memory; social standing; role in the economy and the religious way of life. The great Jewish achievement throughout their history was their success in Judaizing these phenomena, which were not characteristic exclusively of Jews, and of transforming them into a way of life unique to them, and thereby a means of preserving their independent existence.

On the other hand, according to Ankori, religion had never prevented mass Jewish assimilation. Evidence of the truth of this was the astonishing decline in the number of Jews in the world from the classical period (eight million) to the Middle Ages, when they numbered only two million. This decline could not be explained as due to the afflictions which Jewish society suffered, but rather as the outcome of continuous mass assimilation. To further prove his point, Ankori noted that the greatest assimilation occurred in the Gaonic period, when the Jewish world was ruled by *halakhah*, which, nevertheless, did not prevent their absorption in the Christian and Muslim civilizations. This process, which was halted in the Middle Ages and in Eastern Europe, was revived in Central and Western Europe some two centuries ago. His firm conclusion was that wherever there was detachment between Judaism as a religious-spiritual phenomenon and the actual Jewish situation, the bearers of the ideals of Judaism, cut off from its realities, abandoned it and were lost to it. Only Zionism, as an ideology representing the Jewish people and the Jewish state and offering them a political territorial framework, held out a guarantee for the continuation of real Jewish life, and the hope of the survival of Judaism.

Gershon Cohen of the United States and Jacob Katz of Israel took issue with Ankori. For both, the determining factor in Jewish history was not the proportion who assimilated or abandoned Judaism, even if they were the majority, but the number who remained within the fold. It was they who preserved Judaism and gave meaning to Jewish existence in the history of mankind because of the talent (mentioned by Ankori) for absorbing the content of other cultures and Judaizing it. In modern times, they had Judaized the nationalist ideal and the desire to rebuild a state in the historic homeland. The difference between the previous generations and the present one lay in the fact that the former had blended external influences into their religious world, and Jewish unity had survived on this basis. This had now almost totally disappeared. To the cultural differences which had always existed between the various diasporas, was now added the deep rift between religious and secular Jews, and between Jews of different political convictions. What still united the Jews were historical memory, anti-Semitism and the refusal to convert to other religions. It was typical of the times that Gershon Cohen did not mention the State of Israel as a factor uniting the Jews and fashioning their identity.

Katz agreed with Gershon Cohen on the role of religion in Jewish history, but saw it as ending with the eighteenth century. Developments since then had shown that Jewish unity was being eroded. Hence, like Cohen, he asserted that, from the point of view of social cohesion, the Jews were no longer one people. There was no unity between Israel and the Diaspora, no organizational cohesion of Diaspora Jewry, no religious or cultural unity, not even ethnic unity, due to intermarriage. There remained only identification with the Jewish people. Katz proposed clinging to what remained of Jewish unity and cautioned against underestimating it.

We see, therefore, that among Zionists there was an oppressive sense of a widening rift between the Jews of the United States and Israel, marked by a division of opinion on the essence of Jewish identity. Notwithstanding, and perhaps precisely for this reason, the great majority of the participants, excluding several younger representatives of more extreme stands, sought ways of collaborating for the mutual reinforcement of Jewish existence throughout the world.

It is interesting to note that those of the Israeli participants who emphasized the breach between the two Jewish entities on fundamental issues were the most extreme in their demand for coexistence and collaboration. Referring to this dilemma, Professor Avigdor Levontin stressed that there was no accord between the two sides on one central issue.[20] The Israelis could not compromise on the question of rejection of exile, but this did not mean that they were contemptuous of or, Heaven forbid, hostile towards the Jews of the Diaspora. Nor did it mean that normal Judaism could only flourish in Israeli surroundings. And even though the Israelis could not compromise on this particular matter, there were other areas of agreement and mutual understanding.

Nathan Rotenstreich, who had aroused the ire of the American participants at the first dialogue, argued that Diaspora Jews undoubtedly had the moral, even legal right to intervene in Israeli events in order to influence the fashioning of the new society. Israel had come into being through the efforts of the majority of the Jewish people over three generations, and was, consequently, responsible to the Jewish people today and to future generations.[21] Professor Ernst Simon continued in this vein. Like Rotenstreich, he was convinced that 'devoted Diaspora Jewry' had the moral right and indeed obligation to express their views on central questions relating to the state and its peaceful coexistence with its neighbors, the moral character of its society and its status among the Jews of the world. This right to involvement, he said, stemmed from the mutual dependence and because in Israel the historical destiny of the entire Jewish people, and not only of Israeli citizens, was being determined. On all matters, the right to final decision should be reserved for the Jews of Israel, but the voice of Diaspora Jews should first be heard and weighed. He distinguished between the two communities as regards their distance from the focus of the Jewish existential problem: the Israelis were close to it and the Diaspora was further removed, and hence the former suffered from 'shortsightedness' and the latter were 'longsighted'. If both views were combined, world Jewry could achieve a comprehensive view of its problems.

In an interview five years later, in 1966, Simon expressed his beliefs more clearly. There could be no proper ties between Israel and the Diaspora, he declared, as long as Israeli Jews regarded themselves as the bestowers of spiritual largesse and as entitled to receive financial support. This situation could only lead to 'arrogance, groundless spiritual superciliousness and excessive economic abasement'. 'The Jews of the Diaspora', he declared, 'must be allowed to share in Israel's real problems instead of having them covered over with a verbiage of rhetoric and propaganda.'

Simon distinguished between the Zionist myth and the Zionist ideal. The myth had evaporated and no longer held out enlightened and heroic attractions. Those who were continuing along the path of arrogant propaganda in their relations with the Diaspora were doomed to fail. In contrast, the Zionist ideal was alive and well, and could continue to win the hearts of Jews throughout the world only if the true problems and weaknesses of Israel were exposed to them. Beyond this, Simon wanted to base Jewish unity on the differences between the two societies, distinguishing between entity and essence in Jewish existence. In Israel, where the survival of the Jewish entity appeared to be guaranteed, the question of essence was not widely pondered. In the Diaspora, where existence as a separate entity was not certain, there was considerable speculation on fundamental questions. He expressed the hope that just as the Jews of the Diaspora drew encouragement and strength from the existence of the state, the Jews of Israel should be influenced by the soul-searching of Diaspora Jews, if they wished to preserve the Jewish character of Israeli society. 'The Jewish essence in the Diaspora', he thought, 'has the great advantage of pluralism in its modes of expression and organization...whereas here in Israel we have external uniformity and internal disintegration.'[22]

Professor Moshe Davis, himself an immigrant from the United States, summed up the discussion by proposing a kind of Jewish treaty, to be based on mutual acknowledgement: Israel to acknowledge the Diaspora as a perpetual way of life and the Diaspora to accept the fact that the State had a responsible and decisive role in preserving the communal character of the Jewish people. All should acknowledge that religion had a determinant role in preserving the Jewish identity of Diaspora Jews, but that this could not suffice. It was essential to reinforce the ties between the Diaspora and Israel, particularly through the study of Hebrew, and even part-time residence in Israel. It was not possible, he declared, to continue the partnership between the communities by proclaiming the equality between them; only through partnership could this equality be shaped.

Beyond the theoretical plane, speakers from both countries were in agreement, particularly in the practical sphere, on cooperation. The non-Zionist sociologist Nathan Glazer and the historian Yehoshua Arieli agreed that in order to bring young American Jews closer to Israel, it was necessary to convince them that Israel was realizing universal values in the socialism of the kibbutz movement, the integration of different ethnic communities, the building of a democratic society and the extension of aid to developing countries.[23] Arieli, as a Zionist, pointed out the contradiction inherent in this phenomenon. He recognized that an objective process was occurring among American Jews, who were integrating into universal trends and identifying with them. This tendency, of which he personally approved, was, however, problematic from the national viewpoint, since the more the universal aspect of Judaism was accentuated, particularly in Israeli affairs, the less focus was placed on the distinctive national features. Even the Jewish religion, he said, would not be able to check the process of gradual devaluation of national distinctiveness. The solution lay in fostering awareness of the total nature of Jewish history, in which Jews as individuals and as components of a collective were shaped by religious values and national ideals. Mutual balance could be achieved between a community whose Judaism was mainly religious and a state whose Judaism was largely nationalistic. Zvi Ankori and Gershon Cohen, although they differed in historical outlook, agreed that relations between Israel and the Diaspora must be founded on mutual concern. As Cohen put it, it was impossible to maintain a one-way bridge.

Two years later, one of the younger participants, Leonard Fein, adapted these proposals for cooperation based on mutuality into an overall theory of the existential Jewish dimension of mutual dependency.[24] The Jewish community in the United States, he claimed, could not face up to its Jewish identity without links to Israel, and the Jews of Israel were liable to forfeit their Jewish identity some day in the absence of close ties with Diaspora Jewry. This tie only served to emphasize the uniqueness of Jewish existence, since there was no parallel in world history for this mutuality between two communities.

At the same time, it is important to take note of the fact that the American and Israeli views on cooperation and mutual dependence had different implications. The Israelis perceived Israel as the center of Jewish life, on which the Diaspora was dependent, while the Americans were increasingly convinced of the need for balance and equality. Even Rabbi Irving Greenberg, who did not regard the Diaspora as his home, stressed that the Israelis must not delude themselves that the State would be a spiritual center for the Diaspora. The State might be the symbol of Jewish capabilities and heroism, but it would not be the center. The active Jewish intellectuals in Diaspora would become increasingly 'Diasporacentristic'. The best example of dissent on theoretical issues and agreement in practice was the emotion-laden issue of immigration. In principle, those who considered immigration to be the supreme injunction of Judaism and those who wholly rejected the idea were totally opposed. In practice, however, the differences were not so drastic. Ben-Gurion, as noted above, pinned his hopes mainly on the pioneering minority.[25]

Golda Meir, who appealed for immigration, explained, when criticized by the American participants, that she was not demanding that American Jews rise up and go to Israel, but that they recognize the principle of *aliyah*, namely that to live in Israel was important not only for persecuted Jews, but for American Jews as well.[26] Avraham Avihai, of the Prime Minister's Office, reassured the Americans that the Israelis were hoping to attract immigrants in thousands, and no more. Abba Eban[27] and Yigal Allon[28] were essentially of the same opinion. The American representatives could accept this formula without difficulty. This kind of *aliyah* was, in effect, a form of aid to Israel, and could in no way be interpreted as the beginning of the Ingathering of the Exiles.[29] It is noteworthy that most of the young Israelis who took part agreed, both in theory and in practice, with the American stand. The law professor Amnon Rubinstein, Lieutenant-Colonel Mordechai Bar-On, the journalist Nissim Rejwan and Moshe Bitan of the Foreign Ministry stressed that, the importance of *aliyah* notwithstanding, they did not feel that they had the moral right to demand of American Jews that they immigrate to Israel.

Thus, whereas political leaders insisted on the importance of immigration, even if only by a few young pioneers, the young intellectuals refrained from making a similar demand, on personal moral grounds and out of practical considerations. At the same time, one should not underestimate the differences in outlook between them and their American counterparts. These young Israelis were cognizant of the supreme value of the act of *aliyah* and therefore, since they themselves had not immigrated but been born in the country, they refrained from judging others. The Americans, on the other hand, refused to perceive any particular moral dimension in the act of immigration, and left it to the personal decision of each Jewish individual.

This free and open debate between the proponents of the two approaches – 'Jewish normalistic' and 'distinctive normalistic' – ended, like the debate within the Zionist movement, in compromise. Those who regarded Zionism and Israel as the supreme expression of Jewish identity and those who advocated a more comprehensive and egalitarian form of identity continued to be divided, although there was closer agreement on the issue of cooperation and mutual dependence between Israel and the Diaspora. In this area – it being clear to all that relations between the two entities would be mainly practical, solving urgent problems rather than resolving fundamental issues – the distinctive approach prevailed.

At the same time, even when the two sides differed on the question of whether Israel was the national center of the Jewish people, it was at least agreed that the state played a central role in Jewish life worldwide and a considerable role in strengthening Jewish self-identity. This minimalist view was shared by all the intellectuals wrestling with the question of Jewish identity.

5 The Diminishing Status of Israel as a Jewish State

The viewpoint which we have defined as 'general normalization'[1] was never totally unrepresented in the intellectual debate, even in the period covered by the second section of this book. Despite its marginal public weight, it continued to provoke interest. Its decreased significance stemmed from the absence of the political motives which had previously inspired the American Council for Judaism and the Hebrew Committee for National Liberation, as well as the Canaanites in Palestine. At the same time, although they had become less popular, these ideas were, objectively speaking, more in accord with the spirit of the times than they had been in an earlier period. Then, the impact of the Holocaust, the struggle for Jewish statehood and for Israel's survival and the absorption of mass immigration, combined to generate a sense of crisis, based on belief in the uniqueness of the Jewish experience. This being so, concepts of normalization were both intellectually and emotionally unacceptable. They were rejected not only due to the power of the Jewish and Zionist establishment, but also because of their inapplicability. Now, however, the time seemed ripe at last for their acceptance. The period between the end of mass immigration and the Six Day War was one of 'small deeds' rather than heroic endeavor.

It is important to discuss the 'general normalization' approach since it is a prime example of the vitality of certain ideas which surface again and again despite the setbacks they suffer. It is also illuminating to trace the changes in the content and stylistic guise of this approach. It should be noted, at the outset, that we are dealing here, not with political ideologies, but mainly with ideological trends, represented on the whole not by groups but by individuals who varied greatly in their outlook on the world. Nonetheless, there was a paradoxical consensus with regard to Israel's place as shaper of Jewish identity, between the Canaanites in Israel, the 'universalists' in the United States and the neo-Orthodox element in both countries. In all three groups, we discern the attempt to deny or belittle the Jewish value of the Zionist state and to ground both the state and the Jewish people on the normal element of human existence. Those, in particular, who still believed in Judaism's universal social mission, insisted on distinguishing between the state as a normal political organization, and Judaism as a faith or a mission.

In the early fifties, the Canaanite ideology was the bluntest public expression of anti-Zionist ideology. Although this group of young intellectuals and writers was tiny, its ideas roused a storm in Israel and were a cause for concern among American Jews, who tended to perceive this ideology as synonymous with the prevailing mood among the younger generation of Israelis, particularly the labor-related youth movements.

The Center of Young Hebrews, headed by Yonathan Ratosh, was established in late 1951, and its organ was the monthly *Alef*, which had been founded three years before. The Center published a manifesto based on liberal principles,[2] inspired by the American constitution, such as the separation of religion and state, full civil rights for all citizens of the country and denial of the connection between Jewish nationality and the State of Israel. The Young Hebrews, it was stated in the first clause, would act 'to promote the self-determination' of all inhabitants of Israel, irrespective of religion, ethnic group or origin, and for recognition of the singular character of those of the nation residing in the State of Israel out of all Jewry. The distinction between Israelis and Jews living outside the borders of the state led to the demand for 'the liberation of the State of Israel from subservience to overseas Jewish fundraising as regards its internal and external policies, and the liberation of the economy and development policy, from the fundraising orientation'. This trend implied 'the denial of any recognised official status to the Zionist Organization in the State of Israel and the transfer of its assets and the income of its funds, particularly the Jewish National Fund, to the settlers and the development authorities'. The ideological intentions underlying these principles found expression in their views on Hebrew education. They proclaimed the need for a 'secular-national reform of education, in accordance with the principles of territorial self-determination and the Hebrew renaissance', which was, of course, anti-Jewish and anti-Zionist, and entailed 'promotion of the native culture based on Hebrew national culture, drawing sustenance from the original values of the country, and transmitting them to all its inhabitants'.

Fifteen years later, on the eve of the Six Day War, when Canaanism had long since ceased to be a trend in Israeli public thought, Boaz Evron, one of the prominent young ex-Lehi intellectuals who had joined Ratosh, gave a lengthy interview in which he offered his updated interpretation of these principles. Despite his secular outlook, the starting point for his rejection of Zionism was the traditional orthodox approach, namely identification of Judaism with religion. He denoted as 'poisonous deception', the Zionist attempt to perceive the scattered Jews as a nation, although *galut* conditions had highlighted the religious definition of Judaism. This insidious interpretation, he argued, 'encouraged the worst and crudest form of *Hilul ha-Shem* [blasphemy]', because 'religion is related to the absolute. If you replace religion by nationality, the raison d'etat becomes the sole absolute'. This recalls the views of Elmer Berger, Jacob Agus and even Mordecai Kaplan. Moreover, like these thinkers and others, Evron vehemently rejected the Zionist negation of the Diaspora. There was nothing flawed about Jewish existence in the Diaspora, he said, otherwise any playboy in Tel Aviv would be a more complete Jew than Einstein. Hence his conclusion that 'each experience is as legitimate as the other'. He goes on to say that from the point of view of safety and historical fate, it is preferable for the Jews not to be concentrated in one country, and this being so, 'Judaism is safer when dispersed'.

The logic of this argument is valid as long as one accepts the basic assumption that Judaism is a religion and not a nationality, since then national territory is not a precondition for national existence. And, indeed, he claimed that Jews share a religious tradition, which was now in a process of disintegration in middle-class status; and the enmity of the surrounding society. But these manifestations were 'not necessarily connected to nationality' of the Jewish individual living in Israel, who was not exposed to the pressures exerted on Diaspora Jews, and who was not religious, these constituting the majority, 'who, from the point of view of functioning and experience cease to be Jews. It is clear that here and there will remain faint and ever diminishing traces of the spiritual countenance fashioned by Judaism, but these are doomed to extinction'.

These basic assumptions totally divided the Hebrew-national and Jewish-religious experiences. However, there need not be a fundamental conflict between them, if the Zionist outlook, which perceived Jewish existence as a national phenomenon, could be ruled out, thereby putting an end to incessant tension between the national and the religious approaches within Israel and between Israel and the Diaspora. Hence, paradoxically, the easing of tension through separation between the two could reconcile young Israelis to religion, and even bring them close to it. Moreover, *vis à vis* relations between the Jews in Israel and in the Diaspora, only 'a man who considers himself a nationalist Hebrew or a nationalist Israeli, who is not the "bridgehead" of Judaism, can relate to Jews in the Diaspora as equals, whose experience has its own internal justification'.[3]

It should be noted that Boaz Evron no longer represented the Canaanite approach either in the organizational or the ideological sense. The difference between his views on Judaism and those of Ratosh is clearly evident. Ratosh was the most extreme impugner of the Diaspora Jewish experience who ever emerged from the ranks of the Zionist movement. Evron, on the other hand, accepted Judaism as a religion and as a Diaspora experience. All he sought was to separate and to distinguish clearly between the Israeli national territorial entity and the Jewish religious entity, existing mainly outside the borders of the state. In this respect, his outlook can be defined as 'later Canaanite', lacking the blunt anti-Jewish element, but firm in its solely territorial definition of nationalism.

There is no parallel phenomenon to this in ideological cohesion and organizational framework among American Jewish intellectuals. However, there can be no doubt that among the young second generation and particularly the third generation of immigrants, certain trends are discernible, based on identical premises to those of the 'late Canaanites'. They were voiced in a symposium conducted by *Commentary* in 1961.[4] Thirty-one young intellectuals took part, most of them in their early thirties, and all under forty. Among them were thirteen writers and journalists, fifteen academics, two physicians and one public figure. Sociologically and age-wise, they resembled the Canaanites. The young Norman Podhoretz,

Commentary's new editor, wanted to compare their views with those expressed at the 1944 symposium of young writers. He wanted to know whether the mood of alienation from US society had disappeared among young Jewish intellectuals. Podhoretz assumed that this would affect their feelings towards Judaism. He emphasized that since 1944, much had changed in the lives and status of Jews. Unlike those earlier writers who had grown up under conditions of economic distress, the intellectuals of the sixties came from prosperous suburbs. The earlier discussion was overshadowed by the Holocaust, while the second confronted the existence of Israel.

The six questions the editor asked the participants indicate their preoccupations: the reciprocal influences of Judaism and Americanism and the degree of commitment of Jewish individuals to their heritage and their fellow Jews. Podhoretz wanted to discover how the young generation evaluated the contribution of Judaism to American society; their views on the Jewish community, and their ties with it; what was their attitude towards the possibility that their children might convert; and what they thought about Israel as a state and a Jewish society.

As regards their Jewish heritage, these young people did not echo the writers of the forties. Their alienated radicalism was vividly expressed by the journalist, Nathan Polsky, by Professor Werner Cohen and by Philip Green. They repeated the argument of the earlier group in that they dismissed the unique contribution of Judaism to modern society, denying that Marx and Freud, for example, were Jewish creators. Their positive evaluation of their heritage touched on the issue of alienation. Cohen claimed that Judaism had endowed him with the strength to be an outsider, able to fight for his principles, even when he stood alone. Green, a socialist, admitted that he had drawn from Judaism the quality of integrity, which he defined as the ability to withstand dangerous modern trends – nationalism and economic liberalism – which he perceived as threatening the basic values of man and society.

Other participants, however, had chosen to return to Judaism. Malcolm Diamond, a lecturer in the history of religion, argued that Judaism without God was merely tribal paganism. He stressed the need to reform the Jewish faith in the light of the changing times, but could not imagine his Jewishness without religion. Judith Jarvis, lecturer in philosophy, went even further. Severely and acerbically criticizing the new Jewish society in Israel, she emphasized that, when there, she had felt familial affinity only to the Orthodox Jews with their beards and black garb, because they were the only authentic Jews in the Jewish state. The writer Barbara Salomon went even further, in declaring, though without personal commitment, that there was only one Jewish religion – orthodoxy.

Most of the participants stood somewhere between these two stands – neither rejecting Judaism nor defining their Jewish affiliation as a matter of religious faith or ethnic necessity. They saw it rather as based on free individual choice, respect for their heritage and a sometimes inexplicable emotional attraction. The sociologist Irving Feldman declared that in open and democratic American society Jewish existence had lost the collective national significance that had characterized it in the past, particularly in Eastern Europe. In the future, individual Judaism would be founded on individual awareness and identification alone. He defined the sense of belonging to Judaism as purely emotional. The writer Herbert Gold went beyond the concept of individual choice, and sought individualist elements in Judaism itself. He found them in the style of prayer in synagogues, each worshiper appearing to pray independently, the rabbi unable to control the congregation. He found it also in the individual character of Jews, their adventurousness and daring, and their traditional generosity.

The radical journalist Nat Hentoff declared himself grateful for the individualist upbringing he had received in his parents' home in a Jewish suburb of Boston. The academic Michael Maccoby found in Judaism the categorical imperative for each individual to reform himself and help improve society. Barbara Salomon also pointed to the new essence of American Jewish life, which had changed from collective necessity to individual choice. For herself, she admitted that her ties with Judaism were purely emotional, but nonetheless very real, because of their existential nature. 'I feel like a Jewess but do not live like one', she said undoubtedly mirroring the feelings of many others.

The individual-liberal outlook was fully expressed in the reply to the question of reaction to the possibility of conversion by their children. Of the 31 participants, only 20 responded, and of these, only eight totally condemned such a step, while 12 regarded it with equanimity. They did not approve, because of their atheistic vies, but neither did they reject it, because of their advocacy of free choice for their children. If we add to these the one-third who ignored the question, we see the force of individualist liberalism among this group. They did, however, reveal a somewhat stronger commitment to collective Jewish experience in their attitude towards Israel.

Of the 22 respondents, 13 identified totally with Israel in one way or another, four rejected its Jewish character or regional policies, while five were ambivalent. One declared that he admired the heroic endeavor invested in establishing the state, but feared for its continued existence, because Israeli society lacked historical dimension. The abstention of the other participants suggests that the state was still outside their sphere of interests and awareness. The views of Israel's champions are important to us, because of the tension between their individual outlook and their identification with the collective deeds of their fellow Jews. One considered it an objective moral phenomenon, a haven and refuge for the persecuted, although he disapproved of the chauvinistic spirit prevailing there. Barbara Salomon expressed her admiration for the fighting spirit of the Israelis. Another participant said that only in Israel was there hope for the rebirth of Jewish creativity, and was consequently convinced of its importance for Jews and for the entire world. Aaron Asher gave vivid expression to the range of emotions evoked by the state, when he drew an analogy between attitudes towards the Jewish community and the State of Israel. In both cases, he expressed reservations with regard to the establishment, but was unable to detach himself from it. As regards the state, his affection and sympathy were reserved for the new immigrants, and he levelled criticism against the '*sabras*'. He mourned the passing of Yiddish culture, but identified enthusiastically with the ingathering of the exiles. To his surprise, he found himself supporting Israel's policies towards the Arabs, and enjoying military events and celebrations.

One may sum up this symposium by saying, as did Podhoretz, that for the great majority of the participants, Judaism was of minor significance in modern times. As Elihu Katz, who later immigrated to Israel, declared, Judaism is a great thing in the perspective of the distant past, but very small from the viewpoint of modern history. This being the prevailing view, Israel could not be of major importance in determining the role of the Jews in modern history. And the lesser the significance of Judaism, the freer and more normal the lives of Jews in Israel and in the Diaspora. In this respect, there was no difference between the 'later' or 'neo-Canaanites' and the 'American universalism' of the symposium participants.

Another aspect of the trend to 'general normalization' can be identified in the attempt to bestow universal significance on that uniquely Jewish concept *galut*. The intention was to transform Jewish distinctiveness into a general phenomenon. This trend found clear expression in a symposium conducted by *Midstream* in 1963.[5] Discussions were confined to 'The Meaning of Galut in America Today', the problem which had preoccupied the Zionist movement and Zionist public thought since the establishment of Israel and the destruction of the Eastern European community. It may have been because the organizers of the symposium focused on a complex and perplexing problem that most of the people they approached preferred not to respond. Seventeen replies were received, about half the number of those participating in the earlier symposium. This time, the participants were a mixed bag as regards age and public prominence. Two of them had taken part, as young writers, in the 1944 symposium. The editors posed seven questions: some were abstract, dealing with the meaning of the terms *galut*, Zion, and alienation, and the extent to which the territorial solution was relevant to them; the other, more practical questions concerned the status of US Jews and their relations with non-Jews.

The writer Howard Fast and the critic Alfred Kazin, who participated in the 1944 symposium, also took part in this debate. Their replies reflected a trend to return to their Jewish roots, characteristic of certain members of their generation from the early fifties onward.[6] Fast, who, in the forties, had been unwilling to admit that the suffering of the Jews under the Nazis differed in any respect from that of other peoples, had now changed his mind. He acknowledged the uniqueness of the Jewish position. The main obstacle to acceptance of Jews into general society, he wrote, was their Judaism, and the sole feasible solution was for them to cease being Jews. This was the approach of both American and Soviet anti-Semitism. Fast, who had in the past treated his Jewish origin dismissively, was now ready to fight for his basic right to preserve his Judaism. After a long voyage from an assimilated family to a flirtation with Christianity and then identification with communism, Fast now declared that, having been disillusioned by the revolutionary world, he was becoming increasingly Jewish as the years passed. His interpretation of Judaism, however, was purely universalistic, and he focused exclusively on its moral aspects. His universalism, alienated from his sources, was now replaced by Jewish secular-moralistic universalism, rendering him, ideologically and emotionally, a stranger everywhere. He asserted that the United States could never be his true home, but neither could Israel. He was in conflict not with countries or peoples but with a historic era in which the forces of barbarism predominated. Israel, he said, was a miraculous achievement, but it too was a part of the same world, existing in the present and not in the future. If he lived in Israel, he would remain a Jew and would never become an Israeli.

For Alfred Kazin, *galut*, externally manifested in the Jewish dispersion, was the profoundest expression of unique-universal Jewish existence. He hoped that this dispersal would exist for ever because of its universal significance. The Jewish entity, including that in Israel, had absorbed elements of world culture. Hence, he refused to accept the assumption that Zionists in Israel and 'Canaanites' were more Jewish than he, who advocated Jewish dispersal. As far as he was concerned, the concept of exile was much wider and more profound than his sense of alienation from the society around him in the country of his birth. In this respect, his sense of exile was a constant part of his existence as a Jew. Like Fast, he believed that even in Israel he would have felt himself to be in exile. There were varying degrees of intensity to his sense of exile, but the central manifestation of his 'exilehood' was his expectation, as a Jew, of discovering significance in the historical process. Now, however, he was increasingly unsure that there was any logic to the course of human events. This faith was replaced by an existential outlook, recognizing only one sole certainty in this world – death. This was his conviction both as universalist and as Jew, who was in exile within universal society and within Jewish society. Kazin employed distinctly Jewish concepts, but emptied them of traditional and historical content. One might argue that this moral universalism smacked more of the Christian spirit than of the principles of Judaism.

In that same year, in another framework, at the second dialogue held by the American Jewish Congress in Israel,[7] a contemporary of Kazin and Fast, Leslie Fiedler propounded the most paradoxical Jewish-universal formula – 'not to belong', meaning 'to live in exile, to be a stranger, to know at any moment that wherever a man finds himself, he is a stranger'. The dominant trend in present day Judaism, he said, and particularly in the United States, the USSR and Israel, was the reverse of this. There the Jews yearned to belong, and no longer felt themselves to be exiles. It was because of the loss of this sense of exile that they were ceasing to be Jews. The essence of Judaism, according to this revolutionary viewpoint, could be found in a phrase in the Passover Haggadah: 'This year slaves, next year free men'. Judaism meant awareness of slavery and yearning for redemption. When a Jew ceased to be aware that the United States, the Soviet Union and Israel were not the messianic Zion – or when he renounced the belief that this world is unredeemed and that aspirations and hopes cannot be realized therein – he ceases to be a Jew. An intellectual like Fiedler, who had believed in the past in universal assimilation, could not evade the question: Why should not Jews, when afforded the historical opportunity, abandon their Judaism or flee it? His response was almost mystical and determinist. The Jews are the chosen people, by tradition and faith, because they have no option. 'We are Jews, defined as Jews, essentially Jews and there is no escape from this situation', he declared. Hence, the fact of having been chosen is the Jew's slavery, and he is in an almost absurd condition of having no alternative. The only solution that can give meaning to his life as a Jew and a human being is to have a social mission.

Fiedler believed that a Jew should always fight social injustice. In the America of the sixties, during the struggle for black rights, this meant that Jews should side with the minority seeking justice, even if this meant separation from the majority and a kind of return to the ghetto. Although the ghetto walls had fallen, he declared dramatically, he would remain within but would keep a loudspeaker with him to transmit his cry far and wide. Fiedler was not suggesting that by being chosen, the Jew became more moral than other human beings, but was seeking to stress the moral mission which, in effect, constituted his Judaism.

Unlike Fast, Kazin and Fiedler – intellectuals in their forties, who had been disillusioned and now sought Jewish meaning for their sense of alienation – the younger radicals, who had grown up in the 1950s, sought to separate the two emotions. Two of them took part in the *Midstream* symposium: Nat Hentoff and Ronald Sanders. For Hentoff, exile – as a spiritual phenomenon – was the lot of all Americans living in an unjust political and social situation, and there was nothing distinctively Jewish about it, particularly since the Jews were mainly integrated and assimilated in general society. The State of Israel was not Zion, and it offered no salvation from *galut* – it was merely an atavistic national state. These views were shared not only by Sanders, but also by the young writer, Philip Roth, speaking at the second dialogue in Jerusalem in 1963. Roth asserted that Jewish existence in the united States had no Jewish-spiritual meaning, apart from its psychological dimension, reflected in the feeling engrained in Jews in their childhood, that they were 'better'. Nor did he find this meaning in the Zionist Jewish state.

The young 1960s radicals were reverting to the views which Fast, Kazin and Fiedler had expressed in the 1940s. The general normalistic outlook of the younger group was less ambiguous than that of their elders, but neither group attributed Jewish significance to the existence of the Jewish state. In the same year, Arthur Cohen, graduate of the Conservative seminary and disciple of Mordecai Kaplan, published his book *The Natural and Supernatural Jew.*[8] The basic premise was the distinction between the natural-historical Jew, shaped by conditions, and the transcendental, supernatural Jew, liberated by means of his faith from his transient surroundings. Only a Jew of this kind can break out of the confines of his historical destiny to his eternal mission. The belief in God, which is above time and place, creates mutual receptiveness between the believer and his God, and it is from this that the supernatural community springs. *Galut*, as he perceives it, is not a historical accident, solved by the establishment of the Jewish state, but a theological category. It serves as eternal testimony that mankind is still unredeemed, and confirms that the Jew is a messianic creature, for whom there can be no redemption until all mankind is redeemed.

Therefore, while the Diaspora is a historical fact, *galut* is a cosmic event in Jewish tradition: the Titus Gate is evidence of a historical event – the fast of the Ninth of Av is the symbol of a cosmic occurrence. On the mundane plane, therefore, Zionism, through its triumph, spelled the end of Jewish dispersal in the historical sense, since henceforth, Jews are no longer forced to live outside the Land of Israel. The concept of *galut*, on the other hand, is the Jewish doctrine concerning the sinfulness and imperfection prevailing in history. Cohen accepts the Jewish state as a positive phenomenon, enabling Jews to choose between homeland and Diaspora, and helping in various ways to strengthen Jewish existence outside the borders of Israel. Yet, the state of the Jews is not their Jewish mission but rather their exile. Eternal, supernatural Judaism is in exile in Israel as well. Cohen attacked both Zionists and assimilationists, since both, he believed, denied the *galut*. The Zionists wanted to escape it, while the assimilationists wanted to abolish it through their mission in general society and failed to recognize the metaphysical meaning of *galut* existence. The threatened disappearance of the *galut* stemmed from disregard for the supernatural significance of the concept. The natural-historical interpretation of Jewish existence is no longer sufficient, because of the great changes that have taken place. Only if we know how, at every historical juncture, to reveal its eschatological roots will we find purpose to our existence. And so in the face of events which would lead the natural Jew to despair the supernatural Jew knows only faith. The conflict is not between different components of Judaism but within each individual Jew. This means that the differences between state and Diaspora are no longer significant to him, since wherever a Jew lives he faces the same question. This explains his almost neutral attitude towards Israel. It neither harms Judaism nor strengthens it, since Judaism as such is synonymous with galut and the state, though disapproving of it, cannot abolish it.

Whereas Fiedler perceived *galut* as a social mission, and Cohen as a religious-mystical mission, Jacob Petuchowski spoke on behalf of the traditional Reform notion of the mission. He was a Reform rabbi, involved in Jewish community life in the United States, who wrote a book, *Zion Reconsidered,*[9] after a year's stay in Israel. Published on the eve of the Six Day War, it was essentially a continuation of the theories of Elmer Berger and Jacob Agus two decades before. He differed from Berger in that he did not draw political conclusions, and on certain practical issues, such as the use of financial donations for aid to Israel, he differed with him radically. In any event, his views were identical with those of Agus, particularly as regards the universal elements in Judaism, and the role of the State of Israel in Jewish experience.[10]

On his own evidence, Petuchowski wanted to challenge the Zionist interpretation of modern history and Jewish destiny, as accepted by the Jewish masses since the establishment of Israel. He argued that the uncritical emotional attitude of these masses towards the state was highly dangerous since it bordered on irrational and even fanatic chauvinism of the kind which had proved catastrophic in this generation. Like Berger and Agus, he also took issue with the Zionist-national interpretation of Jewish history, which ignored the fact that the national movement was only an infinitesimal part of the Jewish history, the main part of which was focused in the Diaspora and not in the Land of Israel.

In re-evaluating the Jewish experience and the place of Israel within it, Petuchowski challenged several basic assumptions. First, he refuted the view that Israel could be a spiritual center in the secular sense for world Jewry. This was because the Hebrew culture evolving there was not, so he believed, 'Jewish culture' and hence was of no value to Jews living in other secular cultures. Since Jewish culture could be defined only religiously, the center of Judaism was the place where most observant Jews lived, and in modern times, that place was the United States and not Israel. Like Dubnow, he was willing to regard Israel only as an additional center, but in no way as a focus of Jewish life. His objection to the centrality of Israel was based not only on practical considerations, but stemmed from his views on nationalism. Like Berger, he rejected the theory that the Jews were a nation, and reverted to the classic Reform view that in Jewish history there was a progression from tribe to nation, from nation to international religious community. The two theories – the non-centrality of Israel and the non-existence of Jewish nationality – were interlinked. Those who argued for the existence of an international Jewish nation could not envisage its continued existence without a national center. Petuchowski was undoubtedly aware of this, and drew his own conclusions. Firstly, like others before him, he claimed that the term *galut* was religious and not political. Just as there was no *galut* in the political sense, there was no Jewish nation since, as the Canaanites declared, a nation was a territorial entity. Therefore, Israel was home to the Israeli nation and not the Jewish nation. Unlike the Canaanites, however, and unlike Berger, Petuchowski agreed that the concept of religion alone could not encompass the Jewish experience. He reiterated the argument that the Jews were a kind of international family descended from a common forefather. This family consisted of biological descendants and of those who had joined it by choice.

This compromise between religion and nation, reflected in the use of the term 'historical family', led him to an additional compromise. On the one hand, he identified with the classic Reform theory of the mission of the Jewish people as 'a nation of priests and a holy people', which is not dependent on nationality or on a Jewish state. On the other hand, in accordance with liberal-pluralistic theory, he was ready to accept the fact that part of the Jewish family chose to carry out its world mission by establishing a sovereign state. Statehood did not contradict the idea of a universal Jewish mission, but neither did it express it. Therefore, he concluded that there was equilibrium between the two forms of existence in the 'Jewish family' – in the Diaspora and in the state. Only on the basis of this acknowledgement could fruitful reciprocal ties exist within the 'international Jewish family', he said.

At this point, it is worth examining the role of the concept of *galut* in these outlooks as it concerns the normalization of the status of Jews. Ostensibly, what Fast and Kazin, Fiedler, Cohen and Petuchowski share is the assumption that Judaism is founded on abnormality. Thus, they have no common denominator with the purely normalistic approach of the 'later Canaanites' in Israel and the 'American universalists', for whom Judaism was of no collective significance in history, and was a matter for individual choice. This, of course, is valid as long as we are dealing with Judaism as an outlook of faith and not with Jews as a sociological and historical unit. In this context it should be noted that, as awareness grew of the possibility for normal Jewish existence in non-Jewish society to the point where they became an integral part of it, the search intensified at least on the part of some intellectuals, for the essence of Jewish abnormality. They did not find it difficult to reconcile the 'abnormality' of the essence of Judaism with the normality of the Jewish entity in free countries and in Israel. Here, in the denial of significance of Jewish values, lies the common denominator between the advocates of the Jewish mission, particularly its secular proponents, and their opponents. No less determined in their attempt to separate the spirit of Judaism from Zionism, including the State of Israel, were the neo-orthodox thinkers, such as Will Herberg of the United States, Professor Yeshayahu Leibowitz and Professor Baruch Kurzweil of Israel.

Herberg, who had been a Communist in the thirties and forties and became observant after the war, had replaced one extreme ideology by another. In 1952, ten years before Arthur Cohen, he had described Jewish existence as supernatural, its objective to serve the eternal Divine will on earth.[11] Consequently, there was no room for theories advocating pluralism in Jewish life. Judaism had one sole meaning, which was expressed in the concepts and criteria of biblical and rabbinical theology. The essence of the people of Israel was the covenant with God, and this being so, they had no homeland. Each and every Jew, as an individual, belongs to the nation among which he lives, but the Jews, as the 'people of the covenant' were linked to no country, not even the Holy Land. Nonetheless, Zion is the promised land, though not the homeland, of the Jews, and Jewish life and the Jewish mission have a twofold eternal meaning: Zion and *galut*. These two elements, connected and complementing one another, are in a state of perpetual tension. The establishment of Israel was a historical achievement of major importance for all Jews, but to depict it as the commencement of redemption and of the final ingathering of the exiles, was but another example of false messianism. American Jewish life has an exclusively religious identity, and the Jews should be defined collectively as the people of the Torah, in the words of Saadia Gaon. In other words, the only way to guarantee continued Jewish survival is to become a 'people of the covenant' once again, in the traditional-*halakhic* sense of the term. The convictions of the Zionists and their sympathizers, the great majority of US Jewry, that Jewish existence is linked to Israel and dependent on it to some extent – is totally invalid.

Professor Baruch Kurzweil held similar views. 'The primeval sin of Zionism', he wrote, 'is its self-delusion that it is possible to solve the problem of the Jews and of Judaism by means of the ideological apparatus of modern European nationalism.'[12] This is not an error relating to the past, but a delusion which could prove catastrophic in the future. 'If we place our trust in a secular-Levantine interpretation (in whatever guise: socialist, semi-socialist or Canaanite) we are lost.' The blame should be directed at the Zionist presumption that it could extricate Judaism from the crisis which had befallen it in modern society. Kurzweil conceded that 'as long as Zionism was a dream and did not face the test of reality, particularly the political test, it was, like every idea, protected against internal disintegration and could appear as the continuation of Judaism...But as soon as it entered into permanent dialogue with reality, it demonstrated its weakness...since it removed Judaism from the perspective of eternity and placed it in the dimension of the here and now.' Kurzweil went so far as to justify the stand of the extreme Orthodox community, which barricaded itself against the threat of the state which claimed to be Jewish. He acknowledged that this orthodoxy was fossilized, but lauded its instincts. 'They feel that the state sets itself up as absolute and supreme, while they know full well that there is an absolute above the state.'

Kurzweil, who admired the intellect and literary talents of the Ratosh group, was, nonetheless, the first to point out the dangers of Canaanism, and was its most uncompromising foe.[13] He considered it to be logical and extreme continuation of the crisis of faith which had afflicted Judaism in the past century, and the rise of 'neo-barbaric' forces which brought about the decline of European culture. Kurzweil also perceived it as the inevitable expression of the aspiration of the Zionist movement for normalization of Jewish life, which was liable to spell its extinction. Paradoxically enough, however, Kurzweil and the Canaanites shared a basic assumption. Both identified Judaism absolutely with religion, and considered the attempt to identify Zionism with religion as self-delusory and potentially destructive. There was an unbridgeable gap between them, but on pragmatic-liberal grounds, if the state were stripped of its Jewish pretensions and Zionist aims, it was possible to envisage some kind of coexistence between them, though without mutual fruitful contact.

The implied agreement between the Canaanites and the neo-Orthodox on the need for a country free of true or false Zionist-Jewish values was explained by Yeshayahu Leibowitz. He distinguished completely between Zionism and the fundamental problems of the Jewish people. Zionism, he declared, was not an ideology, according to which people should conduct their lives. It was, rather, 'the range of activities undertaken in order to restore the independence of the Jewish people in their land'. In this respect, it had succeeded and had completed its task. Henceforth, the Jewish people should tackle the new phenomenon in their history: the Jewish State, regarding which Leibowitz wrote: 'I am interested only in the Jewish people. The state interests me only insofar as it serves as the state of the Jewish people, since otherwise, it is not only superfluous but harmful, causing regional and international unrest.'[14] This may appear to be the classic argument of Zionism, which perceived itself as a movement for preserving Judaism, but Leibowitz took another view of the matter. He was not seeking in the state the solution to the problem of Jewish existence.

> I am not saying that the state should provide this or that answer, but that its justification (not from the moral and political viewpoint) would stem from its becoming a framework within which the struggle for identity was being conducted, and would thus rouse something in the hearts of those Jews who have some interest in the fact of their Jewishness.

The state, therefore, is not the bearer of Jewish or Zionist values, but serves as the sole place in the world where the true confrontation between 'the conception of Judaism according to its historical essence' and the Canaanite outlook, in its wider sense, can take place. In other words, Leibowitz believed that the Jewish state was merely a territorial framework in which Jews could struggle freely, being liberated from the pressures of their surroundings, to find their historical Jewish identity. In this struggle Leibowitz saw hope for the continuation of Judaism, because only thereby could it be made clear to every individual Jew that 'affiliation to the Jewish people is expressed in struggle over specifically Jewish matters which are not part of the reality of the non-Jewish world'. Leibowitz, somewhat recalling Sorel's anarchistic views, sees the struggle itself, rather than the achievement of the aim, as all. Torah and *mitzvot*, he said, were the sole and exclusive way of belonging not to the Jewish people but rather to a social and political reality, 'whose center is the struggle for specifically Jewish matters, a real struggle and not coalitionary alliance on the acceptance or rejection of Torah and *mitzvot*'.

This, therefore, is a struggle between Judaism, in the historical sense, and Israeli Canaanism in the wider sense. There is no room within it for the Zionist outlook, since Zionism as an ideology completed its historical task when the state came into being, and has no further place among Jews, particularly the younger generation, in the Western world, who abhor manifestations of nineteenth-century-style nationalism.

It was at this point, in their denial of the Zionist significance of the state, in separating the state from Judaism as a faith and set of values, on the one hand, and in perceiving it as a political framework of liberal and pluralistic character, on the other, that Leibowitz and the Canaanites were, paradoxically, in accord.[15]

To sum up: the two approaches, Jewish normalization, and singular normalization, were both resounding failures within the Zionist movement in their attempts to organize and determine the political and ideological framework of relations between the State and the Diaspora. The demand voiced by David Ben-Gurion and Yitzhak Greenbaum for organic organizational links between State and *Golah*, between the Zionist Organization and the Jewish state, was rejected emphatically by Zionist leaders outside Israel. Concomitantly, the call by Abba Hillel Silver and Emmanuel Neumann for the establishment of a Zionist orgnization independent of the state, so as to consolidate Diaspora Jewry into one body, was also rejected outright. To this should be added that the ideas of Simon Rawidowicz· and Mordecai Kaplan, who had no political aspirations, of establishing a worldwide body of the Jews of the Diaspora and the state, under the initiative and guidance of the Zionist movement, never progressed beyond the theoretical state. In this respect a stalemate was created between advocates of the 'Jewish' approach, who perceived the Diaspora as a *golah*, which should be under the leadership of the state, and the proponents of the 'distinctive' approach, who defined the *golah* as a forced exile, which had become a Diaspora out of choice, and should be on an equal footing with the state. The consequence was that, in the political-organizational sense, the Diaspora underwent no changes after the establishment of Israel. This was not so in the ideological sphere: here the 'singular' approach prevailed, as reflected in two issues. One was the official recognition by the Zionist movement of the different status of Jews living in coerced exile and in free Diasporas, and the second, all those who still considered the Diaspora a place of exile agreed with Hayim Greenberg on the distinction between the black night and the moonlit night.

The deep implications of this distinction were reflected in the question of immigration. The loyal proponents of the ingathering of the exiles did not demand mass immigration from the free West and, in effect, concurred with the opponents of immigration in believing that the sole possibility was limited pioneering immigration. The 'achievement' of the 'singular' school of thought in the Zionist movement stemmed mainly from developments within both American Jewish and Israeli society. On the one hand, there was an accelerated process of integration of Jews in non-Jewish society, which despite the inherent dangers, also constituted evidence of their stronger standing in the Diaspora. On the other, the 'radiance' of the Jewish state had been dimmed somewhat, as its social problems increased.[16] As a result of these two conflicting trends, the standing of non-Zionist organizations and personalities was bolstered at this time. They held that the era of Zionism had ended with the establishment of the state, which was to be based on practical reciprocity with the Diaspora. These views won the support of intellectuals in Israel, and of Ben-Gurion in person. Although they drew a clear distinction between national-collective existence in Israel and individual existence of religious character in the Diaspora, they also recognized the intrinsic value of the Diaspora, and sought to win it special status in Israel on all matters pertaining to Jewish affairs. Ben-Gurion, on the other hand, although he had always denied the Diaspora as a spiritual essence, had now become, through his rejection of prevailing Zionist ideology and alignment with Jewish messianic faith, the ally of the proponents of that Diaspora ideology which was the core of the singular normalization approach.

Part III
Return to Jewish
Normalization
1967–82

Introduction

Because Jews are now so very much at home in America ... it was possible for them in this crisis to be boldly Jewish in very angular ways.

Arthur Hertzberg, *Commentary*, August 1967

The Six Day War was a milestone in modern Jewish history, which initiated three processes of vital significance for the Jewish state and for the Diaspora. It opened up a path, albeit strewn with obstacles, to a possible settlement between Israel and the Arab states; it revived the ideological debate and the internal political strife on the issue of Greater Israel, and it changed the nature of American Jewish social development. In those troubled days of May–June 1967, when Jewish families outside Israel sat glued to their television sets, fearful for the besieged state, suppressed emotions of national solidarity surfaced, and inspired an unprecedented financial aid project. Tens of thousands of young Jews volunteered to come to Israel's aid. The intense emotions eventually found an outlet in the outbursts of relief and enthusiasm at Israel's astounding victory. All these happenings combined to create the mythical experience which became an important part of the group identity of American Jews.

This was, to a certain extent, a profounder experience than the founding of Israel, two decades before. The statehood experience had been the culmination of a process of consolidation of Jewish group will, which had begun fifteen years before, with the Nazi rise to power in Germany. In this period Jewish unity and solidarity were strengthened and crystallized, though not without internal dispute, by the endeavour to solve the problem of the German and Austrian Jewish refugees, by the desperate and pathetic attempts to help the victims in Europe and by the great national political, financial and military effort to create a Jewish state. It was not the state that generated the process of national consolidation, but vice versa. Thus, the establishment of Israel did not generate a new process of consolidation but rather brought the process to an end, as we have shown in the previous section.

In the fifteen years between the end of mass immigration and the Six Day War, centrifugal trends within the American Jewish community intensified. These trends, even if not deliberately aimed at sunderance, advocated the right to separateness – the right of the Jew as individual to define his own national identity and the right of the Jewish community to regard itself as an autonomous Jewish center equal in value and standing to Israel. The concept of a Jewish nation as the ideological basis for the existence of Jewish unity was gradually pushed aside, without any ideological or practical substitute being offered.

Consequently, the revival of national spirit came as a surprise to American Jews in 1967. Suddenly, under the impact of a brief period of dread followed by joyous relief, Israel regained its central place in Jewish consciousness. In the Sinai desert, by the Western Wall and in the hills of Samaria, an old-new national-religious myth was born. From now on, a kind of civil religion, as sociologists term it, came into being, attracting believers and non-believers, and placing the Jewish national entity – the State of Israel – at the focal point of their Jewish experience.

Here it should be noted that it was not only the Six Day War that caused the change from centrifugal to centripetal process. A bitter dispute erupted in 1968 between the Jewish and black communities in New York, which soon deteriorated into an open and almost irreparable rift between these two ethnic groups. The Jews, to a large extent, symbolized the success of the American dream, and the blacks its failure. In the previous decade Jewish public personalities, rabbis and students had been in the forefront of the struggle for equal rights for blacks. The tension between the two groups – tinged by manifestations of classic anti-Semitism on the part of the blacks, and compounded by the Jews' exhilaration following the Six Day War, – created an unprecedented situation for the American Jewish community.

This was the atmosphere that gave birth to three new radical trends in the Jewish public in the US and in Israel, namely, the revolutionary radicalism of young Jewish students; the conservative radicalism of disillusioned liberals, and the messianic radicalism of Gush Emunim in Israel. We will also discuss the response of traditional liberal thought and Zionist ideology in the face of the new situation. Thus, we are faced with two kinds of thinking. The first is radical in both the left- and the right-wing sense, trying to change established patterns of thought. The other is moderate, fighting to preserve the traditional principles within the process of inevitable change.

6 Revolutionary Radicalism: The Left-Wing Jewish Student Movement 1967–73

The American Jewish Community along with the ethnic groups of this country is jumping out of the melting pot into the salad bowl.

S. Rosenfeld, *Davka*, Winter 1974

Jewish is Beautiful.

J.J. Goldberg, *Other Stand*, 2 February 1969

Several of the terms employed in this chapter require clarification. Firstly, I have used the term 'radicalism' in its historical sense, to refer to extremist social theories located to the left of center. Secondly, it should be noted that the subject under discussion is radical Jews (with the emphasis on the noun) or alternatively, Jewish radicalism, (with the emphasis on the adjective) rather than the Jewish radicals who were prominent in the student revolt movements in the United States in the early sixties. The attitude of the latter, and particularly their leaders, towards their Judaism was limited to acknowledgment, sometimes reluctant, of their origins. The radical Jews also grew up in this movement, known as the New Left. They adopted its utopian social and cultural ideas, directed against materialistic middle-class society, but they withdrew from it on nationalist grounds. Thirdly, it should be noted that we are not dealing here with the social and political history of Jewish radicalism, but with analysis of its sense of national awareness, born out of a national experience. Many of these young people experienced a profound shock during the Six Day War, and were bitterly disappointed at the reaction of their non-Jewish comrades in their hour of distress. Their disillusionment reached its height in face of the black anti-Semitism of the early seventies.

This movement of radical Jewish students was ideologically diverse and organizationally fragmented. It encompassed mainly student groups: Zionist and non-Zionist, liberal and socialist, secular and religious. Some groups tried to establish collectivist frameworks, in the form of urban kibbutzim or traditional-religious *havurot*. The differences in outlook between the various groups were not always clear, even to the participants themselves. Thus, for example, it is not easy to differentiate between socialism and extreme liberalism; Zionism and Diasporism; nationalism and ethnicity; tradition and revolution. Some of the groups followed Ber Borochov, the socialist Zionist leader of the Poalei Zion Party, who tried to explain the Jewish national problem in Marxist terms. Others were attracted by the revolutionary tradition of the anti-Zionist Marxist socialistic party – the Bund – who endeavoured to build a new Jewish national culture in the future socialist society. Close to them were those who followed the philosophy of history developed by Simon Dubnow; like him they believed that America might be another of the changing Jewish centers in the course of history, such as Eretz-Yisrael, Babylon, Spain and Eastern Europe. All of them were inspired by the idealistic ideology of the Russian populist intelligentsia in the second half of the nineteenth century.

For lack of time and ability to crystallize a common national outlook, it was replaced by a many-faceted intellectual national experience. One can, however, identify three main viewpoints, whose true or supposed roots lay in Eastern European Jewish culture. These were neo-Poalei Zionism, neo-Bundism and neo-Hassidism.

The first and the third of these were the more important because of their attempt to create an ideological synthesis between the traditions of the past and present realities, and because of their public impact. Consequently, most of this chapter is devoted to them.

It is difficult to estimate the size of the movement. We are dealing with about a hundred groups of radical Jews in the important universities in the United States and Canada. About one half of the fifty or so newspapers published by groups of Jewish students represented radical viewpoints. There are no accurate data on the membership of these groups. Naturally enough, and this emerges from the testimony of activists, they constituted a small minority among Jewish university students. The hard core of activists usually numbered several dozen. Several hundreds more attended the meetings and gatherings they organized. Their publications were circulated in tens of thousands and some sources even estimate the total circulation at one hundred and fifty thousand.[1]

The political activity of these groups undoubtedly deviated from the traditional norms acceptable to the American Jewish leadership. Unlike the Jewish establishment, the students expressed themselves frankly, bluntly and aggressively. They sought to convert power into the central factor in Jewish policy, the guarantor of survival, but without resorting to violence. One might say that they tried to endue Jewish political action with normality. As for the content of their activity or the subjects which preoccupied them, they were in broad confrontation with their surroundings. They took issue with their comrades from the new left because of their negative and unfair attitude towards Israel; they denounced the leaders of black power as racists because of their anti-Semitic outbursts; they encouraged the use of overt pressure on the Soviet government to amend their anti-Jewish policies; they criticized their own government vehemently for becoming involved in the Vietnam War and for their military involvement in Cambodia; they denounced the Jewish establishment for neglecting Jewish education, and organized sit-down strikes against it; they protested against Israel's foreign policies, and unwillingness to conduct negotiations with the PLO.[2] Again, they condemned the PLO for its acts of terror against innocent civilians. Nor did they hesitate to demonstrate against official representatives of Israel, as, for example, when Israel honoured Ronald Reagan, then Governor of California, or to publicly denounce Israel for shooting down the Libyan plane in Sinai.[3] Their social criticism was soon extended to Jewish society in Israel as well. It is noteworthy that their attacks on the Jewish establishment did not prevent them from accepting its funds to finance their newspapers. Small sums for this purpose were received from local federations, from the Youth and Hehalutz Department of the Zionist Organization and from Hillel Houses on campuses, which also provided them with various services. Their political methods were indubitably innovative when compared with the American Jewish public tradition. The Jewish establishment, zealous in protecting Jewish rights, refrained from criticizing the policies of the US government on issues not directly pertaining to Jews. It was careful not to express disapproval of Israeli government actions, and refrained from wielding power as a political method. It preferred a policy of conciliation towards the blacks and persuasion *vis à vis* the American administration, rather than the open struggle which the young radicals advocated.

As we have pointed out, the change in the outlook of these young people began with their national experience. It was this experience which spurred them to seek and clarify their individual and group identity. In this case, emotional upheaval preceded intellectual analysis, and revolutionary fervor came before ideological theory. Many of these young people, particularly those who came from homes which had become remote from Judaism, have attested to the existence of a common pattern of 'returning home' to Jewishness.

The process usually consisted of several stages. The tension in the Middle East in May 1967 raised the issue of Israel's survival among young people who until then had concerned themselves mainly with ensuring the democratic character of US society, with the civil rights struggle and with protest against the Vietnam War. After hostilities commenced, they were infected by the profound anxiety for the fate of the Jewish state, which stemmed from their families. There are characteristic descriptions of Jewish parents, sitting tensely beside their radio sets and listening to news from the Middle East. When they realized that their fellow radical students did not share their concern, the Jewish students' anxiety was transformed into a sense of isolation. They suddenly became aware that the few who shared their feelings were usually of Jewish origin. Then isolation turned into a alienation, which found expression in bitterness towards their former friends, who not only failed to support a little country surrounded by enemies, but added insult to injury by denouncing victorious Israel as an imperialist state. In the next stage anger took over, particularly towards the black students, for whose rights the young radical Jews had fought and who had now betrayed them by supporting the Arabs (who were perceived as enslaved Third World Nations). The anger was accompanied by protest at the anti-Semitic attitude towards the Jews. Experience was translated into awareness, and there commenced a search for organizational-ideological frameworks in which they could maintain collective Jewish identity without betraying their radical outlook.[4]

This experience marked the beginning of the transition from the search for personal identity, which had been imposed on them, to the desire to define themselves as a collective entity. Several common elements are discernible in all the attempts at self-definition. The first of these, to paraphrase Ahad ha-Am, may be described as 'imitation not for the purpose of assimilation'. These young people readily admitted that they had been deeply impressed by the awakening of ethnic-national pride among the blacks and the Latino-Americans, and that it had spurred them to seek out their own roots.[5] This search for roots is linked to the second element, sanctioning of the particularist principle in addition to universalist principles.[6] This sanctioning was reinforced by the trend to positive imitation in the national context. It was stated that, since many of the Jewish radicals supported national liberation movements, 'the time has come for us too to acknowledge and support our own particularism'.[7] The positive approach to particularism is related to the third common element, namely the topical interpretation of Zionism as the national liberation movement of the enslaved Jewish people, in the political, cultural and psychological sense, relevant for each and every Jew in the Diaspora.[8]

This led to the fourth common element – the demand for the revival of Jewish culture in Canada and in the United States. These radical circles often cited the argument that the West practised cultural as well as political imperialism. In the United States, Anglo-Saxon culture had prevailed over the cultures of various minorities. Thus, the time had come to break free of this type of imperialism as well, so that each people and community could come to terms with its own historical and cultural heritage.[9]

The final element was the rejection of the capitalist-materialist character of Western society as a whole, and stringent criticism of bourgeois Jewish society in the United States and in Israel.

In light of this negative view of existing society, it is important to clarify the nature of the socialism espoused by these circles. The movement encompassed people of very different views: socialists, liberals of varying shades of opinion, Zionist and non-Zionist sympathizers with Israel. It should be pointed out that of the four important centers of the movement: Montreal, New York, Berkeley and Boston, the first three were predominantly socialist-Zionist. Montreal was characterized by a tradition of Yiddishist and Hebrew Jewish education, and most of the radicals came from families involved in Jewish affairs. The central challenge facing this community was the French-separatist movement, which wanted to establish an independent state in Quebec. The Jews of Quebec were caught in a classic Diaspora situation, between the Anglo-Saxon ruling minority and the French Canadian majority, which felt itself to be oppressed.

In New York, the Jewish labor movement tradition, with its Eastern European roots, was predominant. Whereas the Montreal community was caught in the midst of a national dispute, the Jews of New York found themselves embroiled in a clash between races. The tension between Jews and blacks originated in the 1968 teachers' strike, and was exacerbated by the dispute on the rehousing of tenement-dwellers in Jewish neighborhoods. The two crises were interconnected. In the first, the parents committee in schools in black neighborhoods demanded the right to determine who would teach their children. This meant the dismissal of white teachers, most of whom were Jewish. In the second case, tenants in the Queens neighborhood, most of them middle-class Jews, demanded the right to decide who would live in their neighborhood. The connection lay not only in the racial tensions unleashed between the two communities, but also in the legitimate demand of citizens of a democratic society to take part in conducting community life. The dispute soon deteriorated into a social struggle between blacks, who blamed their poverty on exploitation by Jewish landlords and storekeepers, and Jews who accused the blacks of anti-Semitism and racialism. In fact, the tension has not died down to this day, and it feeds on new controversies, such as the bussing of school-children, or the stand of black politicians on Israel. Berkeley was spared both racial and community disputes and social confrontation, and was characterized by the lack of a Jewish community with its own solid tradition, and by its status as the focal point and vanguard of the American radical movement.

The differences in historical and cultural tradition, and in prevailing social conditions, appear to have influenced the socialist-Zionist views of these four groups of Jewish radicals. Montreal was characterized by a neo-Borochovian outlook, which perceived the predicament of the Jews as resulting from the national dispute in Quebec, their marginal status in the local economy, and their extraterritorial national status. In New York, the neo-Borochovian outlook was combined with C.W. Mills's theory of the 'ruling elite'. This group was also influenced by the writings of the Tunisian-born, French Jewish sociologist, Albert Memmi. Berkeley, on the other hand, was strongly influenced by Herbert Marcuse's neo-Marxist theory of alienation. This group soon developed neo-Bundist tendencies. It is interesting to note that each of the groups consciously related to the Eastern European revolutionary Jewish tradition, seeking therein ideas which would help them interpret their own contemporary existence. Moreover, they sought parallels to the Eastern European situation in the general as well as the Jewish context. In brief, a kind of methodology of radical Jewish thought emerged, blending Jewish socialist traditions of the past with modern socio-psychological theories, in an attempt to find a key to understanding the realities of Jewish life in America and formulating solutions for continued national survival.

For example, the young radicals in Quebec emphasized the marginality of the Jewish contribution to the national economy. They pointed out that there were no Jews among the capitalists developing the economy nor were they part and parcel of the working proletariat.

Their contribution was confined to the non-essential services. Thus, lacking status or a vital economic role, and marked by social weakness, they were liable to be the first victims of the national dispute in Quebec. In Eastern Europe they had been ousted from the economic focal points by the territorial majority, and they were liable to suffer the same fate in Canada.[10] The most far-reaching conclusion was that this situation rendered them incapable of controlling their own destiny, and turned them into individuals whose identity was imposed on them by external forces. In this respect, and despite the freedom and relatively high standard of living of the Jews of the democratic countries, they were in a 'colonized state of being'.[11] The inevitable conclusion was that the sole solution to the problems of the Quebec Jewish community was to move to their own independent state – Israel. Several of the activists of the Montreal group totally despaired of the prospect of reviving Jewish culture in North America and of preventing mass assimilation.[12]

Whereas the Montreal radicals warned that the Jews were the victims of objective national developments, the New York radicals pointed to the nefarious intentions of the ruling White Anglo-Saxon Protestant (WASP) establishment. Moshe Zedek declared that this elite was deliberately dictating to the Jews a state of dependence, and perpetuating their political weakness.[13] The continued existence of a Jewish middle class of businessmen and professionals, despite its economic advantages, was a twofold social trap. On the one hand, there was the danger that any economic recession would harm these strata first, and on the other, in normal times the Jews were hated by the impoverished masses, who were exploited by the ruling elite. This was advantageous to the elite, which used the Jews as the scapegoats for its own exploitative policies. The validity of this theory, he wrote, was manifested in the tension between Jews and blacks in New York.

Aviva Cantor expounded a theory on the oppression of the Jews.[14] Under the influence of Albert Memmi, Cantor defined this oppression, beyond its economic, social and political significances, as 'denial of the basic human right to be yourself'. Throughout their exile, and in the present day, the Jews had been oppressed, and in the United States oppression had created a unique psychological state, reflected in the failure to respond to attack. This policy of restraint, which she defined as the 'sha-shtil policy', was born out of fear. Thus, for example, the Jews had never dared to fight for their rights, as did the blacks. In this sense, the Jews, while enjoying economic prosperity, were more defenceless than any other people in the world. They had perfected two responses in self-protection. The first was the attempt to disappear as a separate national entity through assimilation, and the second was the fostering of a sense of intellectual superiority over non-Jews, as a kind of compensation for constant humiliation. She argued that the ruling white elite in the United States was interested in perpetuating Jewish weakness. Consequently, it accepted their self-definition as a religion, but denied their national identity, because the very act of national self-determination was a source of political power. Moreover, out of the desire to maintain Jewish weakness, the elite opposed the existence and development of their national culture. Aviva Cantor stresses that oppression, as she describes it, is possible only under conditions of exile. While the Diaspora endures, Diaspora Jews must begin to fight for the revival of their culture, as the beginning of the process of national liberation.

Similar views were expressed by Naomi Alboim, who argued that the Jews of the United States suffer from the 'Uncle Tom Syndrome'.[15] They are the 'compradors' and agents of the rulers, fleeing their identity and avoiding an alliance with any ethnic minorities. Hence, their situation is even more degrading than that of other oppressed peoples, because they lack a sense of their own worth. This analysis of the situation led the New York radicals themselves to draw conclusions of Zionist implications, less extreme than those of their comrades in Montreal, but still unequivocal. They rejected *galut* as a national phenomenon, but did not believe in the prospect of the rapid eradication of the *golah*. Therefore, they favoured efforts to revive Jewish national culture in the Diaspora, concomitantly with the process of the ingathering of the exiles. In this, they were close in outlook to the leaders of Poalei Zion in the United States.

A slightly different outlook evolved within the Berkeley group. Here greater emphasis was placed on cultural renaissance than on social reform. Shelley Schreter, one of the leaders of the Berkeley group, under the influence of both Borochov and Marcuse, argued that the liberation of the masses from the ills of the consumer society would be achieved only through the revival of the original national culture of each ethnic group. This culture could counter the process of material atomization of the capitalistic consumer society, which had transformed the individual, in Marcuse's words, into a one-dimensional creature.[16] His comrade, David Biale, agreed with him in essence, but expressed his doubt as to whether the masses were interested in cultural renaissance and were ready to forgo the materialist pleasures of consumer society. He believed that it was necessary first to concentrate on the intellectual elite, since only from it could the national culture emerge: As he said, 'in the technological society, every meeting they [the younger generation] hold, every get-together on Shabbat, every course in Jewish Studies – all these are political symbols just as they are cultural events and the two are inseparable'.[17] Biale also argued the right of the Jews to desire to be themselves, without citing universal values to justify their nationalism. Both agreed that the ideal solution for American society was a socialist regime, based on a confederation of nationalities, each maintaining its original culture.

This accentuation of the cultural-national element in the future socialist conveyed them, through its inner logic, from neo-Borochovism to Ahad ha-Am, and in the end to neo-Bundism.[18] The crux of neo-Bundism was the demand that American society recognize the right of the individual to self-determination based on personal national autonomy. The organizational character and spiritual essence of the Jewish community should change accordingly. It should be transformed from an organization of philanthropic notables to a democratic institution based on popular taxation. The role of the new community would be primarily to maintain comprehensive Jewish education from kindergarten to university.

The authors did not offer their program as an alternative to Zionism. Their neo-Bundism, which they themselves acknowledged, was perceived as the complement to national territorial existence in Israel, aimed at all those who wished to bring about the national revolution in their lifetime, while at the same time remaining in the Diaspora. They were convinced that where political existence was concerned, the Jews should learn from the theories of the Zionist, Ber Borochov, the Bundist, Vladimir Medem and the existentialist Albert Memmi. In the cultural sphere, on the other hand, they should draw their inspiration from Hassidism, from Martin Buber and from Franz Rosenzweig. Thus, neo-Bundism was a formula encompassing all that they considered to be progressive in Jewish tradition. The Berkeley group did not reject *galut*, nor did they advocate eradication of the Diaspora. For them, immigration to Israel was a question of individual choice, and they believed in the rebirth of secular national Jewish culture in the United States.

Within the radical group in San Francisco, which called itself 'Hutzpa',[19] one finds similar views on the Bundist nature of the American version of Jewish existence, coupling conflicting and even hostile elements, such as Yiddishists and Hebraists.

The man who gave neo-Bundism its most extreme expression was Arthur Waskow, who cannot be classified among the Jewish radicals of the seventies. He was a radical of the older generation, almost twenty years older than the younger radicals. In outlook he was anti-Zionist, supporting the principle of Jewish existence in the Diaspora, and he was also an anarchist with religious leanings. His desire to blend the humanistic values in Judaism with universal humanistic values – manifested in the conducting of mass Passover *sedarim* on campuses, which took the form of celebrations of freedom – displeased those circles whose attitude to Jewish tradition was both more profound and more circumspect. At the same time, it should be noted that as the neo-Bundist tendencies of these groups intensified, they became more attentive to Waskow's views, even if not totally accepting. There were certain elements in his theories with which they could identify. Waskow wanted to base Jewish culture on five historical strata, which he selected in the light of his anarchistic predilections: the teachings of the prophets, because of their firm stand against kings and their faith in redemption; Hassidism, because it had risen up against the rationalist rabbinical establishment and legitimized the mystical experience; Bundism, because of its concern for the oppressed masses and its intellectual ability to provide a Marxist interpretation of a singular existence; the lifestyle of the kibbutz in Israel because of its anarcho-communist message, and because it had created a new kind of 'code of conduct' for democratic life; and the teachings of Martin Buber, who had succeeded in combining religious existentialism and Jewish anarchism. Waskow envisaged a society composed of free associations of various kinds. In this society a new socialist Jewish commonwealth would emerge with communal cells ranging from the kibbutz through the cooperative and the cooperative housing estate to the communal school.[20]

There were constructive anarchistic elements in each of the radical groups, manifested both in their opposition to the establishment and their leaning towards communal lifestyles. Hence, one can include within this trend the *havurot* (groups) of students of religious tendencies in Boston and New York, who hoped to transform the *havura* into the nucleus of the free Jewish community.[21] In analyses of the essence of Jewish life in the democratic countries, marked by sharp intellect and rare eloquence, these young people in their early twenties offered theoretical solutions to the dilemma of the relations between the universal and the particularist. Although the ideas in themselves were not original, their blend of socialism and Zionism, or liberalism, socialism (and even anarchism) and Judaism, against the background of the American ethic and culture – were unique. However, when these syntheses came into contact with reality, problems and inner contradictions were revealed. They found it difficult to provide convincing solutions to four problems: evaluation of the French separatist movement in Quebec; the attitude towards black power; their stand on the Jewish Defence League; and the nature of their ties with the State of Israel. In the first two cases, there was a clash between the particularist interest and the universal principle; in the third, a contradiction between Jewish morality and power politics, and in the fourth, a clash between the Zionist utopia and the realities of Israel.

The heads of the Montreal radical group, which was Zionist in orientation, adopted a sympathetic stand towards the separatist movement in Quebec, perceiving it as a national liberation movement, aspiring to win the right to self-determination for the French majority in the province.[22] At the same time, anxious to defend Jewish interests, they opposed the demand of the extremists among the separatists to convert McGill University into a French-speaking institution, a move which would naturally have been detrimental to the Jewish students, almost all of whom were English-speaking. They countered with the constructive proposal of establishing an additional French-language university and reducing tuition fees in all institutions of higher learning, to enable young French-speakers from the poorer strata in Quebec to attend university.[23]

The pro-separatist stance of the radical leaders, who were also editors of the group's paper, aroused debate. Martin Manis wrote that the separatist movement was becoming increasingly intolerant of views other than its own, and displaying growing nationalistic objections to other minorities. He voiced the fear that, in the end, the Jews might become the scapegoats for the nationalist frustrations of the separatists. Manis proposed, in effect, that the Jewish radicals adopt a policy of non-intervention in the struggle taking place in Quebec. He asserted that the true advantage of the Diaspora Jew stemmed from his ability to comprehend historical situations in the light of his own marginal social standing.

This stance was attacked by one of the paper's editors, Peter Shizgal, who declared that, as a Zionist, he could not ignore the inferior status of the French in Quebec, nor could he refute the justice of their demand for self-determination in the territory in which they constituted the majority. Despite the disparity in historical conditions, Shizgal discerned a similarity between political Zionism and the Quebec separatist movement. He did not discount the dangers which Manis had pointed out, but expressed his belief in the possibility of finding a compromise between the extreme demands of the French nationalists and the legitimate rights of other national minorities in the province. Shizgal objected, on practical grounds, to the granting of independence to the province, but favored the idea of national autonomy. This moderate nationalist trend among the French, he asserted, fitted in with Jewish national interests. In the end, he too admitted that he was not content with *galut*, in which the Jews were dependent on the ruling majority, and proclaimed his belief that the Jews could achieve absolute safety and security only in their own independent state.[24]

In his response to Shizgal, Manis raised a question of principle: namely, could Jews who chose not to immigrate to Israel support the separatist movement and, at the same time, maintain their national distinctness? He doubted this because of the nationalistic character of this movement, which would not be able to tolerate national differences within it. Hence, opposition to French separatism did not imply hostility towards French Canadians, but a desire to safeguard the interests of Jewish existence. The ideal solution, therefore, would be a federal political structure, and the preservation of the liberal and pluralistic values of Canadian society.[25] In his comments on this article, Shizgal reiterated that it was precisely Jewish interests that required the Jews to avoid cutting themselves off from the middle-of-the road element in the Quebec population. For the Jews, as a marginal minority, it would be dangerous to tie in their destiny with that of the ruling English-speaking minority.

The New York group conducted a similar debate in the face of black anti-Semitism. The radicals, mostly Zionists, could not ignore the exploitative role played by Jewish storekeepers and landlords in black ghettos. Nor, on the other hand, were they willing to reconcile themselves to black hostility towards the Jews in general. Consequently, some of them tried to find a common class basis for Jews and blacks, and argued that both nations were being exploited in different ways by the ruling white elite. This being so, the hope was expressed that, in the end, Jewish radicalism would find the path to the hearts of black radicals.[26]

Tsvi Bisk (who later immigrated to Israel) took issue with this viewpoint, asserting that the Jews should sever themselves totally from the black community in four spheres: they should liquidate their business concerns in slum districts, cease supporting the black liberation movement, remove Jewish teachers from black ghettos, and cease employing black maids. The historical lesson of Zionism, he said, was that the Jews, by means of the Zionist example, could teach other peoples how to fight for their rights, but must not fight their battles for them.[27] Chaim Cohen, another radical Zionist, was of a similar opinion, pointing to the essential contradiction between the objective interests of the Jewish middle class, with its liberal views in the spheres of education and housing, and the radical demand for social justice for blacks, to be achieved by integrating them in white bourgeois society. His conclusion was that, in the American Diaspora, there was an unbridgeable gap between the political radicalism and the real economic interests of the majority of Jews. Hence, the radical Jew was trapped in an insoluble dilemma between his universalist egalitarian outlook and his awareness of the need to protect the interests of his people. The Jewish left-wing movement in the United States was doomed to live in a constant state of schizophrenia. The only solution was the Jewish state, where it was possible to maintain a normal Jewish majority society and to belong to the left without undermining Jewish interests.

Cohen was not rejecting outright the outlook of the left. He was merely pointing out that any left-wing Jew who remained in the United States must be conscious of the inevitable tension between being Jewish and belonging to the left. Only by being aware that he would constantly face situations requiring choice, could he arrive at the correct decision.[28] To this Richard Morroch replied that the dilemma of the Jewish left was not exclusive to radical US Jews, but was characteristic of radical Jews everywhere, including Israel. The essential problem, he said, was not the existence of discordance between leftist principles and the true interests of the Jewish people, but the distorted and hypocritical interpretation of leftist principles concerning Jews and several universal problems. Consequently, he rejected Cohen's implied conclusion concerning the need to sever the objective connection between the proper Jewish interest and the true universal principles of the left.[29]

The problem of what attitude should be adopted towards the Jewish Defence League (JDL) was related to this issue. This militant body, with radical religious right wing views, had set itself the aim of wielding force to defend the Jewish residents of poorer districts who were being harassed by blacks, and exerting violent pressure on official Soviet institutions in protest against their attitude to Jews. Opinions were divided on this. Some radicals totally rejected the League's methods while others expressed reserved approval. Debby Littman considered the policy of the League to be a crude deviation from the traditional and highly successful method of protecting Jewish rights, as employed by such Jewish institutions as Bnei Brith, the American Jewish Committee, the World Jewish Congress and the Anti-Defamation League in the past half-century. She mocked what she considered the ostentatious and useless activities of the League. The root of the problem, she believed, was not the organization of strong-arm defence, but improvement of the living conditions of slum-dwellers. Hence the problem was not exclusively Jewish but general, pertaining to American society as a whole.[30]

Michael Stanislavsky agreed with her. He claimed that the ideology and deeds of the League were basically anti-Zionist, because they deliberately obscured the differences between the essence of Jewish life in an independent state and life in exile. In Israel the Jews were a normal sovereign nation, employing conventional means to defend themselves. On the other hand, existence in the Diaspora was not normal and was essentially dependent on the ruling majority, the government and legislation regulating law and order. The League members could not be compared to Israel Defence Force (IDF) troops, since the latter operated within the framework of state legislation, while the former were taking the law into their own hands. In the Jewish state there was no anti-Semitism, while in the Diaspora it was a permanent phenomenon, and it would be foolish to believe that it could be eradicated through violent measures. Anyone trying to foster the illusion of the normality of Jewish life in the Diaspora and advocating conduct like that of other peoples was adopting an anti-Zionist stand.[31]

The Berkeley group took a different viewpoint. Shelley Schreter, their spokesman, was ambivalent with regard to the activities of the JDL, ranging from moderate criticism to reserved approval. It is important to note that he rejected outright their ideology but not their activities. Schreter tried to temper the main argument voiced against the League, namely that the use of force ran counter to Jewish tradition. He cited historical examples from the Hasmoneans through the ghetto fighters and Jewish partisans during World War II up to the Israel War of Independence. He went on to point out the important role of this organization in defending the more defenceless Jews in the poorer districts of American cities. The selective use of force against Soviet institutions in New York, he said, could sometimes further political aims. In short, while voicing reservations with regard to the use of force as a blanket solution in any given situation, he criticized the Jewish establishment for their sweeping condemnation of the League's deeds, which he defined as an expression of the *galut* complex.[32] In the same period, the RZA (Radical Zionist Association) published a sharply-worded condemnation of the Jewish leadership for having publicly dissociated itself from the League's actions in a letter to President Nixon. Despite their objections to the quasi-racist ideology of the League, they regarded the conduct of the Jewish establishment as reminiscent of the conduct of Jewish informers against their brethren.[33]

In light of these views, accentuating the importance of Jewish interests, it is not surprising that M.J. Rosenberg's article 'To Uncle Tom and other such Jews' won considerable attention in these circles.[34] The article denounced the black militants and attacked the Jewish radicals of the New Left, who out of their Jewish self-rate complex, and lack of self-respect, were denying their own people and were willing to collaborate with racist elements who were vilifying and injuring Jews. Rosenberg ended his article bluntly by declaring that henceforth he would never join a movement which did not support the just fight of his fellow Jews, and, if faced by the choice, would prefer Jewish interests over progressive anti-Israeli causes. This view was echoed by J. Goldberg, who wrote: 'Jewish is Beautiful'.[35] Thus we see that these young people wrestled with similar problems and dilemmas to their spiritual predecessors, the 'radical Zionists' of the Second and Third Aliyot, who were confronted with the conflict between national interests and 'progressive' universalist principles on the 'Arab question'. In both cases, the final decision was the same – national interests prevailed.

This leads us to the final issue in this discussion – the attitude towards the Zionist entity in Israel. Having dealt with the Zionist analysis of American Jewish society, we now turn to the evaluation of Israeli society. The total identification with Israel in these circles was short-lived, and enthusiasm was swiftly replaced by disillusion, identification by trenchant criticism. This volte-face was linked to the decline of the radical left-wing movement in the United States; internal developments in the radical Jewish movement; and the ideological essence of Jewish radicalism. It has been noted above that Jewish radicalism was linked to the New Left in two ways. It grew out of that movement and took up cudgels against it on the question of its attitude to Israel. As the Vietnam War ended, the left began to retreat from the American public arena. Revolutionary ardor began to yield place to middle-class pragmatism, and collectivist ideals were replaced by personal ambition. This phenomenon, which gradually gained impetus over the years, naturally affected radical Jewish circles. Identification with Israel was weakened, since the quest for individual self-realization prevailed over the desire for personal fulfilment within a collective social and national framework like the State of Israel.

The ideological and emotional development from collectivism to individualism was accompanied by the disillusion of many leaders of the movement as a result of their own personal experiences in Israel. They redirected their criticism from American society to Israeli society, to no small degree out of youthful impetuosity. Furthermore, various problems which appeared to have been solved or to have been in the process of solution in the United States, seemed to them to have been aggravated in Israel. In their home country, the Vietnam War had come to an end, while Israeli government policy was placing obstacles on the path to peace. American blacks were winning equal rights, while in Israel the Arabs of the occupied territories were being increasingly oppressed, and Sephardi Jews were suffering discrimination. In the United States the 'youth culture' had, to some extent, checked the materialistic drive of capitalist society, while in Israel materialism was on the increase and had even affected the kibbutz movement. Whereas in the United States they felt that their struggle to expand Jewish education as a means of bolstering ethnic identity was proving successful, Israeli education seemed to lack any distinctive Jewish content.[36]

This disappointment stemmed from certain political yearnings and convictions, without which one cannot comprehend the character of the movement, nor its historical significance. The New Left in general was imbued with utopian aspirations, and this was true of Jewish radicalism as well. The difference between them lay in the fact that the utopian vision of the New Left was one-dimensional, and of the Jewish radicals tri-dimensional. The New Left aspired to create a new culture based on a different society, while Jewish radicalism sought, in addition, to revive the Jewish national culture in the Diaspora and to transform Israel into the ideal Jewish society. All its youthful fervor; its diverse, self-contradictory, intellectual world; its yearning, its quests and its frustrations – all these were levelled at Israeli society, which was tackling very real existential problems, and which had not yet found the way to deal with very basic issues. The radicals were sorely disillusioned. Some of them decided that, in Israel, Zionism had reached the end of its utopian stage with the establishment of the state, and was now a normal Western society, so that the struggle to change it was pointless, and doomed to failure from the outset. A Diasporist outlook began to evolve in these circles, advocating basic acceptance of the Diaspora as against Israel, and equilibrium between them. It is not surprising, therefore, that the forthright neo-Bundist views of Arthur Waskow won response in these circles.

Others refused to despair of achieving their utopia in Israel at some time in the future, and most of them chose to immigrate to Israel. They believed that Israeli society was undergoing a process of development whose end was still remote, so that all the options were open. They chose to live at the core of events, in the hope that they could help influence this process.[37] There was something paradoxical in the difference between the two attitudes. Those who continued to believe in Israeli society had despaired of Zionism in the Diaspora, while those who were disappointed in Israel believed that the Zionist principle of unity of the people and revival of their national culture could be realised in the Diaspora.

NEO-HASSIDISM

'At twenty I had my first taste of utopia. The year was 1968, a time of apocalyptic expectation. As Jews, we had just seen our messianic hopes fulfilled with the reunification of Jerusalem. As Americans, our whole society seemed on the verge of being torn apart, with the Sons of Light [the opponents of the Vietnam war] locked in battle with the Sons of Darkness. The place was Cambridge, Massachusetts, home of the counterculture.'[38] This description by David Roskies, today a lecturer in Yiddish literature at the Jewish Theological Seminary in New York illustrate vividly the exceptional character of this particular radical trend.

These groups of young people had much in common as regards age, education and ideological basis, namely the revolt against the bourgeois character of American Jewish society, and its materialistic values, the demand for democratization of community institutions, for sexual and racial equality and for social justice. However, there was a clear difference between the secular groups seeking to create a synthesis between nationalism and socialism, and the founders of the 'havurah', graduates of the Conservative movement, who wanted to blend traditional Judaism and modern radicalism. The secular radicals saw themselves as the vanguard of a Zionist-oriented, even pioneering movement, while the traditionalists wanted to create an atmosphere of religious revival through the intimate *havurot*, which they envisaged as the basis for future reorganization of Jewish community life in the United States.[39] They explained that the term 'havurah' traditionally meant a coming together on a religious basis, and was attributed to mystics in the first century CE and in the Middle Ages. But even closer to their hearts was the lifestyle of the havurot of hassidim in Eastern Europe, and particularly the personality of Rabbi Nahman of Bratzlav. According to David Roskies, they devised a kind of neo-hassidic utopia: the *stiebel* as the source of study, impassioned chanting of '*zemirot*', intense prayer, and communal meals. Unlike the Zionist and socialist radicals, who were inspired by modern, established Eastern European ideological traditions, such as the theories of Ber Borochov and

Nahman Syrkin, pioneering Zionism or Bundist ideology, the members of the *havurot* did not apparently examine closely the implication of their socio-religious utopia. At the same time, their sense of themselves as individuals and as a group was clear. They perceived themselves as new Jews – and this was the name of the anthology they published.[40] Thus, whereas the secular radicals emphasized ideological continuity, the traditionalists accentuated the innovative element in their beliefs. This approach affected their stand on Zionism and the State of Israel, as we shall see.

One of the leaders of the Boston *havurah*, James Sleeper, explained that the 'new Jews' wanted to understand the problems of modern man through Jewish eyes. Despite their acknowledgment of existential despair, they did not wish to lose hope of a better and more meaningful life. At the same time, they did not delude themselves that they possessed the answer to the predicament of man in modern society. This utopian yearning, he asserted, created the link between their Judaism and their radical convictions. The connection between the *havurot* and the radical social activists, said Sleeper, was manifest, but by no means simple. The *havurot* and the activist groups agreed that human implications should be taken into consideration whenever social decisions were taken, and were alike in their zealous quest for justice. However, the religious *havurot* tended to focus their efforts on nurturing the moral personality which should initiate social action.

This particular focus on the spiritual and moral aspects of the individual was also influenced by vague mystical proclivities, reflected in the complex and obscure language used by the leaders of the *havurah*. A member of the Boston group, who conducted an accounting with it seven years later considered the root of their failure to be the introversion and self-insulation of individuals and the mystic-transcendental mood which prevailed, leaving no room for clarification of general problems and for social endeavor. James Sleeper asserted in his above-quoted article, that he was a religious communard, seeking to promote small *havurot* who studied, prayed and acted together, thus creating interpersonal understanding. Alan Mintz, one of the chief spokesmen of the *havurah*, confirmed that the founders were attracted to the idea of togetherness as such, and believed that its very existence would vindicate their ideas. He also emphasized that the articles published in the movement's organ, *Response*, exhibited an apocalyptic prophetic tone.[41]

One cannot but note a certain resemblance to the mood of the young members of ha-Shomer ha-Tzair groups who immigrated to Palestine in the 1920s and settled in Upper Bitania high above Lake Galilee. They too were profoundly introspective, marked by utopian, mystical yearnings, and the quest for meaning. They read Martin Buber and studied psychological theories. They too had fled the mass political movements.[42] Arthur Green, one of the founders of Havurat Shalom in Boston, said that the *havurot* were an organic part of the student protest movement in the United States in the sixties. It was not Zionism and knowledge of the Holocaust that inspired them. They were part of the American counterculture.

Green drew a clear distinction between his own views and those of the Zionist activists who were his contemporaries. His radicalism was not inspired by the Six Day War nor by the manifestations of black anti-Semitism in New York, which evoked memories of the Holocaust. Moreover, he took issue with the post-1967 tendency of some secular Zionists to perceive a dimension of sanctity in political policies, and of some religious Zionists to endow religious injunctions with political significance. Green defined himself as a Diaspora Jew, who was linked to Israel and intended to spend a lengthy period there. The idea of the Ingathering of the Exiles excited him, but he refused to regard it as the solution for Jewish survival. To his mind, any attempt to explain the essence of Judaism in terms of national-political territorial existence would bring him close to the orthodox conception of Judaism, since only thus would he be able to justify his existence as a Jew in the Diaspora.[43]

Green's remarks attested to an attempt to devise a comprehensive Jewish approach in the spirit of the synthesis between modernism and tradition, between the Diaspora and Israel, as advocated by the havurot. The second symposium, on Living in Two Cultures, was devoted to this subject,[44] and the aims of the organizers can be learned from their choice of participants. Only those who had no intention of settling in Israel were invited to take part. The author of the programmatic article which introduced the symposium was Alan Mintz, who was a disciple of Mordecai Kaplan. Unlike his mentor, he did not choose to live concomitantly in two cultures – Jewish and general – but tried to merge them through creating a symbolic value system related to Jewish tradition, but with modern orientation. The formula, he said, should be: continuity of traditional symbols, and dialectical modification of the concepts linked to them and their adaptation to modern times. Thus, for example, the *havurah* had been the symbol of religious togetherness from the first century to the Eastern European *stetl*, and because of the continuity and the change inherent in this phenomenon, it was valid for modern times as well. It should, of course, be adapted to new conditions and constantly seek answers outside Judaism as well. In line with the dialectical approach he recommended, he advocated Jewish life based on unity of contrast, on 'creative conflict' between various Jewish ideologies, which were not seeking to compromise, but to fight, each for its own beliefs. This rule, he claimed also applied to relations between the Jews of the Diaspora and the State of Israel. The Diaspora was a real entity which was not anticipating its own liquidation, and as such, must develop its spiritual life and culture without an almost parasitical dependence on the State of Israel. Israel, too, was a real entity, and Jewish radicals could not ignore its existence, nor refuse to accept it as a Jewish national and political being. In the distant future, Mintz hoped, an integrated Jewish entity would evolve, which would contain within it the yearning for social justice, which the radicals demanded, the sanctification of life through religious symbols in which he and his comrades believed, and the realities of national political life, as advocated by the Zionists. All these would be interwoven into one fabric which would offer an existential answer for individuals, for movements and for the Jewish people as a whole.[45] This integrative ideology was aimed primarily at his own contemporaries, since he believed that from them alone would Jewish salvation emerge.

These statements attest to the evolution of Mintz's outlook, and perhaps also the view of some of his contemporaries. One may observe the transition from 'alternative opposition', totally rejecting existing society, to reconciliation with most of its views and acknowledgment of reciprocal influences. Attitudes towards the State of Israel also became more balanced, and the state, and Zionism with it, were now perceived as part of the Jewish whole. Mintz's views on Israel's place in Jewish life underwent an additional change in 1973, after his experiences in Israel during the Yom Kippur War. In an article he published three years later, he described himself as having returned from a journey to 'the center of Jewish history', where he had come face to face with his own personal sorrow.[46] The article was directed against Breira, which we shall discuss below (and which he had helped to found). He criticized his former comrades in Breira on the grounds that, by their opposition to Israeli policy on the question of Middle East peace, they were motivated by an ideology which was exaggerated in its accentuation of the differences and conflicts between the Diaspora and Israel. It should be pointed out that his criticism was indirectly levelled also against some of the members of the *havurot*, who during the crisis of the 1973 war, appeared largely indifferent to Israel's fate. His comrade, William Novak, left the New York *havurah* for precisely this reason.[47] Two years later, Mintz retreated even further from the Diaspora ideology which he had advocated before the Yom Kippur War. Reacting to a book by his contemporary, Hillel Halkin, he revealed that his faith in the possibility of the flowering of a Jewish religious culture in the United States had been undermined.[48] Even if there were indications of a trend to return to tradition, he was not convinced that it would endure, and doubted where it would prove capable of generating a spiritual renaissance. He concurred that the future of Jewish life could be secure only in Israel, but immediately added that he did not believe that the majority of American Jews would draw the logical conclusion, and admitted frankly that he too lacked the strength to abandon his comfortable life in the United States and move to Israel.

Another viewpoint among the ex-*havurah* members was represented by Michael Strassfield, who, together with his wife Sharon, edited *The Jewish Catalog*, which had a wide circulation and did more to disseminate the views of the havurot than the learned articles and communal lifestyle. The *Catalog* aimed at preaching synthetic Jewish culture, as evolved over centuries, and adapting it to modern times. The overall Jewish ideology which underlay it was based on the principle of equilibrium between Israel and the Diaspora, resting on two conflicting symbols and on a socio-political organization. The symbols were Massada and Yavneh, the one representing heroism and struggle and the other passive endurance. These two symbols should be part of Jewish life everywhere in the Diaspora and in Israel,[49] guiding Jewish socio-political organization. In the introduction which the Strassfields wrote to the chapter on Israel–Diaspora relations, in *The Third Jewish Catalog* they tried to sketch a model for these relations, based on the historical past.[50] The basic assumption was that in Jewish history for the past two millenia the Diaspora was the counterpoint to the Land of Israel, and this found expression in three principles: in acknowledgment of the equal importance of the Golah and the community in Eretz Israel; in the granting of priority status in the religious sense to Eretz Israel, on the assumption that Jewish life outside its borders was imperfect; and with the special pledge of the Diaspora to aid the Land of Israel.

Translation of this model for modern application means: whereas Jewish history demonstrates the centrality of Israel, the Diaspora has importance of its own in Jewish life. From this it follows that in Jewish life there are two centers which collaborate on the basis of mutual aid and respect. They are interconnected and interdependent, but are also independent. Unlike Mintz, Strassfield believed that today, as in the Mishnaic and Talmudic eras, it is possible to build two strong Jewish centers, which will nurture one another. Any attempt to base relations between them on one-sided dependence of the Diaspora on Israel, will embroil both in religious and political friction.

NEW LIBERAL RADICALISM

The public fate of neo-Hassidism did not differ from that of pioneering neo-Poalei Zionism and cultural neo-Bundism. Not one of them succeeded in creating a Jewish cultural revival movement in the United States. Some members of each group, however, found their place in two socio-political associations of radical orientation, Breira, established in 1973 after the Yom Kippur War, and A New Jewish Agenda, founded in 1980.

Breira was founded by a group of liberal Reform rabbis, leaders of the *havurot* movement and veterans of radical left-wing circles, both Zionists and non-Zionists. Their supporters included academics of socialist background and secular liberals from the young generation. The organization was mainly concerned with the Middle Eastern dispute and the democratization of American Jewish community life. In the former sphere, their stand was radical and uncompromising in their insistence on the right of US Jewry to express public criticism of the political actions or inaction of the Israeli government. On the Israel–Arab conflict, they explicitly demanded Israel-Jewish recognition of the right of the Palestinians to self-determination, and negotiations with the PLO on the partition of Palestine into two national states. Both because of its content and its openness, Breira's stance aroused considerable furor in the American Jewish public, recalling the storm roused by the American Council for Judaism a generation previously. The Jewish establishment forcefully objected to the principle of the right to open criticism of Israel, which Breira demanded. In the end, the organization was 'outlawed' by other Jewish organizations, and its political views were relegated to the sidelines.[51]

Our interest in Breira relates not to its political stance or views on community politics, but to its attitude to the role of Israel in Jewish life. And here it should be pointed out, in advance, that unlike the American Jewish Council, Briera accepted the existence of the state as a positive Jewish phenomenon, and was not anti-Zionist in viewpoint. The reverse was true. Its leaders included people who identified with Zionism, according to their own radical liberal lights. At the same time, one cannot deny that there was a certain connection between their political stance and their views on the question of the centrality of Israel. It will be recalled that this had been implied by Alan Mintz, who was among the founders of Breira and left it in 1976 due to disputes on relations with Israel. Mintz claimed that the prevailing view in Breira was that of the importance of the Diaspora as a counter-center to Israel both in cultural potential and in political status,[52] and, in fact, perusal of the organization's ideological platform, as ratified at its first national conference in 1977,[53] reveals that Mintz was correct, and that neo-Dubnowist tendencies are clearly evident.

The opening sentence, in which they proclaim that 'we insist on the need for real Jewish life not only in Israel but also in the Diaspora', contains nothing new in itself, and is acceptable to all trends in modern Jewish thought, from Zionists to non-Zionists. However, it is the practical interpretation of this basic hypothesis that clarifies the extent to which Breira was influenced by the concept of centers in Jewish history and the balance between them. Therefore, in defining Israel–Diaspora relations, they assert that 'Jews, all over the world, and throughout the generations, are one people. The State of Israel is a special manifestation of this peoplehood; the communities of the Diaspora are a vital component to the same extent. We believe that the continuity of Jewish life depends on the reciprocal ties between Jews in Israel and in the Diaspora'. In other words, as we shall see below, where the ideological platform of the Reform movement had declared, a year previously, that the existence of the state was vital for the existence of the Diaspora, Breira now allotted equal status to the state and the Diaspora. Hence, the mutuality of Jewish life, on which all agreed, now takes on different significance. This is no longer the mutuality of center and periphery – or preferred center and surrounding centers – but between centers of equal importance.

They went on to declare the total equilibrium between 'the cultural treasures and great moral examples' which Israel had given to the Jews of the Diaspora and 'the richness of the Jewish experience in America'. They insisted on the sovereignty of each Jewish community *vis à vis* all others. They emphasized that the communities should make their feelings known to one another 'as a reflection of responsibility, support and mutual concern'. At the same time, they clearly hinted that in relations between Israel and the Diaspora, 'neither of the sides should try to exploit the other or to intimidate it,' and the meaning is clear: they are referring to the Israel government and the institutions of the Zionist movement.

When they move from principles to the sphere of Jewish practical policy, the theory of total equilibrium becomes explicit. They favored immigration to Israel, but, to the same degree, insisted on the right of immigrant Jews and of Israelis to choose for themselves their country of residence. On so vital and painful an issue as emigration of Israelis and the Russian Jews en route to Israel who dropped out at Vienna, they wrote: 'We regard immigration as a positive act, but also insist on the right of Israelis to settle elsewhere. Similarly, we reject any step intended to place difficulties in the path of those Russian Jews who exercise their right to settle and rebuild their lives outside Israel. We do not believe that Israelis who settle outside Israel or Russian Jews who choose to emigrate to North America have betrayed some special injunction because of this choice.'

Turning to the practical question of the distribution of money raised by the various appeals, they contradicted the theory of total equilibrium and the right of intervention of one Jewish community in the affairs of another. While proclaiming their support for Israel 'as an expression of Jewish self-determination', they explicitly recommended moral and financial support for part of Israeli society, namely 'those bodies fostering the principles of peace, social equality, democracy, civil rights and other values compatible with the tradition of the prophets'. They were referring explicitly to those bodies protecting the rights of the Arab minority.

The document then turns to the question of supervision of the distribution of funds, strongly criticizing the existing system, which distributed money according to political party criteria. They called 'for the establishment of a committee to examine methods of eradicating these types of inequality, and to introduce more responsible and just procedures'.

The Breira leaders formulated a plan of action within Israel, proclaiming their active support for the forces struggling for social justice, true integration of the different communities, equal rights for women, religious and cultural pluralism, civil liberties, etc. In contrast to other Jewish bodies, they sought active status in Israeli society by 'despatching American-Jewish emissaries to aid and take part in activities intended to promote these aims'. They also advocated encouraging American Jewish adults and young people to volunteer for programs to improve Israeli society as a service to their people. Such practical proposals were not unusual and were acceptable to all sectors of the Zionist movement and the American Jewish public. But when they are added to what has been stated above on the right to practical intervention in Israeli affairs, and are accompanied by explicit reference to expansion of financial support for projects promoting certain proclaimed aims, they point to the crystallization of the ideology of extreme diasporism, aimed at changing the order of national priorities by transforming Israel into a society which is not only supported but also guided by the Diaspora.

Despite Breira's 'diasporism' echoing certain views voiced on the eve of the Six Day War by Jacob Petuchowski, their views, paradoxically enough, also reflected the 'Jewish normalization' approach. By demanding the right to active intervention in Israel's actions through open criticism of Israeli government policy and through selective financial aid, they were, in effect, emphasizing the principle of the unity of the Jewish people.[54] Of particular significance in this context, is an article by Arthur Waskow, the most controversial figure among the Breira leaders. In it he proposed reviving the term '*am olam*' in the meaning of scope and time, namely a worldwide association for the renewal of Judaism, based on elections with the participation of all Jews who wished to revive the values of religious and secular tradition. As a first step he called for the establishment of a center of Jewish scholars, which would conduct research and clarification of the cultural, social and psychological problems entailed in Jewish life. The center would also encourage study and dissemination of the biblical Hebrew language to enable the students to understand the source literature. Thus, even though opinions were divided on the centrality of Israel,[55] there was consensus on the idea of the existence of a worldwide Jewish entity, not necessarily in the religious sense. Whether they acknowledged this or not, theirs was a Jewish-national outlook, which can be denoted neo-Dubnowism or neo-Bundism.

The New Jewish Agenda was the continuation of both the havurot associations and Breira. Both ideologically and practically it focused on diasporacentrist trends, and its establishment symbolized a new mood in Israel–Diaspora relations in the early eighties (to be discussed in the concluding chapter).

What then was the importance of the liberal-leftwing radical movement, from the ideological and psychological viewpoints? Its basic trait was activism, expressed primarily in its attitude towards the past, that is to say its perception of historical continuity. One should distinguish between those whose attitude towards the past was spontaneous and those who took a dynamic view of it. The former make every effort to maintain the historical continuity of language, culture, religion and customs, and everything they are seeking to preserve is long familiar to them. As for the latter – the heritage of the past is remote, even alien to them, and they approach it extraneously, out of a desire to extract from it positive support for their present day aspirations and instruments for analysis of the reality within which they live. It was this approach that created the dynamic and activist link between these young people and the historical continuity of the Jewish people. It is no coincidence that when the movement died out, many of its members chose to engage in Jewish activity in academic occupations and in community work.

The truth is that many of them experienced, unwillingly, what Pavel Axelrod had undergone during the pogroms in the Pale of Settlement in 1881/2. Similarly to him, though with different intensity and under very different historical conditions, they were shocked at the cold and hostile attitude of their fellow radical socialists towards the Jewish people in their hour of distress. However, this was not a situation which they had consciously chosen, but rather 'Jewish destiny', maintaining its historic continuity beyond the altering circumstances and change in place. As a result of their shock, they turned deliberately and willingly to the Eastern European revolutionary Jewish tradition. Through praiseworthy intellectual effort, they tried to link themselves to the heritage of Nahman Syrkin, Ber Borochov and Vladimir Medem, and to Hassidism, the various shades of socialist

Zionism, and in particular the Second Aliyah and the Bund. Later, when their revolutionary and Zionist ardor faded, they sought the answer to their queries and their dilemmas in the theories of Martin Buber and Franz Rosenzweig.

In this respect they differed from their predecessors, born in the US and raised on its culture, who were remote from Eastern European culture in any form, as well as from the Eastern European-born Jewish intellectuals who wanted to preserve the stychic historical continuity by preserving Yiddish culture in pluralistic American society. They differed from both in their activist attitude to the past.

Their activist approach was also new in that it combined national radicalism with social radicalism, entailing harsh criticism of American society. In the previous generation, Jewish radicals had condemned this society, but had totally disregarded Jewish national existence, and their contemporaries from the New Left continued this tradition. Those circles which had created the traditional patterns of thinking among US Jews had never presumed to criticize the society in which they lived, either out of a sense of gratitude for the bounty they had received or out of gratification at the public and individual standing of Jews in that country. The younger generation, in contrast, combined their Jewish zeal with social radicalism. In this sense, paradoxically enough, they were the truest representatives of the 'Jewish normalization' school of thought which was emerging in younger circles.

This brings us to the most important contribution of these young people to American Jewish public thought. They declared openly, and without the hesitations which had characterized the previous generation, that the Jews were a nation. This basic acknowledgment of Jewish nationality in the world in general and the United States in particular, (even though they sometimes confused nationality and ethnicity), impelled them to make an unequivocal statement on the legitimacy of the Jewish national interest in the United States. On this point, they would appear to have made an important contribution to destroying a psycho-ideological barrier within the American Jewish community. In conclusion, although their social and cultural achievements within the Jewish community were minimal and their contribution to Zionism infinitesimal, on this emotional and ideological issue – open championing of Jewish interests, not as an act of charity and not as part of the American liberal tradition, as their predecessors had claimed, but as a natural national principle – their contribution was significant.

7 Neo-Conservative Radicalism

To be a Jew is not an act, it is a fate. The existence of Israel is absolutely central to that fate.

Midge Decter, *Commentary*, February 1988.

I am pro-Israel not only because it is a decent, civilized country that is a fine addition to our western civilization...but because it is today, after the Holocaust, the sheet anchor of the Jewish people.

Irving Kristol, *Commentary*, February 1988.

The neo-conservative ideology, which has held the center of the stage in Western public thought for close to two decades, underlying the political and social policies of Western governments, combines outlooks which were once at odds with one another. It is a pragmatic synthesis between the social conservatism and the economic liberalism of the nineteenth century and the theory of the minimal welfare state. Thus, what is new is not the ideology, but the social psychology which generated a militant public mood of promotion of individual principles over all shades of collectivist ideology from Keynesian economics through Roosevelt's New Deal to the social-democratic welfare state.[1]

When we move on to the definition of neo-conservatism as a Jewish public phenomenon and not as the outlook of certain individuals of Jewish origin, the picture becomes more complex. One could say that Judaism as a spiritual-cultural essence and as a socio-political entity is torn between traditional conservatism and revolutionary progress. As essence, it represents the power of tradition within the process of modernization. As an entity it demonstrates the universalist goals of anti-conservative revolutionary forces in Europe. In the past two centuries, thanks to the principles of the French Revolution, and liberal and socialist ideologies – the status of Jews in conservative Christian society has been transformed. Although the links of Jews with progressive forces, particularly the socialist movement, were always complex, the number of Jewish leaders and thinkers (who did not conceal their origins) within the various European socialist movements, attests to the dramatic change in their social standing.

Thus, although Judaism as a traditional essence should have been attracted to the conservative forces in society, in practice, it was the progressive movements which became the allies of the Jews. One might say that the progressive elements who accepted the Jews still objected to the religious or national manifestations of Judaism. The conservatives, on the other hand, were ready to accept Judaism, but had reservations about the Jews. Consequently, throughout the nineteenth century and until the mid-twentieth century, with the exception of Benjamin Disraeli, there were no Jews among conservative leaders and thinkers. In this respect, in our time, we have witnessed an unprecedented phenomenon in Jewish life – Jewish intellectuals have become leading spokesmen and philosophers of the neo-conservative trend in the west, and particularly in the United States. It seems, therefore, that since the waning of the New Left movement in the early seventies, Jewish intellectuals have changed their historic role, and although the voting patterns of American Jews have not changed fundamentally, and the decisive majority continue to support the liberal policies represented by the Democratic party, many Jewish intellectuals have chosen the utopia of the right over the utopia of the left.

There were three stages to this journey from left to right. In the 1950s, they became disillusioned with the Soviet Union and with both the Leninist-Stalinist and Trotskyite versions of Marxism. This led them, in the sixties, the decade of the New Left, to denounce the tendency among young Jews to adopt universal ideas. The ex-leftists preferred to stress the positive elements in American national particularism as a way of life and a democratic, liberal society, and, moreover, were highly apprehensive at the prospect of the spread of international communism. In the late sixties, in the aftermath of the Six Day War and in the light of the tension between blacks and Jews, a Jewish neo-conservatism, which may be described as liberal-conservative in orientation, emerged.

This neo-conservative trend may be seen as part of the Jewish radical phenomenon because of its strong views on four issues: its militant objection to communist imperialism; its dissociation from universalist liberal principles; its accentuation of Jewish-ethnic interests; and its combination of American patriotism and Jewish loyalties. The outcome of this standpoint was legitimization of the middle-class Jewish lifestyle as the reflection of the American ideal, and almost unqualified support for the State of Israel, which became a central factor in their Jewish consciousness.

To understand the neo-conservative outlook in its Jewish context, it is necessary to examine the development of its political and ideological motivation according to the order of appearance of its political and ideological motives, and the way in which it tackled the inherent contradictions it encountered from the outset.

Politically speaking, neo-conservatism was grounded on the viewpoint which perceived the global interests of the United States and the free world as synonymous with the general interests of Jews and the special needs of Israel. In 1957, after the Sinai Campaign, when left-wing Jewish intellectuals levelled fierce criticism at Israel, Norman Podhoretz came to Israel's defence, and in so doing, laid the foundations for the political outlook of Jewish conservatives.[2] He disagreed with certain champions of Israel, who claimed that her Jewish critics were motivated by Jewish self-hatred. He did, however, believe that the critics were alienated from American society in general, of which Jewish life was, of course, a part. He believed that their sense of alienation, stemming from a utopian-rationalist approach, had cut them off from reality and from traditional loyalties. They supported the Hungarian uprising against Russia because it symbolized the fight for freedom, while at the same time condemning the Sinai Campaign, because it represented imperialist aspirations and interests, and failed to grasp the political similarities between the two. Both, he argued were linked to the aims of Soviet imperialism, which stretched greedy arms both to Hungary and to the Middle East. The true moral precepts relating to the survival of nations could be fulfilled only by political means, which are the reflection of national interests. Because of the alliance between Egypt and the Soviet Union, Israel was increasingly important to American global interests, which were synonymous with the values of democracy and liberty, and thus, with the interests of US Jewry. It was incumbent on American Jews, he declared, to explain to their non-Jewish compatriots the links which bind together the United States, the Jews and the State of Israel.

There is a touch of 'Macchiavellianism' in Podhoretz' political realism, but with a difference: he did not separate politics and morals, but utilized politics to promote certain values. But while avoiding the trap of Macchiavellianism, he encountered another pitfall by sanctifying the end through employing Bolshevik means: he hoped that democracy and liberty would prove capable not only of justifying the means employed in their defence, but also of restricting them; he sought to resolve the dilemma of democratic society operating within the political situation. He believed that it was incumbent on the Jews of the Diaspora and the State of Israel to explain this problem to public opinion in the free world.

Neo-conservatism took a positive view of the historical, religious and cultural aspects of Jewish tradition. In 1961 Daniel Bell published an article in which he elucidated his changed views on Jewish historical tradition.[3] In his Marxist-Trotskyist youth, in the late forties, (see the previous Part), Bell had believed that alienation was the existential destiny of the Jewish intellectual in an imperfect society. Now he asserted that identification with the common historical past was an existential injunction for the Jewish intellectual. Bell's return to his heritage was confused and uncertain. His was the uncertainty of a man who, on his own testimony, had no religious faith, no longer believed in the existence of final aims and had no absolute answers to offer to life's predicaments. All that remained to him were memories and a sense of exile. However, *galut* was no longer a universal concept but a Jewish existential condition, which he accepted willingly. He bears the burden and the gratifications of his double life, whose overt, external aspect is American and whose hidden, inner face is Jewish. Bell could not say if and to what extent the decision to identify with his Jewish heritage was binding. But it was clear to him that it stemmed from awareness that, as an individual, he was not alone in this world; part of the overall responsibility of the intellectual relates to his identification with a common heritage, even if it is more a memory than a real experience.

His demand that Jews cling to memory stemmed, in particular, from his concern for the younger generation which was rapidly moving away from its Jewish heritage. But, for Bell, memory is not religious in content, although he is well aware that this is a problematic issue because of the close affinity between Judaism as culture, history and religion. At the same time, Bell was not willing to accept the orthodox tradition because, to him, as an intellectual who formerly held activist social views, that tradition had always maintained a passive stance in history. He also rejected the reform version of Judaism, because as a 'neo-conservative', he was not willing to accept its naive social moral outlook. Like Podhoretz he believed that in the course of history, there was no escape from taking steps which might cause minor injury in order to defeat or prevent great injustice.

In the absence of religious faith and of nationalist convictions, which at the time he had not yet adopted, there remained only memory. He considered recitation of the Yizkor prayer by a minyan of Jews to be the symbol of collective memory, since it combined individual and collective memory. Bell and others like him required determination and firm resolve in order to rejoin the heritage of their people, and this was no easy or simple decision at any time, but particularly for young people in that decade. Norman Podhoretz was aware of the complexity of the problem, and noted with satisfaction, in the introduction to the 1961 *Commentary* symposium that the attitude of young Jewish intellectuals towards the United States had undergone a change for the better. They were now ready to identify with the American way of life, in light of their disillusionment with the communist world. On the other hand, he pointed out regretfully, their qualified view of Jewish society did not differ from that of their predecessors in the 1940s. Like Daniel Bell, Podhoretz asserted that Jewish existence was positive, primarily because it was the expression of free will and choice. Both agreed that the cost of this choice was extracted from the Jews in various ways, but that to be granted a share in four thousand years of Jewish history was worth any price. Beyond this, Podhoretz believed that Jewish history contained within it a great ideal for humanity, and that no individual born into it could deny it or reject it without harming himself. Each and every Jew, he wrote, must feel historic reverence, even if he was convinced that the curtain was about to descend on Jewish life. He himself, on the other hand, was convinced that this life had a future.

For both Podhoretz and Bell, reverence for history and tradition replaced religion, and endowed their Jewishness with meaning. In a conversation with the author of this book, Podhoretz stressed that, while he is not religious, his very existence as a Jew and that of his secular colleagues is of intrinsic existential Jewish value, since thereby they are preserving the Jewish people.[4]

The third fundamental component of this outlook is the lesson of the Holocaust, which is regarded as a kind of categorical imperative. The theologian Emil Fackenheim expressed this conviction most vividly at a symposium on the significance of the Holocaust held two months before the Six Day War.[5] Contemporary Jewish life, he said, was based on three contrasting phenomena. The first was the universal principle, according to which the Jews now enjoyed equality of rights unparalleled in their history in the Diaspora, versus the particularist principle, which has surfaced with the revival of Jewish independence in the historic homeland. The second was modern secularism, on the one hand, practiced by most Jews, and the awareness that Jewish life had no future without nurturing of traditional roots, on the other. The third was the freedom of modern society, which Jews enjoyed in the West and in Israel, as opposed to the tragedy of the Holocaust which had occurred in that same modern world. Despite these recognized conflicts in their modern life, the Jews had succeeded in maintaining a large degree of unity. He offered proof of this unity through negative examples: the failure of the American Jewish Council; the disappearance of Canaanite ideology in Israel; and the marginal role of extreme orthodoxy among the Jewish public. In other words, unity is recognized not in its common content but in the failure of the trends which had attempted to obliterate it. Fackenheim admitted that in the past, he had found it difficult to justify Jewish existence solely in existential terms. But now, faced with a society which lacked faith, the intrinsic will to exist was of historic significance, and he expressed his conviction that the future historian evaluating this phenomenon would not perceive the Jewish will to live merely as a tribal instinct but also as the expression, however partial, of faith. This faith, too, grows out of the negative, out of the memory of the Holocaust transformed, so he says, into a categorical imperative indicating to Jews their future path. He calls this imperative 'the 614th injunction', namely that modern Jews must not allow Hitler his final triumph, and must act and struggle against assimilation and on behalf of the future of the Jewish people.

Immediately after the Six Day War, only three months after formulating the '614th injunction', Fackenheim declared that the Israeli military victory was of religious significance, because it was connected to Auschwitz.[6] This victory, he wrote, was a beam of light illuminating the blackness of Auschwitz. After Auschwitz and because of Auschwitz, Jews must continue to be Jews, to be part of a living Jewish people. This miraculous victory held out hope that there was indeed some meaning to the struggles for continued Jewish existence. Thus, what had been but a wish three months previously, had now become a certainty as a result of the military victory. The spontaneous outburst of Jewish solidarity had bridged all the anomalies and conflicts in Jewish life – from now on the memory of Auschwitz was reinforced by the hope of May–July 1967. From now on, continued existence could be perceived not only as defiance of Hitler, but also as testimony to the intervention of Divine Providence in human actions.

The fourth cornerstone of neo-conservatism – belief in the central role of Israel in world Jewish consciousness and life, was laid after the Six Day War. The man who summed up the development of neo-conservative thought up to this point, and wove it into the fabric of Jewish solidarity during the Six Day War, was the community affairs editor of *Commentary*, Milton Himmelfarb.[7] He drew immediate conclusions in the realm of political philosophy. During the tense days of May and June, he and his colleagues learned afresh that political isolation is an existential condition in the global power alignment. No community or nation can rely on others, but only on itself. Israel had friends and promises galore, but fought alone.

They also learned that only those who are injured and threatened suffer pain, and that the cry of the victims does not disturb the even keel of everyday life. This natural indifference is a universal social law, and does not apply to Jews alone. One need only think of the slaughter of the Armenians and Assyrians in the Middle East during and after the First World War.

This sense of isolation led Himmelfarb to appreciate the positive value of the state in general, and in Jewish history in particular. If Israel had existed during the Second World War, he wrote, not only would a refuge have been available for some of the victims, but the attitude of the Western powers towards Hitler's atrocities would have been different. If a Jewish army had taken part in the war, its existence would have obliged the leaders of the West to bomb the death camps and to caution the Nazis against the outcome of their actions. This growing awareness of the moral value of political and military power accelerated the process of rejection of the universalist illusions which had characterized left-wing Jewish intellectuals. Greater value was now placed on particularist interests and on urgent topical socio-political issues rather than abstract questions. Empirical examination of society as it is, rather than as it should be, reveals that very few principles guide its conduct. It is not universal logic that determines action but particularist interest. In Jewish society, the force of this interest will be nurtured by the reinforcement of the consciousness of Jewish unity and by faith in the providential order in their history.

Fackenheim and Himmelfarb, each in his own way, perceived the Six Day War as the harbinger of redemption. Others shared this view, the most extreme interpretation being that of the theologian, Richard Rubinstein. Under the influence of a certain Christian school of thought, he declared bluntly that, after Auschwitz, he could not longer believe in Divine intervention in history. But it should be noted that he explained that the disappearance of Divine Providence from history did not mean the elimination of religious faith. The reverse was true: in the absence of God as the guiding force, more faith is required, and this can be found within the religious framework and not in devotion to God.[8] He arrived at this conclusion before the Six Day War. Immediately afterwards, he transmuted his religious faith into a theory of Jewish existence, which was too extreme to be palatable to most neo-conservatives, but was fundamentally related to their outlook.[9]

Rubinstein was the most outspoken representative of the neo-conservative theory of power and Jewish interests. He too claimed that the manifestation of Jewish power in the Six Day War had a religious significance, but he went even further both in his religious interpretation and in his concern for the future of Diaspora Jews. He predicted that sooner or later the dominant Jewish force in Greater Israel would generate changes in religious belief. In Israel, with its Jewish majority, a form of Jewish belief would evolve which would differ from that of the Diaspora where Jews were a powerless minority. Israel had no alternative but to become the new Sparta in the Middle East. The religious faith of a community living on the sword must inevitably differ from that of a community of middle-class businessmen and academics. Such views immediately raise the question of whether the Jews are still one people. To this Rubinstein replied in the affirmative. The Israelis, he said, were the true Jews of the twentieth century because they alone underwent a change as a result of the Holocaust. Auschwitz, he believed, symbolized the death of the religious and moral values of Diaspora Jewry. The strategy of the powerless failed utterly when it confronted an enemy armed with technological might and firm resolve to annihilate the Jews. This fact was also valid with regard to the Arab threat to Israel. No society or nation had more reason than the Jews to doubt the values of human morality or international justice. The bitterest irony in the annals of contemporary faith was that the people who gave the world the prophetic vision of universal fraternity and peace was forced to defend its heritage by force of arms in order to survive. In a world in which the balance of terror was the sole guarantee of survival, only nations ready to take risks and to defend their existence by force had any prospect of survival.

Responding to the criticism of Arthur Cohen and Milton Himmelfarb, Rubinstein clarified that his religious-Jewish outlook was based on power and not on faith and trust in God. This led him to adopt the historiosophical position that Jewish existence in the Diaspora was not a positive phenomenon. He agreed with Himmelfarb that there were periods in Diaspora history in which Jewish culture had blossomed and the Jews had made a significant contribution to both western and eastern culture; but this was not the crux of the matter. In his opinion, the final and supreme test of relations between the Jews and other nations was that they were a powerless people living within European Christian society, whose religious faith could not tolerate separate Jewish existence. It was this combination of powerlessness, lack of a homeland and the discriminatory approach of Christianity which had inevitably led to Auschwitz. Powerlessness, according to Rubinstein, meant not only constant dread of external threats but also reliance on others and their goodwill. This was not only morally undesirable and an affront to human dignity, but also useless, since in this world, if the Jews cannot save themselves, they will be lost. Hence his emphatic conclusion that by taking the decision to defend themselves by their own efforts, the Jews had entered the reality of power, violence and interests, and that no other path was open to them. Nations have no friends, only interests. If national security requires a nation to rule another nation, there is every justification for this, and the Jewish people should learn how to live in this world.

Rubinstein, therefore, was the closest of all the neo-conservatives to the Revisionist political outlook propounded by Jabotinsky. Moreover, his theological argument that reliance on the power of the Jewish majority in Israel and dominion over the whole of the Land of Israel would transform religious conceptions, presaged the ideology of Gush Emunim.

The four major components of neo-conservative thought were developed and elaborated over the years. Renewal of the bond with Jewish tradition soon raised the question of the attitude of religion or of Judaism as a spiritual entity to the conservative position.

Whereas Richard Rubinstein endowed Jewish existence with religious significance based on power, Seymour Siegel, professor of Jewish philosophy, drew a
clear dividing line between Judaism as a faith and lifestyle and neo-liberalism as a
social ideology. Echoing Senator McGovern's political platform, Seigel enumer-
ated ten features of 'neo-liberalism'[10]: it opts for individual liberty over the social
order; advocates government intervention in the economy at the expense of private
enterprise; attributes the conduct of the individual to his social milieu rather than
his personal will and heritage, and thus essentially shifts responsibility from the
individual to society; believes that preferential treatment should be awarded on the
basis of ethnic affiliation and not talent; supports left-wing, revolutionary movements; prefers universal principles over particularist values; perceives religion as
everyone's private affair and tries to reduce its influence in the public domain;
downplays the value of tradition and advocates constant innovation; prefers solutions based on rational principles to those related to specific conditions. And
finally, is naive enough to believe that there is a solution to all the problems of
human society. This principle, the cornerstone of the liberal outlook, is highly
dangerous, since such utopian optimism disregards the limitations inherent in
any plan for social advancement, stemming from human nature and the tradition
and culture of each society, which do not always choose rational solutions.

After sketching a group portrait of 'neo-liberalism', as distinct from the classic
'old liberalism', of which he approved, he tried to persuade his readers that neo-
liberalism was totally opposed to the fundamental principles of Judaism. Judaism,
he argued, while trying to guarantee the liberty of the individual, nonetheless
restricts that liberty in the name of the interest and welfare of the community. Consequently, it is not tolerant of law-breaking, immorality, sexual permissiveness,
etc. It is suspicious of any excessive concentration of power in the hands of one
authority since man, by nature, tends to transform power into a means serving his
own interests. Traditional Judaism demands that the individual be responsible for
his own actions and does not accept his submission to extraneous factors. Judaism
is zealous in its pursuit of justice but also realistic enough to understand that in
human society, inequality will always prevail among human beings and can only
be reduced through social legislation. Traditional Judaism welcomes ethnic and
national pluralism and refuses to crowd religious faith into the narrow confines of
the individual domain, seeking to win it public standing and influence. Judaism
does not reject innovation, but integrates it into tradition. It is aware of the frailty
of man, who is driven by his desires, and of the imperfection of human society.
Above all, Judaism is anti-utopian, preferring messianism to utopianism. Messianism means faith in the redemption of man and society through a transcendental
power which stands outside history, while utopianism demands and believes in
change within history to be carried out by man himself.

Siegel was supported by the historians Gertrude Himmelfarb and Jacob
Neusner. Himmelfarb declared that the value which Judaism places on tradition,
law, family, community and religious authority renders it essentially conservative,

and thus, closer to Edmund Burke than to John Stuart Mill. Neusner asserted emphatically that the foundations of traditional Jewish society had always been clearly conservative.[11] Not everyone agreed with Siegel's attempt to transform religion into an instrument in the political struggle between conservatives and liberals in the United States. Norman Podhoretz, who was considered to be a fierce opponent of left-wing liberalism, its conciliatory attitude to the Soviet Union and opposition to Israel, hastened to stress that this fight was being conducted in the name of true liberal principles, and not on behalf of Judaism. He argued that to draw any connection between religious faith and political stances was a vulgar and superficial approach. At the same time, he did not doubt that the true political struggle against 'leftist liberalism' served Jewish interests.[12]

This leads us to another component of this school of thought – the ethnic interest. In 1972, Podhoretz gave succinct expression to this outlook in an article with the blunt title 'Is it Good for the Jews?'[13] It dealt with the liberal demand for preferential treatment in university enrolment for blacks and oppressed miniorities. To discriminate against the gifted for the benefit of the weak ran counter to the American spirit. And if the Jews did not fight for their interests, in other words for what was good for them, they would soon be relegated to the status of a marginal minority suffering discrimination.

Earl Raab, director of Jewish community services in San Francisco, exhorted his fellow Jews to view the naked reality without self-delusion. He defined Jewish unease as a pathological phenomenon stemming from the constant search for the good and the perfect and the inevitable clash between this tendency and the social and political facts.[14] This weakness stemmed not only from good intentions but also from political naivety, which was a highly dangerous trait in the social arena. In order to cure the Jews of this naivety, he proposed that they cast off their delusions as to the character of American society and their own standing within it. They should cease to view Judaism as one of three major religions – Protestant, Catholic and Jewish – which were shaping the cultural image of the United States, as Will Herberg had claimed in the 1950s. They should realize that they had not yet reached the heart of American society. They should accept the fact that they were not liked and that the threat of anti-Semitism had not been extirpated in the United States, and resign themselves to the fact that American society was not and would never be a paradise of social justice. What then, was left to the Jews? America had not only granted refuge to the Jewish masses, but had also built a society based on a universal vision which was in accord with Jewish existence and values. The prevailing ethos of this society was one of openness and constant change, even if there was no certainty as to the direction of that change. In this respect, the aims of this society were consistent with Jewish interests. Raab claimed that there were two types of society: the 'closed society' and the 'open society'. The first was guided by group, class or ethnic considerations, and hence limited the freedom of the individual in the spheres of mobility and achievement. The latter society was open to the talents and energies of the individual. It was, of course, less just in the social sense, but more attuned to the human spirit. It was in the Jewish interests to foster an open society and engage in the struggle to ensure that the United States remained such a society. Raab totally identified the individual interests of Jews in an open and achievement-oriented society with the ideal essence of American society. He was focusing mainly on the interests of American Jews and was dissatisfied with the excessive concentration on Israel's existential problem, which he considered to be one of a number of manifestations of Jewish pathology.

The man who gave this viewpoint intellectual depth was the labor-Zionist, sociologist and historian, Ben Halpern. He declared that he had never been convinced that Jewish and Zionist interests were in complete harmony with the liberal outlook. To his mind, there had been rifts between them even before the volte-face of the American liberal movement. In this respect, Halpern was touching on a question which had troubled the leaders of the Palestinian labor movement in their contacts with Western European socialists, and particularly with the leadership of the British Labour Party. The latter had found it difficult to comprehend the peculiar Zionist combination of nationalism and socialism and to accept it. Unlike Raab, Ben Halpern, in the above-mentioned symposium, distinguished between the interests of Jews and the Jewish interest. On the assumption that these were not always identical, he stressed that the existence and well-being of the State of Israel in the national sense was clearly a Jewish interest. In this sense, there was a clash between this interest and the 'neo-liberalism' which denied the existence of the Jewish people. This brings us to the third and most important element in this viewpoint, namely the standing of the State of Israel in Jewish life. It is the most important element, because it contains the others within it: the return to Judaism, the ethnic and even the national interest, and the lesson of the Holocaust. Discussion of the significance of the state for present and future Jewish existence was based on awareness that, after Israel's establishment, the Jews had reverted to being an active factor in history.

The young professor of literature Robert Alter, a regular contributor to *Commentary*, developed this idea further. Immediately after the Six Day War, he had defined the outbrust of Jewish emotion as a manifestation of national feeling, related to awareness that Jewish history had not ended at Auschwitz and must not terminate with the destruction of the State of Israel.[15] His article was directed at intellectuals who advocated progressive universalist theories, like the critic George Steiner, the psychologist Bruno Bettelheim, and the former journalist, Irving Stone. They had warned against the chauvinistic spirit gradually dominating Israeli society in the wake of the military triumph. Alter countered by arguing that for the Jews of the United States, free of the need to confront powerful hostile forces, it was easy to preach to Israel. Those who were exempt from this battle for survival, those who did not face the struggle with naked political reality, had no right to exercise moral judgment. Criticism of Israel, even when justified, should not disregard the fact that the Jews of Israel had chosen to act in history as a collective body, with all the injustice accompanying this decision. Deviation from moral criteria was therefore the fate of the collective body operating within history.

This had wrought qualitative change in the existential essence of every Jew, whether Zionist or not. In the very act of self-definition of an individual as a Jew, he was entering the sphere in which the State of Israel affected his existence as a Jew. It was the state which had restored to all Jews the normal dimension of human existence – a homeland.[16] Alter expressed his solidarity with Hayim Nahman Bialik's remarks at the opening of the Hebrew University in 1925. In that speech, Bialik had emphasized that one could not separate the material structure from the spiritual renaissance. In the same way, said Alter, one could not separate the Jewish national element from the human general element.

Among the neo-conservatives, Alter was the closest to the Zionist viewpoint, primarily in that he defined the Jews as a nation, a term which most of his co-thinkers avoided. Secondly, as a disciple of Gershom Scholem, he was not only reconciled to the return of the Jews to the historical arena, but welcomed this return, ready to pay the necessary moral price – a view advocated by both left and right within the Zionist movement. And finally, he was close to Zionism in his view of the particularist national element as part of the universal. Hence he totally rejected the views of those liberals who considered Zionism and support for the Jewish state as a manifestation of tribal segregation. He believed that the true universalism was that which did not regard human beings as living in abstract conditions but as peoples with distinctive cultural, ethnic and national heritages. Jewish solidarity was one of the expressions of universal unity.[17] In this way he tried to find not only a synthesis between particularist and universal trends among Jews, but also to establish a balance between the distortions of both. If the sin of the nationalistic Jew was often his chauvinism, he declared, the sin of universalism was sometimes cultural parasitism and social elitism.

The synthesis which Alter favored existed in reality in the combination of the State of Israel and US society. He saw Israel as the expression of the national will of the Jewish people and of illusion-free life, an essential element in national existence.[18] The United States had demonstrated the possibility of a pluralistic society, in which each ethnic minority enjoyed the right to develop and preserve its unique culture without thereby undermining the foundations of the common culture.[19] In this respect, he rejected the views of the young left-wing radicals, who considered American culture to be a kind of expression of Anglo-Saxon colonialism.[20] His national-universal synthesis also shaped his Zionist outlook. He took a balanced view of the historical significance of the Jewish Emancipation. While acknowledging that there was a degree of truth in Ahad ha-Am's statement that life in the free West contained an element of 'slavery within freedom', he emphasized that the rejection of Emancipation meant a return to the spiritual ghetto, and to this he objected. Ever loyal to his synthesis, he argued that Emancipation enabled modern Jews in the West to choose one of two paths: 'slavery within freedom' or 'freedom within freedom'.[21] The experience of the past two centuries had shown how difficult and fraught with hazards was the second path. Zionism had taught the Jewish people which path to follow in order to preserve Jewish distinctiveness within a free society. Alter's Zionism, which was based on a blend of national and universal elements, sought to create an existential synthesis between state and diaspora. He advocated fruitful cooperation between the two, accompanied by the awareness that Israel was the focus of Jewish national life.[22]

Alter's philosophy relates to a central issue in the outlook of the neo-conservatives, namely the relation between the universal and the particular. One might say that the conservatives dissociated themselves from faith in universal moral values, but accepted certain universal rules. These were: the preservation of self-interest, the price of historical action and the reign of force in politics. The man who focused these rules into a clear and unequivocal philosophy was Irving Kristol, a former Trotskyite, who became the spokesman of neo-conservatism in the United States.[23]

The tenth dialogue of the American Jewish Congress, on the Jews and the forces of revolution, was held in Jerusalem in 1972.[24] Kristol took the opportunity to develop his neo-conservative theories, in their Jewish-Israeli context.

His first assumption was that Israel and the United States had a common ideological base beyond the fact that both were states with democratic forms of government. Both were conservative countries, which rejected extreme political and social change, and were alike in that they did not maintain dominant conservative ideologies to explain and justify their way of life. The reason was that the intellectual ideologues could not reconcile themselves to reality and were ceaselessly seeking a different image for their society from the existing one. This was particularly striking among the Jews in both countries. They were involved in an incessant obsessive debate on the fate of those revolutions which had failed or disappointed their followers. In their eyes, both socialism and Zionism had failed. Against this mood, grounded on disillusion with utopia and inability to abandon it, he offered the naked truth. No revolution, he said, was ever betrayed. All revolutions were implemented, but not in the way the revolutionaries had anticipated; this was the decree of history and life. It was hard to accept, he declared, that these were the inevitable consequences of revolutionary political initiative.

Thus, post-1967 Israel was the realization of the Zionist vision – just as Soviet Russia was the realization of the Bolshevik revolution. There was no room, he said, for individual evaluations based on abstract principles. This was a process determined by history, and the views of individuals could not affect it. The founders of Zionism had held different views on the essence of the state, just as the authors of the US constitution had taken a different view of the ideal character of democratic society in their country. There were no non-legitimate phenomena in history, he declared. The outcome of revolutions was a legitimate reality, 'Revolutions', he said, 'do not have abortions. Revolutions all have legitimate children. Sometimes they are pretty ugly'. Kristol evolved a kind of 'neo-Macchiavellianism' according to which there was no room in politics for either dreams or disillusionment. In the past two hundred years, the modern Jews had become 'sick in the head', he said, since, politically speaking, the healthy thing to do was to ask what was good or bad for their interests. For example, the new left was essentially anti-Jewish in the United States and anti-Israel in the international arena. Hence, Jewish self-interest should dictate a struggle against the new left. This was but one example of the universal tenet which should underlie all political activity. The highest stage of political wisdom was the attempt to expand the partial interest and to define it in international terms as enlightened self-interest.

Kristol's statements highlight the central interest of the neo-conservatives – politics. They transformed naked unadorned politics, with its inherent interests and power-seeking, into a categorical imperative for the Jews. By this very approach, irrespective of its content, they introduced a new element into Jewish Diaspora tradition. The Jewish intellectuals and philosophers, bearers of universal moral and religious ideals, the Jewish social utopianists, were now replaced by the secular realists. Richard Rubinstein's theological arguments were converted by Kristol into *realpolitik* which was sober to the point of cynicism, mocking the majority of his fellow Jews for their moral-liberal naivety.

This advocacy of power and interest politics as a means of guaranteeing Jewish survival once again stimulated debate on dual loyalties. The question that American patriots like the neo-conservatives had to ask themselves was to what extent Jewish interests fitted in with American interests in general. On internal questions, such as the quotas for university entrance and 'affirmative action' for minorities, it could still be claimed that there was identity between the interests of the Jews, who certainly believed that preferential treatment should be given on the basis of talent and not ethnic origin, and the good of American society. However, on external issues, such as the attitude towards Israel, the problem was much more complex.

Norman Podhoretz, the loyal champion of Israeli interests, expounded his political hesitations on this question in the autobiography he published in the late seventies.[25] He stated explicitly that he was concerned primarily for the future of the United States and not of Israel. His defence of Israel stemmed from his conviction that this was in the interests of the United States. It was in this light that he interpreted the speech that Patrick Moynihan, US Ambassador to the United Nations, delivered in 1975 in defence of Zionism, after it had been condemned as racist ideology. Podhoretz, hinting that he had helped to write the Ambassador's speech stressed that Moynihan's stance had stemmed not from any special attitude towards the Jews or Israel but from the belief that the UN Assembly's resolution reflected the onslaught of totalitarianism on democracy, Israel being the most vulnerable spot. Thus, the ideological defence of Israel was dictated not only by moral considerations, but also by American interests. This grounding of US–Israel relations on political interests not only made life easier for him as an American Jew, but also enabled him to demand a more emphatic policy of US support for Israel. Podhoretz felt, as he wrote in his memoirs, that, in the end, the United

States, as a world power whose economy depended to a large extent on the import of oil from the Near East, would be forced to compromise with the demands of the Arab states at Israel's expense. He gave expression to this feeling in the heading of his provocative article – written in the wake of the UN resolution – 'The Abandonment of Israel'.[26] In the article he cautioned his fellow countrymen that the isolation and abandonment of Israel might drive her to acts of despair. But this time the state fighting for survival would not choose the path of the Massada defenders, but would act like Samson. Through use of atomic weapons, Israel could engulf the entire Middle East in war and destruction. Podhoretz wrote, in unprecendently blunt fashion, that the blood of Israel would be on the heads of those US administration officials, media people and students who were willing to compromise at the expense of Israel's existence instead of coming unequivocally to the defence of the beleaguered state, the sole democracy in the Middle East, and one of the few remaining in the world.

This substitution of the Samson legend for the Massada myth as a national ethos derived directly from the neo-conservative outlook. The defenders of Massada who had perished by their own hand had committed a supremely moral act, but Samson, who has brought down the temple on the heads of his enemies, had committed an act of power. And from their point of view, it was even more moral than the other act. Podhoretz's views reflected his profound awareness that the establishment of Israel had brought about a significant change in Jewish history. He was deeply concerned for the fate of Israel in light of her growing isolation after the Yom Kippur War. US Jews felt acutely isolated, as attested to by Nathan Glazer's article, 'The Exposed American Jew'.[27]

With the passage of time, and particularly after the 1980 elections and the Republican victory which ushered in the Reagan era, the neo-conservative case gathered force. Before the 1984 elections, Irving Kristol called on Jews to vote for the Republicans because their socio-religious interests and commitment to Israel required this.[28] He compared the rift between Jews and blacks with the affinity between Jews and the white Protestant silent majority. Kristol perceived a similar conservative trend among Jews and Protestants – the desire to return to tradition. He warned the Jews that whereas most of the American public was conservatively-inclined, the Jews were continuing traditionally to support liberal policies, and were liable to remain without political clout. But above all, he noted that if, in fact, collective Jewish existence could not be maintained in the long run, without the existence of Israel, then Jews must support Israel. And Israel's strength and security depended on US might. Consequently the Jews, in their own interest, should support those who wanted to preserve America's standing as the major world power. Israel would survive thanks to the interest-motivated political rather than moral support of the United States, and the latter would continue to be a world power thanks to its conservative and neo-conservative leadership. If the majority of US Jews gave this leadership their vote, this would complete the circle of the mutual existential bond.

After the elections, when it transpired that only 35 per cent of the Jews had supported Reagan, (compared to his 60 per cent share of the general vote), the historian Lucy Dawidowicz, who was a former leftwinger and Bundist, tried to understand this phenomenon,[29] which ran counter to social logic. The Jews were among the most prosperous communities in the United States, but their patterns of voting resembled those of lower-income groups, which felt themselves to be discriminated against. She believed that this pehnomenon stemmed from a sense of political alienation among Jews which could deprive them of the political standing they deserved within the American consensus. She blamed this dangerous trait on the universalist principles which were deeply imbedded in Jewish consciousness and were now hard to eradicate. If we follow this hypothesis, we can identify the third stage of Jewish alienation from their country of birth. The immigrant parents from Eastern Europe had suffered from cultural alienation. Some of their children, in the 1940s, felt ideologically alienated from American society, and now, in the eighties, the Jews were revealing a sense of political alienation from the ruling majority. They appeared to be demonstrating their feeling that this was not their country. Dawidowicz, like others, believed that the Jews did not know what politics were and should learn the art just as they had once studied Torah. Politics meant not only cold realism and abandonment of utopian aspirations, but also avoidance of total commitment to any side, either Republicans or Democrats. She argued that Jewish tradition and history had prepared them for the art of correct politics, based on the rule that in politics there were no enduring loyalties, only changing interests.

This overt 'neo-Macchiavellianism' was based on a moral viewpoint which, since 1967, had linked the lesson of the Holocaust to the existence of the Jewish state. As Israel's political problems increased and her military initiatives roused world public opinion against her, the neo-conservative stand became more emphatic. Emil Fackenheim, who had formulated the 614th injunction, explained in 1983 that Zionism and the State of Israel did not need to seek their justification in the Holocaust. However, their survival of Auschwitz rendered the existence of the state absolute and unconditional, irrespective of its political actions or the debate on its future borders. This was because the state, through its existence and military might, had put an end to the diaspora condition of Jewish powerlessness, which had been exposed by the Holocaust. In this respect, Auschwitz symbolized the end of the epoch of Jewish exile. There was now no escaping the conclusion that the existence of the Jews must rely solely on their political and military power. The state was the supreme expression of this Jewish power and thus, for the sake of their present and future existence, it was incumbent on them to support it unconditionally.[30] It should be noted that Fackenheim distinguishes between 'Diaspora Judaism' and Jewish existence in the Diaspora or even *galut*. *Galutiyut* went up in flames in the crematoria at Auschwitz, while the *tefutzah* would continue to exist by virtue of the state. This view was shared by most of the neo-conservatives.

During the Lebanon War, as political pressure and criticism of Israel intensified, particularly among liberal media people in the United States, many of whom were Jews, the neo-conservatives became even more vehement in their support for Israel. In 1984, Podhoretz accused the Jewish critics of undermining the Jewish solidarity which had been achieved with great effort since the establishment of Israel, and particularly since the Six Day War. He was encouraged by the fact that the Jews had emerged from this trial as well with their unity intact. This, he believed, was because of the awareness of the great majority that thanks to Israel, world Jewry was still a reality.[31] There can be no clearer statement of the link between the lesson of the Holocaust and the significance of the survival of the state for Jews and Judaism than this statement by Podhoretz. However, the neo-conservatives who linked the particularist Jewish interest with universal principles also insisted on the universal human significance of the Holocaust. The subject was raised in the wake of President Reagan's decision to visit the German military cemetery in Bitburg. The protest voiced by Jews of all camps at this act was severely criticized by the President's supporters. The latter argued that the Jews were trying to 'Judaize' the Holocaust and to empty it of its universal significance. The Jews were also charged with unwillingness to forgive. In this polemic the neo-conservatives were in an uncomfortable position, since Reagan's conciliatory visit was attributed to the global interests of the United States and the free world. The perceptive journalist, Midge Decter, wife of Norman Podhoretz, argued against these assertions.[32] There was no contradiction, she wrote, between the Jewish and the universal significance of the Holocaust. The catastrophe had been general, but in the spiritual, moral and quantitative sense, the Jewish suffering had been the most terrible of all. The horror was not theirs alone, but affected the entire Western world. Hence, from both the Jewish and the universal viewpoints, the question was not one of unwillingness to forgive, but of the dangerous tendency to forget. The historic role of the Jews, whether they wished it or not, was to stand guard and to warn against the dangers facing democracy and liberalism from totalitarian forces. Therefore, the visit to Bitburg, an achievement for the German president and an embarrassment for Reagan, had provided the Jews with the opportunity to clarify for themselves and for society as a whole the urgency of the need to remember the Holocaust and to identify with its victims, whose remnants were living in Israel. The immediate conclusion was that any Jew convinced that it was necessary to give in to those trying to destroy the state had forgotten the lesson of the Holocaust.

The Jewish outlook of the neo-conservatives or liberal-conservatives may be summed up as follows: acknowledgment of the right of the Jews to become once again a normal people functioning in history, with all this entailed; the conviction that the continuity of the Jewish people depends on the existence of a political center in Israel; legitimization of the interests of Jews as individuals and the communal or ethnic Jewish interest in the United States and elsewhere, with emphasis on the international solidarity of the Jewish people, centered mainly on Israel, which thereby becomes a national interest; accentuation of the value of religious tradition in preserving the cohesion and continuity of existence of the people; declaration of the individualist principles of classic liberalism as a general Jewish trait; transformation of the lesson of the Holocaust into a new Jewish message to the world, or a kind of mission imposed on the Jewish people, whose suffering serves as a constant caution to mankind against itself.

There is a paradoxical similarity between the views of the neo-conservatives and the young radicals despite the differences between them in social ideology and political methods. The two groups insisted on the right of the Jews to define themselves, for emotional and cultural reasons, as an ethnic group. Although, in the case of the radicals, this demand stemmed from the universalist approach, and where the conservatives were concerned, from insistence on the importance of particularist interests, the outcome was the same. Both groups in effect recognized the existence of an international Jewish national entity, with Israel at its center. For both, the Holocaust was the reality underlying national life, and military and political force was the vital means of ensuring their survival. For this reason, political activism and the wielding of power in internal and external Jewish frameworks was legitimate and essential. And although they differed sharply on evaluation of Israel's policies, for both, Israel's existence was unconditional.

In the final analysis, both outlooks were expressions of the integration of the Jews in American society, not only as individuals but also as a community with its own essence and ethnic interests, in the local sense, and its national interests in the wider international and specifically Israeli sense. Hence, both are original American versions of the 'Jewish normalization' approach.

8 The Alternative Zionism of Gush Emunim

As an ideological movement, a social phenomenon and a political force, Gush Emunim (the Bloc of the Faithful) provided the most comprehensive expression of radicalism in the period under discussion. The Gush was founded officially in early 1974, after the upheaval of the Yom Kippur War, but its roots are embedded in the heady experience of the Six Day War. It was established at a time when the left-wing Zionist radicalism of young Americans was waning. And although there is no causal connection between the emergence of the one and the disappearance of the other, this changeover is of symbolic significance, as if leftist activism had yielded place to right-wing activism, thereby giving the signal for the political upheaval of 1977.

The Gush underwent three stages of development between 1974 and 1987. In the utopian period from 1974 to 1979, there was a messianic note to the rebellion against prevailing conditions, and the eschatological yearning was translated into the socio-political ideology of here and now and the introduction of extra-parliamentary methods of action in the spheres of settlement and public activity. In 1979–83, the political stage, in the wake of the peace agreement with Egypt, the withdrawal from Sinai, the dismantling of the Yamit area settlements and the Lebanon War, the Gush launched an ideological-political campaign in defence of its messianic vision. The uncovering of the 'Jewish underground' in 1984 caused confusion and embarrassment within the ranks of the Gush. In this period, the fundamental differences of opinion were exacerbated, causing an ideological breach.

The Gush as a social phenomenon is difficult to define, and scholars and researchers, who have mostly concentrated on the first stage in its history, have been divided in their views.[1] They are split between those who perceive it as a religious cult or as a militant political group, those who stress its extra-parliamentary activity and those who emphasize its exploitation of the political establishment, and in particular the links of its leaders with the Tehiya party. Research on the Gush's later stages, however, reveals a lack of consensus on basic questions. Thus, for example, in the second and third stages, its political isolation increased as a result of its violent political struggle against the withdrawal from Sinai. The exposure of the Jewish underground intensified the tendency to isolationism, accompanied by eschatological fervor reminiscent of messianic cults, and on the other hand strengthened those elements which objected strongly to the trend to isolation, and called for changes in ideology in order to lay the ideological basis for the establishment of the widest possible common denominator with outside forces. These differences of opinion were particularly striking within the hard core of the Gush

150

leadership, composed mostly of graduates of the Merkaz Harav *yeshiva*. The internal debate on questions connected to political conduct and fundamental principles found expression in the movement's organ, *Nekuda*, which was started in 1979, launching the second stage in the Gush's development.

As the rift between the Gush and Israeli society widened, and the crisis within its ranks grew more acute, *Nekuda* became increasingly pluralistic and polarized in its expression. Within its pages, one can find statements reflecting uncompromising political fanaticism and religious totalitarianism, as well as appeals for balance and discretion. The debate revolved around the nature of public life in Israel, touching on the character of extra-parliamentary activity; the importance of a democratic regime in a Western-type society; the value of humanism and liberalism for modern man; the place of religion in a pluralistic society in the cultural and ideological sense; the true meaning of Rabbi Kook's teachings and the true nature of religious Zionism.

The present chapter deals with only one aspect of Gush thinking – its Zionist conception and view of the place of Israel in modern Jewish life. In this respect, they shared certain views with the radical currents in the United States. Although they differed in their view of the Diaspora, and the value of democracy and pluralism in Jewish society, both movements took a favorable view of the entry of the Jewish people into history and conceded that political existence had a moral price. One can identify within the Gush, as among left-wing radicals, yearnings for a social utopia and, as in neo-conservatism, justification of power politics. At the same time, it differs from them in its essence.

Gush Emunim's philosophy is based on four components: messianic fervor related to belief in the sanctity of Greater Israel; the ethos of a religious utopia, reflecting the desire to build a modern nationalist state based on the *halakhah*; the myth of pioneering settlement inspired by the labor Zionist movement; political activism inspired by Revisionism. In contrast, the radical trends in the United States were one, or at most two, dimensional. Neo-conservatism was essentially political in orientation. The national activism of the students was focused on social and cultural questions. The comprehensive radicalism of the Gush was not only ideological, but also, and mainly, existential. The Gush established a settlement movement and created a political force in which religious and secular elements combined to carry out a joint political-national mission. In the United States the corresponding groups dealt in theory alone, and although as such they influenced the American Jewish public, they did not succeed in bringing about a significant change of direction. The Gush, however, through its actions, determined a historical fact which may, some day, prove to be of far-reaching national significance. All in all, the ideas and actions of Gush Emunim, despite the differences of opinion with it, are the expression of an alternative-Zionist ideology which aspires, through zealous adherence to tradition, political daring and individual devotion, to change the face of Israeli society and to guide Diaspora Jewry in new directions.

The term Hibbat, 'the Zionist alternative' which I use to characterize the ideology of Gush Emunim, particularly in the second and third stages, calls for clarification which takes into account the character of the Zionist movement. Ostensibly, it could be argued that, from the early days of Hibbat Zion, Zionism was a movement which encompassed various groups proposing ideological alternatives. The four main currents: religious Zionism, liberal Zionism, Jabotinsky's revisionist ideology and the various shades of socialist Zionism, each fostered the image of an alternative national society. Moreover, in the Yishuv from the beginning of Zionist settlement to the establishment of the state, separate societies grew up, each with its own lifestyle and culture. Middle-class society coexisted with the labor movement's 'labour society', and national-religious society. Historical experience demonstrated that despite the alternative character of the ideologies and the separate lifestyles, all managed to work together in building the national society. And this as a result of the practical compromise between the various trends, which enabled the voluntarist society to act like a sovereign body, *vis à vis* the world Zionist organization and within the Yishuv. Therefore, with the exception of the Revisionist minority which seceded for political reasons, one may speak of differences within the Zionist movement but not of alternatives. In contrast, Gush Emunim totally rejected all other Zionist viewpoints. Its Zionist alternativity was aimed, in theory and in practice, at abolishing the traditional Zionist pluralism.

The nucleus of this ideology which offered an alternative to all shades of existing Zionism, including religious Zionism, was present in the Gush from the outset, and was evident many years before its establishment, particularly within the Merkaz Harav *yeshiva*. It crystallized into a comprehensive outlook in the second and third stages. At the end of the 1970s, when Zvi Raanan wrote his book about Gush Emunim, he was still wrestling with the question of whether the Gush was proposing a new Zionist ideology, and this was the title of his main chapter. His conclusion was that 'despite their relatively sparse statements ... there does exist in the Gush a religious Zionist ideology, whose innovative element lies not in its various components but in its overall pattern'.[2] In other words, components and content remained unchanged, namely the relations between the religious Zionist and society as a whole, the essence of Zionism as a movement of ingathering of the exiles, and Israel's social image. The innovation lay in the conceptual framework, such as the opposition to modernization; the rejection of normalization and advocacy of Jewish isolation; the devaluation of the universal messianic ideal.[3] Without examining the validity of Raanan's assumptions, it seems indubitably clear that at this stage the Gush paid scant attention to discussion of its Zionist outlook. The change occurred in the later stages, in the wake of the political events preceding and following the signing of the peace treaty with Egypt, which forced its members to adopt a stand. The forum for the debate was *Nekuda*. A movement engaged in a day-to-day political struggle cannot be expected to devote systematic intellectual effort to formulation of its philosophy. The debate was spontaneous and responded to the constant changes. At the same time, it was not devoid of deeper clarifications, confronting principles with political and social actions.

This fascinating intellectual debate recalls, in its fervor, the polemics of the 1950s within the labor movement. In the Gush, materialistic determinism was replaced by divine determinism, and the class struggle by the sacred struggle for the Holy Land, but in both cases, ideology was perceived as a way of life, in which action and theory were interwoven. The alternative Zionist theory began to evolve within Gush Emunim after the signing of the Israel–Egypt peace treaty. The first to propound the idea of a Zionist alternative was Rabbi Shlomo Aviner from the settlement of Keshet on the Golan Heights. After the Knesset ratified the peace treaty, Aviner wrote an article which had strong repercussions within the Gush, with the provocative title: 'The Killing of Messiah Son of Joseph'.[4] In it he proposed abandoning the traditional path which constructive religious Zionism had followed from Kalisher and Alkalai to the Gush.[5] The outcry within the Gush against the withdrawal from Sinai, he said, was diverting attention from the main evil afflicting Jewish society in Eretz Israel. 'A much more severe disease is brewing within our nation', he wrote. 'It has forgotten who and what it is, and hence does not understand the value of Eretz Israel.' The country, he believed, was perceived in terms of territory and not of a spiritual essence linked to the life of the people. In the past, it had been thought possible to establish a Zionist movement which did not draw sustenance from the word of God, he declared, referring to the leaders of religious Zionism as well, such as Rabbi Reines. A movement which was not linked to 'a living source of water must dry up. As long as the light of the Torah moistened the dried-up pool of nationalism, it could save Israel by this power. Now this flow of life has ceased and the nation has nowhere from whence to draw awareness of the value and vital importance of its country.'

So far, Aviner was not diverging from the accepted Gush theory on the sanctity of Eretz Israel, but he went on to assert the need for an alternative to the old religious Zionism. He proclaimed the end of 'the mighty vision of Messiah Son of Joseph and Messiah Son of David, which appears in the writings of our ancient sages', the one representing worldly national action and the other the desire for spiritual elevation and sanctification of the people. Historical Zionism, including the Gush, had distinguished between the two, and this was a great error, since any vision which did not draw its inspiration from Divine light was doomed to die out. 'Messiah Son of Joseph will die unless he is linked to the living source of Messiah Son of David'. No political action of the Gush could succeed unless spiritual renaissance preceded it. Aviner proposed altering the traditional order of events. 'Messiah Son of David must save Messiah Son of Joseph ... simplistic and superficial nationalism is valid when life proceeds as usual, but when evil winds blow ... it sways in the wind like a hut without foundations and falls to the ground.' A new generation must arise to replace traditional Zionism, whose ideals and aspirations no longer suffice. The various setbacks of the Gush on its road to renaissance are of no significance, since 'the Lord is restoring his Divine Presence to Zion through suffering and tribulations, and we will not retreat but will continue to push the carriage of our Messiah until his righteousness radiates forth and burns like a beacon'. Aviner's article roused controversy. His opponents defended settlement activities and did not consider them to run counter to the spiritual renaissance he demanded. The editors of *Nekuda*, in an unprecedented act, added a comment to his article, namely that according to religious Zionist tradition, rooted in the teachings of the Gaon from Vilna, the settlement of Eretz Israel was part of the process of redemption, and Messiah Son of Joseph was not a personality but the symbol of the epoch of action and national construction. Even if some of these deeds had come to nought, as in the wake of the withdrawal from Sinai, this did not mean that Messiah Son of Joseph had been murdered. Destruction was not an irrevocable act and political achievements were the condition for spiritual redemption.[6] Aviner responded that he was not denying the value of settlement activity, but merely trying to emphasize that the condition for settlement of the country by the Jewish people was spiritual rebirth, which should be fostered above all.[7]

Rabbi Aviner was offering a comprehensive alternative to religious Zionism as well as the secular-Zionist outlook, to be realized through a protracted educational process requiring patience and tolerance. He exhorted members of the Gush to obey the laws of the state and to be circumspect in their settlement activities. He also cautioned his colleagues against acts of violence (a veiled reference to the assassination attempts against prominent Arabs in Judea and Samaria – this was before the existence of the Jewish underground was revealed). This view was supported by Rabbi Yaakov Ariel of Kefar Maimon.[8]

Rabbi Ariel called for a new movement which could rehabilitate society and constitute a more advanced stage in the process of 'redeeming the Jewish people in their own land'. It is worth noting the difference between the views of the proponents of the Messiah Son of Joseph theory, and the Messiah Son of David zealots. The former, representing the basic tenets of the Gush outlook, perceived themselves as the heirs of the messianic and Zionist tradition extending from the immigration to the Holy Land of the disciples of the Vilna Gaon in the mid-nineteenth century to the pioneering deeds of the secular and socialist labor movement. Hence, extra-parliamentary action in defiance of government resolutions on settlements did not appear to them to constitute an ideological alternative. On the other hand, Rabbis Aviner and Ariel demanded 'Messiah Son of David now', referring explicitly to the creation of a spiritual alternative to the existing Zionist outlook. The argument that true inspiring nationalism was no longer possible without religious faith, implied a change in the basic values of Zionism as a national movement constituting a common ideological and organizational denominator for all sectors of the people, despite certain fundamental differences between them. Ideologically speaking, there were differences between those who sought an immediate alternative and those who were willing to postpone implementation. A certain paradox is inherent in the practical interpretation of these two viewpoints. The Messiah Son of David zealots, who should have been totally alienated from their surroundings, were the more moderate and open in their approach. Since their aims were mainly educational, directed at the masses, they were ready to acknowledge the value of secular Zionism in the past and even the validity of its existing moral principles. For the same reason they preached respect for the law and for the sovereign status of the Israeli government.

In contrast, the proponents of the Messiah Son of Joseph outlook, in their enthusiasm for settlement activities, created a political alternative to political Zionism which brought them into confrontation with the government and separated them from large sectors of Israeli society. This twofold confrontation soon led them to far-reaching demands for 're-establishment of the Jewish state'[9] to be based on the Divine mission, according to which 'entirely different political views are crystallizing as to the right of the people to exclusive and absolute rule over all parts of Eretz Israel'.

The need to define and consolidate the Zionist alternative intensified among Gush members in the wake of the failure of their campaign of violent resistance to the evacuation of Yamit. The sense of crisis which prevailed among many of the members impelled Yoel Bin-Nun, one of the Gush leaders, to formulate the theory of the comprehensive Zionist alternative.[10] Since the labor Zionist movement had completed its historic task, he wrote, and since Agudat Israel as a religious alternative was anti-Zionist, and hence extraneous to historical events,

> the sole force with the ideological, spiritual and political potential to construct an alternative within a few years is the force leading the combination of the Jewish people living in their own land with the concepts of the Torah. This is the Torah which contains within it both Shabbat and Eretz Israel, love of mankind and acceptance of all that is good and beautiful and rejection of all that is contemptible and degraded, with firm resolve and a spirit of courage and independence and trust in God both within and without.

How then could this religious-utopian alternative submit to the legal authority of a society whose lifestyle was unacceptable and even abhorrent to it? To this Bin-Nun replied that it was impossible to maintain a society without the obligation to obey the law, but 'it should be subject to morality and justice, to the objective of planting the people of Israel in their land ... and establishing internal peace among the people of Israel and between them and their country and Torah'.

This sacred and harmonious trinity: the people of Israel, the Land of Israel and the Torah of Israel (the order having been determined by Bin-Nun himself), is directly related to our subject. The question which arises is: if, in everyday life this harmonious balance is disturbed when one or more of its components is given greater weight due to political considerations, what will happen to the idea of the unity of the Jewish people as preached by Zionism, and as the State of Israel attempts to practice it? For example, granting of preferential status to the Torah could undermine the bond with Eretz Israel, or the people of Israel could supersede the Torah. Then again, emphasis on the supreme importance of Eretz Israel could cause a profound rift within the people of Israel.

Rabbi Yehuda Amital, shocked at the views professed by some Gush members, who attributed apocalyptic significance to the Lebanon War, cautioned against this danger.[11] It should be recalled that Rabbi Amital had been one of the first formulators of Gush ideology as 'the Zionism of redemption'.[12] Now, eight years later, he attacked what he considered the erroneous and dangerous conviction that 'the interests of Israel should take precedence over the interests of the Jewish people, or, to put it more subtly, the interest of Eretz Israel is the true interest of the people of Israel'. This equation, he said, was to a certain degree *hilul ha-Shem* (profanity), since 'there is a scale of values in Judaism, and those who do not differentiate between sanctity and sanctity – will eventually fail to differentiate between the sacred and the profane'. The true order of values should be, 'People of Israel, Torah, Land of Israel'. The State of Israel carried overall responsibility for all Jews, whether observant or not, whether they lived in Israel or in the Diaspora. Thus, when there was a contradiction between the integrity of the people and the integrity of the country, the people took precedence. Since, where Eretz Israel was concerned, the precept of *'yehareg ve-al yaavor'* (unconditional acceptance, lit. better death than sin), was not valid. Amital exhorted his colleagues: 'We often speak of the danger facing Greater Israel, but almost no voices are raised in concern as to the danger facing the whole Jewish people'. And he added a caution, paraphrasing Ahad ha-Am: 'If a stretch of land is destroyed, there is hope for it in generations to come, but when a people is destroyed ...'[13] Rabbi Amital does not deny the redemptive significance of Zionism, but, instead of effort to liberate territory, he demands efforts to save the people from the threat of spiritual degeneration and cultural assimilation. In this respect, his beliefs reflected another aspect of the ideas propounded by Rabbis Aviner and Ariel two years previously. All three advocated an attitude of conciliation and understanding towards secular society, and expressed regret at the rift between the Gush and the labor movement, particularly the kibbutz sector.

Hanan Porat, a former pupil of Rabbi Amital, was one of the first to respond to these provocative statements. The debate between the rabbi and his colleagues and disciples is interesting in itself as a study in different interpretations of rabbinical sources, but we shall concentrate on the Zionist aspect. It was argued against Amital that the very soil of Eretz Israel was imbued with Zionist values because of its religious significance. There was no justification for juxtaposing the value of Eretz Israel and the values of the Torah, education, the people and immigration, Porat declared. He dismissed Amital's argument that the Gush's struggle to create the Greater Eretz Israel was causing a decline in immigration, and said that the reverse was true. 'Immigration to Eretz Israel, which is not impelled by catastrophe and motivated by the search for a refuge from disaster, will be based on love of the country, appreciation of its value and qualities...'[14] Where Amital and his associates believed that the ideal moral nature of Israeli society would be the magnet for Diaspora Jews, Hanan Porat emphasized the mystic spiritual qualities of Eretz Israel. In the wider Zionist sense, national romanticism, an important and basic element in Zionist ideology, was now replaced by religious romanticism.[15] Both types of romanticism, particularly that of the labor movement in its pioneering era, endowed the soil of Eretz Israel with metaphysical spiritual significance. Hanan Porat speaks of Eretz Israel and the people of Israel in Kabbalistic terms:

> I believe that the linking of the people of Israel to their land is like the link between body and soul, and in this link lies the secret of life: the secret of the life of the individual, who takes clods of the earth and breathes life into them and the secret of the life of the nation whose body cleaves to Eretz Israel and whose soul to the Divine presence.

In this respect, he regards himself as the heir to the tradition of the first Zionist leaders and settlers, (the Second Aliyah in particular), and there is some truth to this view. However, according to his alternative Zionist approach, the dedication displayed by the pioneers of the past and the outlook of their spiritual and political leaders were religious in the profoundest sense of the term.[16]

This line of thought was pursued, with greater emphasis and polemical force, by Yoel Bin-Nun and Moshe Levinger.[17] Bin-Nun considered the attempt to determine an order of priorities, ranging from the Jewish people to the Torah and Eretz Israel, and particularly the idea that there could be a fundamental clash between the people and the country, to be 'a concession to the devil', seeking to justify the Diaspora. This view was shared by Levinger, who added that 'only when we grasp, according to the Torah of Eretz Israel, that we are dealing not with three elements but with one spiritual essence – do we understand that the desire for *shlemut ha-aretz* (the integrity of the land) is also the desire for integrity of the people, and the wholeness of the Torah.'

In another context, in a debate with Amos Oz (to be discussed below), Shahar Rahmani defined Oz's arguments against the ideology of Gush Emunim as an 'anthropocentric' approach, namely 'refusal to acknowledge the possibility that there is an absolute truth'. This approach prevents Oz, he said, from acknowledging that 'there is a Creator above him who directs him and acts upon him against his will'. In light of the bankruptcy of secular national ideology, Rahmani declared, it could no longer lead the nation. On the other hand, 'the struggle for Eretz Israel is the struggle for the spirit of the nation, the manifestation of its inner qualities. The return to the inner life of the nation will be expressed, inter alia, in the bond with the country. Reinforcement of the sense of belonging to these regions, our patrimony, will restore our people to awareness of our true nature and our hidden strengths'.[18]

It is illuminating to examine the similarities and differences between this viewpoint and the outlook of the pioneering kibbutz movement, and particularly the Kibbutz ha-Meuhad and its leader, Yitzhak Tabenkin, many of whose disciples were ardent supporters of Gush Emunim. Both movements perceived the settlement of Eretz Israel as a long-term therapeutic process for the Jewish people. The difference, however, was that what the Kibbutz ha-Meuhad regarded as a constructive-social act, was seen by the Gush as the expression of religious faith. Hence, the pioneering ideology of the Kibbutz ha-Meuhad never focused on transcendental absolutes and operated within a given situation with inevitable restrictions, while the Gush linked itself to the absolute force which directs the affairs of men even against their will. Belief in the existence of the absolute force which guides man not only in the path of faith but also in the political and social sphere, is one of the elements of the alternative Zionist outlook. It deliberately sets itself up as the total contradiction to Zionist ideology which was essentially nationalistic and secular, and whose model of operation as a political movement was pragmatic. Moreover, this total dependence is intended to replace such Western concepts as liberalism, pluralism and parliamentary democracy, which had characterized the Zionist movement. Thus, it is no chance that from 1984 on, shortly after the discovery of the 'Jewish underground', *Nekuda* published a series of articles by Moshe Ben-Yosef (Hager), former member of the radical underground group Lehi (Stern group).

Ben-Yosef called for a spiritual revolution led by Gush Emunim, to be based on several principles: total rejection of Western culture which had brought upon the Jewish people two catastrophes – Nazism, the inevitable outcome of German humanism, and liberalism, which grew out of universal rationalism. As against universal principles, he advocated 'geo-climatic' determinism and familial, tribal atavism, which shapes the communal character of groups of human beings. This leads us to the second principle: the moulding of national life in accordance with the *halakhah*. This, however, should be a different *halakhah*, of Eretz Israel and not of the Diaspora, growing out of its unique climate and incorporating the culture of secular Jews as well. Ben-Yosef could envisage no framework other than the 'new *halakhah*' to define Jewish national life and create a spiritual revolution. His conclusion was that 'in order to create a community based on *halakhah* which is not dependent on an alien conceptual framework, we must create the framework for the preparation of a constitution without "religious coercion"; and without "party platforms"'.[19] The Gush should detach itself from the Diaspora 'Babylonian' tradition and return to the Eretz Israeli, 'Jerusalemite' heritage.

Professor Yosef Ben-Shlomo, one of the central ideological leaders of the Gush, formerly affiliated to the labor movement, continued this line of thought.[20] He asserted that in liberal circles, among the lovers of Western culture who flocked to the Peace Now movement, a mood was spreading, which constituted a 'fundamental alternative to Zionism', which could lead to total normalization of Jewish life in Eretz Israel in the spirit of Western culture. This could easily breed a favorable approach to the existence of the Diaspora. Paradoxically, Ben-Shlomo saw some positive elements in this phenomenon, since it indicated that 'secular Zionism, whose aim was normalization of the Jewish people, is approaching the end of its ideological road. The time is ripe to offer our own path'. It was necessary to rescue the Jewish people from Western culture, based as it was on technological achieve-ment, material pleasure and social and intellectual satisfaction. He found the spir-itual dimension in individual and communal Jewish life in the teachings of Rabbi Kook which confronted the condition of modern man through a combination of nationalist elements with universal principles; regarding the individual as an inte-gral part of the national body, and placing Eretz Israel at the center of the people's historical experience.

Rabbi Kook's teachings, he wrote, had shown the way in which the two central phenomena in present day Jewish life should be tackled: the secular way of life which most Jews practiced, and the return to history by means of the State of Israel. Gush Emunim must confront them because there was no other religious viewpoint which could do so. Orthodox Jewry was ignoring them, while tradi-tional religious Zionism as preached by Rabbi Reines did not dare to tackle them.

The call for separation from traditional religious Zionism was therefore the second stage in the development of the Zionist alternative. The first stage was the abolition of secular Zionism, and the second the deposing of the Zionism of the National Religious Party. Rabbi Levinger explained that 'the Zionism of the NRP did not, at the outset, perceive political Zionism at the required religious level, as a Divine state. Religious Zionism did not realize that its Zionist element was much stronger than that of the secular movement...' The NRP and its Zionism had not been inspired by the Divine source, he wrote.[21] Now that historical religious Zion-ism was identified with Rabbi Reines and alternative Zionism with Rabbi Kook, a debate raged within Nekuda between the disciples of these two mentors. Yehuda Zoldin wrote: 'The central question is whether the Zionist movement, which is building the Jewish people in their land, is an integral part of the renaissance of the Torah and the redemption of Israel, or, while furthering the rebirth of the Torah and the redemption of Israel, is not a part of these processes?'[22] Zoldin believed that Rabbi Reines had distinguished between messianic redemption and Zionism, which he regarded as a temporal effort to improve the political and economic con-dition of the Jewish people. According to Rabbi Reines, Zionism was of spiritual value only because it was a factor promoting the existence of the Torah and the religious precepts in Eretz Israel, and no more than that. His heirs, the Mizrahi leaders Rabbi Bar-Ilan and Rabbi Maimon, agreed to this ideological separation of Zionism and religion. And, in the final analysis, the leaders of the present day NRP accepted the separation between Zionist political and social questions and Jewish sources. Hence, throughout its history, religious Zionism had been but the satellite of secular Zionism. On the other hand, Rabbi Kook and his son, Zvi Yehuda, had refuted this separation. Their outlook, wrote Zoldin, can be defined as a messianic and practical religious outlook, perceiving each stage 'in the building of Israel as a stage in the redemption and the rebirth of the nation and its Torah in Eretz Israel. These stages are linked by eternal bonds to the sacred sources of Israel from which they draw their strength'. Hence, politics are connected to the eternal mission of the Jewish people to be 'a nation of priests and a holy people'. In response to those who objected to bestowing religious significance on political policies, considering this attempt to be a kind of 'false messianism', Zoldin retorted that the 'concepts of redemption' were not mere utopian aspirations lacking practical significance. Those who took this view failed to understand that the Torah was a complete and all-embracing outlook, encompassing the affairs of the entire Jewish people throughout their lives, and throughout their history.

Michael Nehorai, in attacking this organic religious viewpoint, cited an unconventional argument.[23] He considered the views of Zoldin and his colleagues to be in complete accord with those of orthodox Jewry. 'The orthodox outlook could not reconcile itself to the existence of a large-scale rescue operation connected to Eretz Israel, and at the same time unrelated to the final redemption, and consequently withdrew from it'. Now redemptive Zionism had become the partner of the orthodox camp, since both agreed that the ideal of the settlement of Eretz Israel could not be detached from the ideal of redemption, 'but instead of seceding like the Aguda, it undertook to sanctify the settlement activity'. Ostensibly, these seem to be different even conflicting viewpoints, but both camps regard the building of a Jewish Eretz Israel as the fulfilment of a Divine injunction, whereby the people are the instrument for realization and perhaps even its victim. In addition, 'the common denominator is the fact that both camps aspire to act in accordance with the precepts of the Torah and the redemption, and these lead them to undermine Zionism, one from without and the other from within'.

Yoel Bin-Nun and Yosef Ben-Shlomo took issue with Nehorai. Their central argument was that the driving force of redemptive Zionism lay not in faith but in history. Bin-Nun asserted[24] that the First World War had ushered in the apocalyptic era in the history of the world and of the Jews. The Zionism of Herzl and of Rabbi Reines was appropriate for the previous, rational era. The new epoch, however, was essentially irrational. 'Zionism in its simple Herzlian sense, ended, in effect, in 1914, and since then has been conducted in an apocalyptic epoch ... those who fail to see that the blossoming of the country and the immigration of millions of Jews are a manifestation of God's will ... may possibly fail to believe in their hearts in the Exodus'. Against this apocalyptic background, one of whose aspect was the Holocaust and the other the building of Eretz Israel, there was no further room for the Zionism of Herzl–Reines and it was being replaced by 'the radical hyper-Zionism' of Gush Emunim.

This radicalism implied not only action within history but also the granting it of special status within Jewish faith. Rabbi Kook, said Bin-Nun, had

constructed an entirely new system, which examines religious thinking not only in light of its internal sources, but also in light of what is happening in the world – both the political and the spiritual worlds. Where Zionism sought to restore the Jewish people to history – and Rabbi Kook accepted this view in principle – he himself wanted to restore to history both philosophy and thought, faith and beliefs. This is the true revolution, for which he was so severely attacked.

Ben-Shlomo[25] did not totally dismiss Nehorai's views. He agreed with him that it was unthinkable to argue that the yearning for redemption in itself justified Zionism, and he also acknowledged that messianism 'can certainly constitute the basis for justification of the opposite path', but he rejected absolutely the assumption that there was no Divine intervention in history. 'I claim that no serious religious thought can regard the great revolution which Zionism has wrought in Jewish history, through hazardously introducing the Jews into the course of external history, as if it were something like the Histadrut medical service, or a charitable fund.'

Such misunderstanding of the significance of the Zionist endeavor was liable to bring about the eradication of Zionism, and just as the Mizrahi, under Rabbi Reines, had agreed to the Uganda program in the name of the ideal of the 'safe refuge' for Jews, his spiritual heirs were liable to accept various 'Ugandas' as alternatives to the process of redemption occurring in Eretz Israel. Ben-Shlomo took this process to mean the re-establishment of unity between religious Zionist Jewry and secular Zionists. He invested considerable intellectual effort in integrating religious belief into historical development through uncovering divine significance within history, and in uniting believers and non-believers and the spirit of the labor movement with the fervor of Gush Emunim. This led him to identify a common denominator between Rabbi Kook and Moses Hess. '[They] share a historiosophical outlook in which religious significance is allotted to political, social and even military acts.... Starting from different basic assumptions (or perhaps not so very different), both arrive at a theory of the Jewish people as the chosen people, and Eretz Israel as the promised land'.[26]

Certain members of the Gush continued to develop the concept of the alternative in directions of their own, leading from the revolt against secular Zionism to redemptive national religious Zionism, and from rejection of NRP Zionism to the teachings of Rabbi Kook, eventually arriving at rejection of his views. These were the active members of the 'Jewish underground' (who were sentenced to imprisonment), and their supporters within the Gush. In 1985, when the Gush appeared to be in a state of profound crisis in the wake of the revelations about the activities of the underground, Moshe Simon declared that what set the Jewish people apart from other nations was the fact that 'it is defined as bearing one sole unchanging mission...this mission preceded nationhood'.[27] There is no room here for history, as Ben-Shlomo and Bin-Nun claimed, because 'it was not the nation which created the mission, but the reverse. This nation was created in order to realize the pre-existing ideal'. The root of the crisis of the Jewish people lies in its denial of its utopian-religious mission 'to build a heavenly society which, in its everyday life, will demonstrate the integrity of man and the best of the eternal values of the prophets of truth and justice'. Those who rejected this mission, he said, would some day deny their own homeland, and he discerned indications of this in the 'tired' and outdated slogans of Zionism.

More explicit in his conclusions was Yehuda Etzion, one of the leaders of the underground.[28] He openly criticized Rabbi Kook and his movement, Degel

Yerushalayim (Banner of Jerusalem) for having removed themselves *a priori* from all political involvement in society and thereby abandoned Zionism to secular Jews. 'We are not non-joiners of the orthodox community. We are not "joiners from outside" like the Rabbi and Degel Yerushalayim...nor do we force ourselves on it (and into it) like Rabbi Cahane.' Etzion proposed that he and his friends define themselves as 'graduates of Zionism', maintaining awareness 'that there is no escape from creating an alternative.... Just as we have outgrown the childish innocence of anticipating miracles, we have also outgrown the approach which seeks to pour our redemption into a secular vessel...of 'peace and security.'...out of trust in the Redeemer of Israel we will strive for our Hebrew peace – for national wholeness – the renewal of the worthy kingdom of Israel'. This is a combination of the religious messianism of some of Rabbi Kook's disciples with the concept of the revival of the Hebrew kingdom as advocated by the former members of Lehi within Gush Emunim, and particularly the late Shabtai Ben-Dov. They sought an absolute alternative not only to secular Zionism and to the National Religious Party, but also to the disciples of Rabbi Kook 'who are assimilated in the Zionist secular experience'. This outlook entailed total separation from secular society and from those religious Zionist circles which were involved in it. It also led to certain political conclusions of clearly totalitarian nature in the sphere of popular education, and in attitudes to democracy and parliamentary rule. Etzion's fellow-conspirator and cellmate, Dan Beeri, noted this, and cautioned him against excessive religious pietism which could deteriorate into social and political autism.[29] Beeri's use of these terms reflected profound concern at the infiltration of anti-Zionist orthodox ideas into the Gush, as a result of its advocacy of radical alternative ideologies of an anti-democratic nature. This phenomenon, pointed out by Zvi Nehorai in his debate with Rabbi Kook's pupils, greatly concerned the more moderate members of the Gush.[30] This development marked the culmination of the comprehensive alternative theory, since it now perceived the Torah as an outlook totally at odds with the social outlook underlying the state. There were at least two reasons for this: the logic of the internal development of alternativist thought, and the growing disillusionment with the social and political actions of the Zionist state.

The inner logic of the trend to orthodoxy emerges clearly from Yedidya Segal's statements in his debate with Yisrael Eldad.[31] The latter wanted to emphasize the general nationalist element in the Gush outlook, linking the religious to the secular wing within it. To illustrate, he asked Segal what appeared to be a rhetorical question: Who was closer to the Gush – the secular Professor Yuval Neeman or Professor Yeshayahu Leibowitz, a devout Jew. To Eldad's surprise, Segal replied unhesitantly and openly: 'Leibowitz, notwithstanding'. He went even further, predicting the possibility of an alliance between activist orthodox forces and the *dohakei ha-ketz* (apocalyptics) within Gush Emunim. 'We have need of the great force inherent in orthodox Jewry in order to continue the process of redemption. Redemption does not end in conquest and settlement, but in renewal of the revelation of Sinai, the return of the people of Israel to God. And who will be our allies in the struggle to achieve this if not those Jews who have preserved the purity of their house of prayer without giving access to the dregs of western-secular thought'. He undoubtedly includes Zionism within these dregs.

Whereas these remarks mainly reflect a religious outlook, with political undertones, Moshe Simon, two years later, proposed an anti-statist ideology in the name of the supremity of the Torah. Having once proclaimed that the Jewish mission had preceded the people and that this mission entailed the establishment of a religiously whole society in Eretz Israel, he now openly declared that parliamentary democracy could not be allowed to interfere in matters which related to the people's mission. He regarded parliamentary democracy as synonymous with the existing state of Israel, and declared, like Yeshayahu Leibowitz, though for different political motives, that 'a nation which considers the state its supreme value, is a fascist nation, while a nation whose land is its supreme value is a patriotic nation'. This situation existed because the state of Israel was estranged from Eretz Israel.[32] This stance signified not only withdrawal from Zionism but also political isolation. Yitzhak Hanshke argued that both the left and the right wings of the political establishment of the state were incapable, because of their inherent contradictions, of being leading forces in the process of settling and redeeming Eretz Israel.[33] 'Whether we will it or not, we must return to the uncensored Torah, the Torah we know from the bet midrash with all its details and minor rules and regulations. This Torah contains the injunctions of conquest and settlement of Eretz Israel'. In short, the 'comprehensive alternative' gives preference to Eretz Israel over the State of Israel; and to the Torah over Zionism; and seeks to replace parliamentary democratic society with a totalitarian monarchic regime.

Other members of the Gush advocated an inclusive alternative, namely an alternative which did not set itself apart, socially and politically, and did not hold aloof from external secular points of view, but tried to include all of these in one ideological setting. This trend was succinctly expressed by Dan Beeri, also a member of the Jewish underground, in his above-mentioned article, 'Zionism More than Ever': 'Zionism awakened profound forces, beyond the dreams of its activists, and the tortuous realization of the Zionist objective has been intertwined with historical events of aweinspiring dimensions, out of all proportion to the vision, lives or stature of the leaders of the Jewish national renaissance movement'. In distinguishing between the Zionist movement as a historical phenomenon and its historical implementers and leaders, Beeri was seeking to refute the 'comprehensive alternative' argument that, because of the 'deviations' of secular and religious Zionism, it had forfeited its validity as an ideology. According to Beeri, the reverse was true: 'The existence of all Jews wherever they may be, for at least the past forty years, has been imbued with Zionism: the Zionist movement is a vector, the straight line and point of equilibrium of our lives, and we have no choice in the matter'. Zionism, therefore, does not belong to a certain movement or to a sector of the people, and consequently does not reach its end when those who once led it, like the labor movement or the secular forces, deviate partially or wholly from its principles. And despite its disillusionments, Gush Emunim must not stand apart from the people, and become a religious sect like the *haredim*. They should avoid sectarianism, and break down the ideological barriers. At the same time, they should act openly and respect the right to be different. Above all, they should strive to create 'a qualitative intellectual expanse, and to define their basic premises while avoiding ideological and social coercion'.[34] Beeri explained the term 'intellectual expanse' in his next article[35] in which he described the self-segregation of the secular and the religious camps as a diaspora phenomenon. The religious camp was fostering a Jewish clergy, marked by its own garb, customs and psychology. Religious clericalism and secular rationalism were playing into each others hands and the sole solution was 'the living Torah, breathing life into the Israeli corpse. But this will not come about unless a revolution takes place in our spiritual makeup. In other words: the Torah must function not as a religion but as an ideology. And it is no accident that the term "ideal" plays so important a part in the teachings of Rabbi Kook... Henceforth all our human powers must be directed at the new pioneering endeavor'. Children should be made acquainted with the modern world and all its scientific and human dimensions, 'that world which we are exhorted to reform and improve in the spirit of the Kingdom of Heaven. We should offer not the bogey of a dry, clerical and totalitarian '*halakhah* state' but the reborn Jewish nation...Our political, social and scientific concepts should refructify Jewish thought, like the Aristotelean philosophy of the Middle Ages'. His views on the 'Who is a Jew?' issue illustrate his intentions.[36] Beeri considered Reform conversion to Judaism to be mere conversion.

> It is important to explain to the secular public that Jewish identity, which they consider to be self-evident, is no light matter, and no person from outside can purchase or adopt the mighty subconscious burden of all the historical and cultural deposits on which Judaism is based, even in the absence of a religious outlook. The essential substitute for this existential force is sincere acceptance of the yoke of Torah and its injunctions, adoption of the fate and mission of the many generations of the Jewish people and sincere readiness to pay the price.

A similar approach was adopted by Rabbis Yehuda Zoldin and Menahem Fruman.[37] Both disapproved of the Gush's seclusion from the outside world, and also emphasized that the values advocated by the secular left, such as humanism, liberalism, democracy and socialism, were of importance for national religious thought as well, and should not be dismissed lightly. 'We should view with regret and not with malicious satisfaction the great decline of Israeli socialism to the point where it has lost its identity.' Hanan Porat was also anxious to dissociate the Gush from its extremist right-wing image. He wanted it to become 'a backbone, a golden mean...'[38] This approach also encompasses Ben-Shlomo's above-mentioned synthesis between the socialist-secular Zionism of Moses Hess and the mystical religious Zionism of Rabbi Kook. Such cooperation was possible only on the basis of mutual acknowledgement, as Eliezer Schweid put it:

where secular families accept the ethos of obligations, recognition of the commitment of the individual towards the group (family, community, nation), awareness of the supreme goal of man lying above the individual sphere, if they have an affinity with Jewish education, faith and tradition. For religious families, the condition is that they accept, first of all, the humanistic ethos of tolerance, openness and empathy, have an affinity with general knowledge and vocational occupations in the sphere of science, and affinity with the whole spectrum of humanistic life.[39]

When the Jewish underground was uncovered, Eliezer Schweid demanded that the Gush clarify several fundamental ideological and political issues, as the precondition for possible cooperation between the two cultures.[40] What limits did the Gush set to practical, extra-parliamentary pressure on the elected government? Was democracy a value in itself? What were the relations between the authoritarian element in *halakhah* and humane considerations? To what extent was it possible to base decisions on social and political matters on messianic aspirations? The above quotations from the writings of different Gush thinkers provide a direct answer to these questions.

Gush Emunim had reached a watershed: it had to choose between isolation and integration, between dialogue with the surrounding society and a monologue with itself. Essentially, this is the choice between Zionism in its original, true sense and anti-Zionism in its religous-activist guise. Those who advocated the comprehensive alternative removed themselves thereby from the consensus of the post-Six Day War radical trends. The proponents of the inclusive alternative held certain views in common with the student movement and the neo-Conservatives in the United States. All three trends offered an alternative, but they did not reject Jewish and other traditions. Thus, the young generation turned to Eastern-European socialist tradition and Hassidism. The secular conservatives sanctified Jewish tradition and based their thinking on classic liberalism. On the other hand, the 'inclusive' trend in Gush Emunim, after their change of heart after exposure of the Jewish underground crisis, accepted such Western universal ideas as democracy and liberalism and emphasized their links with the tradition of the labor movement. All three groups are aware that the return of the Jews to the historical arena after the establishment of the state is of great Jewish significance but has a moral cost. Hence, all of them see political power, in varying degrees, as an organic phenomenon of the new Judaism, and, for all, the national or ethnic-cultural element, in its quasi-national significance, is a basic component of their Jewish outlook. All are attempting to shape a collective Jewish identity in an era when political, cultural and religious modernism have reached most Jews in the world. Although each of them disapproves of certain elements in Western-universalism, they do not deny its positive heritage, but rather seek, each in its own way, to create a synthesis between this heritage and their own Judaism.

9 Conservative Liberalism

Conservatism has also been good for our people. My students today are more aware of their Jewishness than my contemporaries were at the same age.

Eugene Borowitz in a conversation with the author, February 1988

The events of 1967/8 which bred Jewish radicalism also influenced the liberal trend among American Jews. The enthusiasm which followed the Six Day War reinforced the particularist element within it, while the shock caused by manifestations of black hostility sapped its universalist convictions.

American Jewish liberalism encompasses three movements: the Reform movement, which also denotes itself liberal Judaism; the progressive circles aligned politically with the Democratic Party; and the young liberal radicals who were mostly committed to the civil rights struggle. All three sectors highlighted the importance of the human and moral dimension for both American and Israeli society. American liberalism, it should be noted in passing, differs from nineteenth-century Central and Western European liberalism, not only because of the absence in the United States of conservative socio-political forces in the European sense, but also because American political culture lacked a significant and vital socialist movement. Consequently, in various periods, liberalism in the United States was a kind of 'substitute' for Western European social-democratic ideas. This was the case in the thirties, in the New Deal era, when the Democratic Party under Roosevelt was a political coalition of immigrant groups, and in the sixties and seventies, when liberalism brandished the banner of civil and social equality. It was natural for Jews to identify with liberalism as long as it did not threaten their direct and indirect interests. And, as noted above, 1967/8 marked a turning point in this respect.

Regarding this matter, the Reform movement is of particular interest. It displays a certain similarity with developments in the Jewish socialist movement. At the end of the nineteenth century, when the Reform movement in the United States totally rejected nationalist theories, the central force in Russian Jewish socialism was the Bund. It demanded cultural autonomy for the Jews, but denied the existence of a Jewish nation. Thus, where the Bund advocated autonomous culture, the Reform movement based itself on religious belief. In the 1930s and 1940s, when labor Zionism was becoming increasingly influential in the Jewish community, the Reform movement also adopted a more positive attitude to Jewish nationalism. At the end of the sixties, when the State of Israel, with a social-democratic party at its helm, won its great national victory, the Reform movement reached the third stage in its progression from the universal to the particular. Concurrently, secular progressive and radical circles, which had not gone so far as to identify with neo-

166

conservative or liberal conservative ideologies, also re-examined their stand. This self-appraisal was also affected by the ever-present neo-conservative challenge, which forced them to relate to newly-emerged Jewish particularist issues. This was not an easy task, and only four years after the events of 1967/8 did liberal thought begin to formulate a public stand adapted to the new circumstances without totally abandoning traditional principles.

In 1972, Robert Gordis, editor of the Conservative quarterly Judaism,[1] organized a symposium on the relations between Judaism and liberalism. The discussion revolved around the question of whether the traditional Jewish dedication to liberal and progressive ideas could and should continue. This question was addressed by Arthur Lelyveld who, at the dialogue held in Jerusalem on the eve of the Six Day War, had declared Judaism to be synonymous activity on behalf of social morality.[2] Lelyveld sought to defend true liberalism against those who distorted it – whether they came from the dogmatic left or the radical right. In his opinion, true liberalism was based on four principles: human liberty as an end and a means, pluralism of thought and faith, direct social critique, and the constant search for ways of reforming society and improving human life. As an advocate of these principles, he abhorred manifestations of black anti-Semitism, the illogical sentimentalism of the young proponents of the counterculture, and the crude radicalism, motivated by self-interest, of the neo-conservatives.

It was clear to Lelyveld that his condemnation of the dogmatism of the liberal left might be interpreted as pointing the way to liberal conservatism, and hence he made an effort to undermine this outlook. He stressed that the conservatives were fostering a sense of second-class citizenship, which was reminiscent of persecuted Jewish communities in Eastern Europe. He also cautioned that such an ideology, based solely on Jewish particularist interests, was essentially anti-Jewish, since Judaism, despite its pragmatic traits, had never limited itself to promoting Jewish interests, but advocated justice for all. Jewish existence was manifested not only in the practical effort to survive, but also in messianic-moral visions.

Lelyveld's attempt to restate the need for equilibrium between particularist interests and universal principles won the support of the historian Arthur Hertzberg. One year later, in the course of the debate on relations between the Jews and the forces of revolution, he tried to sustain this approach by citing historical examples.[3] Hertzberg argued that for the past two centuries, since the Enlightenment and the French Revolution, there had been an essential conflict between left-wing radical forces and the Jewish outlook. On the other hand, there were reciprocal relations between Kerensky-style pragmatic liberalism and the Jews who were being enfranchised at this time, even though this same liberalism was at the helm of the February Revolution in Russia. Therefore, Hertzberg asserted, the Jews should beware to an equal degree both the traditional anti-Semitism of the right and the new radicalism of the left, and choose the middle path of practical liberalism. At this point, Hertzberg commented that his own identification with the oppressed elements in society stemmed not only from his liberal outlook, but also from his Zionist convictions. Zionism had always demanded equal rights for the oppressed Jewish people, and consequently could not remain indifferent to the plight of others. Later on, in an exchange with Irving Kristol, the outspoken champion of 'Jewish interests', Hertzberg offered another interpretation of the same concept. Jewish politics, he said, should be guided by self-interest, but this was true in a society in which the Jews had a vested interest in stability and order, on the one hand, and social reform on the other. Therefore, in contrast to the dogmatic outlook of the conservatives, who, he said, related Jewish interests to specific political forces, he recommended a pragmatic approach, a constant assessment of the situation and decision-taking on the basis of political utilitarianism.

The subtle difference in Jewish outlook between the conservative liberals and the liberal-conservatives was defined seven years later by the director of the American Jewish Congress, Henry Siegman. The conservatives, he said, exhorted the Jews to live for themselves but not to be themselves, hoping thereby to help the Jews rather than to teach them to be better Jews. This, he said, was impossible since in his words 'It is on being for ourselves rather than being ourselves. It is the difference between making it better for Jews, and making better Jews. Like it or not, a significant part of being ourselves has something to do with not being only for ourselves'.⁴

Awareness of the need to strike a new ideological and political balance with regard to the liberal and conservative forces in society was accompanied by the demand for equilibrium between tradition and change in modern Judaism. Professor Joseph Blau of the Department of Theology at Columbia presented this view to the annual convention of Reform rabbis.⁵ Blau cautioned his audience against the ideological oscillations between rational universalism and atavistic particularism. The Reform movement, he said, must maintain a balance between the two. What was required was a 'tradition-oriented universalism'. Excessive emphasis on particularism could obliterate the progressive elements in the Reform movement, while accentuation of universalism could undermine the Jewish elements.

The concept of a distinctive homeland was necessary to the maintenance of this equilibrium, he said. It was also essential to foster a Jewish culture with its own special language, Hebrew, and to emphasize the universal elements within Jewish festivals, while at the same time avoiding assimilation of the customs of other peoples. The ethical aspect of the Reform movement, and its universal message, should also be reinforced. In conclusion, Blau believed that it was the tension between the universalist and particularist trends within the Reform movement which guaranteed the preservation of the delicate balance between the two. Through this tension, a reasoned progressivism could be achieved, guiding the Jews along the path from the past to the future.

Rabbi Eugene Borowitz, professor of theology at the Rabbinical Seminary in New York, consistently tackled the fundamental issues facing the liberal-Reform movement. Borowitz was chairman of the committee which composed 'A Centenary Perspective', the declaration of the basic tenets of the Reform movement on its hundredth anniversary in the United States, which were endorsed at the 1976 San Francisco conference. Between 1973 and 1984 he published three wide-ranging books on problems of Jewish faith and existence. His writings reflect clearly the changes in the outlook of the Reform movement in the United States after 1967.

Unlike the neo-conservatives, who regarded Jewish particularism primarily as a collective interest, and unlike some of his colleagues, who considered it a Jewish value, Borowitz emphasized its universal significance. What the Jews offer mankind today, he said, was not the idea of Judaism, but the very fact of its existence and survival. This emphasis on peoplehood was the foundation of the new universalism. Thus, the survival of the Jews, and their refusal to assimilate, had a meaning for mankind as a whole. It is not necessary to be a Jew in order to grasp the greatness of the Jewish ethnic steadfastness. In a world which takes a cynical view of ideologies, ideological sermonizing is useless, and only living examples can have any impact; the Jews provide such an example. Hence, the 'Jewish mission' is to continue to exist apart. In the past, the Reform movement had subordinated its particularism to universal ideals. Now the time had come to restore the proper balance between the two.[6]

This new equilibrium, as he defined it, was purely dialectical, containing the positive tension and unity of contrasts between love of the Jewish people and love of mankind. Through its acknowledgement of these facts, he asserted,[7] the Reform movement was responding to pressing needs.

The 'Centenary Perspective' stated explicitly that the Reform movement had previously understood service to mankind to be the epitome of Judaism. Only in the past few years had the movement become aware of the virtues of pluralism and the value of particularism. The movement had also once considered its obligations towards its people and towards mankind to be compatible, but they were now seen to be at variance. There was no simple way of resolving this tension, but the movement should confront it without forgoing either of its obligations, in the awareness that love of mankind without devotion to the Jewish people meant self-destruction. On the other hand, to be committed exclusively to the affairs of the Jewish people without being involved in universal issues was a betrayal of the vision of the prophets.

Borowitz continued to ponder the 'new equilibrium' between particularism and universalism in the context of the social action of the Reform movement, in an article entitled 'Rethinking Reform Jewish Social Action'.[8] The Reform movement, he wrote, was based on two assumptions: that the quintessence of Judaism was universal morality, and that it found expression in liberal social policy. In other words, the Reformists tended to believe that their efforts on behalf of social progress in line with radical liberal concepts was, in effect, the realization of Jewish values.

In the past few years, Borowitz admitted, although most Jews supported political liberalism, their attitude towards the social theories of the Reform movement had changed. This change, he felt, might be the outcome of the disillusionment of

Jewish liberals, who had overestimated the impact of their endeavors, sincerely convinced that the millenium was at hand. Instead, they had encountered black anti-Semitism and the hostility of liberal or left-wing radicals. Borowitz himself had no doubt that a particularist rather than a universal mood now prevailed among the public at large, and particularly among Jews. They were now concerned primarily for their own survival and that of their fellow Jews. This existential mood, stemming from changes wrought by time, has been reinforced in the past few years by academic research on Jewish history and the sources of Jewish faith. This research has questioned whether Judaism has always been rooted in universal ethics. It discerns a much more particularist perspective than that attributed to Judaism by reformist liberal thinkers.

Notwithstanding, Borowitz remained true to his beliefs in the need for balanced liberalism. To his mind, the Jewish affinity with liberal-universal action, even if it did not stem directly from their faith, should be based on their historical experience. And as such, this affinity must be pragmatic, namely, closely linked to changing circumstances. This experience indicated that such universal principles as emancipation, liberal pluralism, freedom of thought and of faith, were in harmony with Jewish interests. All these were important for the survival of the Jews on condition that they took a skeptical view of their social efforts and ceased to believe that these efforts would usher in the Messianic age.

This skeptical realism led Borowitz to dissociate himself from universal-liberal principles. Judaism, he asserted, could not accept each and every moral principle in full, since they were often at odds with Jewish needs. This being so, they were not always consonant with Jewish obligations. Thus, for example, mixed marriages, while they represented individual freedom of choice, conflicted with the precept of Jewish survival.

In short, the universal ideal that the individual must devote himself to promoting the common good, cannot easily be realized in history. In the final analysis, one cannot escape the conclusion that a true universal stance must stem from a stable particularist starting point. In other words, it is advisable not to practice universalism without first shoring up the foundations of Jewish particularism.

According to that same yardstick of equilibrium, Borowitz examined Israel's standing among world Jewry. At a 1980 symposium,[9] he expounded his views on the relations between universalism and particularism, liberalism and conservatism. His formula was clear, if not simple. Messianic liberalism, he said, was dead, but for practical reasons and out of Jewish considerations, he and many Jews like him had refrained from joining the conservative ranks. He argued that, practically speaking, it had been demonstrated that the Jews had achieved individual freedom and won a national state thanks to their activity aimed at eliminating social injustice. They had won emancipation as a result of consecutive legislative activity, aimed at abolishing age-old traditions of discrimination. The establishment of the Jewish state was the outcome of a political struggle and was not born out of faith in the stability of the prevailing order. In other words, Borowitz perceives liberalism as synonymous with social action and the political struggle to achieve just ends. These two principles have always operated to the advantage of the Jews as individuals and as a community, and there is no reason to assume that this situation will change in the future. Borowitz's opponents argued that practical considerations indicated that Jews should align themselves with the conservative camp, both because the Jews were the most prosperous ethnic minority in the United States, and because such a step was in Israel's interest. If Jewish life were normal, like that of other peoples, said Borowitz, he too would consider this the logical path of action, particularly since the present tendency of the masses was towards conservatism. However, Jewish life was abnormal, and the survival of the Jews was the most resounding evidence of this. The Jews had survived because they had closed ranks against social forces and objective processes in the name of the values they advocated. The Jews were unique in modern society in their struggle on behalf of moral values at the behest of the great thinkers of modern Judaism. In the future, as in the past, Judaism and the Jews must withstand general trends, since only thus can they safeguard and justify their singular existence.

Borowitz was aware that the existence of the Jewish state was a central factor in the called-for change in the social and political thought of the reform movement. However, his approach to the state was in no way simple, because of his desire to find the true balance between emotional links to the state and religious faith which was independent of Israel. The book he published in 1973 on 'The Masks Jews Wear'[10] explored the significance of the Six Day War in Jewish life. On the one hand, he perceived the Jewish response as a kind of religious experience which had restored to the fold many assimilated or indifferent Jews, by enabling them to remove their 'Marrano masks'. He believed, however, that the Jews of the United States, in their enthusiasm for the State of Israel, had replaced the 'Marrano syndrome' of assimilation by another 'Marrano syndrome' – of total dependence on the Jewish state. He objected vehemently to this phenomenon, because, he declared, to the best of his understanding, the state could not serve as a substitute for Jewish faith, the moving force of Judaism. In other words, there could be no doubt that the existence of the state was more important for the Jews than for Judaism. He arrived at this conclusion not only because of his own religious beliefs, but also because he held that the classic spiritual Zionism of Ahad ha-Am was now irrelevant.

Hebrew culture, he claimed, was the natural dimension of Jewish life in Israel, but could not supply the needs of Jews in the Diaspora, because Jews living in a non-Jewish milieu required a culture which would foster their distinctive qualities as Jews. Consequently, they had no need of an additional secular-universalist culture. Thus, the definition of Judaism as a Zionist-nationalist concept ruled by faith, with the State of Israel as its *raison d'être*, is but another expression of the Marrano syndrome. This Judaism covers its true face with a mask of Hebrew language and culture, but conceals the fact that its values stem from divine transcendental and not temporal sources. Therefore, Borowitz argued, some day the Jews in Israel and in the United States would understand that their existence was not dependent on secular nationalism, but rather on divine faith. This 'distinctive' approach, stressing religion rather than nationalism or the state, was gradually modified in a Jewish-nationalist direction.

Three years later, when Borowitz composed the Centenary Perspective, he defined the relations between Israel and the Diaspora as the expression of transcendental nationalism, which could serve as an example for other peoples of how to rise above parochial interests and dedicate themselves to a noble task. In other words, Borowitz had reverted to the idea of the 'mission', but this time in ethnic or national guise. It is the tangible links between the state and the Diaspora, of profound moral significance, that transform particularist tendencies into a universal value. And, therefore, by holding their special national dialogue with Israel, Diaspora Jews 'transcend common nationalism'.[11] Borowitz uses the concept of transcendental nationalism to define the standing of the state in Jewish life. The state is vital for the Diaspora, but not indispensable, because in the Jewish religious sense, even if the state is an important value, it is not a supreme value. And because the Diaspora possesses its own inner forces, and notwithstanding the fact that it is, in many respects, nurtured by the state, Diaspora Jews are capable of supporting it without being dependent on it. This explains why, several years later, Borowitz wrote that if, Heaven forbid, the state should disappear, this would not spell the end of Judaism.[12] This, it should be noted, was his personal view, which was not expressed in the official manifesto of his movement, probably because it appeared to question the accepted view on the centrality of the State of Israel in Jewish life. As his views evolved gradually but consistently from the universal-religious outlook to the national-religious viewpoint, he also modified his ideas on the existential dependence between Israel and the Diaspora.

In 1984, in *Liberal Judaism*, Borowitz summarized his socio-religious outlook.[13] This work, aimed at the general public, is written with a clarity which enables the reader to grasp the author's views and to trace the development of his movement's outlook.

The first part of the book – The Jewish People – deals with modern Jewish identity in relation to the historic changes of the past half-century. It starts out from the assumption, now generally accepted, that Judaism cannot be defined solely in religious terms. With intellectual integrity, Borowitz points out that only about half of the Jews of the United States are affiliated to religious movements. In the large cities, the great majority of the Jews are not members of temples, and among those who are, a large percentage attend for social rather than spiritual and religious reasons. Israel, on the other hand, evokes loyalty more than the Torah does, despite the fact that it is not a purely Jewish state. Part of its population is Muslim, part Christian, and most of its Jewish citizens are not religious.

Taking these facts into account, Borowitz modified his definition of Judaism as mainly a religion. He now asserted that Judaism is as a synthesis between religion and nationality. These terms, he said, were not congruent with the concepts of

American culture and ideology. Fortunately, however, the term ethnicity had recently been sanctioned, and it was now permissible to refer to the Jews as a religious-ethnic group.[14] He apparently believes that the differences between these concepts are merely semantic, particularly in the case of Jewish ethnicity. The events of the past fifty years: the Holocaust, the establishment of Israel, disillusionment with dogmatic liberalism, have strengthened the Jewish sense of national affiliation, and there has also been a change in attitudes towards the Jewish state. Borowitz continued to claim that Zionism could not offer an overall alternative to Jewish life in the Diaspora. While he remained convinced that the state could not serve as a spiritual center for Jews living in different cultures, he now allotted Israel a central role in the international Jewish national-religious experience. Israel, he said, 'crowns our folk existence'. After the Holocaust, it was the truest manifestation of the Jewish will to live, containing within it the best yearnings and visions of the Jews throughout the centuries. Its loss would be 'a shattering blow' to world Jewry.

In the eighties, Borowitz changed his mind about immigration to Israel. Having acknowledged that the best place to realize a collective Jewish way of life was in the sovereign Israeli society, he came to view *aliyah* as an act which every good Jew should contemplate.[15] He seemed to be moving towards the outlook of several of his colleagues in the Reform movement, with whom he had debated in the seventies. This outlook may be defined as a kind of new 'practical Zionism' reminiscent of the old Hibbat Zion. Its proponents believed that the continued existence of the Jewish people as a single religious-national entity could be guaranteed through perpetual collective effort aimed at promoting immigration and the study of Hebrew as a living language, the establishment of institutions in Israel, and the strengthening of ties with the kibbutz movement. A debate on the definition of Israel-Diaspora relations was conducted at the American Reform movement's centenary conference in San Francisco in 1976, between this group, then in the minority, and Borowitz, spokesman of the majority. The minority group argued that the existence of the state was indispensable for the Diaspora whereas the majority defined it merely as 'vital'. The minority group pressured the conference into inserting into the ideological platform a favourable reference to immigration.[16] The movement proclaimed its willingness to encourage the immigration of those Jews who wanted to seek self-fulfilment in Israel.

In their polemics with Borowitz, his opponents cited arguments which he himself accepted several years later. In the course of the deliberations,[17] Rabbi Gerald Goldman of New Jersey claimed that Jewish history in the past century, and particularly since the Holocaust and the establishment of Israel, had set the Jews even further apart from other peoples. Whereas the Holocaust had cast a shadow of doubt over Jewish existence, the state was now maintaining this existence. This meant that it was not faith but history which had rendered Jewish existence unique. Hence, too, the neo-conservatist conviction that the return of the Jews to history was the most important phenomenon in their history in the past few generations. But it was precisely because of this return to the universal historical arena that the particularist aspect of Jewish existence had come to the fore. This process had also influenced attitudes towards religious belief. The Reform movement, therefore, should revert to the traditional stance as regards study of Torah, observance of the Sabbath and of the festivals. In this way Jewish values would become the Jewish lifestyle.

Shortly after the Reform movement manifesto was composed, Rabbi David Polish published an article whose title was self-explanatory: 'We Do Not Take Israel Seriously Enough'.[18] After the Holocaust, he wrote, the Jewish people would have disintegrated without the State of Israel, and its spiritual fortitude would have been sapped. The Holocaust had proved that the state was indispensable, not as a refuge for persecuted Jews but as solace in a world in which devilishness is possible. The spiritual and existential significance of Israel also has religious implications. If the state had been annihilated, as had appeared momentarily possible in 1973, then after Auschwitz there would have been no escape from total denial of the existence of God and from the conclusion that the Jews are a nation bearing the mark of Cain and forever accursed.

Polish contradicted the outlook which underestimated the importance of Israel's role as rescuer of Jews and of Judaism. Although Israel is not synonymous with Judaism, he said, its very existence breathes new spirit into Jewish life in the cultural and organizational sense. Unlike Borowitz, Polish remained loyal to Ahad ha-Am's Zionism. The original Zionism, he said, was always a synthesis between the needs of Jews and the needs of Judaism. He did not deny that this synthesis was problematic in the modern world, but its annulment, he said, might undermine and even destroy Jewish unity and cohesion, both politically and spiritually.

The historian Michael Meyer, addressing a Reform rabbinical convention in Jerusalem, demanded that it intensify its involvement in Israel.[19] This was necessary, he said, first because of the need to struggle for the spiritual image of the state, which had not yet been given final form, and second because of the movement's historical mission – to 'put forward a guiding ideal which embraces both tradition and modernity...' – an ideal whose embodiment in Israel 'would possess great attractive force to Jews everywhere'. In this, unlike Borowitz, he was expressing belief in the essential centrality of the state for Jewish communities in the Diaspora (though he preferred the term 'heart'). Meyer was aware of the incongruence between the standing of the Reform movement in the Diaspora and in Israel. In Israel religious orthodoxy held sway, but in the Reform movement lay the sole hope of bridging the gap between the religious and secular camps. In order to solve this dilemma, he recommended greater practical involvement of the Reform movement in Israeli affairs. For Meyer, appreciation of the historical importance of the Reform ideology is linked to acknowledgement of Israel's role as the heart of the people, and he perceives modern Judaism as consolidating into 'a religious people focused upon Zion'. This people will combine 'both particular and universal values', and continue to maintain messianic faith. This viewpoint, it should be noted, is shared by all Reform thinkers; they stress that since the establishment of Israel, the pinnacle of political Zionist achievement, only religious faith can fill the Zionist ideal with new, revivifying content. In their way of thinking, if not in content, the Reform thinkers do not differ from the leaders of Gush Emunim.

Most emphatic in his Zionist convictions was Rabbi Richard Hirsch, (who put them into practice by immigrating to Israel).[20] In contrast to Borowitz, he postulated mutual existential links between the State of Israel and the Jewish people. The crux of the Jewish question in modern times, Hirsch emphasized, was not the existence of the individual, but the survival of the group. Israel is the sole place on earth where the Jews, even though most of them are living in the Diaspora, are free to shape the cultural and social aspects of their national life. This is the sole and final historic opportunity given to the Jews. Collective Jewish character and Jewish destiny will be determined in the Jewish state. And immigration is needed, not because there is no future in the Diaspora, but because this is the only way of safeguarding the future of Israel, the chief instrument for the continuation of Jewish life in the Diaspora.

Two years later, in 1981, at a congress of Reform rabbis in Jerusalem, Hirsch reiterated even more emphatically his view that the Diaspora could not survive without the State of Israel. No other Jewish community has similar standing to Israel. It is expressed in the desire to re-establish a center for the Jewish people by means of a society based on Jewish values, to revive Jewish culture through the Hebrew language, and to protect the rights of Jews everywhere. Hirsch did not negate the Diaspora, and acknowledged the right of every Jew to live wherever he chose. And precisely because of the centrality and importance of the state for the Jews of the Diaspora, it was incumbent on them to strengthen the state. The supreme effort they could make in this context was immigration.

In conclusion, it should be emphasized that, if we exclude the religious-messianic dimension in their thinking, the Reform rabbis who were the main spokesmen of the liberal-conservative trend were indistinguishable in their social and political outlook from secular intellectuals with a similar approach. This was clearly illustrated by the symposium on Jews and liberals conducted by *Commentary* in 1980.[21]

Thus, conservative liberalism became the public viewpoint of the left wing of the Jewish center, just as liberal conservatism or 'neo-conservatism' characterized its right wing. Paradoxically enough, these ideologies bore an ideological affinity to one another, but diverged in the practical political sphere.

In the debate between them, there is no diametrical opposition between universalism and particularism; nationality and religion; the centrality of Israel and the autonomy of the Diaspora; political force and political ethics, etc. The partial consensus resulted mainly from the liberal shift in the direction of the conservative views. The political and social developments in the period under discussion, and the conservative challenge, spurred the liberals to conduct a moral stock-taking, based on acknowledgment of the need for reform without abandonment of the intellectual force and intensity of feeling of the liberal tradition. Hence, the liberal stance, because of its tendency to compromise, was sometimes vague, while the views of the conservatives were extreme and uncompromisingly clear.

On the political plane, however, there was a wide discrepancy between the two outlooks. Here the philosophical realism of the conservatives was manifested as political dogmatism, while the relative idealism of the liberals took the form of social pragmatism. The liberal-conservatives aligned themselves, ideologically and politically, with conservative trends in the American public, while the liberals, aware of the complexity of their relations with the liberal forces in society, proposed examining each political situation on its merits. Thus, as regards Israel's policies, the conservatives, on principle, totally separated political and moral issues. Political interests, they asserted, are always power-based. The liberals, on the other hand, recognized the inevitability of injustice in politics, but sought to limit it by operating moral principles. Consequently, the liberals demanded the right to openly criticize Israel's policies, while the conservatives totally rejected this possibility.

Despite these differences of opinion, the two currents of opinion were in agreement regarding the role of Israel in shaping the collective Jewish character. Both welcomed the return of the Jews to the historical arena, while recognizing the 'moral cost' of this return. They acknowledged the centrality of Israel for world Jewry and appreciated the moral value of its very existence, achieved thanks to the collective Jewish will to survive, and the terrible lesson of the Holocaust.

10 From Concentration to Centrality

For one thousand and eight hundred years we were a people without a state.
Now we are in danger of being a state without a people.

A.J. Heschel at the Zionist Congress, 1972

After 1967, the non-radical Zionist outlook – that way of thinking which did not dream of creating a social and cultural utopia, was not dazzled by the splendor of political power and was immune to messianic fervor – continued to follow its consistent policy of adapting itself to changing circumstances. In this process, which had led from Hibbat Zion to political Zionism, and thence to synthetic and constructive Zionism and onward to power Zionism struggling for a state, the Six Day War was yet another milestone, ushering a new era, one of the most paradoxical in its history. On the one hand, this was the first time that the Jewish masses in the West had displayed spontaneous, direct national emotion, undisguised by humanitarian, philanthropic, altruistic or religious considerations. On the other hand, it very soon became clear that this national identification reflected a sense of common destiny but not the desire for a common way of life. Moreover, it was precisely the radicals within American Jewry, the element who stressed the ethnic-national interest of the Jews, in both the local and the international sphere, who considered themselves to be totally rooted in the culture and the society of their country of birth. Underlying this paradoxical phenomenon of simultaneous identification and repulsion was the possibility of a dialectical development which could prove dangerous to Zionism. In other words, when the Jewish people acknowledge the first principle of Zionism – unity on a national basis – but reject the second principle – territorial concentration in the national homeland – what remains of Zionism? Up to the Six Day War it was argued that Zionists had no reason to fear the specter of dual loyalty and that their political support for Israel was unconditional and guaranteed. After the Six Day War it became clear that this fact was valid for all Jews. And thus Zionism forfeited its 'monopoly' in this sphere as well.

The 27th Zionist Congress was convened in Jerusalem in June 1968, when enthusiasm at the military triumph was still at its height, and as tension between Jews and blacks in the United States was mounting. The Congress tried to tackle this dialectical dilemma by formulating an innovative definition of Zionism. The 23rd Congress in 1951 had defined the role of Zionism after statehood as 'the consolidation of the State of Israel, the ingathering of exiles in Eretz Israel, and

177

fostering of the unity of the Jewish people'.[1] Now, seventeen years later, it was decided that the aims of Zionism were: 'The unity of the Jewish people and the centrality of Israel in Jewish life; the ingathering of the Jewish people in its historic homeland, Eretz Israel, through *aliyah* from all countries; the strengthening of the State of Israel'.[2] The modifications were as follows: strengthening of the state was replaced by the preservation of the unity of the people. The historical concept of ingathering of the exiles was replaced by the call to gather the Jewish people from all countries into Israel. Thus, in theory as well as in practice, the traditional stand of the leaders of the American Zionist majority was accepted. On the other hand, in order to reflect the new situation, and to counterbalance the trends to change, a new and significant ideological concept was created – the centrality of Israel in the lives of Jews throughout the world – which was unrelated to the concept of *galut*, and may even be seen as substituting for it as the existential need of a diaspora which did not consider itself a *golah*. The veteran leader, Emmanuel Neumann, in his address, analysed the terms diaspora (*tefutzah*) and center. He asserted that the semantic debate about the terms *kibbutz galuyot* – ingathering of exiles – and *kibbutz hagaluyot* – ingathering of all the exiles – which had begun in 1951, was superfluous. The Jews of the United States did not consider themselves to be in exile (*galut*) and in need of 'ingathering', he said. No attempt at rephrasing the term would alter their convictions. Hence, he welcomed the new definition, because it advocated the continued ingathering of the Jewish people in their historic homeland, without specifying that this applies to communities living in *galut* or communities which do not regard themselves as *galuyot*. This phrasing clearly implies the centrality of Israel in the life of the Jewish people, the unity of the people, the essence of its identity and the need for Jewish–Zionist education.[3]

Another American Jewish leader, Israel Goldstein, called the attention of the delegates to the term 'centrality of Israel' and all its theoretical and practical implications. He pointed out that it had recently become customary to define Zionism as the uniting of the Jewish people around their center, Israel. In his opinion, this phrase might sound more moderate than it actually was, being opposed to all the accepted conceptions of nationalism. 'Nationalism, as accepted today, is connected to geographical borders, and thus, Zionism, which postulates a Jewish nation with Israel as its center, will have to fight for its place as an enlightened movement.' Above all, in his view, Zionism must display and emphasize that same universal idealism which was manifest from the outset in the Return to Zion movement. As for the practical aspect, the Zionist definition must clarify that it was not enough for Israel to constitute the center and impart its spirit and influence to the Jews of the Diaspora. Jewish life in the Diaspora must accept this influence, and be directed towards Israel. Zionist education must be Hebrew and Israel-oriented, and immigration to Israel must be the most important precept of Zionism.[4]

On the basis of this key concept of the centrality of the State of Israel, the heads of the Zionist Organization attempted to restore the Zionist movement to its previous central status in the Diaspora. The Chairman of the Zionist Executive, Louis Pinkus, issued a somber warning, reflecting the anomalous situation of the Zionist movement. He cautioned that the lack of 'Zionist Jewish presence' in the Diaspora was a spreading phenomenon, and said that if it was not checked, 'a void would be created in Jewish life which would eventually lead to the rejection of the two fundamental principles – the continued existence of the Jewish people and the centrality of Israel in national life'.[5] This view was reiterated, less bluntly, by the President of the Zionist Organization, Nahum Goldmann. The Zionist movement, he said, must mend its ways and return to 'classic Zionism', if it wished to regain its image as a militant movement, uncompromisingly demanding the full realization of the Zionist program. A mass movement, he said, by its very nature, could not be a movement of realizers. The pioneers had always been few in number and as such, had enjoyed unique standing in the past and should be granted such standing in the present. However, this did not mean that the movement as a whole should cease to be extreme. It should 'gain entry to associations and organizations where we have a foothold and fight for full Zionist and Jewish education'.[6] In other words, it should revert to the classic historical attempt to 'conquer communities'. In practical terms, this policy led to the decision to permit general Jewish organizations with international standing to join the World Zionist Organization directly, and not through national federations.[7] This made possible the acceptance of the Reform and Conservative movements into the Zionist movement, with special status.

The Zionist movement had built a Jewish national society in Eretz Israel, won a sovereign state, and successfully absorbed mass immigration, but it had failed to attract pioneering immigration from the West. It now promoted the concept of the centrality of Israel as its last existential justification. As formulated by Zionist leaders, this concept was three-dimensional: politically, it meant that the Jews of the Diaspora supported the state, while the state, in its turn, offered succor to Jews in distress; socially and educationally it meant leadership of the Diaspora Jewish communities by means of Jewish-Zionist education; and it also operated on the personal-emotional level.

The 28th Zionist Congress, which convened in 1972, reaffirmed the centrality of the State of Israel in the life of the Jewish people in general and the life of each individual Jew.[8] The Zionist movement was seeking to capitalize on the post-1967 fervor and to make Israel the focus of Jewish life, determining the nature of Jewish identity. At that time, when the majority of Diaspora Jews regarded Israel with almost religious reverence, this appeared a valid assumption. However, it constituted an official admission that Zionism had no autonomous existence but was totally dependent on the state, and hence the constant references to the need to preserve the Jewish-Zionist character of the state. In fact, two decades after their debate with Ben-Gurion, the leaders of the Zionist movement were conceding that he had been right and that the state could not, in practice, replace the Zionist Organization, but was the bearer of the spirit of Zionism.

Arthur Hertzberg provided a lucid explanation of the concept of the centrality of the state. 'What is meant by this term,' he wrote, 'is that the building of Israel is the central and dominant purpose of all of world Jewry'. But 'the "centrality of Israel"', he explained, 'as understood in the free Diaspora, does not mean that the Diaspora regards itself as in the process of building itself into the state. It means, on the contrary, that the labors for the state are the prime preservative of the Diaspora'.

At the time he wrote, in 1976, Hertzberg considered such mutual support to be the ideal means of guaranteeing the survival of the Jewish people. 'I am a Zionist,' he declared, 'not because I may carry an Israeli passport, but because I am a citizen of world Jewry, *am Yisrael*. The task of Zionism in our time is to educate our children for that pervasive citizenship, and to create the modes of joint endeavor, with Israel as the center, which will create and retain that citizenship.'[9] However, this worldwide-Jewish citizenship, he said, could not be maintained, in the long run, solely through links with the political center. Diaspora Jews could only resist the growing attractions of assimilation if they cultivated their sense of exile. In 1979, Hertzberg clarified that, as far as he was concerned, exile was not only a political reality, but also a spiritual condition. He was not referring to the universal meaning of this term. His exile is specifically Jewish, and reflects the existential problem of the Jews in the free Western countries, who live not in two cultures, as Kaplan claimed, but in one secular Christian culture, which is drawing them in. To be in exile means to be in constant danger of cultural evanescence, and to have a sense of exile means to resist this assimilatory centripetal force at all times. As the external condition of political exile disappears, the awareness of inner spiritual exile is more sorely required. 'Only those Jews who know that they are in exile can live in it with some hope that their Jewishness will continue. Those who imagine that they have found a permanent home in the exile are destined soon to evaporate as Jews.'[10]

There is, of course, a direct connection between the sense of exile and awareness of the centrality of the State of Israel. As the one grows, the other becomes more profound, and vice versa. Here we observe one of the clearest manifestations of the concept of Jewish normalization. However, Herzberg's optimism with regard to Jewish survival in the Diaspora was to prove short-lived.

In the preface to the Hebrew edition of his articles on Judaism and Zionism, Hertzberg declared frankly that he was losing hope that the existence of the Jewish state would check the process of normalization of Jewish life in the United States, and persuade American Jews to acknowledge that they were a minority living in exile. He admitted that in the past he had thought that such self-awareness would stimulate the expansion and deepening of Jewish education, thus inspiring the minority to immigrate to Israel, and preserving the Judaism of the majority. Now this hope as well had faded almost completely, and been replaced by despair. 'Sometimes I feel like a traveller on a luxury ocean liner, which is gradually and imperceptibly sinking into the sea as the band plays.' The last hope of saving Diaspora Jews lay neither in 'negation of the Diaspora' according to Herzlian political Zionism, nor in Ahad ha-Am's concept of the spiritual center, nor in faith in the political center in Israel, but in constant, indefatigable effort on behalf of immigration. When immigration becomes the central issue in Jewish life, Israel will cease to be the 'vendor of the honors and of absolution and will become the supreme expression of the Jewish will to live'. Immigration as a communal activity 'must now take pride of place in the Jewish experience, and guarantee its future existence'. Because nothing can compare with the act of immigration in highlighting the distinctive nature of the Jewish people in their own eyes and those of the world, 'which will watch us with wonder and say: this is really a strange people, deliberately trying to break away from comfort and even luxury in the West for the sake of their spiritual authenticity'.[11]

The Reform rabbi and veteran Zionist David Polish arrived at similar conclusions though by a different route. Whereas Herzberg progressed from the importance of Israel for the survival of the Diaspora to the value of immigration for the individual spiritual salvation of Diaspora Jews, Polish started out from a different, even opposite viewpoint. Though both agreed that a sense of exile was essential to Jewish survival in the Diaspora, Polish did not perceive Israel as central to Jewish life[12] for two reasons: one stemmed from his religious convictions and the other from his outlook as a Diaspora Jew. The messianic, universal mission of the Jewish people could only be carried out, he declared, when the Jewish people took a positive view of both their types of existence: the territorial-political form in Israel and the international Jewish communities. In addition to religious faith, he proposed a kind of autonomistic diaspora ideology, according to which the advocacy of Israel's centrality conflicted with the Diaspora's desire for autonomy and might even undermine it. Polish argued that the imperialist or colonial system, based on a political-cultural metropolis with dependent protectorates, was defunct. He condemned Zionist colonialism of this type because he thought that the authoritarian, paternalistic spirit accompanying it could destroy the autonomous spirit of the Diaspora. The danger was that the State of Israel might remain a center without a periphery.

His objection to the concept of the centrality of the state stemmed from fear that world Jewry would identify with the state, to the point where this identification became a value in itself, replacing religion and its institutions, such as the synagogue. This concern deepened into anxiety in the wake of the Yom Kippur War. Polish feared that, if the Diaspora continued to be totally dependent on Israel, destruction of the state would mean the end of the Diaspora as well. He believed it essential to seek to establish equilibrium between the state and the Diaspora, which, as the recent war had demonstrated, were closely interconnected but not totally dependent on one another.

His view of the balanced dependence between State and Diaspora was rooted in a Zionist outlook made up of elements of Ahad ha-Am's spiritual Zionism, the moral mission of the Reform movement and Mordecai Kaplan's 'new Zionism'. He even reverted to the idea of setting up a consultative assembly of world Jewry.

In other words, like Kaplan, he emphasized the centrality of Zionism rather than of Israel. But whereas Kaplan annulled the Diaspora, for Polish, like Hertzberg, 'Galut is Galut'.[13]

Several years later, haunted, like Hertzberg, by fears that assimilation was on the increase, Polish abandoned the idea of the centrality of Zionism and accepted the centrality of the state, which he considered to be the central historic event in Jewish history. Israel's very existence, he declared, was an elixir of life for the Diaspora, giving meaning to national life and the incentive to live.[14]

The fact that Polish now saw the state as central to Jewish life indicates that he was as pessimistic as Hertzberg regarding the future of the Diaspora. He too believed that the golden age of Western Jewry had passed and that, increasing efforts should be invested in the struggle for Jewish education, and the encouragement of immigration to Israel. He did not actually negate the Diaspora, but he now doubted its ability to survive in the long term.

Ben Halpern, the consistent secular Zionist, had reached these same conclusions years before Hertzberg and Polish. Current events did not change his view that there could be no rational resolution of the constant tension between the Jews and their environment except 'evacuation' to Israel of those sections of the people unable or unwilling to continue living with the eternal Jewish problem.[15] For the majority, who would continue to wrestle with the question of Jewish existence, the United States was undoubtedly the most congenial and tolerant place in the world.[16] Since there is no rational solution to this existential problem, either in the national-secular sense, which had vanished after the Holocaust, or in the religious sense, which was relevant only to a portion of the people, the concept of the centrality of Israel had no real, everyday significance for Jews in the Diaspora, according to Halpern. Thus, all that remain to them are the myth and the ethos of *galut* – a state of perpetual collective solitude in the midst of non-Jewish faiths and cultures.

It is his view that 'Jewish isolation is neither a triviality nor a condition of individual maladjustment. Its roots are deeply embedded in history and extend to a communal experience of great age and wide variety'. This applies not only to the religious Jew whose faith sets him apart from his surroundings, but also to the secular Jew whose aloneness, according to his outlook, be it in exile or in Israel, is a product of this history and experience, 'and the myth-image by which the Jewish ethos has made their meaning concrete for successive generations has been the linked symbol-set of Exile and Redemption'.[17] These words, written in 1983, emphasized that in more than a generation his basic position had not changed. At its center stood the myth and the ethos of exile and redemption, which are the key to the self-understanding of the secular Jew beyond the recognition of his personal isolation and his identification with the Jewish milieu close to his residence in the exile. Furthermore, he pointed out, 'True self-understanding requires a full openness to the Jewish communal experience everywhere and at all times, and to its continued creative unfolding – most authentically in Israel and under the age-old protean imagery of Exile, wherever Jews still live with the consciousness of their unique historical ethos'.

Thus, there cannot be a cohesive national ethos in a diaspora which does not recognize its condition of *galut*, and because of the fundamental difference between the Diaspora and Israel, Ben Halpern stresses again that the sense of *galut*, exile, is the sole idea which can unite Israel and the Diaspora. It derives, not from the individual's isolation or failure to adapt, but from the historic essence of Jewish existence. Therefore, the myth of collective isolation is the basis for the ethos of unity and is common to both the Jews of Israel and the Jews of the Diaspora.[18] What therefore separates Israel and the Diaspora? Life as a total Jewish experience in all spheres: economic, social, political and cultural. All the problems of Jews living in Israel stem from the fact that they are Jewish, and consequently, this is the authentic total Jewish experience.

To judge by this theory, the significance of the State of Israel as a spiritual or political center of world Jewish life is not the core of his outlook. Israel, according to Halpern, is the epitome of authentic Jewish life, and cannot be emulated elsewhere because the Diaspora cannot maintain a Jewish totality. Israel is the historic alternative to the Jewish world which once existed in the Diaspora. And all that now remains is the historic collective myth of solitude and the essential ethos of *galut* linking the integrated Jewish existence in Israel to incomplete existence in the Diaspora. Israel is also the magnet attracting those few who refuse to reconcile themselves to the tensions of life in exile, and who thereby realize and maintain the historic unity of the Jewish people.

For Isadore Twersky as well, the centrality of Israel was not a key concept. For Twersky, a Zionist and an Orthodox rabbi, it was a positive fact, accepted unreservedly by the great majority of Diaspora Jews.[19] He was concerned, however, at the prospect that Israel might become merely a normal political and national center. He argued that the role of Zionism as a revivifying force in Jewish history, was to find the balance between the religious and spiritual significance of Judaism and its territorial national essence. Twersky yearned for the renewal of the dialectical tension between these two distinctive forces in Jewish history. And, in so doing, he warned that national political force should not be allowed to become the *ersatz* for the spirit of Judaism. The historical function of this force is to serve as an incentive, precluding excessive spirituality and, at the same time, guarding against spiritual atrophy. The risk could be averted, he thought, if the Jews perceived Zionism as an integral part of Judaism, and understood that its problems as a movement of construction and renewal were also the problems of Judaism. The central problem was to ensure the overall revival of Judaism in a spirit of appreciation of the Jewish heritage. Twersky did not delude himself as to the anticipated dimensions of the spiritual renaissance among the Jews of the Diaspora, aware that it will be confined to '*She'erit ha-peletah*' (a last remnant). In Israel, on the other hand, it could become a general movement. On this point, the difference between state and Diaspora is connected to political normality, which in itself, cannot guarantee the survival of Judaism, but facilitates the rebuilding of Jewish society. It is in this way that Zionism should be understood, and the centrality of the state valued.

Paradoxically, one discerns a certain similarity between Halpern and Twersky in their grasp of the international Jewish condition and their evaluation of the role of the state in this context. Both rejected the idea of the normalization of Jewish existence. Twersky's outlook derived from his religious convictions, and Halpern's from his historical consciousness. Both believed that the sole hope for the revival of authentic Jewish life lay in Israel. Again, both agreed that Jewish life with original content could exist in the Diaspora only among the select few. Thus, for both men the importance of Israel for the Diaspora lies not in its centrality, which is a kind of corrective, enabling the continuation of Jewish life, but in the overall Jewish alternative it represents.

Common to all four representatives of the traditional currents of American Zionist thought: Hertzberg, Polish, Twersky and Halpern, is an alternative, relative and dynamic approach. All four expressed doubts as to the survival of a creative and self-renewing Jewish entity in the free diasporas. None of them believed that western Jewry would disappear completely, but all agreed that under prevailing conditions, it was doomed to shrink. They did not believe that Israel's value lay in its role as the center of Jewish life, since only those who believed in the eternity of that unique Jewish world experience could argue that the center was of great spiritual, moral or political significance. For those who doubted that the Diaspora would endure in perpetuity, Eretz Israel and immigration, even of limited scope, were the alternative to a shrinking Diaspora.

The Zionist skepticism of American Jewish thinkers, which ran contrary to the 'Zionization' process within the Jewish public, was shared by some of their counterparts in Israel. This mood of skepticism, which generated not defeatism but a search for new meaning for traditional views, was lucidly expressed in an interview given by Gershom Scholem three years after the Six Day War.[20] Asked whether he considered Zionism to be the solution to the Jewish question, he said: 'In my writing you will not find a word suggesting that Zionism is a "solution" to what is called "the Jewish question".' It is not a solution but a form of action. 'When you begin to move forward you choose one direction and not others, and pay the price for your decision and action. This is the significance of action in history.' He considered Zionism to be 'a noble attempt to tackle the Jewish problem. One can do no more than tackle a problem on the historical plane. The Zionists were not afraid to take historical responsibility upon themselves, and therein lies their greatness'.

Scholem's claim that there is no solution to the 'Jewish problem', even through Zionism, does not mean that he denies the existence of a Zionist goal, which is, first and foremost, to stem those trends to normalization which intensified in Israeli society after the Six Day War. Normalization, by its very nature, contains within it 'Canaanite' elements, which are anti-Zionist and anti-Jewish in character.

In Scholem's view, on the other hand, 'the State of Israel is of value only because of Jewish continuity'. To sever this historical continuity could diminish the universal significance of the state for Jews everywhere. In contrast to the leaders of the Zionist Organization, he held that it would be a mistake to assign Israel the task of reviving the sense of exile of the Diaspora. 'This task cannot be carried out by a state which has renounced religious and metaphysical components, since these components alone could endow it with influence....'[21] In other words, Scholem, like Halpern, thought that it was the ethos of *galut* and redemption that had preserved the Jewish people. But as a believer, in his own way, Scholem considered this ethos to be a manifestation of religious and metaphysical faith, while Halpern saw it as a manifestation of overall cultural isolation.

Thus, Scholem was more pessimistic than Halpern as to the prospects for Jewish survival, since Halpern believed that Jewish existence was being preserved thanks to the objective isolation which was imposed on Jews, while for Scholem, the sole ray of hope was belief in redemption. However, this hope was absent from both the Diaspora and Israel. It was the misfortune of the Diaspora, he wrote, that those living there 'deny its realities' while large parts of the Jewish people, living in the West 'find countless excuses for... eradicating the consciousness of exile'.

Something even graver had happened to the self-realizing Zionist movement. 'The flower of our country's builders, perhaps inadvertently, have emptied the concept of galut of the germ of redemption which was contained within it.' This could be explained, and perhaps even justified, against the historical background, in light of pressing needs, the struggle for livelihood, for security and for physical survival, but yet, 'together with the bonds of exile, they have also cast off the promise of redemption, and thereby transferred the problem of *galut* in different, but no less threatening guise, to the fields of the homeland', creating in Israel itself a fundamental imbalance.[22]

According to this viewpoint, the idea of Israel as the center of Jewish life is of scant importance, and central importance is attributed to the yearning for redemption, since this yearning alone can make Diaspora Jews aware of their true condition and restore the State of Israel to its historic-religious heritage. Scholem was by no means convinced that this was, in fact, what would happen. The reform of Diaspora Jews, he wrote, depended 'neither on us nor on our historical logic but on the air they breathe'. Yet his skepticism does not lead him to despair. In referring to Israel, where he discerns an imbalance between revolution and tradition, he writes that the situation there 'has not yet been put right'. And rectification in Israel, unlike the Diaspora, depends not on the milieu but on the Jews themselves. Hence, the very possibility of independent activity within history holds out hope for the creation of a society in which the religious spirit prevails, and where self-awareness will consist of recognition of its ideal anomalous essence.

Ephraim Urbach also favored anomaly, considering it to be the distinctive feature and power of the Jewish people among other nations, of the Zionist movement within the Jewish people and of the State of Israel among other nations. But, in contrast to Scholem, he did not perceive the state as a metaphysical entity or Zionism as a messianic movement. It was enough for him that the establishment of the state had been the joint effort of various diverse sectors of the Jewish people.[23] For Urbach, the centrality of Israel was an axiom, but, unlike Ahad ha-Am, he conceived this centrality in the political rather than the spiritual sense. The history of relations between Eretz Israel and the Diaspora demonstrates that it was due to the loss of sovereignty and independence in their own country that Eretz Israel ceased to be the center for Jews. 'Without these elements, all attempts are doomed to failure and all historical conceptions regarding the center and the periphery are idle speculations.' From the days of the Tannaim (the Sages of the Talmud), through Samson Raphael Hirsch to the present time, it has been repeatedly stated that spiritual centers can exist outside Eretz Israel as well. Examination of the historical facts show that 'even in periods in which the centrality of Eretz Israel was undisputed, the centrality was expressed through something which could not exist in the Diaspora – namely sovereignty, the independence of the Jewish people in one place alone, Eretz Israel'. The historical lesson, according to Urbach, is that 'objective factors will determine whether Israel is to become a center and these are: political independence and sovereign institutions'. Links with such a center become a religious obligation rather than a question of choice. For example, in ancient times the Shekel was donated to the Temple as a national duty, and not through some appeal for funds. Herzl had received the idea of the Zionist Shekel but his idea had been cast aside and become a marginal issue, replaced by the fund-raising campaign, which was a very different thing.

Responding to criticism, Urbach clarified that he had no intention of belittling Israel. 'Its centrality, I say, does not depend on its quality and image. But they can, of course, add validity and significance to that centrality, which is objective and given. It did not drop manna-like from Heaven nor was it given on a silver platter. It is the fruit of a great and supreme effort which entailed great sacrifice'. Unlike Scholem, who considered the essential heroic effort to run contrary to the Zionist concept of redemption, Urbach appreciated its intrinsic value. At the same time, unlike pro-Zionists in the Diaspora, who were also content to regard Israel as a political center, Urbach did not believe that Israeli centrality could guarantee the lasting existence of the Diaspora. At the opening session of the 28th Zionist Congress in 1978, he declared that 'those who present the existence of the Diaspora not as the outcome of fleeting circumstances, but as stemming, as it were, from the Jewish national character, and therefore equal in value to the center in Eretz Israel, are denying not only political Zionism but also the conception of *galut* and nation in the course of Jewish history'.[24] For Urbach, Zionism was grounded on immigration, and he saw the collective effort to encourage it and absorb it as the main aim of national activity in the Diaspora. Precisely because of his desire to transform Israel into a place to which Jews would not only turn but also immigrate, he was obliged to add to the concept of the political center a dimension without which immigration could not take place – namely the social image of the state. But here again, he was referring to social quality rather than to metaphysical essence.[25]

This attempt to prove that the political dimension of Zionism was sufficient in itself to transform Israel into the center of Jewish national life was taken even further by Jacob Katz. Where Urbach had expressed reservations and linked the image of the Jewish state, as regards social values, to the essence of Zionist ideology, Katz distinguished between them. From his study of history, Katz concluded that the two utopias which Zionism had envisioned – based on romantic-religious and secular-modern ideals – had not been achieved. Religious Zionism had not succeeded in consolidating a traditional Jewish society in Israel, safe from the threat of cultural assimilation. Secular Zionism had not achieved its goal of building a progressive modern society, free of the anomalies which had characterized the Jewish people, so it claimed, in the course of its long exile. Katz did not deny the historical value of the Zionist utopia. What attracted the first waves of immigration to Eretz Israel, he said, was not the Jewish plight, but the Zionist utopian vision. All in all, 'the utopistic expectations linked to the Zionist immigrations and the establishment of Israel were not fulfilled. What developed was a kind of communal Jewish destiny with validity extending above and beyond the decisions of individuals or of groups'.[26] His conclusions, based on a study of Jewish history, led him to formulate two definitions of the essence of Zionism after statehood and the Six Day War. A Zionist, he declared, was one who accepted the view that the existence and survival of Israel are essential to the survival of the Jewish people. Any attempt to introduce into the Zionist ideal extraneous ideals or ideologies, such as religious beliefs, socialist ideologies or liberal convictions, is problematic. Katz does not deny that these ideas have helped Zionism in the past in the process of implementation and might do so in the future. But he takes issue with the view that they are an integral part of the Zionist idea, which is essentially political in nature. Hence, the great triumph of Zionism was the establishment of the state. Now the state is the sole entity able to preserve the unity of the Jewish people, and this is its historical role and national contribution. One should not seek more than this, and those who do so in the name of some ideology, could arrive at denial of Zionism, and renunciation of Judaism.[27]

This trend to identify Zionism exclusively with Jewish sovereignty finds its most extreme expression in Yeshayahu Leibowitz, whose views have remained unchanged for decades. 'I define Zionism thus: we were weary of the rule of gentiles over the Jewish people...it is possible that gentile rule is very good today...but some Jews are tired of being ruled by *goyim*, and this is the essence of Zionism'.[28]

The views of religious Zionist thinkers on the essential link between Zionism and Jewish and universal values vary widely. Gershom Scholem was 'convinced that behind its secular front, Zionism contains potential religious content, and that this religious potential is stronger than the present actual content, which finds expression in the "religious Zionism" of political parties'.[29] Urbach confined his discussion to the importance of the social-value dimension in Zionism. For Katz, the various extraneous ideologies play a merely auxiliary role, while Leibowitz draws a sharp distinction between Zionism and value systems of any kind. According to the extreme viewpoint – the state is not central to Jewish life, either because it has no metaphysical message, according to Scholem, or because this is in no way its task, as Leibowitz believes. Urbach and Katz consider that centrality stems from the political sovereignty acknowledged by the Jews of the world.

This view was not shared by secular thinkers, who were united in the awareness that, in respect to the Zionist outlook, political sovereignty in Israel was not enough. Yehoshua Arieli, who took part in the above-mentioned debate with Urbach and Katz, agreed with them that the centrality of the state among Jews stemmed from its sovereignty. However, the sovereign dimension did not fully reflect the essence of the state. Jewish society in Israel, he asserted, by its very nature, had a greater interest in Diaspora Jewry than the Diaspora had in Israel, because of the particularist nature of national existence in Israel. Moreover, an integral part of the essence of Israeli sovereignty is acknowledgment of responsibility for the fate of Diaspora Jewry, and this was the manifestation of the abnormal character of Jewish society in Israel, namely its mission *vis à vis* the Jews of the Diaspora. Israel's centrality also derives from the nature of Jewish life in the Diaspora, which lacks the necessary power to preserve its integrity without the State of Israel. Because of the principle of comprehensive responsibility, Arieli stressed the existence of interdependence of all sectors of the Jewish people, and did not deny the right of all diasporas to autonomous status. It was in the interest of the state, he declared, to promote the emergence of internal forces in Jewish communities in order to strengthen them. As long as the Diaspora remained Jewish, it would support the state, he said. Ten years later, in the face of the growing controversy between religious and secular factors on the character of the State of Israel, Arieli cautioned any attempt to transform Israel into a religious state, which would entail renunciation of the secular and pluralistic aspects of Jewish society, and would spell the end of Zionism. Since the state would no longer be a cohesive, rallying force for the Jews of the Diaspora.[30]

Somewhere between the concepts of the sovereign center and the Zionist mission, Nathan Rotenstreich formulated his theory of the preferential status. The term 'centrality of Israel', which was endorsed by the Zionist movement in 1968 and 1972 had, he said, become a tired cliché. This was mainly because of various crises and difficulties, the ideal or idyllic type of Jew envisaged by Ahad ha-Am's utopian imagination, had not come into being.

In place of centrality in the moral-cultural sense, Rotenstreich preferred the term 'priority, preferential status, Israel as primate'. This meant, in practical terms, that 'if there is a conflict of interests between the Diaspora and the State, the State's interest takes preference.... There is a difference between helping one's brethren in times of trouble and the injunction to redeem captives...and support for the struggle for the historic-collective place of the Jewish people.'[31] It should be recalled that this was written in the wake of the Yom Kippur War, and in the face of the increasing pressure among US Jewry to extend aid to their brethren in Israel in their plight. It was for this reason that Rotenstreich emphasized that this was no ordinary plight, but a national problem brought about by the conscious collective decision of the Jewish people to restore their national sovereignty. In other words, he sees at the center of the stage not the spiritual-qualitative center, but the collective national effort. And Israel was not merely *primus inter pares*, but decisively prior in status, 'because it is thanks to this sovereignty that the Jewish people has achieved its standing in world history, with all this implies'. It should be noted that the Israeli–American dialogue of 1977 ('the contemporary significance of Zionism – definitions and new directions'), adopted Rotenstreich's definition of Israel's preferential status. One of the resolutions passed by that body stated that 'Zionism affirms the role of Israel as the homeland of the Jewish people and as occupying a special and primary role in the life of that people everywhere, while acknowledging the existence of other valid and ongoing centers of Jewish creativity'.[32]

The status which Rotenstreich accorded the state brought him back, paradoxically enough, to the idea of the spiritual center. Ten years later, in a discussion of the negation of the Diaspora, he wrote: 'We note that the very existence of the state does not serve as a motive for secession from the Diaspora. In a certain sense, this extistence does not take the form of a spiritual center, but it replaces a spiritual center – that is to say, maintains Jewish inertia'.[33] There is a twofold paradox inherent in this statement: the first relates to the historic fate of the Zionist movement, whose ideology, according to Rotenstreich, 'did not foresee it. One could almost say, with all the differences entailed, that just as it did not predict the Holocaust, it did not foresee the problems of the prosperous Jewish communities'. The second paradox stems from Rotenstreich's own view of the preferential status of the state, which, as it were, substitutes for centrality. Any attitude which grants it national priority over other considerations, in the given condition, recognizes it as a spiritual center, a center to which the Jews of the Diaspora are linked by emotional, political, charitable, religious and cultural ties. But despite these ties, Jewish national life is not cast in uniform national molds.

The interpretation given here to the term 'substitute for a spiritual center' leads to Rotenstreich's next conclusion, namely that in light of the existence of affluent Jewry and the absence of the possibility of maintaining a 'spiritual center', national sovereignty cannot suffice, as Urbach and Katz believed, but should be supplemented by the abnormal essence of Jewish life. He held that the abnormality derived from the standing which the state had chosen for itself. This was because 'the State of Israel as a Jewish state, that is to say, as a state which is not detached from the Jewish people, refutes normalization in the simple or unequivocal meaning of the term. The 'abnormal normality' of the Jews maintains this link between Israel and the Jewish people'.[34] This 'abnormal normality', which incidentally, is not far removed from the term 'Jewish normalization', which we have used throughout this book, is not only an expression of a specific existential condition, but also has significance in terms of social values. For example, Rotenstreich regarded the materialistic drive of Israeli society, its abandonment of the principle of Jewish labor, as a dangerous manifestation of normalization. This was because the loss of moral distinctiveness would not only distort the image of society, but also undermine the standing of the state among Diaspora Jews.[35]

Hence, Rotenstreich sought to revive the pioneering spirit of the past, which had inspired the youth movements of the socialist labor movement, since he saw it as 'one of the factors able to influence and guide in our times'.[36] This new pioneering elite would be motivated not by hatred leading to awakening of will, but by the historical vision of the Jewish people, by awareness of the need to maintain the collective survival of the Jews, and the need to maintain reciprocal ties between the individual and the public domains of the Jewish people. This appeal for the revival of the pioneering spirit contained a partial historical truth. On the one hand, this spirit was nurtured more by the national-social utopia, but had developed in a milieu of distress and suffering, from which it drew the emotional drive for action and the readiness for sacrifice. This background no longer exists in the Western countries, and thus, what is required is a pioneering elite motivated by historical awareness and a sense of historical mission. Rotenstreich was attempting to transform the pioneering activism of the few into the central deed of the Jewish people, contributing to the moral rehabilitation of Israeli society and the national strengthening of the Diaspora. Therein, he thought, lay the possibility of preserving Zionism as an ideological movement and not merely a remnant of the past

Shlomo Avineri and Eliezer Schweid, disciples of Jacob Katz and Nathan Rotenstreich, who grew up with the state, continued the line of thought of their mentors. According to Avineri, the centrality of Israel in Jewish life derived, primarily, from the fact that it fulfils the function of religion and of the Jewish community in giving public expression to collective Jewish identity. Consequently, 'today, in the wake of the process of modernization and secularization, it is the normative expression of the preservation of this collective survival of the Jewish people'. Avineri saw 'the crux of the significance of the Zionist revolution, historically speaking, in the renewal of a Jewish public domain in place of the community and its religious institutions'.[37]

This definition of the essence of the central status of the state, he asserted, establishes the basic distinction between sovereignty and life in the Diaspora. Referring to the question of 'negation of the Diaspora'[38], Avineri said that if this negation meant that no kind of Jewish life could exist outside the borders of the state, it was unacceptable. But there was a fundamental difference between the Diaspora and Israel on the level of values relating to Jewish life. Whereas life in the Diaspora is a fact which will undoubtedly endure, life in Israel, despite its insecurity, is a value. The existence or non-existence of an organized Jewish community in any place in the world, even the United States, is not decisive for the contribution of Judaism. The important thing is that the Jews in those places be permitted to live as free individuals. This was not true of Israel. What matters in this case is the existence of the corporate body, and not the welfare of the individual. If, Heaven forbid, something terrible happened to Israel, the effect of the catastrophe on the Jews of the Diaspora would be far-reaching, not only because of the fate of the Jews living there, but because of the meaning of the existence of Israel for Diaspora Jewry.

Eight years later, in the wake of the Pollard affair and the initial response of Jewish leaders, Avineri added to his objective definition of the *galut*, a subjective interpretation. He said that *galut*, as a symptom of insecurity, apprehension and apologetics is part of the Jewish soul.[39]

The conclusion of Israel's objective status in Jewish life, as Avineri saw it, is the need for the moral essence and values of the state. The choice is between Israel as a just and enlightened society, evoking pride in the hearts of Diaspora Jews, and Israel deteriorating into a society in which it is hard to take pride. This is a question which should concern not only the Jews of Israel, but Jews throughout the world. Avineri, unlike Rotenstreich, does not abandon the idea of the spiritual center as envisaged by Ahad ha-Am, and casts responsibility for its construction on Israeli society. Only they can transform Israel into the central value in the lives of Jews. At this point, paradoxically enough, he concludes that Israel can become the normative center for Diaspora Jews only if its life differs from theirs. 'Israel will continue to be the focus for normative identification for the Jews of the world only if it is fundamentally different from world Jewry. If Israel is only a mirror of what is occurring among world Jewry, if it is only yet another western consumer society', then the Western Jew who perceives therein only a facsimile of his own life will be unable to identify with it.[40]

Avineri took Urbach's theories to extremes. As regards patterns of thinking, if not content, his approach resembles that of Gershom Scholem. Both advocated radical change in Jewish life, and both pinned on this change and its distinctiveness the centrality of Israel. Scholem, however, spoke of the metaphysical-religious essence of the state, while Avineri warned against the loss of the original social values of Zionism.

Eliezer Schweid went even further than Avineri in distinguishing between the significance of life in Israel and the essence of Jewish Diaspora life in Western society. He wanted to adapt the old idea of 'negation of the Diaspora' to the new reality and to transform it again into the central ideal of Zionism, fashioning an alternative way of life to that of the Diaspora. As he saw it, negation of the Diaspora is an ideology aimed at consolidating a new Jewish morality as a value in itself,[41] unconnected to and unconditional on a specific historical situation. With threefold foundations: the value of national force, namely rule over power factors of various types and readiness to use them for the defence of Jewish life; national independence, signifying the aspiration of Jews to undertake responsibility for their survival as a nation; national distinctiveness, aimed at bestowing on the Jewish people a comprehensive framework within which their original creation can be maintained and developed without imitation and self-effacement and with proper balance between the particularist and the universal. Today, those who do not accept these three positive values of Zionism can claim, with a large degree of justice, that there is no *galut* in the free world. On the other hand, 'those who accept the values of Zionist morality will not doubt the claim that the Zionist analysis of the condition of the Jewish people in the Diaspora is still valid'. In other words, the Golah has no political independence. The political power of the Jews is worthless when there is a discrepancy between Jewish interests and the interests of the countries where they live. The Jews do not control their own fate, and have no chance of maintaining their original culture in the long run; the free Diasporas cannot become the 'new Babylon'. The conclusion is, therefore, inevitable:

> In the present-day galut as well, Jewish life is parasitic. As a people, insofar as the Jewish people is still acknowledged to have its own unique framework, they are nurtured by the creativity of others, lean on the strength of others, need them to the point of self-abnegation, and exploit their endeavours. This is a vulnerable way of life. Any strong social upheaval will expose the tensions of competition and hostility between the Jews and their surroundings and uncover their weakness and inability to defend themselves.

It is worth noting that for Schweid, in the historical sense and in the present context as well, negation of the Diaspora is not negation of the Jews living in the Diaspora.

> On the contrary, those who advocate negating the Diaspora as negation of the condition of the Jewish people can also appreciate the great and vital potential inherent in the people. They also know that the ingathering of the Jewish people into their country is not a one-time event, but a historical process. In order for this process to proceed, it is not enough to step up immigration. What is required is as strong an infrastructure as possible, in other words, we must strengthen Jewish association in the Diaspora and particularly Jewish education.[42]

Moreover, as long as the majority of the Jewish people live outside their homeland, the validity of the Diaspora also affects collective Jewish life in Israel. This finds reflection in the weakness of the state in the international arena, and in 'internal assimilation' in the cultural sense, which is occurring within Israeli society. No part of the Jewish people can liberate itself from *galut* through emancipation or auto-emancipation. Until the vision of the ingathering of most of the exiles is realized, the entire Jewish people, in varying degrees, is in *galut*.[43] The question under debate is evaluation of the prospects for the continued existence of the Jewish people in the Diaspora and the selection of the means and methods of bolstering it. The ability and the scope are limited, but it is important to do the little that can be done.

This is not to say that Schweid believes in a kind of Ahad ha-Am-like 'spiritual center'. This is because of the basic assumption that culture cannot be imported. 'Culture is, primarily, an everyday lifestyle, patterns of behaviour, the symbols and values shaping them and lending them meaning, and anything that man creates in his spheres of action. In all these respects, the Jews of the Diaspora can only live within the context of the national cultures around them.'

Both Rotenstreich and Schweid, therefore, hold that a spiritual center had some prospect as long as authentic Jewish life existed in the Diaspora, as in Eastern Europe. The center is a factor aiding the existence of a national culture, but it does not create it. This dissociation from the idea of a spiritual center does not imply approval of the normalization trend in Israel–Diaspora relations. The reverse is true. The conclusion of this analysis is very clear. Israel can be a factor stemming the tide of assimilation and bolstering Jewish identity only if the base of its relations with the Diaspora is the Zionist goal, demanding implementation. If the basis is only a static reality, a Diaspora seeking to institutionalize itself on a permanent basis and a state content with its role within the Jewish people, there will commence a process of estrangement between the Jews of Israel and of the Diaspora. 'This will be inevitable because, even as regards identification, the focus of interest will not be the same. Even if the Diaspora endures for several more generations, it will develop separate identity from that of Israel.'[44]

At the same time, intensely aware of the danger threatening the Jewish people, Schweid, in the fortieth year of statehood, clutched at the conviction that systematic and constant educational efforts, shared by Israel and the Diaspora, and a constructive dialogue between all the ideological currents in Judaism, could gradually create a true spiritual center in Israel, reflecting the aspirations of Jews for independence and unity.[45] Thus, Schweid is the most emphatic opponent of the 'distinctive normalization' approach, based on the unique ties between the Israeli center and the Jews of the world. He is an ardent advocate of 'Jewish normalization' based on non-acceptance of the perpetual existence of the Diaspora. Here, like Rotenstreich and Avineri, he sees the continuation of Zionism as conditional on the striving to realize Jewish normalization in the original social sense, in the spirit of the historical endeavour of the pioneering labor movement.[46]

The negation of Diaspora life and the building of a society with a normal national moral foundation 'are interconnected and face the Jewish people, and in particular the Zionist movement, with an arduous task, bordering on the utopian', namely to shape a society founded not on Western normalization but on a special Jewish-Zionist formula, combining the Jewish cultural heritage and the social vision of the Zionist labor movement.

The views of those who believed that Zionism could not survive without social utopia were summarized by the historian Shmuel Ettinger, who claimed that precisely because Zionism as a national movement with collectivist aims operates in the present in an individualistic society, it cannot continue to exist without proposing an overall ideological moral approach, which will restore to public awareness the value of labor, and the importance of quality for individual and society.[47]

In conclusion, in the attempt to revive the assumptions of classic Zionism in the new situation following the Six Day War, politicians and intellectuals were divided. The idea of the centrality of Israel, adopted by the Zionist Organization, was grasped by politicians as a unique and revolutionary idea and as a means of reviving the political and cultural hegemony of Zionism in the Diaspora. But this idea, while revolutionary, was also open to compromise. It was entirely based on acknowledgment of the disappearance of exile and the eternity of the Diaspora, since the status of the center is dependent on its periphery.

The intellectuals, on the other hand, did not take a simple view of matters. For them, the idea of the center in the political and cultural sense could not suffice to maintain the Jewish–international entity. They extended and deepened the concept of *galut*. Theirs was a *galut* which was no longer a *golah*, and its significance was even greater because of the disappearance of the Jewish plight. It was *galut* because the welfare of the individual was in conflict with the integrity of the group; because the Jewish collective will and expression were waning there; because of the lack of authentic Jewish culture and the total dependence on the surrounding society. And they even extended the concept to cover society in Israel, mainly because it had abandoned the Zionist social utopia.

There was no connection between this *galut*, which was socio-historical and particularist, and *galut* as a universal existential or even metaphysical religious concept. Its focal point was not the alienation of man in society nor the exile of the Divine presence, but the special condition of the Jewish people as an objective fact and the threat of disappearance because of its subjective shortsightedness. Thus, they negated the Diaspora with varying degrees of intensity, but out of the same concern.

Paradoxically, the overall negation of *galut* relating to the Diaspora and to Israel was more valid *vis à vis* Jewish unity than the idea of the state as center. It reinforces national self-awareness, strengthens the inner cohesion of the Jewish communities in the Diaspora, unites Israel and the Diaspora in a shared yearning, and rouses the few activist forces to rebel against the *galut* experience. Thus, there is a kind of reconciliation between this negation of the Diaspora and the desire to revive autonomous Jewish community life there, to extend and intensify Jewish education, to struggle against discrimination, etc. And the supreme expression of this effort was immigration to Israel. Thus it emerged that in the historical situation in which the *golah* disappeared as a Jewish phenomenon, negation of the Diaspora became the consciousness maintaining the *tefutzah*. It became the central concept in Jewish life, and placed Israel at the heart of Jewish life.

Part IV
Return to the Tangle of Normalization
1982–90

11 Renewed Search for Identity

INTRODUCTION

This last section, dealing with the 1980s, has no clear chronological boundaries. It commences not with historical events, but with trends which emerged in the late seventies and early eighties, and which are not easily definable because of their ambiguity and because they are still in the embryonic stage. Thus, this concluding section also marks the opening of a new era in the annals of Jewish public thought in the United States and in Israel.

In the absence of such momentous historical events as the Holocaust, the establishment of Israel and the Six Day War, the limits of the new era are set by public developments which may prove in the future to have been of historic significance. I am referring to the Israeli political upheaval of 1977, which encouraged the neo-conservative mood within the American Jewish community; the 1982 Lebanon War which aroused renewed criticism of Israel's Middle Eastern policies by radical liberal Jewish circles; the controversy on the right of Jewish emigrés from the Soviet Union to choose their destinations; the storm which erupted in 1985 around President Reagan's visit to Bitburg, and the protracted campaign of protest against the election of Kurt Waldheim as Austrian Chancellor; the Pollard affair; and finally, the storm of protest against the proposal to change the definition of 'Who is a Jew' in the Israeli Law of Return.

The motives behind the public debate on all these issues are not related solely to the events as such, but should be assessed against the background of constantly evolving ideological and emotional factors originating in previous eras. On the national plane, the debate can be defined as a struggle between trends promoting national unity and those seeking deliberately or inadvertently to undermine it. These conflicting trends are inherent in the issues under discussion: such as the autonomous status of Diaspora Jews in relation to Israel; the right to criticize Israel's official policies; the question of 'Who is a Jew', etc. All in all, the present era is marked by uncertainty and even confusion. In this respect, it is reminiscent of the first period surveyed in this book, the forties and early fifties.

GENERAL NORMALIZATION: POST-CANAANITE LIBERALISM

The term 'post-Canaanite liberalism', used to define the various standpoints in the 1980s which advocate 'general normalization' of Jewish existence, contains within it both continuity and change. On the one hand, the Canaanite ideology of the forties and fifties, as a romantic-cultural myth and a political utopia linked to the Semitic world, has run its course. On the other, the liberal element, which perceives citizenship and nationality in American terms, and was a prominent component of Canaanite philosophy after statehood, has endured. We are now witnessing a new phenomenon in Jewish public thought, an attempt to define nationhood not on the basis of the combination of people and religion, as the Zionists believed, and not in terms of the Semitic cultural heritage, as the early Canaanites believed, but on a territorial-political basis, as in the western countries. In this respect, this approach is influenced directly and obliquely by the views of Hillel Kook, as expressed forty years previously. Hence, it should be stressed, there is a fundamental difference between post-Canaanite liberalism and traditional Zionist liberalism. Proponents of the liberal outlook within the Zionist movement, and even those who supported the socialist ideology, were not ready to forgo the identity between the state and Jewish nationality. Even Marxists, like ha-Shomer ha-Tzair, who favored a bi-national state, did not substitute territorial-political nationality for historical-ethnic nationality.

The transition from liberal *Canaanism* to Canaanite *liberalism* is particularly striking in the case of Boaz Evron. After the Six Day War, Evron abandoned the Canaanite philosophy propounded by Yonathan Ratosh.[1] The shock of the 1967 events brought it home to him that the rules of normalization did not yet totally apply to Jewish existence. He realized that 'the Jewish plight', to which Zionism had drawn attention, still existed. And, he said, he now understood that the formal definition of nationality on the basis of territory and language was not appropriate to the Jewish people in light of the spontaneous emotional reaction of the Jewish masses throughout the world, when the State of Israel was in danger. Consequently, he concluded that there was no point in 'denying the fact of the existence of the Jewish people'; but, he added, paradoxically, once this people had established their state, 'at that same moment the principle of political territorial-linguistic organization began to operate'. In other words, Evron's 'reconciliation' with Zionism, to the point where he was ready to identify with it as long as the state was in danger, was merely temporary. He was also convinced that in the Israeli case, the political principle would eventually and inevitably triumph over the ethnic-religious principle, since the triumph of this principle was essential for the existence of the state as a normal political entity in the Western liberal style.[2]

For Evron, messianic Zionism, which had come to the fore in Israel since the Six Day War, was undermining Israel's moral foundations. It was a kind of 'Shabbateanism', whose consequences, once expectations were belied, could be no less ruinous than those of the original Shabbatean movement. In order to preserve the spirit of Judaism, it was necessary to create separation between the state and the Jews outside its borders, or, as he phrased it, 'to refute the myth of "one people" in order to ensure Jewish continuity and sanity'.[3] Evron's territorial normalization is based to some extent on Canaanism, but with some modifications. He now acknowledges Judaism not only as a religious denomination, as Ratosh defined it, but also as an established cultural civilization, creative in various languages.

'There is no possibility of distinguishing ancient Hebraism from the vast and rich reservoirs of Jewish culture. One cannot leap over two and a half millennia and cast them aside; awareness of Hebrew nationhood will always be associated with Judaism'.[4] Evron was relinquishing the Zionist nationalist-unitarian approach in favor of a Jewish cultural unitarian outlook. In this he was undoubtedly influenced, directly or not, by the secular Jewish outlook of the pre-war Bund. He recognized the justice of the claim that a Jewish national entity had developed in Eastern Europe. At the same time, and for this very reason, the Jews of the world should not be considered as constituting one people, since the development of Jewish communal collective depended on the milieu. According to this Bundist-Hebrew viewpoint, just as a Yiddish national entity had evolved in Eastern Europe, a Hebrew nation had come into being in Israel. The connection between them and the other Jewish communities which are unable and even unwilling to be included within a single national definition, is culturally based. In other words, even in Evron's radical normalistic approach, the anomalous element of Jewish life is now lacking. The cultural connection between people of different nationality and Jewish origin, according to Evron, is not only religious, as is the case with Catholics or Muslims. He regards culture primarily as a secular phenomenon. How else can one understand the connection he postulates between Eastern-European secular Yiddish culture and the Hebrew culture which emerged in Eretz Israel, and exists in the State of Israel.

In conclusion, there are two levels to the territorial-Hebrew essence, as Evron sees it. One is political, and stripped of any Jewish or Zionist significance, not only because of Evron's views on Judaism and his objections to Zionism, but also for universal-existential reasons: 'The raison d'etre of the state is its existence, just as in the case of a private individual'.[5] The second level is spiritual, based on the belief that the Hebrew culture of most Israelis is linked to the historical dimensions of Jewish culture, and hence to those people of Jewish origin who are citizens of other countries whose links are the same.

Professor Joseph Agassi's national liberal views are close to Evron's Hebrew nationalist outlook. In his book *Bein Dat u-Leom: li-Krat Zehut Leumit Yisraelit* (Between Religion and Nationality: Towards an Israeli National Identity),[6] he makes a theoretical contribution to clarifying the differences between the Jewish-Israeli and Diaspora-Jewish entities, and is clearer and more explicit than Evron. Whereas Evron perceives the liberal state in American terms, as an institution consolidating a nation, Agassi, under the influence of his mentor Karl Popper, and his friend Hillel Kook, recognizes the liberal nation as an entity in itself, and as an ideological concept and social institution which consolidates individuals into a group with collective identity.[7] The nation, as he sees it, is a social territorial phenomenon, and the liberal nation is pluralistic as well. The Jews of Israel belong to the pluralistic Israeli nation, while the Jews of the world are affiliated to the nations in whose territories they live, on condition that these are liberally spirited, i.e. do not consider the Jews to be an alien element.

So far there are almost no differences between the two, and naturally enough, Agassi, like Evron, totally rejected the Law of Return for disrupting the normal order of liberal nations by fostering extra-territorial national links between the Jews of Israel and those of other nations.[8] He concedes that 'the Law of Return was just, necessary and even visionary at the time the state was established', but 'today it is being forced on the Jews of the world, at least the Jews of the free countries', and he advises them to dissociate themselves from it. At the same time it should be preserved for Jews in distress, who qualify as refugees. Thus far Agassi, in his own special way, has remained within the framework of general normalization. But he goes on to advance theories closer to 'singular normalization'. Unlike the veterans of the Hebrew-Canaanite tradition, Agassi is not a dogmatic territorialist. He too holds that nations are territorial entities, and that Jews living in countries with liberal regimes, the majority of the contemporary Jewish people, are part of those nations. But he goes on to establish that 'it is easy to agree that the Jews are a distinctive people, since each people has its unique qualities'. At least where the Jews are concerned, Agassi distinguishes between the nation as a territorial phenomenon and the people as a super-territorial entity.

Thus, he does not agree with Evron that Judaism is a religious denomination. 'Throughout the generations,' he writes, 'the Jewish people has been an abnormal people, not only because of the lack of territory of its own, but also because they are a nationality-religion.' Since the establishment of Israel, the total normalization of the Jewish people has been made possible by separation of nationality from religion. Separation of the Israeli nation from the Jewish religion will make the relations between Jews and non-Jews in the state and between Israeli Jews and Jews of other nationalities more human. In the former case, there will be civil equality among them, and in the latter the state will cease making demands of Diaspora Jews, such as immigration, which they cannot satisfy. The establishment of internal normalization in the State of Israel will facilitate 'creative cooperation between Israel and the Jews of other nations – on matters of religion and Jewish culture'. Moreover, in the spirit of Ahad ha-Am and under the influence of Martin Buber, Agassi proposes a general debate on the possibility of setting up a world Jewish religious center in Israel, or even various centers of this type, as well as the similar possibility of establishing secular Jewish cultural and spiritual centers. He foresees the setting up of a Jewish-spiritual center in Eretz Israel, on condition that it is separated from the Israeli official establishment.

In short, the 'general normalization' of Jewish existence, for Agassi, is partial and not all-embracing. 'The Jewish nation is the political heir of the Jewish people', but 'the Jewish people has not disappeared as a religion and a historical entity'.[9] Under the impact of the American ethnic culture, he determines that even in the United States there is a distinctive quality to Jewish life in comparison to that of other groups, such as the Italians or the Irish. These latter ethnic groups separate religion and ethnic origin, while among the Jews 'religion and ethnic culture go hand in hand. Hence, we can refer to the Jewish people as against the

Israeli nation'. This suggests that the rules of normalization which are valid for Israeli Jews do not apply to the Jews of other nations. The existence of the Jewish people as a cultural religious-secular entity continues to be abnormal.

Moreover, Agassi argues that 'the links of the people to the nation and the religious and cultural ties between the dispersed people and the nation residing in its own land could be highly desirable', on condition that 'the national identity of a member of the nation is not eroded as it is in Israel today'. The very existence of this connection, even when subject to the conditions Agassi specifies, indicates to what extent, in the universal sense, the existence of the Jewish people is anomalous. And since Agassi does not believe in the prospect of the ingathering of the exiles, and, at the same time, accepts the idea of Jewish cultural unity, he thinks that the ambiguous nature of the normal Israeli Jewish existence and abnormal Diaspora existence could endure perpetually.

The idea of normalization in the territorial-liberal tradition, as expressed by Evron and Agassi, evoked response among liberal intellectuals in the United States. Professor James Diamond,[10] who studied Canaanite ideology as a historical phenomenon, admitted frankly in summing up his research that his intention has been to convince his audience that in the long term it would be in the interests of Israel and the Jewish people in the Diaspora to separate the Jewish religion from the Jewish state. In other words, Zionism and Judaism should be totally separated, and the state should be grounded on purely secular elements. Israel should cease to be an ethnic state and become a pluralistic state granting services to its citizens. Diamond does not demand, for the time being, the 'de-Zionization' of the state, because of the far-reaching political ideological implications of this thought, and hence its impracticality. The Canaanism he proposes is not an alternative to Zionism, but an ideological direction in which the state should develop, until it becomes a pluralistic secular democracy.

The separation of Judaism and Zionism in the value sense, would protect the moral character of Judaism, which would no longer be involved in political action in history. And, practically speaking, it would demand the rescinding of the Law of Return, which now does more harm than good.

The transformation of the image of the state would also alter relations between Israel and the Diaspora. Jewish life in the Diaspora would now be of exclusively religious significance, while life in Israel would be conducted on a secular basis. These two approaches – Judaism as a faith existing on the metahistorical level and Zionism as a political entity involved in historical action – should not be interwoven. It is inconceivable that, in the long run, a modern state would be capable of being guided by biblical myths, such as those of Gush Emunim, or the halakhic injunctions of Orthodox Jewry.

The separation of Zionism and Judaism would also have a salutary effect on Jewish life in the Diaspora. Since the Diaspora will be unable to ground its future on the secular Jewish state, it will be forced to resort to utilizing its own inner forces. This inward-directed gaze will summon forth latent forces and strengthen its confidence in its own efforts. The separation of religion and state is therefore of twofold significance: separation of Judaism and Zionism and separation of the State of Israel and the Diaspora. This will foster unity among Jews living in a condition of two-dimensional normality: political liberal normality in Israel and pluralistic normality in the Diaspora.

Diamond's contemporary, Bernard Avishai, immigrated to Israel in the sixties, and, like many of his friends, was disillusioned, left the country and became an 'apostate', attacking the Law of Return. He objected to it because it presupposed the existence of a Jewish nation. As one who had despaired of Zionism, he could not accept this view. He also considered it an insult to every non-Jewish citizen of Israel and to Israeli Jews as well. The Hebrew culture and language of the majority in Israel, he believed, would suffice to preserve the Jewish character of the state.[11]

Thus it is evident that the anti-Zionists presume the existence of an Israeli nation, a community of citizens, but do not deny the existence of Judaism as a religion, as a people with a common history or culture maintaining historical continuity and unity between its various strata.

Paradoxically enough, there are points of contact between the post-Canaanite liberals and the radical Zionists. Just as, forty years previously, there had been a consensus between Hillel Kook and Yonathan Ratosh on the question of territorial normalization, even though their ideological starting points were very far apart, now the principle of normalization served as a common denominator for their heirs. The barrier between the two approaches was the attitude towards the Law of Return, with everything it implied for Jewish and Israeli life. Midway between them stood the group which established the Israeli Congress,[12] which removed the desire for normalization from the domain of individual thought and transformed it into a public need. The very name of this body, echoing the 'Zionist' Congress, reflected the shift from Zionism to Israelism.[13] Its manifesto refers to 'a normal people in a normal state' identified as Israelis and not as Jews, and it warns that 'Israel must be normal, democratic, modern, if it seeks life'. The words 'Zionism' and 'Jew' are not mentioned.

In a letter to one of the heads of Gush Emunim, in which he clarified the Congress's views on the Jewish character of the state, Yigal Elam asked: 'What does "Jewish state" mean? We believe that there can be only one interpretation – Israel will be a Jewish state in the same sense that England is English, and France is French'. In other words, its cultural character will be determined naturally by the culture of the majority of its citizens. According to Elam, 'the Israeli Congress arose in order to combat the atavistic concept of "a nation dwelling apart...", a concept which undermines the foundations of the State of Israel and endangers its future. Our task is to pose the concept of the democratic state as an element without which it is impossible today to maintain a state, to explain its application to Israeli reality and to create a bridge between it and the Jewish view of nationality and culture, as fashioned by the Zionist revolution'.[14] Elam does not refer to the Law of Return. In private conversation, he reveals that he takes a neutral view of this law because, practically speaking, it is less important than the shaping of the democratic-liberal Israeli entity. At the same time, he is not far from Shulamit Aloni in his views on this issue. She holds that the idea of the ingathering of the exiles, which is expressed in the Law of Return, is a kind of 'affirmative action – correcting a historic injustice', the significance of which is to grant members of the Jewish people the right and opportunity of returning to their historic homeland. The Law of Return, she says, applies to Jews as individuals and not as a people. It should not be ignored since it grants 'extra-territorial priority to people with affinity to the Jewish people in the laws of entry into the country, but once these people are living in the sovereign state and within its sphere of jurisdiction, one law applies to all'.[15] Henceforth all citizens are Israelis. Consequently, the state is not the national home of the Jewish people but of its own citizens. The Jewish people does not enjoy special status there. Only Jews as individuals are granted the right to return under the provisions to the Law of Return. Hence, this law should not be regarded as the expression of discrimination on a national basis, but as a humanitarian gesture towards individuals belonging to an ethnic group which has experienced extraordinary suffering throughout history.

As noted, on the other side of the dividing line stand the radical or maximalist Zionists. Their Zionism is based on negation of the Diaspora, and the more extreme the negation, the profounder their recognition of their own Israelism. In this respect, it reinforces Evron's and Elam's interpretation of historical Zionism as a movement for the normalization of Jewish national existence, the crux of which is existence itself, which requires no justification save the will of the Jews.

The first and most extreme spokesman of this outlook was Hillel Halkin, who in 1977 published a book which had considerable impact, particularly in the United States, entitled *Letters to an American Jewish Friend*.[16] Halkin was born in the United States and was a member of the radical Zionist movement of the 1960s, but unlike most of his comrades, he immigrated to Israel and has remained there.

Halkin's Zionism may be defined as radical in its efforts on its own behalf, and minimal in its external significance. It starts out from the assumption that Judaism no longer has a universal message to offer the world, nor are the Jews different from or superior to other peoples, ethically and intellectually. Now that they have forfeited their distinctive qualities, the rules of normalization valid in an open society are applicable to them as well, and will expedite their integration within that society. Judaism as a particularist religious culture, he says, can be comprehended and lived only in a closed system. Territorial and political Zionism is re-creating the framework which is gathering in the remnants of Judaism, which was laid open by the stormy development of modern history. For him, Zionism, meaning life in Israel, is primarily a Jewish existential matter, and he does not deem it necessary to seek any meaning and justification beyond this argument. He believes that, at best, the Jews in Israel will succeed in developing a national-secular culture without outstanding content or achievements as compared to other national cultures, but this Israeli culture will be Jewish, just as Albanian culture is Albanian and Finnish is Finnish. It is no coincidence, of course, that Halkin, in order to emphasize his minimalist approach, chose to mention two peoples on the margins of international events. He was challenging those Zionists, like Buber and Ben-Gurion, who believed in the universal mission, and feared the transformation of Eretz Israel into another Albania.

Halkin, as a national existentialist, proclaims that 'we are what nature has made us.... It is not our business to decide whether we deserve to exist or not. It is our business to exist'. Even more explicitly he says: 'I don't know why one should be a Jew. I don't know whether the world needs us. I don't know whether God needs us. I only know that we need ourselves. For that you don't need reasons'.[17]

Halkin's Zionist existentialism is not lacking in historical significance. The reverse is true. He is awed by the four thousand year old historical drama of a people which entered its land, was expelled from it, and returned after a long saga of suffering and achievement. This people, he says, has returned to the same historical places, the same language and the same disputes with neighbors as in the distant past. And if, thanks to Zionism, 'if we have ourselves, if we are willing to be ourselves, we do not need their reasons either ... And yet, just between the two of us, since no one is listening and we are free to say what we want, are we not a most marvelous people?'[18]

It appears, therefore, that the normalization which Halkin favors is a kind of return to the province, to the place where we can exist as a people without being subjected to constant existential and value trials. And thus, as against the traditional Zionist aspiration for normalization, with its moral, spiritual and even utopian dimensions, Halkin proposes what I may call, an 'existential normalization'.

Amos Oz expressed himself in the same spirit and in similar terms. He too, like Halkin, is gripped by 'the secret of the Zionist enchantment', and he regards Zionism as 'a great achievement (in contrast to the sober prognoses of two generations ago)' but also as 'a crushing failure (in contrast to the dazzling dreams)'. He accepts this dual significance of Zionism, perceiving this to be its charm. And hence he suggests that the Jewish people should be content with existing achievements since 'we have achieved several gains which have few parallels in history. Not only a patch of territory guarded by aircraft and tanks, but two other aspirations as well have been realized: we have more or less achieved a larger degree of responsibility for our own destiny, and we have attained the beginning of the cure of the disease of the Jews'.[19] Five years later, in Autumn 1982, travelling the length and breadth of Israel, and faced with the resentful frustration of the people of the development towns and the messianic fervor of Gush Emunim, he pondered:

> Perhaps it was a lunatic proposition: to transform, in two or three generations, a mass of persecuted, intimidated Jews, consumed with love-hate towards their countries of origins, into a nation serving as a shining example to the Arab surroundings, a model for the entire world. Perhaps we aimed too high...perhaps it was a wild pretension beyond our powers or, indeed, any human powers. Per-

haps it is necessary now to cut ourselves down to size and to renounce the messianic dreams.[20]

He found the answer to these questions in the provincial immigrant town of Ashdod, 'a little Mediterranean town...a pleasant unpretentious town with a port and lighthouse and power station and factories and many pleasing boulevards. It does not pretend to be Paris or Zurich and does not aspire to be Jerusalem'.[21]

So far it seems that the post-Canaanite liberals, with their various traditions and shades of ideology, no longer advocate the total normalization of Jewish life. They have accepted the fact that it cannot be judged according to general criteria. Boaz Evron, unlike his spiritual progenitors, acknowledged the continuity and unity of Jewish culture; Yosef Agassi seized on the existence of the Jewish people as a super-territorial entity; Yigal Elam does not object to the Law of Return; James Diamond does not deny the Jewish character of the state; Hillel Halkin offers a Zionist interpretation of the course of Jewish history; and Amos Oz argues that Jewish society in Israel has not yet achieved normality and requires a protracted process of therapy.

But it is the writer A.B. Yehoshua who has devoted the most thought to the perfection of this concept, in the Jewish context. In the past ten years, Yehoshua has been the tireless champion of the 'right to normalization', arising out of his radical Zionist outlook.[22] He understands the term 'normalization', first and foremost, in its profoundest Jewish sense as self-responsibility. He writes: 'Normality does not mean emphasis on worthy content or values, but the indication of the existence of a framework in which a man is considered responsible for his actions'. As a result, from the historical viewpoint,

the abnormality of Jewish existence in the Diaspora... lay in the renunciation of responsibility for the central and important spheres of life. It stemmed from the very fact of Jewish dispersal and their submission to ... other peoples.... This renunciation is a negative moral decision.[23]

In other words, the value is not normality but self-responsibility. Thus, once the Jews were afforded the opportunity to undertake responsibility for themselves in their own country, Jewish life in the Diaspora became immoral. The tragic expression of this immoral decision is the role of the Jews themselves in the Holocaust which befell them. Therefore, says Yehoshua,

when I request that, on Holocaust Memorial Day, instead of bewailing the evil deeds of the goyim, we state simply that this is the end which awaits a people who cling leechlike to other peoples, I am seeking to draw attention to our own responsibility, in addition to the responsibility of anti-Semites, for our intolerable historical condition.

The responsibility that Yehoshua seeks to impose on a people which evades responsibility is not confined to the present day, when, after the establishment of

Israel, Jews have been given the chance to take responsibility for their lives. He believes that *galut* as escape from responsibility, is a pathological-historical phenomenon unique to the Jewish people. To his mind, '*golah* was not forced on us, we forced it on ourselves. It should not be considered an accident or a catastrophe, but a profound internal national distortion'.[24]

This suggests that the source of the distortion is the strong national aspiration to be a unique people. The refuge of those evading normality is *galut*, since there alone is it possible to remain a chosen people. However, he sees this psycho-national condition as more complex than the choice of exile itself. The Jewish people is in a constant state of tension between practical advocacy of the Diaspora and its theoretical negation as a permanent state. 'A paradoxical, almost pathological situation is created. The Jewish people are attracted to the *golah* ... hate it and do everything possible to endure there, but at the same time they postpone the return to their own land due to their ever-improving quality of endurance.' The Jewish people feel guilty for not returning to their country, and consequently praise and laud it more and more, sanctify it, all this in order to justify the fact that they are not worthy to return there. On the other hand, 'they describe it as a nightmare, a dangerous country "which consumes its inhabitants", in order to justify their fears of return'.[25]

Yehoshua defines this internal conflict as a neurotic condition, from which there can be no escape as long as *galut* endures. The cure for the Jewish national neurosis is twofold: a matter of will, namely immigration to Israel, and an involuntary, perhaps inevitable matter: the gradual disappearance of the Diaspora through assimilation. Faced with these two alternatives, Yehoshua calls for immigration and regards assimilation almost with equanimity. He argues that the continued existence of the Diaspora creates difficulties for the state. In the short term, its disappearance would harm the state, but in the long term, it will remove the threat of an alternative Jewish society, which prevents it from being an absolute national entity, as are other peoples.[26] And meanwhile, as long as the Diaspora exists, it is necessary to educate the Jews there, and particularly the young, for immigration; and at the same time, to create a kind of 'tactical detachment' between the two entities in order to highlight the fundamental difference between them, 'to establish clearer borders between total Jewish existence, namely Israel, and Jewish existence'.

The first step in the direction of this tactical separation is the semantic alteration of national identity form Jewish to Israeli, though not in the meaning of the term perceived by the heirs of the Canaanites. He writes: 'The recent confusion and obfuscation around the term Israeli, stem from the fact that we confuse the element of citizenship contained in the term with the element of identity'. There is nothing unique or abnormal in this, since 'very many concepts of national identity contain this duality within them ... for example, the term "Frenchman" is both a concept of identity and of citizenship'. Through this semantic modification, for the time being, he hopes to achieve two aims which will help the society achieve normality. Firstly, the distinction between the civil and the national entities guarantees the continued existence of the historic Israeli nation. Unlike Boaz Evron and Yoram Kaniuk, Yehoshua rejects the US-style national-civil idea. Secondly, in replacing the term Jew, a late term used to define Judaism as a religion, by the term Israeli, which is an ancient expression of the comprehensive existence of the people, he is approaching the separation of religion and nationality. Yehoshua, however, is aware that the time for general normalization has not yet arrived. He acknowledges that any true secular stand, which proclaims the legitimacy of secular Judaism, must recognize that a Jew can also be a Christian-Jew or a Muslim-Jew. But somehow, is seems to him that

within the zealous secular community there will be few who will be ready to acknowledge the right of a Jew to cross this border... I too, confess, for all my loyalty to the principle of secular Judaism...I cannot as yet accept the right of any Jew to change his religion to Christianity or Islam and remain a Jew.[27]

Thus, en route to total national normalization, reflected in separation of State and Diaspora, religion and nationality, he creates a kind of twofold compromise. He distinguishes clearly between the terms Israeli and Jew, with emphasis on the fact that the term Israeli, because it is ancient and because of its totality, contains the term Jew within it. Then, again, he distinguishes between the Israeli state and the Jewish Diaspora without renouncing the Zionist idea, the crux of which is the demand for immigration. Through this advocacy of compromise, Yehoshua becomes the spokesman of incomplete normalization, aimed at changing the course of Jewish history, but also aware, with varying degrees of intensity, that it cannot totally detach itself from that history.

SINGULAR NORMALIZATION – NEO-DUBNOWIAN DIASPORISM

In the early eighties, the 'singular normalization' approach, which had all but disappeared in the decade after the Six Day War, resurfaced. It was first manifested at the end of the seventies in the theories of members of Breira. But, as has been noted above,[28] this organization was relegated to the sidelines, because it was publicly critical of Israel's Middle Eastern policies, and particularly its attitude towards the Palestinians. On the other hand, at this time the focus is not on an organization with radical political tendencies, which generally antagonized the establishment, but on a group of people of standing and high reputation, of different age groups, whose independent views were compatible with the establishment's interests. And thus, borne on the spirit of the age, and without clashing with the leadership of the communities, this outlook penetrated the core of Jewish public thought and established itself there.

We are dealing here not with a coherent ideology but with the point of view of certain individuals which, different shades of opinion notwithstanding, is based on two shared presuppositions: the existence of total balance between Israel and the Diaspora and their equal importance for the future of the Jewish people; the lack of need for Zionism as an ideology maintaining the cohesion of the Jewish people and helping them to survive. In this respect, this is post-Zionist thought, leaning deliberately or inadvertently towards the views of Dubnow, inspired by his historiography to believe that the Diaspora has infinite capacity to restore its powers and to build new centers to replace those destroyed, and by his view that the national existence of the Diaspora has an intrinsic and absolute value beyond that of territorial political existence.

The neo-Dubnowian outlook has two starting points: moral, and social and practical. Its most extreme spokesman was the reform rabbi, Roy Rosenberg, who echoed the theories of Jacob Petuchowski. He defined *galut* as the manifestation of humanistic Judaism, and consequently took a positive view of the loss of Jewish political sovereignty, and particularly of the destruction of the Temple. *Galut*, for him, is a challenge and not a plight.[29]

Michael Lerner, editor of the liberal Jewish journal *Tikkun*, translates the old universal reformist outlook into American terms. In his programmatic introduction to the first issue of the journal,[30] he declared that his contemporaries, those who had come to maturity in the sixties and seventies, and their juniors, 'speak as a different generation of Jews. For us, America is home, not host – and we do not feel outsiders to this reality, but a constituent part of it'. He went on to list the most important phenomena in Jewish life, stating that the first of these was the movement for the liberation of Jewish women. In second place is Israel, to which he attributes a messianic role in the course of history.

Lerner's axiomatic statement that America is home, and his order of priorities which indicates that as far as he is concerned, domestic matters are more important than general Jewish affairs, were given a different slant by the essayist Leon Wieseltier. He recognizes that Israel has a special place in American Jewish life and admits that the cultural future of the Jewish people is connected to the Hebrew language and to the place where it is a natural part of life. But at the same time, he demands recognition of the historical fact that Israel and America are the two great attempts of the twentieth century to create new conditions. America, he writes, is not merely a new address for Jewish refugees from Russia. Philosophically and politically this is an innovation in Jewish history – a diaspora which is not a *golah*. Anti-Semitism is a different phenomenon there; the psychological state of the Jews is different. This is the American contribution to what Zionists call the normalization of the Jewish people. The classic Zionist idea of negation of the diaspora, he says, 'if not yet dead, is certainly dying'.[31]

The death of classical Zionism, according to Wieseltier, signifies not only the disappearance of classic anti-Semitism, but also the replacement of classical nationalism by ethnicity. In the United States, he wrote, every citizen was defined by national origin, Italian American or Irish American, but there was no such thing as an authentic American American, apart from the Indians. 'In America you are an American because you remain a Jew, in other words because you remain a member of your group'.[32] Thus, it is not that the Jews as a minority have integrated in Anglo-Saxon American culture, but that American culture and its manifestations are composed of minorities. The classic and modern Zionist argument, namely that the threat to the survival of the Jewish people stems from the fact that it is a minority everywhere, is totally spurious. The waning or even death of Zionism, as Wieseltier sees it, also derives from the faith that among the Jews of the United States there are internal forces capable of filling their ethnic entity with original cultural content.

This view was shared by his two contemporaries, Professor (of Yiddish literature) David Roskies, and Professor (of Jewish Philosophy) Arnold Eisen. Roskies, graduate of the '*havurot*', proposed emulation of the model of Yiddish culture, not its content and language, this being inconceivable in the new reality, but its form of self-perception. He sought an American Jewish culture relying, like the Yiddish culture, on its system of prototypes: a culture treating itself with irony and humour not out of any desire to ingratiate itself with non-Jews, but in order to be able to confront God or its historical destiny; a culture taking a serious and knowledgable view of Jewish collective existence; a culture committed to the radical self-expression of the individual; and a culture which would bind all these together into a vision of utopia. Thus, even when Roskies does not believe in the revival of the Yiddish language and cultural content in the American milieu, he proposed grounding the American Jewish ethnic culture on the fundamental patterns of self-perception and relations with the surrounding world which shaped Yiddish culture. He believes that these foundations have already permeated the writing of American Jewish novelists, even though they are not always aware of this. These elements, he says, must be brought to public consciousness in order to fashion an American Jewish culture through them. This, of course, will increase the differences between American Jewry and Israeli Jewry.

The divergency between Israel and the Diaspora that Roskies wishes to foster, is perceived by Eisen as almost complete separation. Also a former member of the *havurot*, affiliated to their Zionist wing, he immigrated to Israel, but several years later returned to the United States. While still in Israel, in the mid-eighties, he described it, in light of its material and spiritual achievements, as 'a spiritual center for world Jewry'.[33] Three years later, however, back in the United States, addressing the Memorial Foundation for Jewish Culture on Israel's fortieth anniversary, he spoke in a different way.[34]

Forty, he said, was the age for self-scrutiny in respect to relations between Israel and the Diaspora. And, in sharp contrast to his former views, he concluded that Ahad ha-Am's existential-national model was no longer relevant. Similarly, Simon Rawidowicz' views were no longer valid, and Herzl's theories were outdated. Israelis and Diaspora Jews, he declared, took a totally different view of Jewish existence. Diaspora Jewry was not ready to accept the Israeli assertion that there was some decisive advantage to Judaism within an entirely Jewish society.

Life in the Diaspora, in a state of cultural fragmentation, where Judaism was confined to the home and to the synagogue, was also Jewish life, in no way of less value than the Jewish totality in Israel. Nor did he accept the view that Jewish Diaspora life in the free world held the advantage. The two forms of Jewish life were in total equilibrium, he said: they were simply two versions of the same thing. His conclusion was that in due course cultural reciprocity would develop between them, based on import and not on export. Each side would take from the other what it required but would not be subject to orders or directions from outside with respect to its own specific needs. Hence, there was no need for mutual intervention on the part of the political or public establishment.

Eisen, we see, was opposed to overall Jewish efforts to resuscitate and preserve Jewish culture. He leaves this to the free initiative of the communities themselves, advocating a kind of 'free culture', on the lines of the 'free economy'. Above and beyond methods or paths, what the Diaspora and Israel have to offer one another is themselves. If the greatest gift that Zionism has bestowed on the Jewish world is the concept of a people, the time has come for the parts of this people to acknowledge one another and to be reconciled to separate and different patterns of existence. Thus, since 'all Israel are responsible for one another', Israel is not responsible for the survival of the Diaspora and the latter is not responsible for the existence of Jewish refugees in Eretz Israel. These patterns of mutual relations are outdated. In the fortieth year of statehood, the time has come to promote heterogeneity, and to preserve diversity within unity.

The view that the American Jewish community is endowed with strength of its own and the conviction that it is capable of becoming independent of its surroundings and of Israel, was expressed explicitly by the young sociologist Steven Cohen.[35] He denounced the prevalent tendency among Diaspora Jews to debate the question of their survival as Jews and called, instead, for a Jewish creative effort to direct attention inward. The Jews should be less concerned with what non-Jews think of them and more preoccupied with their own self-awareness. Cohen believes in the possibility of building a kind of Jewish cultural autonomy in the United States within the framework of the Jewish federations. He also holds that the American community, as the most prosperous and influential Jewish community in the world, has a central role to play in shaping Jewish history by developing a network of relationships with all the Jewish centers throughout the world, including Israel.

The central thesis of the thinkers who emerged from the ranks of radicalism and found their way back to the heart of the Jewish establishment is the idea of modular-Jewish unity in which the components, scattered throughout the world, are also integral units, each in itself. There is a close but not organic link between them. And, perhaps for this reason, the idea of the existential dependence of the component on the whole or the dependence of the whole on its parts, including Israel, was not acceptable to them. At least to outward appearances, they view the relations between Israel and the Diaspora without passion and without uncertainties. In this respect, distinctive normalization for them is not only an ideological outlook, but also an emotional condition. This is not the case with their seniors, members of the previous generation, who came to maturity during the Holocaust and experienced the establishment of Israel. For them, Jewish unity is an organic phenomenon, in which overall and partial existence are interwoven and inseparably linked. Thus, while they are organically united in their consciousness, there is considerable tension among them on the significance of this unity. For fear of confronting the issue, they prefer not to lay down categorical rules but to evaluate the situation on the basis of prevailing facts.

The first of these is the sociologist Daniel Bell, who moved from the radical left of the 1940s to advocacy of the theory of the alienation of intellectuals in the fifties, and in the late sixties arrived at identification with Jewish tradition and history. Bell, unlike his predecessors, does not speak of the Diaspora, but emphasizes the existence of two effective centers of the Jewish people: the communities in Israel and in the United States. He does not accept the extremist Zionist view that there is only one center and everything outside it is *galut*. To his mind, the two coeval centers are unique in Jewish history, and came into being after Jewish life had undergone drastic change over two centuries, the lifestyles and social trends which characterized it in the past no longer existing. Jewish life is no longer confined to an institutionalized community organization framework. It is now voluntaristic and pluralistic. The trend to deliberate assimilation, motivated by the desire to abandon inferior and debased status, has vanished due to the growing tendency of Jews to enter general society where they are increasingly accepted. Socialism, which once held out promise for Jews, has degenerated, and the influence of Zionism, particularly in its socialist manifestations, is waning. There have been changes in non-Jewish society as well. The United States is no longer ruled by the Anglo-Saxon Protestant culture, and throughout the world the large nations, excluding Japan, are pluralistic in the ethnic-cultural sense.

In what way, therefore, is Jewish existence distinctive within this universal pluralism? According to Bell, for historical and psychological reasons, Israel is 'a symbolic center' of Jewish life and, for practical reasons, a place of refuge for Jews. In other words, Bell was coining a new definition. Bell does not underestimate the importance of the symbolic center. He attributes significance to its political-sovereign essence, but stresses that, in parallel, there is a Jewish power-base in the United States, which can provide the economic and political aid required for sovereign Jewish life. The two centers serve as examples of the success of Jews in establishing a state of their own and developing vibrant Jewish life within non-Jewish society. And thus, while the cohesive-political center is balanced against a center which is amorphous and pluralistic, the equilibrium between them is not disturbed, and neither one should be considered a pontifical center with the other as a province. They are interdependent and equally responsible for the survival of the Jewish people. Bell, therefore, aspires to a balanced synthesis between what he defines as an Israeli nation and the American Jewish community.

These definitions are reminiscent of Agassi's above-mentioned theories, although they were never completely in agreement. Agassi postulated the existence of an Israeli nation composed of all the citizens of the State of Israel, while Bell was apparently referring only to the Jews of Israel. This can be deduced from the emotional conclusion of his article:

> We remain one people united by blood (in many senses of the word) and by collective memory. The survival of the Jewish people is one of the mysteries of the history of human civilization. No other people, dispersed, as we have been, so widely and for so long, have maintained a collective continuity. No other people, decimated by pogroms and Holocausts, have risen like the fire-bird, again and again, to maintain the covenant. We are the joint legatees of Jewish history. That is our common condition, and our common responsibility.[36]

Bell's views on the two centers, therefore, are closer to those of Simon Rawidowicz, though again not totally identical. Rawidowicz spoke of the unity between Israel and the Diaspora, located at opposite poles, while Bell refers solely to two significant centers: Israel and the United States. And herein, it would seem, lies the difference between the two approaches.

The acknowledgment of the existence of two centers raised fundamental questions as to the basis on which relations between them should be founded. Bell's contemporary, Professor David Sidorsky, has recently focused on this issue.[37] He believes that pluralism, in the limited sense, means acceptance of coexistence, and in the wider sense, acknowledgment on principle of the individual's right to self-perception. He wishes to apply this rule to the relations between Israel and US Jewry: it is his view that the relations between the two communities, over the years, demonstrate that each takes a pluralistic view of the other. Israel has chosen the limited interpretation while US Jews adhere to the wider meaning. Israel is reconciled to the existence of the Diaspora and recognizes its autonomous leadership. To this should be added the fact that the basic debate on 'negation of the Diaspora' which was once a stormy and controversial issue, is now a marginal question. At the same time, there is a difference between the two communities as regards self-perception. American Jewry accepts Israel's self-perception as central to the continued survival of Judaism, while Israel, on principle, does not acknowledge the self-perception of the US Jewish community as equal in value. According to the Israeli approach, it represents the vanguard of the Jewish people both in its sovereignty and in its struggle for the continued existence of the Jewish people.

In this sense, the diasporas are not equal to Israel, but are her auxiliary forces, and even if the issue is not negation of the diaspora, the diasporas must display loyalty and unconditional support. The fact that Israel does not accept the concept of the equal value, on the national plane, of a sovereign state and a voluntarist-pluralistic community, irrespective of its power and importance, and that the US community, despite its self-esteem, feels itself connected to Israel, creates constant tension between them. This tension can only be resolved on two conditions:

the first, which is inconceivable, is that the Jews of the United States will renounce their self-perception, meaning that they will abandon their faith in their historic mission and accept immigration to Israel as the foregone conclusion. Then, of course, Israel will accept diaspora life, even without mass immigration. The second condition, which is more feasible, is that Israel's self-awareness will change.

This change, he believes, will occur gradually thanks to the process of normalization in Israeli society. The improvement of the security situation and of economic conditions will weaken the demand that the periphery mobilize its forces in order to strengthen the central position or the vanguard of the Jewish people. And, as a natural consequence, the tension inherent in this system with its two different self-perceptions will disappear. This development will also temper the excessive expectations of each community *vis à vis* the other. This too will facilitate the normalization of relations between them. Sidorsky is aware that this is a possibility for the long term, but he sees no other prospect of mutual acceptance. Until then, while awaiting the objective process which will bring about the hoped-for change, practical ways should be sought of achieving pluralistic coexistence between Israel and the American Jewish community.

Leonard Fein, editor of *Moment*, continued this line of thought. Of all the thinkers mentioned here, he is perhaps the most closely linked, personally and ideologically, to Israel. At the same time, he is firm in his opinion that a self-respecting US Jewry must reassess the classical Zionist outlook which allots a marginal role in Jewish history to the Jews of the Diaspora. What is needed, he believes, is a new theory which will permit mutual coexistence of American Jewry, now beginning to acknowledge their own value, and classical Zionism, obliged to adapt to the new conditions – otherwise a crisis might erupt and split the Jewish people.[38] It is more important to seek such a theory than to engage in fruitless effort to disguise the differences between them.

Fein attempted to formulate this theory in his book *Where are We?*[39] There he tries to base American Jewish group identity, beyond its religious features, on memory of the Holocaust, on the liberal-humanistic social mission, and on identification with Israel as bearer of an optimistic message to the Jewish people. Israel, he says, is central to the survival of Judaism, but is not the objective of this survival. It has a significance of its own. Even though the establishment of the Jewish state after the Holocaust restored the meaning of Jewish communal existence, this existence is not dependent on Israel. At the same time, Israel, for the Jews of the United States, is first a faith and only then a place. Hence, it is not part of the idealistic yearning of the US Jews, who dream of another time but not of another place. He has an uneasy feeling about immigration, and is by no means confident that the Zionist prognosis regarding the assimilation of US Jewry is not valid. But, at the same time, he declares that the Jews of the United States feel at home. He admits that Jewish self-responsibility in the Diaspora is limited when compared to the Jewish state, but argues that Jewish history teaches that Jews must not invest everything they have in one sole place. Because of this, US Jews have adopted a Babylonian ideology.[40]

The foundation of the Jewish existential theory which will replace the classical Zionist theory is, therefore, Fein's distinction between Israel as a place and as a faith. For classical Zionism and its modern versions, Israel was always a place, which demanded national endeavor, self-denial and self-sacrifice. One could say that 'Palestinocentrism', in its various forms, is the main foundation of Zionism. On the other hand, faith requires not action but only dedication. One can, therefore, believe in Israel and even consider it to be the prime element of Jewish life in the Diaspora, without being obliged to take action which requires self-denial. Thus loyalty to Israel is transformed from public effort to strengthen the state into faith, which is a component of Jewish life in the Diaspora. This faith, together with knowledge of the Holocaust and a sense of mission, is what sets the Jews of America apart from other ethnic groups, thereby reinforcing the foundations of Jewish life in the United States.

These ideas had found practical expression several years previously in Fein's forthright defence of the right of the Jewish community to absorb Soviet Jews, and even to encourage them to emigrate to the United States.[41] To his mind, those American Jews who support the Zionist stand are not convinced of the possibility of Jewish survival in the United States. Their activity within the communities is carried out on behalf of Israel and not for the sake of the communities themselves, and those who believe that Israel is the true center of Jewish life are, in essence, turning the Diaspora into a periphery without intrinsic value. This, however, is not the case; the Diaspora is a center in its own right, and must, therefore, help those Jews who choose it freely, and thus place their trust in it as their Jewish way of life.

JEWISH NORMALIZATION – NEW ZIONISM

> *Jews need not yield to current tendencies; We can also resist them. Zionism is the call to that resistance.*
>
> Michael Walzer, *Zionism in Transition*, 1980

Certain of the basic tenets of modern Jewish thought are continuations of the theories of Mordecai Kaplan. His well-known book, *A New Zionism*, was published in the 1950s, when the standing of the Zionist movement was at its lowest ebb, and the Diaspora was uncertain as to its survival as a Jewish entity. In the late seventies and early eighties as well, Israel's aura had dimmed somewhat and the Diaspora, though no longer in dread of losing Judaism, was profoundly concerned at the possible disappearance of Jews. Kaplan was anxious to inspire the Jewish people, enervated by a generation of catastrophes and almost superhuman effort, to undertake action to safeguard their integrity and their very survival. The 'new

Zionists', too, are trying to remake Jewish reality in accordance with collective and comprehensive concepts. They have inherited Kaplan's views on the identity of Judaism and Zionism; they are trying, in their own way, to promote the view that Judaism is a collective international entity, both secular and religious in character. This is, in a way, a new version of Kaplan's 'Jewish civilization' without his organizational proposals.[42] One may therefore, say that whereas Kaplan's theology did not succeed in altering the traditional faith of American Jews, his ideology still influences Zionist-Jewish thought in that country.

The term 'Zionist-Jewish' thought is an innovation because of the juxtaposition of Judaism and Zionism, in the historical, cultural and religious sense. It is therefore no coincidence that the main spokesmen of this trend include rabbis and scholars from the Orthodox and Conservative trends. Prominent among them are the Conservative Professor Jacob Neusner, the orthodox Professor Daniel Elazar, and Rabbi Irving Greenberg, who advocated his own version of orthodoxy. The secular representatives of the trend, with the exception of Professor Howard Adelman of Canada, have made no attempt to formulate an overall Zionist-Jewish or Jewish-Zionist outlook.

Jacob Neusner is the most prolific writer among them, and has had considerable impact. His views are based on those of his predecessors, but he lends them his own interpretation which is often extreme. He agrees with Kaplan that Zionism is the precondition for Jewish survival, in Israel and in the Diaspora, but utterly rejects the 'Jewish civilization' theory, because he considers impractical the idea that Diaspora Jews could live simultaneously in two cultures, general and Jewish. He accepts Rawidowicz's theory of equilibrium between Eretz Israel and the Diaspora. But the State of Israel holds central position in Jewish life, as far as he is concerned, because of its significant role in altering the historical and political status of the Jewish people. Neusner, like Ben Halpern, sees *galut* and redemption as the two central historical symbols in Jewish history, but endows them with essentially religious content. He is the most extreme advocate of the Jewish-religious significance of the place – Eretz Israel. But with the same fervor, he is ready to support Jewish existence in the Diaspora. Neusner is aware of the paradoxical elements in his thinking. In his foreword to a compilation of articles on Jewish and Zionist subjects he published in the seventies, he wrote:

> I am three things, but logic dictates I should be only two of them: American, Jew, Zionist. You can combine the first and the second, or the second and third. But how to join all three in one person, living here? As a Zionist I affirm America – but as Golah, and myself as living in Galut. As an American I can imagine no other place in which life is worth living. As a Jew I know how in a life of Torah to keep these other two convictions in uneasy balance.[43]

In 1972, under the intoxicating impact of the 1967 events, Neusner, disciple of Mordecai Kaplan, declared: 'We are Zionists because we are Jews' – Zionism being integral to the understanding of Judaism. In the past, he continued, Zionism had grown out of Judaism, but in the present age Judaism is subordinated to Zionism. Here he went beyond Kaplan, but his practical interpretation of this theory echoes Kaplan. Zionism, he said, means not only activity on behalf of Israel but above all, 'spiritual involvement with the Judaic tradition that underlies Zionism, that forms the Jewish people and gives meaning to its existence, purpose to its endeavours, hope to its future'.[44]

Fifteen years later, in a historiosophical essay entitled Zionism and Judaism,[45] Neusner asserted that there was a unity between the aspirations of Zionism as a national movement and the fundamental Jewish faith as shaped 450 years before the Christian era, in the Pentateuch. This identity between them is based on three basic postulates: the Jewish people as one people; its insoluble link with the Land of Israel; and the right of the Jewish people to renew their political life in that Land. Moreover, Zionism was unique in its idea of the return to Eretz Israel, without which it would not differ from mere territorialism. Neusner argues that the distinctive quality of Judaism in its formative period lay in the basic assumption that the integrity of the Jewish people could find expression only in Eretz Israel, and he adds that the Jewish perception of themselves as the people of the covenant and the chosen people was linked to the ties between the Jewish people and the Land of Israel.

It was this Jewish-Zionist perception which preserved and exacerbated the Jewish sense of alienation. Although other ideological strata had been added to Judaism as a faith and a way of life over the centuries, these basic postulates had endured until recent generations. Zionism had merely reformulated this emotion, and, at a time of profound national crisis, also offered the correct answer. His conclusion is that, on the basis of faith and historical development, 'Zionism is Judaism and Judaism is Zionism'. In a letter to the editor of *Commentary*, he warned against the trend emerging among Jewish intellectuals to separate the Jewish state from Zionist ideology,[46] in a spirit of esteem for the former and contempt for the latter. Those who did this were, in effect, belittling the most important phenomenon in Jewish history since the destruction of the Second Temple and disregarding the need for Zionism as a theory of Jewish existence.

Neusner was not trying to devalue the state, which he perceived as the jewel of the Zionist crown and the focus of Jewish attention. According to his views, at the present stage in the life of the Jewish people their collective identity is connected to Israel not only as a place, but also, and mainly, as a political state. And this is because Israel has changed and reshaped the essence of Jewish life. Since it came into being, 'political Israel' has replaced 'theological Israel' in Jewish consciousness. Henceforth, the Jews are a nation among other nations and the same rules of conduct apply to them, for better or worse. The restoration of the political dimension to Jewish existence obliged the dispersed people to recognize that the main collective effort of the Jews is to aid the state in all spheres. He cited this argument, in the mid-seventies, against Breira, the organization which questioned the authority of the State of Israel to lead the Jewish people, and, on the basis of this same argument, he criticized the leadership of American Jewry in the mid-eighties for insisting on the right of Jews leaving the Soviet Union to choose their destination. He charged them with damaging the core of the Jewish collective interest – the strengthening of the State of Israel. And to those who complained that Israel had not fulfilled the expectations of individuals, Neusner responded two years later that it was not fair to judge the state by individual criteria, since Zionism was not intended to solve the problems of the individual Jew, but to guarantee the survival of the Jewish collective.[47]

At the same time, despite the central place of Israel in the national life of modern Jewry, and despite its Jewish-Zionist theological significance, it cannot serve as a cultural center for the Jews of the Diaspora. This was too great a pretension from the outset; moreover it is not capable of offering Diaspora Jews a special way of life. Hence, in the present and future, as in the past, Ahad ha-Am's theory of the spiritual center is invalid. The Jews have no center other than the place where they live and struggle for their Judaism. For the Jews of Israel, the state is the framework and center of their lives as Jews, but this is not the case for Diaspora Jewry.[48]

Beside the state, the political core and bulwark of the Jewish people, as he defines it, Neusner sets the Diaspora, which shapes the autonomous Jewish experience. It should be noted that Neusner defines as *golah* any place outside Eretz Israel where Jews live.[49] In this respect, he is one of the sole Zionist thinkers in the United States who insists on this term. *Golah*, being outside Zion, and *galut* – the inability of the individual to be what he deserves to be – are purely religious terms for him. The distance from Zion, which is a place, but also a utopian religious idea, and the detachment from a way of life based on the Torah, are therefore *golah* and *galut*. In this respect, *galut* is not a universal human condition as postulated by radical secular intellectuals, but a universal Jewish condition, which also includes the Jews of Israel as well.

Neusner is aware that in this respect he is deviating from the accepted Zionist outlook, which perceives *golah* and *galut* as an actual historical condition which is a threat to Jewish survival. But, at the same time, he knows that continued Jewish existence has need of Zionism as an ideal framework and of the State of Israel as a political center. Hence his ambivalent attitude towards 'negation of the Diaspora' and its logical conclusion: the demand for immigration. To his mind, negation of the Diaspora is the strongest justification for Jewish sovereign existence in the State of Israel. But, to the same extent, sanctioning of Jewish existence in the Diaspora gives the seal of approval to the present unalterable historical situation.[50] The same is true of immigration. He believes that Zionism without immigration is not Zionism, but a Zionism which demands immigration alone is not realistic. It is unacceptable to him also because it deliberately ignores innovations and developments among Diaspora Jews in general, and in the United States in particular.[51]

In other words, he recognizes the objective tension between the Zionist ideology which created a Jewish reality in Palestine and the historically-rooted reality of American Jews who have no clear perception of themselves, but have a strong drive for survival. The term 'tension' is used here deliberately rather than 'conflict' because Neusner reaffirms the unity of the Jewish people and rejects any view which presents any single alternative as better than others. As he sees it, without Zionism, this natural tension may develop into an unbridgeable rift.[52] Neusner, therefore, sees Jewish existence as fraught with constant tension between Israel and the Diaspora. He agrees to the prime importance of several issues: the centrality of Jerusalem, the urgent need for immigration, the priority of Israeli interests in the sphere of Jewish public responsibility. But, to the same degree, he insists on the rights and the inherent value of Jewish existence in the Diaspora.

It is noteworthy that Israel is allotted central place not in its own right but because of the role it plays in maintaining the unity of the Jewish people. In 1977, when associated with Breira and in light of the attempts of radical groups in Israel and the United States such as Gush Emunim and the Jewish Defense League to endow the state with messianic significance, he reiterated its instrumental essence and the value of the Jewish people, rather than the State of Israel.[53] This view of the functional value of the state led him, ten years later, to attribute even greater value and importance to Zionism as a faith than to the state as an existential entity. In his book *Death and Birth of Judaism*,[54] he enumerates six forms of Jewish life created after the disintegration of halakhic society from the eighteenth century onward: Reform, Conservative, neo-Orthodox, Yiddishist, Bundist and Zionist. Zionism was the pattern of thinking and lifestyle which guided Diaspora Jews and showed them the way, he writes, and it retains something of its former qualities, since it bids Jews to preserve the unity of the people. On the other hand, Israeli nationalism, which is developing naturally and spontaneously in Israel, has nothing to say to Diaspora Jews. Hence, the state is of Jewish significance as the center of Jewish life, only if it is seen as located at the heart of Zionist ideology, as serving it rather than epitomizing it, and as maintaining the unity of the Jewish people.[55]

In short, Neusner's 'neo-Zionism' is based on a combination of paradoxical assumptions: he is a Zionist who sanctions the Diaspora; he sees Zion as a place without parallel in the Jewish sense, but also perceives the United States as a place worthy of residence; he acknowledges that he lives in the *golah*, but his *galut* is also his home; he favors granting Israel prior status as a universal Jewish interest but insists on the value of the Diaspora; he knows that Zionism has no meaning without the demand for immigration, but insists on his basic right to refrain from responding in person to this demand; he sees the State of Israel as the center of Jewish life, but does not think that it can serve as a guide for world Jewry. These contradictions can be reconciled only if we consider this outlook to be one of the outstanding expressions of 'Jewish normalization', a combination of terms which is itself paradoxical, and suggests that what is normal in Jews is abnormal elsewhere.

In light of the above, it is worth reading Neusner's provocative and controversial article 'Is America the Promised Land for Jews?'[56] It contains several assumptions which appear to be at odds with the views analysed here. The article asserts that America is a better place than Jerusalem in which to be a Jew. He declares that US Jews have changed from 'American Jews' to 'Jewish-Americans', with emphasis on the last word. This view conflicts with his basic conception of Zionism, which he reiterated constantly even after this article was published – namely the unity of the Jewish people. Neusner did not even bother to clarify, as did William Safire, in the wake of the Pollard affair,[57] that in the sphere of foreign affairs and security, the Jews emphasise American issues, and in religious and cultural matters, they stress the Jewish element. In a personal letter to the present author, Neusner stressed that this article was unconnected to his response to the Pollard affair. The article was written several months before the Pollard sentence, and the timing of publication was random. Since I have no reason to doubt his statement, his remarks in the article on his general outlook are even more puzzling, and can only be regarded as an uncharacteristic deviation.

Neusner's claim (which has political implications) that there is identity between Zionism and Judaism, was further elaborated by Professor Daniel Elazar, who immigrated to Israel from the United States in the seventies.[58] His starting-point, in the early eighties, was that the era of secular-messianic ideologies has reached its end. Following in the footsteps of Daniel Bell, who had predicted this at the end of the 1950s, Elazar concluded that Zionism as a messianic-secular ideology with many different variations, has also ended its important and even decisive task. Henceforth, Zionism should be regarded as a current in Jewish faith, like any other. As such, it defines the Judaism of most of the Jewish inhabitants of Israel, and has become a kind of civil religion for the state. As one of the currents of Judaism, Zionism is no longer a revolutionary movement with a comprehensive ideology, offering an alternative to existing patterns of Jewish life, but is now an ideology which is in harmony with them.

According to Elazar, two traditional Jewish outlooks have always been at war within Zionism: Sadduceeism and Pharisaism. The modern Sadducean approach sees Israel as the political center of the Jewish people and is content with this, while the Pharisean outlook, which Elazar has adopted, seeks to restore to Zionism, in accordance with the anti-doctrinarian and practical approach of the Pharisees, the operative vision, based on '*yir'at shamayim*' (piety). This vision is grounded on biblical principles: the covenant – *brit* – of the Jews among themselves and between them and their God, which gives meaning to their Jewish existence; the grace – *hesed* – which reflects the emotional links among Jews. In the Zionist sense, hesed means constant concern for the continued existence and unity of the Jewish people: 'a survival and unity that is always in doubt but at the same time is never doubted'. The third principle is the constant need of Jews to wrestle with God in the proper way, rejecting doctrinarianism while preserving faith. The final principles are justice and law – *tzedek-u-mishpat* – which are the foundations of a just society. According to Elazar, this Zionist pharisaic tradition must become the way of life of world Jewry. It is also a political tradition, he says, as opposed to political ideology, of Judaism. Zionism has undergone three stages in its attitude towards the Jewish people, he declares. First it aroused its political consciousness, then it established the Jewish polity. Now it has reached the third stage of traditional Jewish policy. The roots of this policy lie in the Bible, in medieval philosophy and in Zionism, parts of which are linked to biblical sources. In this context the Jews of the United States have a contribution to make. They were educated in the American political tradition, which is not only anti-doctrinaire, but linked, in many respects, to the spiritual traditions of the Bible. In conclusion, Elazar's neo-Zionism is the continuation of messianic-secular Zionism, because it does not dismiss its achievements but tries to establish a new outlook on that old foundation. With the end of the secular-Zionist era, comes the era of Pharisaic Zionism. This, according to its practical non-doctrinarian essence, is reconciled to the existence of the Diaspora and the numerous forms of expression of Judaism, Israeli Zionism being one of its forms. At the same time, in principle, the center of Pharisaic Zionism is the State of Israel, because only there and by that means can the five principles be realized, particularly the Jewish covenant and fraternity which preserve the integrity of the Jewish people. It could be said that Elazar seeks to pour the biblical political tradition into the mold of Zionism through the operative vision of the Pharisees and within the Saduccean political framework. This entire viewpoint, as a public-national way of life, is influenced by the American political tradition.

At this point, one cannot refrain from commenting that Elazar, while rejecting one ideology, created another. Close examination of messianic-secular Zionism, as he defines it, with all its political currents and shades of opinion, demonstrates that it was not doctrinaire, as he claims, and that its method of operation, from Hibbat Zion through Weizmannism to the constructive Zionism of the labor movement, was impelled by the 'operative vision' no less than was the 'Pharisaic' path. Thus, there is a certain element of exaggeration in his emphasis on the fundamental contrast between the path of secular Zionism, which believed in the 'earthly Messiah' and traditional Judaism which dreamed of celestial redemption. The inescapable conclusion is that the innovation in Elazar's new Zionism lies not in the method but in the view of Jewish national existence in a religious-pluralistic light.

The third of the religious Zionist thinkers is Irving Greenberg.[59] He sees Jewish-Zionist identity as the creation of modern times, particularly since the Holocaust. The identification of Jews with Zionism stems, he argues, from the terrible lesson of the Holocaust and the tragedy of the helpless.[60] From this starting point, he develops an overall historiosophical outlook. Jewish history, he says, is divided into three main periods: the biblical, in which the covenant between the people and their God was forged; the rabbinical, beginning with the destruction of the Second Temple and ending in the eighteenth century, marked by the struggle to ensure the survival of the Jewish people as a religious community conducting its life according to rabbinical halakhic laws; and the political power era, beginning with the Holocaust and the establishment of the Jewish state. He writes that in the Holocaust the Jews learned that power corrupts and absolute power corrupts absolutely, but absolute powerlessness is even more corrupting. On this foundation, he constructs a theory of 'Jewish political culture'. This is a system based on various Jewish institutions and their leaders, dealing with the affairs of the Jewish community – *kelal* – the name of the organization which Greenberg heads in the spheres of both political action and monetary aid. Israel as the state of the Jewish people is the center of these circles of power.

If we accept Elazar's distinction between the Sadducean and Pharisaic political traditions, then Greenberg, unlike Elazar, tends more towards the former. In this, and in his view of the Holocaust as the turning point and beginning of a new era in Jewish history, Greenberg was in concurrence with the neo-conservatives. For both, the lesson of the Holocaust is the mandate for continued Jewish existence, which is guaranteed by Israel. In this respect, this is indubitably an etatistic or Sadducean Zionist viewpoint. Greenberg's Jewish-Zionist outlook, however, goes further than the views of the main spokesmen of neo-conservatism. He places greater emphasis on the unity of existence of the Jewish people, in the historical, political and civil sense. The Holocaust and the establishment of the state are, for him, the events which augured a new era in Jewish history. The political and organizational framework which has Israel at its center has created a Jewish *kelal* on a universal basis. And finally, the close connection of American Jewish citizens to the State of Israel reflects 'positive dual loyalty', which is one of the features of democratic pluralism. He perceives dual loyalty to the United States and to the State of Israel as a principle, acknowledgement of which is the next important step on the road to more complete union between democracy and nationalism.[61]

Whereas Greenberg stresses the positive value of dual loyalty as the balancing factor between democracy and nationalism, Professor Howard Adelman, from Canada, raises the question of the unity of the Jewish people to a higher plane.[62] The survival of the Jewish people, he says, depends on the creation of a real link between each Jewish individual and the State of Israel. In effect, he is proposing to the Jews of the Diaspora, who see themselves as belonging to the Jewish people, dual nationality – of their own countries and of Israel – through at least part-time residence in Israel, through paying taxes to the Israeli government, and taking part personally in Israel's defence. It is important to note that Adelman stressed not the state but the Jewish nation. The state is but a means of nurturing and bolstering national identity. The nation, for him, is even more important than territory.

But he acknowledges that the country is the spiritual basis of the nation. Hence, Eretz Israel is inseparably linked to Jewish national identity. Without it, this identity could be given racist genetic interpretation if, of course, one tries to comprehend Jewish nationalism solely on a secular basis. Adelman's 'dual nationality' derives, therefore, from loyalty, in the following order: to the Jewish people, to Eretz Israel and to the State of Israel. The spiritual basis of the people is its country, and the framework which enables its national existence is its state. Here

222   *The State of Israel in Jewish Public Thought*

Adelman is proposing a new interpretation of Ahad ha-Am's philosophy, adapted to the Western liberal-pluralistic civil society, in which most Diaspora Jews live. If we assume *a priori* that the State of Israel is part of the Western world and that it is not feasible to anticipate any profound political differences with the United States, then dual loyalty, as proposed by Greenberg, or dual nationality as advocated by Adelman, linked to an external political-spiritual center, are compatible with the liberal-democratic pluralism of enlightened Western society.

In parallel to the theories cited above, there evolved a kind of collective neo-Zionist outlook. In 1979, the Zionist Executive decided to hold seminars on Zionist thought in the larger centers in the Diaspora.[63] There were two underlying intentions: to revive interest in Zionist thought in order to adapt it to changing circumstances, and to consolidate a young intellectual Zionist leadership in the Diaspora. And, in fact, the participants included young academics, most of them third-generation American and Canadian Jews.

The central idea broached by most of the participants, in different versions, was recognition of the need for auto-emancipation of Diaspora Jews through Zionist ideology. Professor Steven Cohen demanded the liberation of the Diaspora from its dependence on the Israeli establishment. He defined the prevailing system as 'ecclesiastical' and doomed to failure. The Diaspora, he declared, needed a different approach, which would encourage the dynamic forces in the communities to engage in Zionist activity. To replace the ecclesiastical Zionist organization, he proposed setting up a federal Zionism. According to the federal principle, Jewish organizations in the Diaspora would have the initiative and responsibility for Zionist action. The transition from ecclesiastical Zionism to federal Zionism, he said, was the road to the traditional Zionist aspirations, since Herzl's days, of conquering the Diaspora communities.[64]

Another aspect of the same desire for Diaspora auto-emancipation was proposed by Professor Steven Katz. He focused on the Zionist term 'self-realization' in an attempt to adapt and apply it to reality in the Diaspora. In his opinion, Zionism as an ideology and the Jewish state as a real political entity impose on Jews a certain self-definition. They perpetuate the sense of *galut*, reinforce the sense of being different, and aggravate the feelings of alienation. This new objective situation raises weighty questions as to the essence of Jewish existence in the Diaspora in general and the United States in particular. This speculation leads to the search for personal and collective identity, which Katz denotes 'self-realization' in the Zionist sense, on which depends the future of US Jewry and the State of Israel.[65]

Professor Mervin Verbit went even further in claiming that the ideological innovation of Zionism lay in the very idea of auto-emancipation and not in the desire to establish a Jewish state. The state is one of the components of the idea of auto-emancipation. Hence, what characterizes Zionists today and distinguishes them from non-Zionist Jews, is the inseparable combination of three features – namely, the indispensability of Israel's existence, its centrality in Jewish life, and the responsibility of the Jews for their own destiny.[66] Auto-emancipation is their common denominator, with all this implies for Israel–Diaspora relations. And it is the double justification of both the Zionists in Israel, who argue that Jewish life in the state differs from life in the Diaspora, and also of the Diaspora Jews who believe that by force of their own responsibility for their own lives they are able to maintain their Jewish formula within the framework of general culture. He believes that the combination of these two contradictions, each valid in itself, creates the singular nature of Jewish unity.[67]

The neo-Zionist adherence to the idea of auto-emancipation, translated, in organizational terms, into the demand for autonomous status of the Diaspora *vis à vis* the state, raised the question of its centrality in Jewish life. On this question, the participants in these seminars were divided. Several of the advocates of the centrality of Israel were not content with the traditional arguments, such as the status of Israel as a political center or psychological focus, and sought to augment them according to their own lights.

Mervin Verbit considered the centrality of Israel to be a vital concept enabling Judaism to function within history. The annals of the Jewish people record numerous centers which arose and were destroyed. But none of these evoked in Jews so fierce and protracted a desire to restore it to life as did Eretz Israel. The historical force of this aspiration means that contemporary Jewish existence which fails to acknowledge the centrality of Israel, will be incomplete. Verbit's conclusions are an important part of his neo-Zionist outlook. For him, because of its central position, Israeli society has priority over all other Jewish communities, and Israel is the prime Jewish interest. On the basis of these assumptions, he stressed that for a Zionist like himself, who was still living in the Diaspora, Israel was home. Therein lies the distinction between the concept of centrality for the Zionist and for the 'pro-Israel' Jew. For the former, centrality is the expression of commitment and responsibility towards the entire people, while for the latter it is a theory which can be held as long as it does not clash with existential interests. That which demands total dedication of the Zionist, is a 'leisure-time activity' for the pro-Israeli non-Zionist.[68]

At the same time, Verbit stresses that the value of centrality does not diminish the value of Jewish life in the Diaspora. And the fact that there is a connection between Israel as a Jewish center and as a home for all the Zionists of the Diaspora does not transform Zionism into an immigration movement. Verbit cautioned against the unequivocal and uncompromising demand for Zionist realization. Exclusive focus on this injunction, he said, would reduce Zionism from a wide popular movement into a kind of sect, and it could thereby forfeit its new historic role of aiding Jewish collective existence in the Diaspora. Hence, the greater the emphasis placed on the idea of centrality and the historic role of Zionism, the less importance is attributed to the Zionist value of immigration.

This trend, originating in Kaplan's philosophy, was carried further by Sidney Schwartz, who perceived Zionism as a noble objective in itself without connection to immigration because it fortifies Judaism in every sense. Therefore he argued, in original and paradoxical fashion, that the Zionism of the Diaspora cancels the sense of *galut*. It renders the Diaspora a natural place for Jews as individuals and as a collective body. And only the assimilationists, who are anxious to sever their ties with their people because they regard their Judaism as a barrier against total absorption into surrounding society, suffer from a sense of exile.[69]

The importance that Schwartz attributed to the Zionist movement led him to his next argument. While recognizing the centrality of Israel, he saw the Zionist movement as a counterbalance. Since the state, because of its political essence, is obliged to operate within the world of power politics and has conveyed the Jewish people into this sphere of human activity, the Zionist movement in the Diaspora has a role to play which will countervail political action by strict observance of moral principles. Schwartz was seeking to create a kind of Jewish national equilibrium between the centrality of the state as bearer of Jewish interests and the role of Zionism as guardian of Jewish moral values. On the basis of this view, he arrived at the conclusion that the main function of Zionism is not to deal with the immigration of Jews to Israel but with their spiritual elevation in their diasporas.

The assumption that Zionism, in its new formulation, negates the Diaspora, was not universally accepted. Verbit stressed that, in the final analysis, Zionism is the desire to return home to Eretz Israel. If one's home is set apart from one's place of residence, the latter becomes an exile. This view was expounded more explicitly by Henry Weinberg. Like Neusner, he argued that Zionism must observe the sharp distinction between Israel and the Diaspora. Zionism, to his mind, cannot accept life in the Diaspora as the norm. It must negate the *galut* without belittling the Diaspora and its present day achievements.[70]

At this point, Weinberg cited an interesting argument. As a matter of principle, he declared, the perpetual sanctioning of *galut* life is at odds with the right to self-determination, on a national-political basis. This means that Israel, although not yet the spiritual center of the Jewish people, is the center of self-determination. And as such, together with Zionism, it has bolstered the national awareness of the Jews of the Diaspora. This success has generated a dialectical paradox. The great majority of the Jewish people are content with this situation, and only a few among the Zionists feel the need to give personal interpretation to 'negation of the Diaspora' by immigrating to Israel. Practically speaking, it is necessary to abolish the distinction between Zionists and non-Zionists, where the wider masses are concerned, and to retain it only with respect to the elite, with their subtler national awareness. Zionism in the sense of the ingathering of the exiles, is the supreme national goal, but the way to achieve it consists of preserving the practical equilibrium and close cooperation between Israel and the Diaspora. In this respect, in the attempt to translate the fundamental approach into the language of action, there was no difference between Weinberg and Schwartz, who rejected 'negation of *galut*'. At the same time, definition of Jewish existence in the Diaspora as a *galut* experience is important as a criterion for distinguishing between the various approaches.

The main spokesman of the trend which rejected Israel's centrality was Professor Abraham Rothstein from Canada.[71] He postulated a connection between the auto-emancipation and autonomy of Diaspora Jews and denial of the term *galut*, because, he said, the term itself implies inequality and dependence. The Jews of the Diaspora must decide for themselves whether they are in exile or not, and whether they have a future. Discussion of these issues should be conducted in the United States, in Canada and wherever Jews live, outside Israel, but not in Jerusalem. The Diaspora must consider its own interests above all, without reducing its support for Israel. This being so, he proposed that the attitude towards *yordim*, (emigrés from Israel) be changed, since they are playing an important role in Jewish education in North America. Zionism and the Diaspora have entered a historic 'post-apocalyptic' era, and this implies not the end of Jewish history but the end of *galut* in North America.

This view of the total independence of the Diaspora led him, two years later,[72] to negate Israel's centrality. Like David Polish, he declared that, in history, the relations between center and periphery are always destined to collapse; either the periphery is oppressed by the center or else it breaks away sooner or later. The ideal solution, therefore, is to establish equilibrium as advocated by Simon Rawidowicz, namely a number of centers, none of them predominant. Rothstein was, thereby, essentially calling for independence of the Diaspora *vis à vis* Israel, instead of demanding autonomy, as did most of the other participants.

The trend to rejection of the central status of Israel and recognition of the independence of the Diaspora won considerable support in Zionist circles in London.[73] In a discussion on the adaptation of the 1968 'Jerusalem Program' to new conditions, several speakers called for its reformulation. It was said that the two basic concepts in the program – the unity of the Jewish people and the centrality of Israel – required clarification, because the concept of unity did not reflect the Jewish pluralistic reality, and because there is an inherent conflict in the very concept of centrality. Centrality is intended to bolster unity and collaboration among Jews. However, this approach is based, by its very nature, on the principle of inequality between Israel and the Diaspora. According to this principle, they argue, equality and unity cannot endure in the long term. Furthermore, subordination of Jewish Diaspora life to Israel could eventually prove detrimental to world Jewish existence. For example, transferral of most of the Israel Appeal funds to Israel limits the scope of Jewish education in the Diaspora. The conclusion was that Zionism has reached a watershed, and must now choose between the inclusive outlook, encompassing the entire Jewish people while maintaining the balance between Israel and the Diaspora, and the exclusive path, which is the choice of the minority, since it entails immigration to Israel.

The discussion concluded with citing of a previous statement by Israel Finestein, which provided the foundation for a certain understanding between supporters and critics of the Jerusalem Program.[32] Finestein declared that the Jewish people, the State of Israel and Zionism had entered upon a new era in their history. The people had gained a state of their own, the state had completed the trial period of its political existence, and Zionism must now become a spiritual movement concerned with self-identity and the meaning of Jewish existence in the world. Hence, Zionism should no longer be identified solely with the demand for immigration, and the Diaspora should not be defined as a *golah*. By using such definitions, Zionism could forfeit its influence over the majority of the people who have no intention of moving to Israel and do not perceive themselves as living in exile. In line with this reasoning, Finestein interprets the term centrality not in the political sense, but as the expression of the desire to preserve the unity of the people.

Furthermore, historiosophically, he expressed doubt as to whether the aspiration to establish a territorial center was a central phenomenon in Jewish history. At the center, he believed, lay the tension between action and reaction, between the idea of *Kelal Israel* (the community of Israel) and the fact of Jewish dispersal. This tension can be translated into modern terms by reviving Ahad ha-Am's theories, namely reinforcing Jewish spiritual unity above and beyond its political significance.

Similar views, though from an American angle, were expressed by Professor Michael Walzer. Jewish life in the United States, he asserted, had become normal according to the principles of general ethnic self-determination, just as Jewish life in Israel is normal according to the territorial-political definitions accepted throughout the world. In this general normalization, particularly where US Jewry are concerned, lies the danger of loss of specific and unique identity. This brings us back, he believes, to the question of the survival of Judaism, as presented by Ahad ha-Am. In seeking an answer to this new form of assimilation, Walzer reverted to Greenberg's formula that in order to travel the road to Zionism, the people must first return to the sources of Judaism. Zionism, as he sees it, is primarily a movement of resistance to ethnic normalization. Israel, with its vibrant Jewish life, can help US Jewry in this struggle, but the bulk of the efforts must be carried out by those forces within it who believe in the value of Jewish self-identity.[75] Walzer accepts in full Ahad ha-Am's analysis of the Jewish condition, but agrees only in part with the solution Ahad ha-Am proposes – the creation of a spiritual center. Israel is an auxiliary factor in the struggle against assimilation, but not the leading force.

This view was not confined to intellectuals and academics. Stuart Eizenstat, one of the prominent figures in US Jewry, formulated it in both theoretical and practical terms, after the shock of the Pollard affair and in direct response to articles by Neusner and Avineri which had roused controversy among US Jewry.[76] Neo-Zionism, in the second half of the eighties, as he understands it, is based on the synthesis between the views of Herzl and Ahad ha-Am. The Holocaust demonstrated tragically the validity of the Herzlian prognosis, but the present condition of the free Diasporas requires a return to the Ahad ha-Am philosophy, to be based on the following principles: first, recognition of the unity, mutual dependence and right to exist of Jews and Judaism on a universal basis, with Israel as the epicenter of Jewish life, helping to realize these aims. Secondly, just as American Jews acknowledge the distinctiveness and centrality of Israel, Israelis must accept the American Jewish existence. This means, as Eizenstat states explicitly, that a Jew can be a Zionist even without immigrating to Israel, if his thoughts and his heart are directed there. Thirdly, the Jews of the United States must cease to be passive spectators of Israeli events. They must not content themselves with financial contributions; it is incumbent on them to be involved partners in Israeli life with its whole range of problems. At the very same time, Henry Siegman, Director of the World Jewish Congress, proposed establishing a new Zionist movement in the spirit of Mordecai Kaplan, to encompass all the active sectors of the Jewish people connected to the State of Israel. The prime task of the Zionist–Jewish congress to be convened in Jerusalem would be to determine the national stand towards the Arab–Israel dispute.[77] Professor Ismar Schorsch, Head of the Theological Seminary of the Conservative Movement, welcomed the establishment of a conservative-Zionist party and assigned a role to conservative Jewry as a whole, entailing greater involvement in Israeli spiritual, social and political affairs.[78]

On the basis of the above, one may deduce that whereas intellectuals and academics emphasized the 'auto-emancipation' of the Diaspora, intellectuals who were active in public life stressed the mutual ties between the Diasporas and Israel and sought, in various ways, to encourage greater involvement of world Jewry therein.

In summary, neo-Zionists, while differing on two basic questions – the centrality of Israel and the *galut* nature of the Diaspora – agreed that in the internal political sphere the Diaspora had the right to self-determination with regard to Israel, and that, on the national plane, Israel has a central role to play in preserving the Jewish identity of the people. In this respect, they were the new, and perplexed, spokesmen of Jewish normalization.

In concluding this section, which could serve as the summary of the entire study, one can say that, although it is difficult to anticipate future trends, it is already possible to point to certain new directions, not necessarily drastic changes in understanding of the essence of Jewish life, but new interpretations of old ideas. This is not to suggest that the ideas of this generation have come full circle, but to hint that on several central issues, public thought has reverted to the quandaries of forty years ago, and the need to choose between Jewish normalization and singular normalization, with general normalization as a side issue. These basic approaches are taking on new forms. In neo-Zionist thought the autonomist trend is coming to the fore, in non-Zionist thought the ethnic element is gaining ground, while in anti-Zionist thought the territorial factor is growing in importance.

On questions of principle, it seems evident that the proponents of general normalization are no longer totally committed to territory as the shaper of collective national consciousness. The recognition of the history unity of the different strata

228 The State of Israel in Jewish Public Thought

of Jewish culture, and not only on a religious basis, and the assumption that there is an extra-territorial Jewish people, attest to the change in this outlook, which is bringing it closer to the Jewish consensus. Forty years ago, in contrast, those who upheld similar views placed themselves, in the ideological and political sense, completely outside this consensus. On the other hand, on the more practical plane, on such issues as the Law of Return, applicable only to Jews, the rift between them and the other approaches has only widened.

As regards the two central approaches – Jewish and singular – their profound differences on the question of the negation of *galut* and the national essence of the Jewish people have almost totally disappeared. On the one hand, there is increasing awareness that free and open Western society is not a *golah*, and on the other, belief that the Jews are an extra-territorial nation has been reinforced. This rapprochement has been caused, in large measure, by the sanctioning of ethnic culture and mentality in a pluralistic society and the intensive involvement of Diaspora Jews in Israeli affairs.

One may say, therefore, that an ideological consensus is emerging, which acknowledges the significance of history, namely a continuum of culture, belief, will and aspiration, as the basis for Jewish collective consciousness. And this, in one way or another, serves as a kind of recognition of the justice and the triumph of Zionism, despite the recent chorus claiming that Zionism's hour has passed. Even those champions of singular normalization who now consider the Zionist movement to be superfluous can be confident of their views thanks to this achievement.

On the other hand, in the theoretical sphere, as hinted above, there is increasing controversy between the two approaches. The debate on the centrality of Israel, as the 'preferred center'[79] (a definition which does not imply denial of the existence of other centers but bestows on Israel special national status) has had far-reaching practical implications. I am referring to the polemics on the freedom of Jewish emigrés from the Soviet Union to choose their destination. The disagreement between those who demanded, in the name of national interests, that the emigrés be directed to Israel, and those who defended the fundamental and practical right of American Jews to encourage them to emigrate to the United States, is a clear expression of the difference between the two approaches.[80]

In parallel to this dispute, an academic debate is being waged between demographers, sociologists and public leaders on the capacity of the Jewish people in the Diaspora for survival. This debate, too, is related to the two conflicting ideological standpoints. Opinions are divided between those who argue that the Jewish people is dwindling because of the low rates of natural increase, the high proportion of mixed marriages and the gradual but constant process of assimilation, and those who claim that these evaluations are invalid, and that the US Jewish community has been displaying great and unexpected vitality in the past few years. Evidence of this is the flourishing of Jewish studies at universities, the preservation of traditional symbols by the young generation, and the tendency of mixed couples to join Jewish congregations.[81]

This public-academic debate between the optimists and the pessimists is both directly and obliquely connected to the controversy between the Jewish and distinctive approaches. To begin with, some of the same people have been taking part in both debates. Secondly, there can be no doubt that the views of both pessimists and optimists have implications for those who believe in the need to build an independent center in the United States, and those who see Jewish existence there as dependent on closer ties with Israel, as the center of Jewish life. These lead to logical conclusions with respect to immigration to Israel among those Diaspora Jews who are clinging to their Jewish identity and wish to hand it on to the generations to come.

As noted above, in the introduction to this section, these trends in public thought are connected to developments in the political sphere and to internal Jewish controversies. Beyond the specific interest of each of these events or questions, they indicate the ambiguity or diversity of meaning of Jewish life in the universal sense and the indecisiveness of the trends of Jewish public thought. Thus, for, instance, the political support which Jewish leaders extend to the Israel government, even though some, or even most of them, do not identify with its policies, is one of the clearest expressions of 'Jewish normalization'. The Jewish public, and all its organizations, has, in effect, accepted the principle advocated by US Zionists, concerning unconditional support for Israel, which at the time, before the Six Day War, set them apart from non-Zionists. Moreover, even those who publicly criticize the Israel government and claim the right to voice their opinions in order to influence its policies, are expressing, in reverse fashion, the very same trend of Jewish normalization, which highlights the national features of Jewish existence.

On the other hand, the debate on the unqualified right of Jews leaving the Soviet Union to choose their destination is evidence of the intensification of the non-Zionist trend within the US Jewish leadership, or, in other words, the strengthening of the 'singular normalization' approach. The interest of the Jews outweighs the Jewish interest. In other words, in contrast to the first (political) example, whereby the leadership, in the name of national interests, denies the right of Diaspora Jews to express public criticism of Israel, here it insists on the individual's right to free choice, while acknowledging the national importance of immigration to Israel.

The polemics on the question of Soviet Jewry are related to a more historically significant development, namely the relations between Israel and the Diaspora. One of the characteristic features of this period is Israel's loss of standing, and the growth in self-awareness and self-confidence among Diaspora Jews. The non-Zionist choice of most of the emigrés from the Soviet Union attests loudly and clearly to this development, but does not predict any clear trend in Jewish life. The question is whether these emigrés are choosing the United States because of the Jewish lifestyle there or because of the American standard of living. Moreover, if the American Jewish way of life does not succeed in protecting these emigrés against the almost total exposure to the temptations of assimilation, this will be one of its greatest failures. The same existential ambiguity is inherent in the political protest of Jewish organizations against President Reagan's visit to Bitburg, and their campaign against the election of Kurt Waldheim as Austrian Chancellor. These two campaigns indubitably demonstrate the prestige and self-confidence of Diaspora Jews. This is also additional evidence of the profound change in the feelings of the Jews living among non-Jews. Yet, the fact that, on these sensitive moral issues, the US President and the Austrian people prevailed, proves once again how delicate is the collective situation of the Jews among other nations.

This leads us to the Jewish response to the Pollard affair as additional and final evidence of the ambiguous nature of Jewish Diaspora life. Was this a traditional *galut* reaction, as Shlomo Avineri sees it, or merely the expression of concern on the part of those committed to Israel and concerned for its status in American public opinion. Although the institutional Jewish response should not be perceived as evidence of a '*galut* mentality', among US Jewry, one cannot disregard the fact that this feeling was manifested in the Jewish public mood.[82] One of the important distinctions between the two basic approaches – Jewish normalization and singular normalization – is the acceptance or negation of the Diaspora. The Jewish stance on the Pollard affair demonstrates, therefore, that the conflict between the two has not yet been resolved.

Thus, these two approaches have been constantly weighed in the balance of Jewish public thought for the past 40 years. Today, the scales appear to be weighted in favor of the singular approach, but this is probably not the last word. These lines are being written at the height of the public storm on the definition of 'Who is a Jew?' in the Law of Return. Whatever the outcome of this ideological struggle, it will have a far-reaching impact on the Jewish world. Henceforth there are three paths: greater cohesion and the reinforcement of Israel's central role in Jewish life; acceleration of the process of separation and seclusion of each community, reflected in the United States in the attempt to build a kind of cultural autonomy on an ethnic basis; and the third, and most likely, scenario – which is a blend of the other two – accentuation of Jewish unity and the distinctive character of US Jewry. From this blend will emerge a formula of 'singular Jewish normalization' for a community who are ever aware of their dual national loyalties: loyalty to their homeland and loyalty to their people, some of whom have returned to their own territory, but most of whom still reside outside it; who have returned to the arena of history but whose survival cannot be explained only in historical terms.

This assumption, which derives from this study of 'public thought', is borne out, to some extent, by S.M. Cohen's research into Jewish 'public opinion' in the last ten years. Cohen divides American Jewry, in its attitude towards Israel, into 'three broad categories' related to commitment and involvement. He states that one-third are 'relatively indifferent' to Israel; another third are pro-Israel 'in reflexive but not particularly thoughtful, committed or active fashion'. The last third are, in his words, 'passionately pro-Israel, occasionally or even frequently expressing their passion through visible concrete behavior'.[83]

Since pro-Israelism is the major public expression of Jewish identity in America,[84] Cohen's division appears very close to the three major approaches in the present book: general normalization; singular normalization and Jewish normalization. The differences between Cohen's last two categories are not significant, and I suggest that the quest for collective identity today entails the merging of singular and Jewish Normalization.

In his most recent book, on the social forces that have shaped Jewish Identity in the last two centuries, the historian Michael Meyer arrived at a very similar conclusion. 'Never in modern times have Jews in the West been more committed to Jewish peoplehood,' he writes, 'and most of them see Israel as its chief embodiment.'[85] And, despite the tensions between Diaspora Jewry and Israel, which are elaborated at length in this book, he argues that 'Zion has retained its influence as the most powerful symbol of Jewish unity and common destiny'.[86]

In the public sphere, S. Eizenstat suggested that Jewish identity should be based on a balance between identification with Israel and a return to the values and practices of the Jewish religion.[87] In the face of a growing trend towards assimilation among the Jews in the open and free society, he asserted, this is the only possible mode of national existence.

I concur with this view and that is the reason why I cannot entirely agree with David Vital's pessimistic prediction that the Jewish nation is on the decline and that its national-communal structure 'lies shattered today, almost beyond repair'.[88] The long history of the Jews proves that, whenever they reached a watershed in their national and religious existence, a time when cultural assimilation, religious discrimination, and political persecution threatened their integrity and unity – new forces arose within the society to combat the threat.

Since history is replete with dialectical paradoxes, any historian, engaged in predictions, must do so with skepticism and humility, and remember that 'The work is not upon thee to finish, nor art thou free to desist from it'.

Afterword
1992

Afterword, 1992:
In Defence of Perpetual
Zionist Revolt

Never in modern times have Jews in the West been more committed to Jewish peoplehood. And most of them see Israel as its chief embodiment.

Michael Meyer, *Jewish Identity in the Modern World*

The full reckoning is not yet over.

Y. H. Brenner, *From Here to There*

The historian sometimes resembles a playwright who constructs his drama out of the materials of real life, and in so doing, feels the desire to play a role in his own drama. During the years in which I have studied the subject of this book, I have felt the increasing desire to become involved in it. And as my research came closer to the present day, I felt a growing need for direct commitment, and became convinced that the very nature of the study demands it. Hence, I have decided to become an actor in this intellectual drama – by adding my own concluding remarks.

Examination of Jewish public thought in the past 40 years, and analysis of the developmental trends, show, so I believe, that the sole common denominator is the Zionist world outlook.

Zionism today is in a state of profound crisis. The Zionist Organization appears to be powerless, and its way of thinking seems outdated. This sorry situation stems not only from the fact that the movement lacks authoritative and influential leaders, and its institutions are perceived as ineffectual, but because it has not succeeded in capturing the imagination of contemporary Jews by offering a central ideal, suited to the new realities in which they live.

Like every long-lived social movement, Zionism, in its century of existence, has undergone so many crises that its history can be classified accordingly. The Hibbat Zion era ended in a crisis of leadership, which began in the early 1890s. Pinsker died in 1891, disillusioned with the prospects for Jewish settlement in Palestine; the waning of the second wave of immigration in that same year (because of restrictions imposed by the Ottoman authorities) seemed to confirm his pessimism. Herzl's inspiring debut in 1897 ended in bitter polemics on the question of settlement in Uganda, and he died after only seven years of activity within the Zionist movement. The days of glory of Weizmannite Zionism – from the Balfour

235

Declaration in 1917 to the establishment of the Jewish Agency in 1929 – also terminated in a profound political crisis with the British Government and in a dispute within the Zionist movement, which led eventually to the reluctant resignation of Weizmann from presidency of the movement. The *sturm und drang* days of the 1930s, when immigration flowed into Palestine and settlements sprang up all over the country, ended in the partition controversy which threatened to split the Zionist movement, and in the 1939 White Paper, aimed at repudiating Great Britain's commitment to the Zionist movement by establishing a Palestinian state. The mass mobilization of US Jewry for the political struggle for statehood and their financial aid to immigrant absorption came to an end in a spirit of mutual recrimination and estrangement between Israel and the Diaspora, which lasted from the mid-fifties to the Six Day War.

The four decades of statehood have also been marked by periodic crises, but there is a fundamental difference between pre- and post-state crises. The former resulted from the weakness of the Zionist movement and political circumstances, which it was powerless to change; the latter were caused, paradoxically enough, by its achievements. Moreover, the crises stem from the dual achievements of Zionism and of Diaspora Jewry. In the past two generations, a period in which Zionism became the greatest collective achievement of the Jewish people throughout their history, the Jews of the free world have won individual achievements, on a scale unparalleled in Diaspora history. These two developments are not necessarily at odds, but in certain historic situations, there is a basic conflict between them. Thus, the collective achievement of establishing a state and the guaranteeing of its survival in this troubled region places a heavy burden on the individual. The revolution wrought by mass immigration, which, for the first time in Jewish history, brought together Jews from east and west at the core of Jewish historical action, led to the cultural transformation of that society. The new reality, reflected in lifestyle and quality of life, is of great concern to many of those who have achieved personal success in the West and in Israel. When Jews in search of individual success and prosperity prefer to emigrate to the United States instead of to Israel, Zionism's prestige is dimmed and the reputation of the state suffers. But this is so because the Zionist state reflects the collective will of the people by observing the Law of Return. And finally, the fact that Zionism has succeeded in restoring to the Jewish people their ancient political and spiritual center, arouses in successful Jews abroad great expectations, which, because of their intensity, can be transformed swiftly into deep disillusionment.

This disillusionment, still confined to a minority of Diaspora Jews, is expressed in the tendency to question the very principle of the centrality of Israel in Jewish life. It is altering the focus of the Jewish collective effort, which was once directed towards Israel and on Israel's behalf, towards the development of other Jewish centers coexisting with Israel and of equal standing. These ideas, although still held by a minority of Jews, should not be dismissed lightly, because they enfold a threat.

At the present state, these ideas seem to confirm Dubnow's views on the proliferation of Jewish centers and the shift from place to place throughout history. Yet, in a world in which Jews are integrated and involved in the culture of their countries of residence, this neo-Dubnowianism could develop into a kind of neo-Bundism, and to gradual erosion of acceptance of the existence of one Jewish people throughout the world. In other words: this trend will not lead to the flowering of Jewish cultural autonomy in the countries where Jews live, as Dubnow or the Bund leaders believed, but will cause the total assimilation of Jewish ethnic groups into the pluralistic societies of their countries of residence, and the loss of their national common denominator. This trend, essentially anti-Zionist, is confined, ideologically, to an intellectual minority, but is latent and subconscious, in the social sense, among the Jewish masses in the Diaspora and in Israel.

In light of this trend, is Zionist ideology still necessary? This query leads us to one of the central issues for understanding of the roots and ideology of the Zionist movement. It is worth pondering to what extent this movement is the outcome of necessity and how much it is the product of free ideological choice. In other words: which ephemeral historical elements and which metahistorical elements exist and operate within it?

Zionism was undoubtedly born out of the political and economic predicament of the Jews of Eastern Europe, and was greatly influenced by the national and social ideologies prevailing in nineteenth-century Europe. But it was not only necessity or cultural milieu which determined its essence and its destiny: it is a fact that want and persecution led the masses of Jewish emigrés from Eastern Europe to the United States and not to Eretz Israel. The awakening of nationalist feeling in Europe aroused other forms of Jewish nationalism apart from Zionism. Jewish territorialism sought to establish a Jewish state in a more congenial territory than Palestine. Autonomism, the brainchild of Dubnow, advocated the establishment of Jewish cultural autonomy in Jewish centers in the Diaspora, and even the Bund had its own socialist-national outlook. Zionism was distinctive among these ideologies in that it offered an absolute alternative, based on freedom of choice.

The basic principles of this choice were: return to the historic homeland in the Land of Israel, settlement on the land and control of all economic spheres, creation of a Jewish majority in the country, and revival of the Hebrew language as the national tongue of the people. All these goals were contradictory to the processes developing objectively throughout the world, namely the flow of migration from the agricultural nations to the industrial ones. Elsewhere, the masses were moving from village to city, and among the Jews the trend was to increasing socio-cultural integration in their countries of residence or places of migration. From this we may learn that Zionism, in essence, is not only the fruit of reality, but also the personification of a rebellion against reality. This revolt was expressed in ideas and in actions.

The 'rebels' were the naive settlers of the First Aliyah, who chose the difficult path of founding colonies and rejected the easier path of urban life in the older

Jewish urban communities. They were followed by the young activists of the Second Aliyah, who launched a struggle on behalf of 'Hebrew' labor' in defiance of economic logic. With their inspiration and guidance, the Third Aliyah settlers implemented the idea of 'constructive socialism', both by founding the General Federation of Labor, which differed from any other labor federation in the world, and by establishing the cooperative settlement movement. By these actions they rebelled against reality in the name of utopia and created a model of realistic utopianism, which became a driving and constructive social force, which eventually also made a decisive contribution to the establishment of the state. These Zionist rebels included the teachers who revived the Hebrew language, through protracted efforts, as well as the leaders of the Zionist movement who succeeded, by unconventional means, in transforming objective weakness into subjective political force.

This 'rebellious' trait of Zionism highlights an additional paradox inherent in the movement. This movement, which restored the Jewish people to its history, did so by means of its will and by measures which were, to a large extent, superhistorical: thus, it is not the changes wrought by time and place which will determine its fate, but the will and aspirations of the Jews. This statement does not answer the cardinal question: Is Zionism necessary to Jews in their present situation? I believe that we can answer this question only after clarifying the basic ideological essence of Zionism.

From the outset – the Hibbat Zion era – Zionism was a pluralistic movement, which succeeded in concentrating within it, on the basis of a possible consensus, conflicting ideological currents and political groups: religious and secular, political and practical, socialist and middle-class, liberal and totalitarian. The basis for compromise, agreed upon by most of those participating in the movement, were the principles of the Zionist revolt, as follows: the return to Eretz Israel, the historic homeland of the Jewish people; creation of a Jewish majority in Eretz Israel, as the expression and guarantee of change in the historic status of the people; creation of a normal Jewish economy, as the condition for independence of the national society; and the revival of the Hebrew language as the supreme stage in cultural renaissance. Beyond these basic tenets, opinions were divided on all ideological and political issues. Even on the question of attitudes towards the *golah*, there was no single viewpoint. Ostensibly, Zionism, which aimed at establishing a society which would be the antithesis of the Diaspora, should have negated it absolutely. But this was not the case. Zionism negated the Diaspora in the sense that it denied its ability to survive in the long term by its own powers, as an entity with Jewish identity, but in practice there was no consensus as to its fate, namely that it was destined to disappear.

On this point, Ahad ha-Am and Herzl differed from the outset. Ahad ha-Am sought a way of preserving the Jewish character of the *golah*, because he did not anticipate its physical disappearance; while Herzl, who despaired of the idea of Jewish integration in European society, advocated the exodus of the majority of European Jews. Paradoxically enough, therefore, although Herzlian Zionism became the predominant trend in the pre-State Zionist movement, it was Ahad ha-Am's views on the future of the Diaspora that prevailed. In other words: the various trends in Zionism, from the moderate to the activist and radical, perceived immigration to Eretz Israel as a practical solution only for part of the Jewish people.

Furthermore: the demand for territorial concentration in Palestine, and the creation of a Jewish majority, was not perceived as dependent on the immigration of the large part of the Jewish people. Zionism always took a selective view of the Diaspora, related primarily to the predicament of Eastern European Jewry. The Jews of Western Europe, and particularly the United States, were not considered candidates for immigration; and the Jews of Asia and Africa did not constitute a problem at that time. In the 1930s, when the plight of Europe's Jews worsened, Weizmann and Greenbaum anticipated the immigration of one to two million Jews from that continent. Shortly before his death, in 1940, Jabotinsky envisioned a Jewish state of five million Jewish citizens and two million Arabs. After the 1942 Biltmore Conference, Ben-Gurion spoke of the immediate immigration of two million Jewish refugees to the future Jewish state. But, by the fifties he was no longer confident that the vision of the ingathering of the exiles would be realized where US Jews were concerned.

At the same time, inherent in Zionism was a qualitative 'negation of the *golah*' which stemmed from the fundamental Zionist view of Diaspora life and the alternative which Zionism hoped to offer. Ahad ha-Am negated cultural assimilation, or what he denoted 'slavery within freedom', the condition of the Jews of the free Western countries. Chaim Weizmann condemned the lack of aesthetic sense among Eastern European Jews in the widest meaning of the term. Jabotinsky abhorred *galut* life, as lacking dignity and self-pride. The labor movement rejected the parasitic element in Jewish life in the Diaspora, the total and undignified dependence of the Jews on their surroundings. In short, 'negation of the *golah*' in Zionism, with the exclusion of Herzl, was relative, and linked to time and place. This being so, one cannot accept the reverse of 'negation of *golah*,' namely 'negation of Zionism' which is based on the argument that in the light of the fact that the Diaspora did not wane after the establishment of Israel, Zionist ideology is no longer valid. This view of confrontation between the Zionist and Diaspora ideologies emphasizes their mutual negation. It should be stressed that this view does not imply opposition to the state or even its depreciation. The reverse is true. The very connection with the state becomes the argument against Zionism.

Since Israel came into being, its ties with Diaspora Jews have strengthened, despite problems and upheavals. Israel is today the central public interest of Diaspora Jews, a kind of 'religion', common to secular and religious Jews. But, together with this profound identification, there is a natural tendency to distinguish between the value of the state and the value of Zionism in the context of Jewish interests. Whereas the distinction between the sovereign State of Israel and the Zionist Organization, whose members are citizens of other countries, is essential for political reasons, the distinction between the Jewish state and Zionist ideology is artificial and spurious.

The Zionist-Jewish combination is built into the essence of the state and finds expression in its everyday life. It constitutes the territorial-national framework, guaranteeing the continuum of Jewish life, with its religious and secular aspects. As an open refuge for all Jews in trouble, it maintains in practice the value of mutual responsibility. The centrality of the state in the consciousness of Jews, reflected both in their concern for it and their quarrels with it, their support for it and their reservations, reinforces Jewish unity and identity, which is the basis of Zionism, as laid down by Herzl. Thus, when the Jews of the Diaspora define their devotion to the state as a form of Zionism, this view should neither be belittled nor dismissed as hypocritical and self-indulgent.

Ostensibly, it is the almost unconditional support of Diaspora Jews for Israel which demonstrates the validity of Zionist ideology for our times as well. One could interpret this identification, against the general background and the objective developments of today, as an inner need. There is an element of truth in this, but it is not the whole truth. This need stems from the unique lives of Western Jewry, who are preoccupied with the question of their own freedom, but it lacks the element of the conscious rebellion, which was once the symbol of Zionism. In other words, the Jews of the West are living in a society which not only allots respected status to the Jewish religion, but also sanctions ethnicity. Ethnic pluralism is the cultural-psychological norm in the free countries. And as such, it offers a new and different path to assimilation in non-Jewish society. Henceforth, in order to become part of general society, there is no longer any need to convert to Christianity or to deny Jewish culture. On the contrary: to maintain a degree of ethnic distinctiveness is the respected and accepted way to total assimilation.

The significance of this trend is that, in the final analysis, the traditional-Jewish character, which on principle, was separate and distinct, will be forfeited. One might say that the ethnic trend among Jews is an expression of objective processes occurring within the general society. These processes may cause the Jewish sense of unity to deviate from the idea of the center in Israel, towards the Dubnowian theory and thence to the Bundist ideology. Anyone who rejects this possibility must choose Zionism instead.

Because of the need for Zionism, for the preservation of universal Judaism, it is incumbent on us to clarify its suitability for this task, by examining the essence of the Zionist praxis as a movement operating within history. Let it be stated at once: Zionism was never a religious faith or an ideological doctrine, though such elements existed in many of the ideological groups which composed it. In general, however, Zionism was always the reverse of doctrinarian. Its power lay in the ability to adapt its ideals to changing conditions and to select the right means and instruments for their implementation: all this without losing sight of the main goal. Therefore, over three generations – from Hibbat Zion to statehood – it changed its priorities and shifted its trends without deviating from its path. First, political

Zionism replaced Hibbat Zion; then constructive Zionism, headed by Weizmann and implemented by the socialist labor movement, dominated it in the 1920s; from the mid-thirties, in the period of national emergency, the main concern was the struggle for the survival of the Yishuv, which developed into the fight for statehood; after the state was established, it became a movement whose overt and proclaimed aim had been achieved and Jewish sovereignty became its main concern. Each period was characterized by its unique mood.

The Hibbat Zion period was colored by the romanticism of intellectuals who 'saw the light'; political Zionism – by the aspiration for normalization; constructive Zionism – by social utopianism; in the time of national emergency, the mood was one of readiness for combat; and in the era of statehood – the desire to consolidate the patterns of life of an independent society. I believe that we are now on the threshold of a new movement – post-sovereignty.

As we approach the year 2000, Jewish life is characterized worldwide by two conflicting features. On the one hand world Jewry has never been so united in the political sense, and on the other Judaism has never before been so divided culturally. Political unity is fostered by concern for Israel, concern for Soviet Jewry, a vigilant stand against neo-Fascist tendencies, etc. But all these are issues which, by their very nature, are transient. The cultural dimension, on the other hand, is durable and profound. In effect, Judaism is split up in a number of ways: the religious and secular camps, the former divided into a number of trends, which are increasingly divided on questions of conversion, mixed marriages and the Law of Return; Jews who are an integral part of their countries of residence and those who are citizens of their own sovereign state; Jewish communities speaking different languages, who not only enjoy the culture of their countries but contribute to it as well.

The present balance between political unity and cultural division may be disrupted some day because of the changing character of the former and the durability and increasing intensity of the latter. In face of these trends, those Jews who wish to preserve their Jewish identity as a people with its own distinctive character, require an ideology of revolt against objective reality. Of all the trends and movements which have struggled in the past to preserve Jewish distinctiveness and continue to do so, Zionism is the most comprehensive. Extreme orthodoxy represents only a small part of the people, and the more fanatic this minority becomes, the more it promotes division. The modern religious trend, Reform and Conservative, have attracted only a part of the Jewish people. Secular Jews are left without guiding ideology apart from their political support for Israel. Zionism as a pluralistic movement succeeded in the past and can do so in the present, in embracing various conflicting trends on the basis of a common denominator. But in order to do so it needs to place at the core of Jewish consciousness an idea which has been deeply repressed until now.

In its century of existence, Zionist thought and action has emphasized the trend to national normalization. This was true of the idea of the return to the historic homeland, the return to physical labor and productivization of the masses, as well as the establishment of a socialist society, the political struggle for the right to self-determination, the desire to achieve sovereignty for the Yishuv, etc. The distinctive anomalous element was reflected mainly in the measures adopted in order to implement these trends. Thus the return to nature became an ideal, and physical labor became a value ('the religion of labor'), the class struggle was transformed into constructive socialism, the national commitment of the labor movement took the form of effort to achieve a cooperative utopia, and the migration movement aspired to become an 'ingathering of the exiles'. The anomalous means maintained normal tendencies and without them the goals could not have been achieved. Without agricultural settlement, 'Hebrew labor', the kibbutz movement and the ideology of ingathering of the exiles, the state could not have come into being and could not have survived. But in the course of history, the anomaly of the means has been overwhelmed by the normality of the tendencies, and society in the Jewish state increasingly resembles other societies. Now, in light of the prevailing situation, the time has come to reverse the order of things. The Jewish people should face the challenge of anomalous trends which should be achieved through normal deeds.

For those Diaspora Jews who wish it, the consolidation of the sense of distinctiveness in a society which is becoming increasingly uniform entails elevating ethnic consciousness to the sphere of overall national consciousness. Such consciousness will constitute a kind of declaration that the Jewish people is one, although Jews, for the most part, are not concentrated in their national territory; are not, for the most part, religious; speak many languages and live in diverse cultures; and this being so, the Jewish people does not intend to submit to objective developments. Just as their forefathers fought in the name of religious injunctions, they now rebel in the name of national principles. Such a revolt demands intensified awareness of *galut*.

Golah, in the political and economic sense, disappeared when the Jews were given a choice between immigrating to their national home or remaining in their countries of birth. For those who chose the Diaspora – the sense of *galut* is the condition for their Judaism – *galut* not in the overall social meaning, namely a place where injustice prevails, nor in the traditional-religious sense of exile of the Divine Presence (*Shekhina*) and anticipation of the messianic era, but *galut* as the historic experience of an extraordinary people, who are a minority wherever they live and struggle for collective survival. This sense of *galut* is not universal, but distinctively-national.

The rebellious desire of the Jews to maintain their national unity, leads, by internal logic, to acknowledgment of the State of Israel as their center; a scattered people, without a cultural and territorial framework, needs a focus where its parts can come together. No diaspora can substitute for Israel's historic function. But, according to that same principle of unity, just as the Jews of the Diaspora must promote the center, Israel must encourage autonomous, cultural and ideological trends in the Diaspora. This will create the abnormal balance between mutual dependence and independence.

Acknowledgment of the centrality of Israel requires that a distinction be drawn between the state as an etatist organization with vital normal functions and natural weaknesses, stemming from the very fact of its activity within history, and the state as guarantor and preserver of Jewish values, as an 'open refuge', as the guardian of historical tradition, bolstering the unity of the people and demonstrating the change in the status of the Jews.

The special connection of Diaspora Jews to the state demands of them that they recognize immigration to Israel as the most important act of bonding and the supreme expression of the revolt against reality. Immigration, even when limited in scope (and perhaps precisely because of its restricted nature), should be the jewel in the crown of 'rebellious Jewry'. In addition, study of the Hebrew language should play a central role. The effort invested in study of a language which is neither fashionable nor useful, is the most important popular expression of the communal will to survive.

And finally, the last 'abnormal' principle, binding together all the others, is the equal right to mutual intervention. On all the distinctive issues, namely, the standing of religion in society, Jewish education, natural increase, immigration and migration and the guaranteeing of the Jewish character of the state, the Jewish people in the Diaspora and in Israel have the right to intervene. But fertile thought on these matters can develop and exert influence only within the framework of an all-Jewish movement.

One hundred years ago, the Hebrew writer M.Z. Feuerberg wrote an essay entitled 'Where to?' ('*Le'an*') and the question reverberated in the world of Eastern European Jewish intellectuals. The answer proposed by Hibbat Zion saved the national identity of the Jewish people. I believe that the time has come to rouse a new Hibbat Zion movement. Ostensibly this is a paradoxical and non-historical thought. The Jewish people are now living under totally different conditions to those of the 1880s, when Hibbat Zion came into being. At the same time – although the past century has witnessed the creation of large Jewish concentrations in the West, the Holocaust which destroyed both Jews and the Jewish predicament, and the establishment of a state which bestowed a measure of normality on Jewish existence – there is a certain resemblance between the two historical conditions, reflected in the choice granted to the Jewish masses. In the past, they were free to choose between emigration and Aliyah, and now they are free to choose between Judaism and assimilation.

In this situation, where freedom of choice is compounded by relative ease of assimilation, the predicament of the Jews is easing, and the predicament of Judaism, as Ahad ha-Am called it, is growing more acute. What is needed is a new Hibbat Zion, since the previous movement was established primarily in order to relieve the plight of Judaism in the face of the danger of individual assimilation, detachment of Jewish centers from one another and loss of individual and group self-respect. In no previous period in our history have these dangers been as real as today.

At the same time, let it be pointed out that this call for a new Hibbat Zion is directed towards the idea rather than the movement, since the historical Hibbat Zion was a movement which failed and an idea which triumphed. It failed because it did not produce from its midst a national leadership, failed to unite Jews of Eastern and Western Europe in a joint endeavor, and was unable to recruit the required funds in order to help the First Aliyah settlers, who were eventually saved by the national paternalism of Baron Rothschild. As an idea, however, it succeeded, and to this very day its national principles are valid, and lie at the core of the Jewish public discussions. These principles should be deepened and reconsolidated and the relevant organizational and practical conclusions should be drawn.

Three of Hibbat Zion's principles are of vital significance for present-day Zionism. This movement removed the meaning of Jewish identity from the exclusive sphere of religious definition, by determining that Judaism is a national entity with its own distinctive social, cultural and spiritual nature, consolidated throughout the course of history. Religion was perceived in this context as a spiritual-cultural element, but not as a faith on which nationalism is dependent. The second principle is the assumption that the national cohesion of the dispersed and divided Jewish people will be achieved through the settlement of Eretz Israel, which will be gradual, protracted and perhaps even never-ending. The third principle was the attribution of supreme importance to national education, both as the conduit of Jewish culture to the individual and as a barrier against mass assimilation.

Examination of these ideas in light of contemporary Jewish realities indicates that they are as valid today as ever before.

The understanding of Jewish existence according to the widest possible definition is the sole formula for preserving Jewish unity. The Jewish people today are split and divided into various categories. As regards political status, some are living in their national territory, in their own state, while the majority are citizens of other countries. Religiously speaking, the majority are non-observant and the minority are believers. Among the secular Jews, one should distinguish between those with passive awareness, whose Judaism consists of acknowledgment of their origins, and those with active links to Judaism, who choose to affiliate themselves to national frameworks. Among religious Jews, there are at least three central currents: Orthodox, Reform and Conservative, which are in conflict with one another. To these internal schisms should be added the external divisions, reflected in cultural pluralism and geographical distance.

Under these circumstances, only an all-embracing formula of Jewish nationalism can create a unifying value framework. The other formula – advocated today by orthodox radicalism, and supported by some activist religious-Zionists – namely that the distinctiveness of the Jewish people lies in its faith and in the Torah – is highly dangerous. Its inner logic can only lead to numerical reduction of the Jewish people and their eventual fragmentation into the separate categories listed above.

The result will be not only the end of Jewish existence as a universal entity, but also the transformation of Jewish faith into a religion like Christianity or Islam, composed of numerous and diverse sects. Instead of endangering national cohesion, the secular nationalists and the religious Zionists should seek a compromise in the ideological rather than the political sphere. In this context, we have much to learn from the troubled, though not unsuccessful, efforts of the historic Hibbat Zion movement.

The new formula for compromise should be based on recognition of mutual interests. The secular Jews, who are interested in national survival in the Diaspora, inter alia, out of fear of the evolvement of an Israeli nation of provincial character and marginal cultural standing, should recognize that in the Diaspora today true Jewish identity is religious, while religious Zionists must admit that nowhere in the world is Jewish orthodoxy so strong and influential as in Israel. This illustrates that the wider definition of Jewish nationalism reinforces the Jewish religion. The reasons for this phenomenon are interesting in themselves but are outside the scope of the present discussion.

This comprehensive approach, based on compromise, which composes the lowest common denominator of unity in national diversity, should be built on three practical principles. The first one is the right of mutual participation of Israel and the Diaspora in their common principal issues, like 'who is a Jew', in the past, or the national nature of Israel as a Jewish or a bi-national Jewish-Arab state, in the future. The second principle should be the recognition of the Diaspora Jewry that Aliyah by choice of the idealistic few is the highest expression of Jewish unity, and therefore it is the responsibility of the Diaspora leadership to encourage and nourish it. The third principle is in the acceptance of the idea that without common basic Jewish education in Israel and the Diaspora, which will combine tradition and modernism in Jewish culture, the unity of the Jewish people will be severely endangered in the future.

These principles hold out the hope that Zionism, which was once a movement for the liberation of the Jewish people and freed them from forced exile, from humiliation and persecution, from self-hatred and inferior status, can become a movement for national existence, fortifying the rebellious desire of those Jews who wish to be Jews.

But this is only a historical likelihood for the future. As in the present, the stormy currents of contemporary events surprise the historian who is anticipating long-range processes. The unforeseen dramatic developments in the Soviet Union that changed dramatically the status of the Jewish people there, restored to Zionism its liberation task.

The Jews in the ex-Soviet republics are facing now a classical national problem which resembles in many aspects the situation that ignited Zionism a hundred years ago. The status of the Jews there – changed from Soviet citizen, which aspired to a universal meaning, to a national minority – is abnormal because of the lack of a national territory and language. A minority who are identified with the communist regime in the past and with Russian colonialism in the independent national republics.

Political tensions, severe social and economic problems in Russia, and the fact that the Western countries, chiefly the US, are closed to mass immigration, are the components of a classical 'Zionist situation'. The only place for the Jews who are forced by objective conditions or by hardships motivated by subjective strivings to leave those countries – is Israel.

This drama has repeated itself several times in the history of the Jewish people over the last three generations. It happened in the middle of the 1920s, when the immigration quotas were implemented in the US; in the middle of the 1930s when the gates of most Western countries were closed to Jewish refugees from Nazi Germany and anti-Semitic East-Central European countries; and after the Holocaust when the survivors and the Jews from Arab countries had no other place to settle except Israel.

In such a situation, the desire of the individual Jew to solve his plight by emigration turned into an act of *aliyah*, which is identical with national liberation. That is, because it not only entails providing sanctuary to the individual in distress, but also implies a fundamental change whose repercussions are wider and further-reaching in their national character, by changing his personal and collective status from a minority, with its dangers, to a majority with its responsibilities.

The renewal of the 'Zionist situation' and solution, which might go on for an entire generation, will bring out far-reaching changes in the Jewish world and history. First of all, this continuous process will establish Israel on the eve of the third millennium, as the biggest Jewish community in the world. And if the trends of inter-marriages, low birth rates, and assimilation among the Jews in the Western world continue in the future as they are in the present, in one or two generations the majority of Jewish people will live in Israel.

This foreseen process of Aliyah on the one hand and the diminishing of the Diaspora Jewry on the other hand will strengthen the status of Israel as the undisputed center of the Jewish people at least in two aspects. The first, since the process of Aliyah and absorption, as far as we can see today, is a lengthy and onerous task that can only be carried out by the whole Jewish people, it follows that the state of Israel will, for the next generation, be the center of the overall Jewish collective effort. The second aspect derives from a possible reaction towards the process of growing assimilation. In the past, in face of a danger of national deterioration, a part of the Jews became more active and determined in fostering their religious and national identity. So might it be in the future. For most of those Jews, Israel as a center will become a prominent and important one. This will be a multi-dimensional center: different types of concerned and active Jews will be able to identify themselves with Israel on either religious belief, cultural aspirations, psychological propensities, or political interests, as their needs dictate.

The whole process will draw on the uniqueness of Jewish existence and presumably will thus strengthen the recognition of 'Jewish normalization' in the thought and opinions of the Jewish public. If this assumption proves to be correct, then those issues which have caused public controversy in recent times, mainly around the tension between an 'illusory Babylon' and a 'true Jerusalem', will be put aside for the foreseeable future.

That does not mean the existence of a Jewish collective entity without inner conflicts. Two can already be singled out: one on the intellectual-philosophical level; the other one on the political-pragmatical level. On the first is the tension between Israel as a 'civil religion' with the legacy of the Holocaust as the main component of Jewish collective identity; on the second level is the dispute over the future of the Jewish community in the former Soviet Union. These are the different assumptions of the 'neo-Dubnowists' in Russia and the US who believe in the possibility of building a new Jewish center there, and the Israel–Zionist opinion which rejects this idea on ideological and pragmatical bases.

But these tensions in the decisive 'Jewish Triangle': American, Russian and Israeli Jewry, will neither weaken nor endanger Jewish unity. They will even strengthen the desire for a life of partnership, if only the Jewish people will agree upon a minimal outlook of collective identity.

Notes

INTRODUCTION

1. The data have been taken from the *American Jewish Year Book*, 1948–87, and particularly the following articles:
   Sidney Goldstein, 'Jews in the USA' (1981), p. 56.
   U.O. Schmelz, 'Jewish Survival', ibid., p. 76.
   U.O. Schmelz, S. DellaPergola, 'World Jewish Population', (1982), p. 277.
   On the debates between 'optimists' and 'pessimists', see also:
   Calvin Goldscheider, *The American Jewish Community*, Brown Studies, 1986;
   Paul Ritterband, *Modern Jewish Fertility*, Leiden, 1981.
   U.O. Schmelz, 'World Jewish Population in the 1980's – A short outline', in:
   S. DellaPergola, L. Cohen (eds), *World Jewish Population: Trends and Policies*, Jerusalem 1992.
   U.O. Schmelz and Sergio DellaPergola, 'World Jewish Population 1990', *American Jewish Year Book*, vol. 92, 1992, p. 493.

CHAPTER 1: THE TANGLE OF NORMALIZATION, 1942–50

1. 'Under Forty', *Contemporary Jewish Record*, February 1944, pp. 3–36.
2. I have found only two reactions to the symposium. It was criticized by the theatre critic William Schack, and the Zionist writer Shlomo Grodzensky: W. Shack, 'Hard to be a Jew', American Version, *Contemporary Jewish Record*, October 1944; S. Grodzensky, 'Iddish Americaner Zelbst Portret', *Der Iddisher Kamfer*, 25 February 1944.
3. Elmer Berger, 'Why I am a Non-Zionist', 1942, p. 29. See also: Elmer Berger, *The Jewish Dilemma*, New York, 1945.
4. It should be noted that from the political and even the ideological viewpoint, the denial of nationalism, Hannah Arendt's views are reminiscent of Berger's. See: Hannah Arendt, 'Zionism Reconsidered', *Menorah*, Autumn 1945; H. Arendt, 'The Jewish State: Fifty Years After', *Commentary*, May 1946. See also E. Munz, 'Nationalism is the Enemy', *Commentary*, August 1946.
5. Elmer Berger, 'Integrated Americans of Jewish Faith or a Permanent National Minority', *Council News*, 1 August 1948.
6. Yonathan Ratosh, *Reshit Yamim*, Tel Aviv, 1982, pp. 172–8.
7. In Yakov Shavit, *me-Ivri Ad Knaani*, 1983, pp. 191–200.
8. Solomon Zeitlin, 'What then are the Jews in the Light of History?' *Menorah*, Autumn 1947.
9. E. Berger, *The Jewish Dilemma*, pp. 39–41.
10. Jacob Agus, 'Masochism and Anti-Zionism'. *Reconstructionist*, 28 June 1946.
11. J. Agus, 'Goals for Jewish Living', *Menorah*, Winter 1948.
12. 'Goals for Jewish Living, A Symposium', *Menorah*, Spring, 1948.
13. J. Agus, 'Ends and Means of Jewish Life in America,' *Menorah*, Winter 1949.
14. Louis Finkelstein, 'Reflections on Judaism, Zionism and Enduring Peace', *The New Palestine*, 21 May 1943; and 'Zionism and World Culture', ibid., 15 September 1944.

15. Reuven (Robert) Gordis, 'Der Drang noch a ganzer Yiddishkeit', *Zukunft*, March 1950.
16. Louis Katzoff 'Religious Civilization or Civilizational Religion', *Conservative Judaism*, October–January, 1948–49.
17. Leon S. Lang, 'Judaism, A Guide Governing Human Relationships', ibid.
18. Solomon B. Freehof, 'Reform Judaism and Zionism – A Clarification', *Menorah*, Spring 1944.
19. S.B. Freehof, 'The War of Theories', *Liberal Judaism*, June 1943. See also 'Leo Baeck Meets the Jewish Press', Liberal Judaism, January 1948; M. Frank, 'Leo Baeck, Prophetic Spirit', ibid; Felix A. Levy, 'The Case of Zionism', Liberal Judaism, 1943.
20. 'Israel Redivivus' - Editorial, *Liberal Judaism*, June–July 1948; M.N. Eisendrath, 'Anticipation and Realization', *Liberal Judaism*, August–September 1949.
21. Abba Hillel Silver, 'Liberal Judaism and Israel', *Liberal Judaism*, January 1949.
22. Salo Baron, 'At the Turning Point', *Menorah*, April–June 1944.
23. S. Baron, 'Prospects for the Diaspora', *New Palestine*, 20 June 1947.
24. M. Kaplan, 'The Predicament of the Modern Jew', *Jewish Frontier*, November 1944.
25. Ira Eisenstein, *Reconstructionism and Zionism*, New York, 1943, p. 30, and 'Zionism in American Life', *New Palestine*, 18 August 1944.
26. Milton Steinberg, *The Creed of an American Zionist*, New York, 1945, p. 24; see also Eugene Kohn, 'Is it our Duty to Remain Maladjusted?', *Furrows*, March 1943; Emmanuel Gamorah, 'Diaspora vs. Exile', *Reconstructionist*, 28 May 1943; Max Artz, 'Jewish Identity in the Modern World', ibid., 23 June 1944; Milton Steinberg, *A Partisan Guide to the Jewish Problem*, New York, 1945, chap. 16.
27. M. Kaplan, 'The State of Israel and the Status of the Jews', *Reconstructionist*, June 1949. See also: L.W. Crohn, 'Auto-Emancipation Today', ibid., 16 June 1950; S.M. Blumenfield, 'Israel and the American Jew – Design for Cultural Independence', ibid., 15 December 1950; E. Kohn, 'The Reconstructionist Position', *Conservative Judaism*, October–January 1948–49.
28. See polemics between Emmanuel Novogrodsky and Yaakov Patt, *Unzer Zeit*, December 1946.
29. Emmanuel Scherer, 'Zin und Geist fon Brissel', *Unzer Zeit* September 1947.
30. 'Unzer Shtellung – der Bund vegen Medinas Yisroel', *Unzer Zeit*, July–August 1948.
31. See Yosef Bromberg, 'Tzvei Resolutzies'; Jacob Pat, 'In Shpigel fun Virklechkeit', *Unzer Zeit*, September 1948.
32. Emmanuel Scherer, 'Unzer shtellung, unzer Entfer', ibid.
33. See 'Die Tzveite Velt-Konferents fun Bund', *Unzer Zeit*, October–November 1948.
34. Y. Trunk, 'Die Historische Vortzlen fun Bund un Tzionism', *Unzer Zeit*, February–March 1949.
35. See Z. Breen, 'Yuden noch der Milhomeh', *Zukunft*, March 1945 (symposium). See also, S. Niger, 'Hemshech meint nisht az altz zol bleiben bein alten', *Zukunft*, March 1950.
36. H. Leivick, 'Die Beshutfusdikeh sheferishkeit fun Yisroel un die Yidden iber der Velt', *Zukunft*, May–June 1949.
37. Simon Rawidowicz, 'Tzvei vos zeinen Eines', *Zukunft*, May–June 1949. See: 'Two That Are One', in S. Rawidowicz, *Israel the Ever Dying People*, London and Toronto, 1986, pp. 147–61.
38. Joachim Prinz, 'Basic Zionism', *New Palestine*, 15 September 1944.
39. Ben Halpern, 'At Home in Exile', *Furrows*, January 1943.
40. See the debate between Ben Halpern and Eugene Kohn, one of the leaders of the Reconstructionists, in the wake of the above-mentioned article: E. Kohn, 'Is It Our Duty to Remain Maladjusted?'; B. Halpern, 'How to Observe the Commandment of Exile', *Furrows*, March 1943.

41. 'Yidden noch der Milchomeh', *Zukunft*, March 1945.
42. Hayim Greenberg, 'Golus Yid', *Yiddisher Kempfer*, 31 August 1945.
43. A. Mennes and H. Greenberg. 'Religieh un Yiddishkeit', *Yiddisher Kempfer*, Passover 1945.
44. Hayim Greenberg, 'A Farfalshter Bagriff', *Yiddisher Kempfer*, 24 February 1950.
45. Hayim Greenberg, 'Yiddisher Andershkeit', *Yiddisher Kempfer*, 29 December 1949.
46. Shlomo Grodzensky, 'Die Shechina in Golus', *Yiddisher Kempfer*, 23 January 1942, 'A Broche of an Aveida', ibid., 7 May 1943.
47. Shlomo Grodzensky, 'Medinas Yisroel un der Americaner Identum', ibid., 6 May 1949; 'Tzurik Tzum Tzionism', ibid., 23 September 1949; 'Arum un Arum', ibid., 10 January 1950.
48. Jacob Lestschinsky, 'Vos es Felt', ibid., 16 July 1943; 'Sach Hakol fun Golus, Experiment', ibid., 24 December 1943; 'Golus un Yiddishkeit', ibid., 22 April 1947; Golus un Hutz Laaretz', ibid., 27 August 1948.
49. Baruch Zuckerman, 'Die Problem "Yisroel Baamim" in der Neye Tekufa', *Zukunft*, January 1950; Baruch Zuckerman, 'Vegen dem "Am Ehod", Yesod in Tzionism', *Yiddisher Kempfer*, 16 June 1950; Baruch Zuckerman, 'Kibbutz Galuyos', ibid., 23 June 1950.
50. E. Berkovits, 'Dual Loyalty', *Jewish Spectator*, March 1950, pp. 12–14.

CHAPTER 2: CONFUSION FOLLOWS TRIUMPH

1. See 51st Annual Convention, 2–5 July 1948, ZOA, New York, XXXV/2–5; Emmanuel Neumann, *The Turning Point*, ZOA, New York, 1948, pp. 5–6; Noah Orian (Herzog), 'Rabbi Abba Hillel Silver's leadership in the American-Jewish arena, 1938–1949', (Hebrew) PhD thesis, Tel Aviv University, 1982, pp. 426–7.
2. Executive session 26.6.48, Z/45, Central Zionist Archives.
3. Executive session, 18–19.8.48, Z/45, CZA.
4. See: Yosef Gorni, Ahdut ha-Avoda, 1919–1930 (Hebrew), Chapter 10.
5. Zionist Actions Committee session, 24 August 1948, S5/323, CZA.
6. See the political biography of Yitzhak Greenbaum: Roman Prister, *Le-lo Peshara* (Uncompromising) (Hebrew), Tel Aviv, 1987.
7. Emmanuel Neumann accepted the need for compromise on this matter, but changed his mind shortly afterwards, and ceased to demand separation of state and Zionist Organization functions, and transfer of the Executive to Jerusalem.
    See Emmanuel Neumann, *be-Zirat ha-Maavak ha-Zioni* (In the Zionist Arena, Memoirs) (Hebrew), Jerusalem, 1978.
8. See speeches by Yaakov Hazan and Rabbi Meir Berlin, Actions Committee Minutes, see note 5 above.
9. On this, see: Emmanuel Neumann, *be-Zirat*, chapter 22; D. Ben-Gurion, *Yoman ha-Milhama* (War Diary, 1948–9), (Hebrew), vol. 2. pp. 665, 772, 892, 909; Noah Orian, op. cit., p. 505; Melvin I. Urofsky, *We Are One! American Jewry and Israel*, New York, 1978, p. 208.
10. See correspondence between Jacob Blaustein and David Ben-Gurion, September–October 1956; July–September 1961 (in American Jewish Committee Archives, Jacob Blaustein files). See also Naomi W. Cohen, *Not Free to Desist*, Philadelphia, 1972, pp. 309–15. On the particular sensitivity of the American Jewish Committee to the question of dual loyalty, see Menahem Kaufman: 'The American Jewish Committee's image of the Jewish state, 1947–1948', (Hebrew), Yahadut Zemanenu, (Contemporary Jewry), vol. 3, 1986, pp. 171–86.

11. Zionist Actions Committee, Jerusalem, 5–15 May 1949.
12. Ibid., 19–28 April 1950.
13. See notes 11 and 12. Speeches by Yaakov Hazan, Yaakov Riftin, Yitzhak Ben-Aharon of Mapam; Isaac Remba, Joseph Schechtman of the Revisionists.
14. Ibid.
15. Twenty-third Zionist Congress, Jerusalem, 14–30 August 1951. Minutes published by the Zionist Organization, Jerusalem, pp. 94–5.
16. Ibid., p. 167.
17. Private conversation with Arie Dulzin.
18. Zionist Actions Committee meeting, 1950.
19. Twenty-third Congress, p. 129.
20. Actions Committee, April 1950.
21. Meeting at Prime Minister's Office, 25.7.50. Ministry of Defence Archives, 161/62, File 656 – Zionist movement and US Jewry, 1948–63.
22. Twenty-third Congress, p. 583.
23. Knesset records, vol. XI, 1952, pp. 1886–28.
24. Ibid., p. 1921.
25. Knesset records, vol. XII, 1952, p. 2877. The vote itself was dramatic. The first vote was a tie: 27:27. The second vote produced a majority of 37 for, with 27 against.
26. Knesset records, vol. XIII, 1952, pp. 24–61; 132–48.

CHAPTER 3: THE ZIONIST MOVEMENT IN QUEST OF ITS IDEOLOGICAL ESSENCE

1. See Gorny, 'The Paradoxical Ambivalence of David Ben-Gurion in Relation to Zionism' (Hebrew), in: *Ha-Ziyonut u-Mitnagdeha ba-Am ha-Yehudi* (Zionism and its Jewish Opponents), Jerusalem, 1990.
2. 'Medinat Yisrael veha-Tenuah ha-Tziyonit', 5 May 1949, in David Ben-Gurion, *Hazon va-Derekh* vol. I, pp. 119–20.
3. Speech at the Zionist executive, 25 April 1950, *Hazon va-Derekh*, vol. II, p. 163.
4. Ibid., p. 174.
5. See Naomi Cohen, 'Not Free to Desist', Jewish Publication Society, Philadelphia, 1972.
6. 'Yahadut America u-Medinat Yisrael', 19 May 1951, *Hazon va-Derekh*, vol. III, p. 150.
7. Speech at the Zionist Executive, 11 May 1952, *Hazon va-Derekh*, vol. IV, p. 43.
8. 'Maamad ha-Histadrut ha-Tziyonit be-Yisrael', 5 May 1952, ibid., pp. 13–22.
9. Response, ibid., pp. 23–4.
10. Letter to Shimon Dilgin, Ben-Gurion Archives, Ministry of Defence, 161/62, File 656.
11. Private conversation with Hayim Yisracli, then Ben-Gurion's secretary. See also: Michael Bar-Zohar, *Ben-Gurion*, vol. 2, Tel Aviv, 1977, pp. 999 on.
12. 'le-Birurah shel Sugiya', correspondence between Ben-Gurion and Nathan Rotenstreich, *Hazut C*, Zionist Library, Jerusalem, 1957, p. 29.
13. 'Zika le-Netzah Yisrael', *Hazon va-Derekh*, vol. V, p. 63.
14. 'Medinat Yisrael ve-Atido shel ha-Am ha-Yehudi', *Hazut D* (1958), p. 145.
15. Ibid., pp. 167–9.
16. Speech at writers convention. Cited in Michael Keren, *Ben-Gurion and the Intellectuals*, Dekalb, Ill., 1983, p. 67.

17. See above, note 15.
18. 'Zika le-Netzah Yisrael', *Hazon va-Derekh*, vol. V, p. 62.
19. *Hazut* D, p. 167.
20. 'Medina le-Mofet – Matara ve-Emtzaim', *Hazon va-Derekh*, vol. V, p. 81.
21. 'Bein Yisrael la-Gola', *Hazon va-Derekh*, vol. IV, p. 87.
22. See Ben-Gurion's address in: 'American Jewish Dialogue, June 1962', *Congress Weekly*, 24 September 1962.
23. *Hazut* D, p. 167.
24. Twenty-fifth Zionist Congress, p. 53.
25. Letter to Harry Cohen, 27 June 1961, see above, note 10.
26. See above, note 12.
27. It should be noted that after his final resignation in the wake of the Lavon Affair, Ben-Gurion avoided discussion of the Diaspora question, and dedicated himself wholeheartedly to the question of Israel's moral image, as he understood it. Indirectly, of course, the shaping of Israel's image would affect the Diaspora.
28. See M. Kaplan, 'Alumni Address' in: R. Leibowitz, Kaplan and the Development of Reconstructionism. New York, 1983. Mordecai Kaplan, 'Zo Simha Shlema', first published in 1925, and again in full in *Yahadut Zemanenu* 3, Jerusalem, 1986, p. 25. Mordecai Kaplan, *Judaism as a Civilization*, New York, 1934.
29. Mordecai Kaplan, *A New Zionism*, New York, 1955. Second enlarged edition, New York, 1959. Quotations are from the second edition.
30. Ibid., p. 11.
31. Ibid., pp. 21–2.
32. Ibid., p. 26.
33. For a comprehensive survey of these questions in American Jewish religious thought, see Arnold M. Eisen, *The Chosen People in America – A Study in Jewish Religious Ideology*, Indiana University Press, 1983.
34. Ibid.,
35. Mordecai Kaplan, 'ha-Mifneh he-Hadash ba-Tziyonut', *Hazut* D, 1958. On his indirect debate with Ben-Gurion, see his 'The Jewish People in Search of an Ideology' in *Judaism without Supernaturalism*, New York, 1958.
36. Ibid., p. 29.
37. Ibid., p. 34.
38. See 'A Proposed Platform for the Greater Zionism', *A New Zionism*, pp. 187–9. The proposals were intended to serve as the basis for discussions at the ideological convention of the American Zionist Organization, organized by Emmanuel Neumann.
39. See B. Sherman 'Comments on the Greater Zionism', *Reconstructionist*, January 1959. Kaplan's reply appeared in the same issue.
40. 'Why a Greater Zionism?' in Kaplan, *A New Zionism*, op. cit., pp. 174–8.
41. M. Kaplan, 'Can Zionism Reconstitute the Jewish People?' *Reconstructionist*, October 1963. This was the most concise expression of the ideas Kaplan had broached at the 1957 convention, and in his 'Greater Zionism' platform in 1959.
42. See Eliezer Livneh, *Medinah ve-Gola*, Zionist Organization, Jerusalem, 1953. See also Ben-Zion Dinur's speech at the ideological convention, *Hazut* D, pp. 172–3. Ephraim Broide, ibid., pp. 213–4. Yitzhak Tabenkin, ibid., pp. 198–9.
43. See speeches of Yisrael Bar-Yehuda and Zvi Luria at the 23rd Zionist Congress, 1951, pp. 105–10, 213–17.
44. Trude Weiss-Rosmarin, 'America is not Babylonia' in: H. Ribalow (ed.), *Mid-Century Anthology of Jewish Life and Culture in our Times*, New York, 1955.
45. T. Weiss-Rosmarin, 'Living in Two Civilizations', *Reconstructionist*, 18 February 1955. See also Kaplan's reply: 'The Advantage of Living in Two Civilizations', ibid., 4 March 1955.

46. See the *Jewish Spectator*, September 1954, January 1955.
47. Views similar to those of Weiss-Rosmarin were expressed by Professor Abraham Halkin, who had immigrated to Israel, and the veteran Zionist, Benno Weiss. See A.S. Halkin, 'American Judaism – A Balance Sheet', *Judaism*, Spring 1954. B. Weiss, 'Ben-Gurion's Dispute with American Zionists', *Commentary*, August 1954.
48. See *Reconstructionist*: Joseph Ross, 'The Jew in American Society', 29 October 1954; Anniversary issue, 18 February 1955; Trude Weiss-Rosmarin, 'Living in Two Civilizations', 18 February 1955; M. Kaplan, 'The Advantage ...' (See note 45), 4 March 1955; S.M. Blumenfield, M. Kaplan, 'Ahad ha-Am', 20 April 1956; M. Kaplan, 'The Need for Reconstructionism', 18 May 1958; M. Kaplan, 'Why a Greater Zionism?' 28 November 1958 and 9 January 1959; R.L. Rubinstein, 'The Significance of Zionism', 29 April 1960; M. Kaplan, 'Zionism and Jewish Religion', 11 December 1959; M. Kaplan, 'Israel – Diaspora and Zionism', 4 November 1960; M. Kaplan, 'The Paradox of Israeli Jewry', 16 December 1960; Ira Eisenstein, 'What is Zionism?' 2 June 1961; M. Kaplan, 'Aims of Reconstructionism', 15 June 1962; R.L. Rubinstein, 'The "Supernatural Jew"', 3 May, 1963; M. Kaplan, 'Can Zionism ...' (See note 41), 4 October 1963; M. Kaplan, 'Israel, the Diaspora and Zionism', 24 January 1964; M. Kaplan, 'Towards a Zionist Judaism', 26 June 1964.
49. Ludwig Lewisohn, 'The Future of American Zionism', *Commentary*, August 1950.
50. Maurice Samuel, 'The Sundering of Israel and American Jewry', *Commentary*, September 1953.
51. M. Samuel, 'Why Israel Misunderstands American Jewry – Some Ways of Closing the Rift', *Commentary*, October 1953.
52. See articles by Samuel in *Congress Weekly*, 17 May 1954; 27 May 1954; 31 May 1954; 14 June 1954.
53. Reuven (Robert) Gordis, 'Yehuda ve-Yisrael', *Hazut* D, p. 179–190. See also Robert Gordis, *Judaism for the Modern Time*, New York, 1955, chap 6, pp. 103–25.
54. Minutes of 23rd Zionist Congress, p. 149.
55. Ibid., p. 164
56. Ibid., p. 583.
57. Nathan Rotenstreich, 'Ribonut o Kinus', in: *Al ha-Temura – Prakim bi-Sheelot ha-Am veha-Medina*, Tel Aviv, 1953.
58. 'le-Verur Musagim al Mahuta shel Galut Yisrael', ibid.
59. Mevukha – Pri ha-Emet', ibid., pp. 63–8. 'ha-Ometz Lihiyot Miut', ibid., pp. 69–72.
60. 'Mesilot Makbilot', ibid., pp. 91–4.
61. 'Raayon ha-Merkaz ha-Ruhani ba-Mivhan', ibid., pp. 85–108.
62. 'Bein Am li-Medinato', ibid., pp. 109–19.
63. See S. Rawidowicz, 'Bein Yisrael le-Yisrael', *Hazut*, A 1953, and Rotenstreich's reply, 'Ahdut she-Yesh Ima Mamashut', ibid.
64. 'li-Vhinat ha-Autoemancipatzia ha-Yehutid', *Hazut* B, 1956.
65. D. Ben-Gurion, 'Munahim va-Arakhim', *Hazut* C, 1957, p. 7. N. Rotenstreich, 'Todaat ha-Tzorekh ba-Moledet', ibid., p. 12. D. Ben-Gurion and N. Rotenstreich, 'le-Verura shel Sugya', (correspondence), ibid., pp. 27–9.
66. Ibid., p. 29.
67. Ibid., p. 13.
68. Ibid., p. 15.
69. Ibid., p. 20.
70. Ibid., p. 26.
71. Ibid., p. 22.
72. See: Ben Halpern, 'ha-Idea shel ha-Bayit ha-Ruhani', *Hazut* B, 1956.
73. Ben Halpern, 'Exile', *Jewish Frontier*, April 1954.

74. Ben Halpern, *The American Jew, A Zionist Analysis*, New York, 1956, pp. 149, 158, 159.
75. 'The Meaning of Galut in America Today', *Midstream*, March 1963.
76. *The American Jew* op., cit. p. 159. See also 'Golat America be-Tokh Am Olam', *Hazut* C, 1957.
77. Ben Halpern, 'Medinat Yisrael ki-Medina Tziyonit', *Hazut* D. 1958, p. 154.
78. Ibid., p. 162.
79. Arthur Hertzberg, 'ha-Omnam Yoshev ha-Yehudi ba-Galut?'; Heyot Yehudi be-Golat America – Masot u-Reshimot, Jerusalem, 1981, p. 43.
    The two prominent Zionist leaders Nahum Goldmann and Moshe Sharett had almost the same opinion on this issue. See: *Hazut* 4, p. 215; pp. 222–4.
80. Twenty-third Congress minutes, pp. 151–2.

CHAPTER 4: THE INTELLECTUALS IN SEARCH OF JEWISH IDENTITY

1. On this see Uriel Tal, *Mytos u-Tevuna be-Yahadut Yameinu*, Tel Aviv, 1987, pp. 129–67.
2. See: Sarah Schmidt, 'A conversation with H.M. Kallen', *Reconstructionist*, November 1975. S. Schmidt, 'Messianic Pragmatism: The Zionism of H.M. Kallen', *Judaism*, Spring 1976.
3. See *Judaism*, Winter 1959.
4. Milton Konvitz, 'Zionism: Coming Home or Homelessness', *Judaism*, Winter 1956.
5. See Julian Morgenstern, 'What are we Jews', *Central Conference of American Rabbis*, October 1965. Robert Gordis, 'Towards a Renaissance of Judaism', *Judaism*, January 1952; *Judaism for the Modern Time*, New York, 1955, p. 124; 'Yehuda ve-Israel', *Hazut* D, p. 189.
6. Conference, 'Jewish Identity Here and Now', ed. S. Dawidowicz, M. Himmelfarb, American Jewish Committee.
7. Ibid.
8. The following dialogues took place, and were published in the *Congress Bi-Weekly*:
    I. Israel and World Jewry (1962), September 1962.
    II. The Jewish Intellectual and Jewish Identity (1963), September 1963.
    III. Variation on the Theme: Religion, Culture, History (1964), September 1964.
    IV. Variation on the Theme: The Post-War Generation in the United States and the Post-Independence Generation in Israel (1965), October 1965.
    V. The Nature of Jewish Distinctiveness (1966), April 1967.
9. It should be noted that this dialogue was held a year before the Six Day War.
10. Third Dialogue.
11. Ibid.
12. Fourth Dialogue.
13. See Fourth Dialogue, remarks of Shlomo Avineri.
14. See remarks of Edwin Wolf, President of the National Foundation for Jewish Culture, Second Dialogue.
15. First Dialogue.
16. Fifth Dialogue.
17. Third Dialogue.
18. Fifth Dialogue.
19. Third Dialogue.
20. Fifth Dialogue.
21. First Dialogue.
22. See *Unease in Zion* (ed. Ehud Ben-Ezer, *New York Times Book Co.* 1974, pp. 307–8).

23. 'Jewish Identity Here and Now', Third Dialogue.
24. Fifth Dialogue.
25. Ibid.
26. First Dialogue.
27. Third Dialogue.
28. Fourth Dialogue.
29. See remarks of Will Maslow, Paul Cowan and others, Fourth Dialogue.

CHAPTER 5: THE DIMINISHING STATUS OF ISRAEL AS A JEWISH STATE

1. See Chapter 1.
2. Yakov Shavit, 'me-Ivri ad Cenaani', pp. 182–6.
3. Boaz Evron, 'Separation and Equality', in: Ehud Ben-Ezer (ed.), *Unease in Zion*, Jerusalem, 1974, pp. 165–74.
4. 'Jewishness and the Younger Intellectual – A Symposium', *Commentary*, April 1961.
5. 'The Meaning of Galut in America Today', *Midstream*, March 1963.
6. On this, see the following articles in *Mid-Century, An Anthology of Jewish Life and Culture in Our Times*, H.U. Ribalow (ed.), New York, 1955; Irving Howe, 'The Lost Intellectuals'; Leslie A. Fiedler, 'Plight of the Jewish Intellectuals'; Ludwig Lewisohn, 'To the Young Jewish Intellectuals'; Charles Angoff, 'Troubled Intellectuals'.
7. See 'Second Dialogue in Israel', *Congress Bi-Weekly*, September 1963. Fiedler, like his two colleagues, was disillusioned with communism and sought to return to Judaism as he understood it. In this respect see his confession published in *Mid-Century*, note 6 above.
8. Arthur A. Cohen, *The Natural and Supernatural Jew*, New York, 1962, pp. 6–7, 186–7, 191, 291–4, 313.
9. Jakob J. Petuchowski, *Zion Reconsidered*, New York, 1966, pp. 11, 70, 75, 86, 107, 120, 131–3.
10. See remarks of Jacob Agus on the meaning of *galut*, in the *Midstream* symposium.
11. Will Herberg, 'Jewish Existence and Survival – A Theological View'. *Judaism*, January 1952.
12. See *Ein Shaananim be-Tziyon*, (Hebrew) pp. 211–12; 216–17, or *Unease in Zion*, Jerusalem and New York, 1974.
13. See his study, 'Mahuta u-Mekoroteha shel Tenuat ha-Ivrim ha-Tzeirim', in: *Sifruteinu ha-Hadasha Hemshech o Mahapecha*, Tel Aviv, 1959, pp. 270–300.
14. *Ein Shaananim be-Tziyon*, op. cit., pp. 114, 121, 123.
15. See Yeshayahu Leibowitz, *Yahadut, Am Yehudi u-Medinat Yisrael*, Jerusalem, 1975, pp. 235–42. From his statement at the same gathering, one gathers that Leibowitz was particularly cautious because of the apparent similarity between his views and those of the Canaanites. He took care to point out, ibid., p. 239, that his own demand for separation of state and religion resembled that of secular Jews and not Canaanite theories.
16. For example, the role of the Jewish state was not discussed in the debate on Jewish faith. See 'The State of Jewish Belief – A Symposium', *Commentary*, August 1966, Milton Himmelfarb (ed.). The following questions were posed to the participants: (a) Do you believe in the revelation at Sinai? Should all the 613 *mitzvot* be observed? If not – which can be waived? (b) Are the Jews the Chosen People, and how can one justify this choice in the light of the various ideologies of national or racial supremacy? (c) What is the distinctiveness of the Jewish religion in comparison with others, what distinguishes the believer from the non-believer? (d) Does Judaism represent

any particular political viewpoint? Can a man be a good Jew and, at the same time, a racist, communist or fascist? (e) Is the theory of some Christian theologians about the 'death of God' relevant to Jewish theology, and what modern belief constitutes the gravest threat to Judaism?

CHAPTER 6: REVOLUTIONARY RADICALISM

1. See: J.N. Porter and P. Dreier (eds), *The Roots of Jewish Radicalism*, New York 1971; J.A. Sleeper and A. Mintz, *The New Jew*, New York, 1971; Sherman Rosenfeld, 'Blowing in the Wind', *Davka*, Winter 1971; Jay Rosenberg, 'My Evolution as a Jew', *Other Stand*, 6 October 1970.
2. As regards the political approach to the Israel–Arab dispute, these groups were close in outlook to Zionist circles in Israel which were to the left of Mapam. Almost all the radical press published Amos Kenan's article, 'Letter to all Good People', with its emotional appeal to the leaders of the Third World to acknowledge Zionism as a national liberal movement.
3. Editorial, 'Tragedy in Sinai', *Genesis*, 2 March 1973.
4. See: Jay Rosenberg, 'My Evolution as a Jew', *Other Stand*, 6 October 1970; Susan Schechter, 'To my Real and Imagined Enemies ...', in *Chutzpah, A Jewish Liberation Anthology*, New York, 1977; Ruth Balser, 'Liberation of a Jewish Radical', ibid.; Josh Kay, 'Leftist Odyssey', *Jewish Radical*, August 1973.
5. See Introduction, *Chutzpah*.
6. Editorial in *Other Stand*, vol. 1, no. 1, 1969.
7. *Doreinu*, vol. 1, no. 1, 1970.
8. See: Eliot Yagod and David Kaufman, 'National Liberation and the Zionist Model', *Other Stand*, 19 February 1969; Editorial, *Davka*, November–December, 1970; Hilliard Aronovitch, 'Particularism and Universalism', *Echo*, November 1967, October 1968.
9. Editorial, *Genesis*, no. 2, 13 February 1970.
10. J. Goldberg, 'Quebec, Jews on the Powder Keg', *Other Stand*, 4 November 1970; Zoltan Kemeny, 'An Open Letter to the Jewish Community', ibid.
11. Peter Shizgal, in: 'Response', 20 January 1971. See also the Borochovist explanation of the political weakness of US Jewry in an article by Shelley Schreter, formerly one of the leaders of the Montreal group, who had moved to Berkeley: 'American Jew, Cambodia and Israel', *Jewish Radical*, May 1970.
12. B. Schaicovich, 'The Diaspora Revisited', *Other Stand*, 3 March 1971.
13. Moshe Zedek, 'Borochovism', *Jewish Liberation Journal*, February 1971.
14. Aviva Cantor-Zuckoff, 'The Oppression of America's Jews', *Jewish Liberation Journal*, November 1970.
15. Naomi Alboim, 'Alienation ...' *Other Stand*, 11 November 1970.
16. Shelley Schreter, 'Where We're At and Why', *Jewish Radical*, January 1980.
17. David Biale, 'Critique of Schreter', *Jewish Radical*, February–March 1970; David Biale, 'The Trialog', ibid., Winter 1971.
18. Baruch Ballin and David Biale, 'On Jewish Revolution', ibid., Spring 1971.; see also editorial, ibid., Winter 1971.
19. Jeffrey (Shaye) Mallow, 'Politics of Language', *Chutzpah*, 1971, p. 149.
20. Arthur Waskow, *The Bush is Burning*, New York, 1970, pp. 127–41.
21. J.A. Sleeper and A.L. Mintz, *The New Jews*, New York, 1971.
22. Lina Vardi, 'A Limited Liberation', *Other Stand*, 25 November 1970.
23. D. Kaufman, P. Shizgal and J. Goldberg, 'Operation Sell-Out', *Other Stand*, 19 March 1969.

24. M. Manis and P. Shizgal, 'Jew and Independence: An Exchange of Views', *Other Stand*, 24 February 1971.
25. Martin Manis, 'Response', *Other Stand*, 10 March 1971.
26. Itzhak Epstein, 'American Jewry: On the Barricade or on the Fence?' *Jewish Liberation Journal*, May 1969.
27. Tsvi Bisk, 'Uncle Jake, Come Home', ibid.
28. Chaim Cohen, 'On Being Left and Being Jewish', *Nitzotz*, May 1972.
29. Richard Morroch, 'Left and Jewish – a Response', ibid., October 1972.
30. Debby Littman, 'Jewish Militancy in Perspective', *Other Stand*, 24 February 1971.
31. Michael Stanislavsky, 'The J.D.L. Anti-Zionism', *Other Stand*, 10 March 1971.
32. Shelley Schreter, 'On Jewish Militancy', *Jewish Radical*, Winter 1971; Cherie Roller, 'The J.D.L. on Patrol...' *Genesis*, 2, 1 March 1971.
33. RZA 'Comments on J.D.L.', *Doreinu*, March 1971.
34. M.J. Rosenberg, 'To Uncle Tom and Other Such Jews', *Village Voice*, reprinted in *Other Stand*, 19 March 1969.
35. J.J. Goldberg, 'Harlem on My Back', *Other Stand*, 2 February 1969.
36. 'Israel and the Galut – a Symposium', *Jewish Radical*, October 1971, January 1972; 'Israel and the Golah – A Symposium', Genesis 2, May 1973.
37. See on this: Tsvi Bisk, 'Uncle Jake, Come Home', Jewish Liberation Journal, May 1969; Shelley Schreter, 'Towards a More Self-Conscious Zionism', *Jewish Radical*, January 1972.
38. David G. Roskies, *The People of the Lost Book*, Orim, Yale, Autumn 1986.
39. See speech by the young Hillel Levine of Havurat Shalom to the Jewish communities conference in Boston in 1969 .. Hillel Levine, 'To Share a Vision', *Response*, Winter 1969, p. 70.
40. *The New Jews*, eds James A. Sleeper, Alan L. Mintz, New York, 1971.
41. Ibid.
42. See method of organization and operation of the havurot in Boston and New York in articles by Bill Novak, Stephen Lerner, and Jacob Neusner in *Response*, Winter 1970/71.
43. 'The Response Symposium', *Response*, Fall 1972.
44. 'Living in Two Cultures', *Response*, Fall 1972.
45. Alan Mintz, 'Towards an Integrated Jewish Ideology', *Response*, Fall 1973.
46. A. Mintz, 'The People's Choice? A Demurral on Breira', *Response*, Winter 1976/7.
47. See William Novak, 'On Leaving the Havurah', *Response*, Summer 1974.
48. See critique of Hillel Halkin's book, 'Letters to an American-Jewish Friend', Jewish Publication Society, Philadelphia. *Response*, 1977/8.
49. Michael Strassfield, 'Towards a Creative Diaspora', *Response*, Summer 1980.
50. 'Models for Diaspora–Israel relations', *The Third Jewish Catalog*, compiled and edited by Sharon and Michael Strassfield, Philadelphia, 1980, pp. 298–329.
51. See Joseph Shattan, 'Why Breira', *Commentary*, April 1977; readers responses to the article, ibid., June 1977. Debate by Rabbinical Council of the Conservative movement on the right to criticize Israel publicly, *Judaism*, Winter 1977.
52. See note 48.
53. See 'Tefutzot Israel', published by the American Jewish Committee, December 1975.
54. See A. Waskow, 'The Future of Jewish Peoplehood', *Forum*, Fall 1978.
55. See Arnold J. Wolf, 'American Jewry and Israel', *Judaism*, Winter 1977; Jacob Neusner, 'What has Israel Done for us Lately? *Inter-Change*, April 1976; and exchange between Noah Lucas and Bernard Avishai, *Inter-Change*, January–March 1977.

CHAPTER 7: NEO-CONSERVATIVE RADICALISM

1. See Norman P. Barry, *The New Right*, London and New York, 1982.
2. Norman Podhoretz, 'The Intellectual and Jewish Fate', *Midstream*, Winter 1957.
3. Daniel Bell, 'Reflections on Jewish Identity', *Commentary*, June 1961.
4. Interview with Podhoretz, February 1988.
5. 'Jewish Values in the Post-Holocaust Future', *Judaism*, Summer 1967.
6. Emil Fackenheim, 'Jewish Faith and the Holocaust – A Fragment', *Commentary*, August 1967.
7. Milton Himmelfarb, 'In the Light of Israel's Victory', *Commentary*, October 1962. See also his book, *The Jews of Modernity*, New York, 1969.
8. See his remarks in 'The State of Jewish Belief – A Symposium', *Commentary*, August 1966.
9. See his statements at the Sixth Dialogue of the World Jewish Congress (WJC) 1968: (a) *Congress Bi-Weekly*, 24 February 1969; (b) 'Judaism and Liberalism – Marriage, Separation or Divorce – A Symposium', *Judaism*, Winter 1972; (c) 'Homeland and Holocaust ...' *The World Yearbook of Religion*, ed. Ronald Cutler, 1968, vol. 1, pp. 39–110; 'Dilemmas of Jewish Power – Symposium', *Jewish Frontier*, May 1980.
10. 'Judaism and Liberalism – Symposium', *Judaism*, Winter 1972. Siegel reiterated this view in 1980 at a symposium conducted by *Commentary* – see note 13.
11. See 'Liberalism and the Jews – A Symposium', *Commentary*, 10 January 1980.
12. Norman Podhoretz, 'A Certain Anxiety', *Commentary*, August 1971.
13. Norman Podhoretz, 'Is It Good for the Jews?' *Commentary*, February 1972.
14. E. Raab, 'The Deadly Innocence of American Jews', *Commentary*, December 1970. See also: 'The Black Revolution and the Jewish Question', ibid., January 1969.
15. Robert Alter, 'Israel and the Intellectuals', *Commentary*, October 1967.
16. R. Alter, 'Israeli Culture and the Jews', *Commentary*, November 1976.
17. R. Alter, 'The Jewish Community and the Jewish Condition', *Commentary*, February 1969.
18. See Alter's introduction to the book which Ehud Ben-Ezer edited, *Unease in Zion*, New York, 1974.
19. R. Alter, 'Teaching Jewish Teachers', *Commentary*, July 1968.
20. See: R. Alter, 'A Fever of Ethnicity': Norman Podhoretz, 'The Idea of a Common Culture', *Commentary*, June 1972.
21. R. Alter, 'Emancipation, Enlightenment ...', *Commentary*, February 1972.
22. R. Alter, 'New York and/or Jerusalem', *Commentary*, August 1977.
23. See: James Nuechterlein, 'Neoconservatism and ... Irving Kristol', *Commentary*, August 1984. The article deals with Kristol's book, *Reflections of the Neoconservative*, New York, 1984.
24. See: *Congress Bi-Weekly*, March, 1973.
25. Norman Podhoretz, *Breaking Ranks*, New York, 1979, pp. 352–3.
26. Norman Podhoretz, 'The Abandonment of Israel', *Commentary*, July 1976.
27. Nathan Glazer, 'The Exposed American Jew', *Commentary*, June 1975.
28. Irving Kristol, 'The Political Dilemma of American Jews', *Commentary*, July 1984. A debate ensued between Kristol and readers. See: 'Jewish Voters and the "Politics of Compassion"', *Commentary*, October 1984.
29. Lucy S. Dawidowicz, 'Politics, the Jews and the' 84 elections', *Commentary*, February 1985.
30. Emil Fackenheim, 'The Renewal of the Zionist Impulse', *Forum*, Spring 1983; and, 'Diaspora and Nation; the Contemporary Situation', ibid., Winter 1983/84.
31. Norman Podhoretz, 'State of World Jewry', *Commentary*, December 1983.

32. Midge Decter, 'Bitburg: Who Forgot What?', *Commentary*, August 1985. See also the documentary collection on the Bitburg controversy: Geoffrey H. Hartman (ed.), *Bitburg in Moral and Political Perspective*, Bloomington, Indiana, 1986.

CHAPTER 8: THE ALTERNATIVE ZIONISM OF GUSH EMUNIM

1. See, on this, the following books: Zvi Raanan, *Gush Emunim*, Tel Aviv, 1980; Danny Rubinstein, *Mi le-Adonai Elai, Gush Emunim*, Tel Aviv, 1982; articles by: Uriel Tal, 'Yesodot ha-Meshihiyut va-Politit be-Yisrael', (1984), in *Mitos u-Tevuna be-Yahadut Yameinu*, Tel Aviv, 1987, pp. 115–28; Janet Oday 'Gush Emunim, Shorashim ve-dumashmauyot'; Shulamit Har-Even, 'Degem Sotziologi Mul Metziyut'; Nathan Rotenstreich, 'Emuna Datit u-Tefisa Politit'; Eliezer Goldman, 'Meshihiyut Pashtanit' – all of these in *Tefutzot ha-Gola*, nos. 79/80. 1977. Michael Rosnak, 'Gush Emunim - ha-Omnam ha-Tziyonut ha-Datit shel Yameinu?' in *Tefutzot ha-Gola*, 1976, nos. 77/78; Amnon Rubinstein, *mi-Herzl ve-Ad Gush Emunim*, chapter 8, Tel Aviv, 1980.
2. Zvi Raanan, op. cit., p. 57.
3. Ibid, pp. 173–4.
4. Rabbi Shlomo Aviner, 'Harigat Mashiah Ben-Yosef', *Nekuda*, 27 June 1980.
5. See comment by editor of *Nekuda*, ibid.
6. See articles by: Hillel Weiss, 'Besorat ha-Boser', *Nekuda*, 11 July 1980; Avraham Mintz, 'Harigato shel Melekh Heshbon', ibid., 30 September 1980; Rabbi Yisrael Ariel, 'Hulsha ke-ideologia', ibid., 5 December 1980.
7. Rabbi Shlomo Aviner, 'Mashber Kaful', ibid., 15 August 1980.
8. Yaakov Ariel, 'Darush Binyan Hadash', ibid., September 1981.
9. Eli Sadan, 'Leyased me-Hadash et Medinat ha-Yehudim', *Nekuda*, 30 October 1981.
10. Yoel Bin-Nun, 'Lo Taguru', *Nekuda*, 7.4.82.
11. See also: Eliezer Waldman, 'ha-Oz Ligmor et ha-Melakha', *Nekuda*, 6 August 1982.
12. Yehuda Amital, *ha-Maalot mi-Maamakim*, Jerusalem, 1974.
13. Rabbi Yehuda Amital, 'be-Milkud ha-Shlemut', *Nekuda*, 24 December 1982.
14. Hanan Porat, 'Matai Ein Holkin Kavod la-Rav', *Nekuda*, 12 November 1982.
15. See my article: 'ha-Yesodot ha-Romantiyim ba-Aliyah ha-Sheniya', *Asufoth*, 10, 1966.
16. Hanan Porat, 'ha-Pulmus im ha-Rav Amital al Eretz Yisrael', *Nekuda*, 28 March 1983.
17. See Yoel Bin-Nun, 'Iy Efshar le-Rabea et ha-Maagal'; Moshe Levinger, 'Galut Ruhanit be-Eretz Yisrael', *Nekuda*, 14 January 1983.
18. Shahar Rahmani, 'le-Omko shel ha-Ahshav', *Nekuda*, 27 February 1983. See also articles in the same spirit, by: Yaakov Ariel, 'be-Hair ha-Nurot ha-Adumot'; Moshe Shapira, 'Anahnu ha-Humanistim ha-Amitiyim'; Dov Biegun, 'Ma Gorem le-Bilbul ha-Daat'. Uri Elitzur, 'Ani lo Yoter Tziyoni ve-Ata lo Yoter Shafuy', *Nekuda*, 27 February 1983.
19. Moshe Ben-Yosef, 'Gush Emunim Alul Lihyot le-Khat', *Nekuda*, 23 March 1984. The idea of the 'new halakhah', as a national way of life was the basis of the outlook of the late Shabtai Ben Dov, who was also a Lehiite. See his article: 'ha-Problematika shel ha-Yahadut ha-Datit', *Nekuda*, 22 February 1980.

   Moshe Ben-Yosef published the following articles in *Nekuda*:

   'Bein Mashiah Achshav le-Raayon ha-Meshihi', no. 74; 'Tziyonut Hilonit be-Kelim Datiim', no. 79; 'ha-Maavak le-Hisardut min ha-Shoah ha-Liberalit', no. 80; 'Min ha-Hazon el ha-Nihilism', no. 91; 'ha-Emancipatzia Kevar Hehriva et ha-Bayit ha-Shlishi', no. 94; 'me-Ever la-Sekhel ha-Yashar', no. 98; 'Karati ve-Ein Oneh', (a talk with Yosef Ben-Yosef by Ofra Amitai), no. 100.

20.   Yosef Ben-Shlomo, 'ba-Maavak ha-Ideologi Im ha-Yamin ve-Im ha-Smol', *Nekuda*, 5 April 1985.
21.   Moshe Levinger, 'be-Ein Hazon Ein Ahdut', *Nekuda*, Elul, 1984.
22.   Yehuda Zoldin, 'Tefisat ha-Rav Reines Nidheket mi-Pnei Tefisat ha-Rav Kook', *Nekuda*, 24 June 1985.
23.   Michael Zvi Nehorai, 'ha-Tziyonut ha-Datit Nesoga bi-Fnei Geulatiyut Haredit', *Nekuda*, 15 September 1985.
24.   Yoel Bin-Nun, 'Derekh ha-Orot Mul Derekh ha-Setiya', *Nekuda*, 15 September 1985.
25.   Yosef Ben-Shlomo, 'Tziyonut shel Geula o Tziyonit shel Kupat Holim', *Nekuda*, 23 October 1985.
26.   Yosef Ben-Shlomo, 'Achen, Esh ha-Geula Yokedet be-Atzmoteinu', *Nekuda*, 27 May 1987. See also article by Mordechai Horovitz (also former laborite), 'le-Lo Meshihiyut Ein Tziyonut', *Nekuda*, October 1987.
27.   Moshe Simon, 'Am ha-Mitkahesh le-Yeudo', *Nekuda*, 15 September 1985.
28.   Yehuda Etzion, 'mi-Degel Yerushalayim leTenuat ha-Geula', *Nekuda*, 20 December 1985. See also his previous article: 'le-Hanif Sof Sof et Degel Yerushalayim', *Nekuda*, 22 November 1985.
29.   Dan Beeri, 'Tziyonut Yoter mi-Tamid', *Nekuda*, 21 January 1986. Dan Beeri is a convert to Judaism, born in Switzerland. His role in the underground was minor, and his sentence relatively light. He wrote the article after his release from jail.
30.   See article by Rabbi Moshe Shapira, 'Gush Emunim Tzarikh Lahazor bi-Teshuva', *Nekuda*, 11 July 1986.
31.   Yedidya Segal, 'be-khol Zot Leibowitz', *Nekuda*, 21 June 1984. See article by Eldad: 'Bein Professor Neeman le-Professor Leibowitch', *Nekuda*, 16 April 1984.
32.   Moshe Simon, 'Medinat Yisrael Mitnakeret le-Eretz Yisrael', *Nekuda*, 11 July 1986.
33.   Yitzhak Hanshke, 'Medina Al-Tenai', *Nekuda*, 28 August 1987. See also article by Rabbi Moshe Tzuriel: 'bi-Zekhut Yozmat Geula', *Nekuda*, 8 December 1986.
34.   See note 29.
35.   Dan Beeri, 'La-Akor et ha-Galut ha-Mithadeshet mi-Tokhenu', *Nekuda*, 3 October 1986.
36.   Dan Beeri, 'ha-Paradox shel Mihu Yehudi', *Nekuda*, 13 February 1987.
37.   Yehuda Zoldin, 'Pahot Imutim Yoter Mifgashim', *Nekuda*, 30 May 1986; Menahem Fruman, 'Likhbosh et Yetzer ha-Zilzul', *Nekuda*, 13 March 1987.
38.   Hanan Porat, 'Lo Hitzlahnu Lihiyot be-Ofen Rahav Nosei Orot', *Nekuda*, 11 July 1986. This approach also underlies his book: *Et Anat Ani Mevakesh*, Bet El, 1988.
39.   Eliezer Schweid, 'bi-Svakh ha-Shever, ha-Kituv veha-Harada', *Nekuda*, 23 March 1984.
40.   Eliezer Schweid, 'ha-Mahteret veha-Ideologia shel Gush Emunim', *Nekuda*, 6 July 1984.

CHAPTER 9: CONSERVATIVE LIBERALISM

1.   See 'Judaism and Liberalism', *Judaism*, Winter 1972.
2.   See *Congress Bi-Weekly*, 3:7, April 1967.
3.   See: Tenth Dialogue of the American Jewish Congress, 31 June 1972; 'The Relations between Jews and Revolutionary Forces', *Congress Bi-Weekly*, 30 March 1973.
4.   See: 'Liberalism and the Jews, A Symposium', *Commentary*, January 1980.
5.   See: Joseph Blau, 'Problems of Modern Jewish Thought', *Journal of Reform Judaism*, Fall 1978. Also ibid., William Cutter and Alan Henkin, 'Universalism and Particularism'.

6. Eugene Borowitz, *Reform Judaism Today*, New York, 1978. Book Three, pp. 182–84.
7. Ibid., Introduction, xvi–xvii.
8. Eugene Borowitz, 'Rethinking Reform Jewish Social Action', *Journal of Reform Judaism*, Fall 1980.
9. See: 'Liberalism and the Jews, A Symposium', *Commentary*, January 1980.
10. Eugene Borowitz, *The Masks Jews Wear: The Self-Deceptions of American Jewry*, New York, 1973, pp. 152, 167, 173.
11. *Reform Judaism Today*, p. 80.
12. See: 'What we Learned from the 1970's', *Sh'ma*, 11 January 1980.
13. Eugene Borowitz, *Liberal Judaism*, New York, 1984.
14. Ibid., p. 36.
15. Ibid., pp. 95, 135.
16. See: Richard B. Hirsch, 'Jewish Peoplehood – Implications for Reform Judaism', Central Conference of American Rabbis, *CCAR Yearbook*, 1979, p. 164–73. See also R. Hirsch, 'Confronting the New Historical Mood', *Forum*, Fall 1978, in which he refutes the negation of the Diaspora and insists on the mutual dependence between Israel and the Diaspora. See also: 'The Reform Movements', *Zionist Forum*, 1977, no. 26.
17. See: Gerald A. Goldman, 'One Hundred Years: What we have Learned'. *CCAR* Spring 1977, p. 25.
18. David Polish, 'We Do Not Take Israel Seriously Enough', *Sh'ma*, 16 September 1977.
19. Michael A. Meyer, Am ve-Emuna le-An? *CCAR Yearbook*, 1981, pp. 98–103.
20. Ibid., note 16.
21. 'Liberalism and the Jews, A Symposium', *Commentary*, January 1980.

CHAPTER 10: FROM CONCENTRATION TO CENTRALITY

1. Twenty-third Zionist Congress, Jerusalem, August 1951, published by the Zionist Executive, Jerusalem, p. 583 (Hebrew).
2. Twenty-seventh Zionist Congress, June 1968, published by Zionist Organization, Jerusalem, p. 503 (Hebrew).
3. Ibid., 106–7. See also speech of Rose Halprin, ibid., p. 110.
4. See ibid., p. 48.
5. Ibid., pp. 393–4.
6. Ibid., pp. 148–9.
7. Ibid., p. 514, clause 47.
8. See 28th Zionist Congress, January 1972, published by Zionist Organization Executive, p. 577.
9. A. Hertzberg, *Being Jewish in America: the Modern Experience*, New York 1979, pp. 272, 278.
10. 'Negating the Diaspora – A Symposium on the Zionist Idea'. *Jewish Frontier*, December 1979.
11. See: Arthur Hertzberg, op. cit. pp. 11–19. See also his address to a meeting of the Jewish Memorial Fund, 1982, 'The Jewish Intelligentsia and their Jewishness', *Jewish Ideas*, World Zionist Organization, no. 7, 1983, pp. 51–63.
12. David Polish, 'The Tasks of Israel and Galut', *Judaism*, Winter 1969. D. Polish, 'Israel and Galut', *Jewish Frontier*, March 1974.
13. David Polish, *Renew Our Days – the Zionist Issue in Reform*, Jerusalem, 1976, pp. 262–7. 'We do Not Take Israel Seriously Enough', *Sh'ma*, 16 September 1977;

'Negating the Diaspora', *Jewish Frontier*, December 1979; 'Golah and Moledet', *Forum*, Spring–Summer, 1978.

14.   See the document which Polish submitted to the ideological committee of the Zionist Organization in New York in 1985. Summary report, Jerusalem, 1985, pp. 12–15.

15.   See 'Negating the Diaspora – A Symposium', *Jewish Frontier*, December 1979.

16.   Ben Halpern, 'A Program for American Jews', *Jewish Frontier*, November 1971. See also: Jacob Cohen, 'Jews and Blacks, A Response to Ben Halpern', ibid., September 1971.

17.   Ben Halpern, *The American Jew, A Zionist Analysis*, first published 1957. Second edn, Postscript, New York, 1983, p. 179.

18.   See: Ben Halpern, 'Exile and Redemption, A Secular Zionist View', *Judaism*, Spring 1980. This was a response to Sharon Miller, 'The Zionist Thought of Ben Halpern', *Judaism*, Summer 1978.

19.   Isadore Twersky, 'Survival, Normalcy, Modernity', in: *Zionism in Transition*, ed. Moshe Davis, New York, 1980.

20.   Gershom Scholem, 'ha-Tziyonut – Dialektika shel Retzifut va-Mered', *Ein Shaananim be-Tziyon*, pp. 291–2. See as well: 'Zionism – Dialectic of Continuity and Rebellion', *Unease in Zion*, pp. 263–96.

21.   Ibid., p. 317. See also 'Yisrael veha-Golah', *Devarim be-Go*, 1974, pp. 133–44.

22.   'ha-Galut Nitrokna mi-Nitzanei ha-Geula', *Devarim be-Go*, pp. 219–22.

23.   E. Urbach, 'The Contemporary Meaning of Zionism', in: The 12th American–Israel Dialogue 1976, *Congress Monthly*, March–April 1977.

24.   E. Urbach, 'Muda'ut shel ha-Merkaz veha-Tefutzot be-Toldot Yisrael ule-Ahar Kum ha-Medina (1974)' *Al Tziyonut ve-Yahadut, Iyunim u-Masot*, Jerusalem, 1985, pp. 120–1. See also 'Darka u-Mashmauta shel ha-Tziyonut be-Yameinu', ibid., pp. 3–12.

25.   See: Ephraim Urbach, 'Zionism, The Moral Challenge', *Zionism in Transition*, p. 372.

26.   Jacob Katz, 'ha-Tziyonut veha-Zehut ha-Yehudit', *Leumiyut Yehudit – Masot u-Mehkarim*, ha-Sifriya ha-Tziyonit, 1979, pp. 82–4.

27.   Jacob Katz, 'The Core of Zionism, The 12th American–Israel Dialogue (1976)' *Congress Monthly*, March–April, 1977.

28.   Yeshayahu Leibowitz, *Al Olam u-Melo'o – Sihot im Michael Shashar*, Jerusalem, 1987, p. 28.

29.   Gershom Scholem, 'Hagigim Al Teologia Yehudit', *Devarim be-Go*, pp. 588–9.

30.   Yehoshua Arieli, 'On Being a Secular Jew in Israel', *Jerusalem Quarterly*, Winter 1988.

31.   Nathan Rotenstreich, 'Tmurot ba-Yahasim she-Bein Medinat Yisrael ve-Golat Yisrael (1975)', *Iyunim ba-Tziyonut ba-Zman ha-Zeh*, ha-Sifriya ha-Tziyonit, 1977, pp. 38–43.

32.   *Congress Monthly*, March–April, 1977.

33.   Nathan Rotenstreich, 'Shlilat ha-Golah Az ve-Ata', *Gesher*, Summer 1985.

34.   Nathan Rotenstreich, 'Al Normaliyut u-Vaayoteha (1975)', *Iyunim ba'Tziyonut ba-Zman ha-Zeh*. p. 81. See also: *Bein Medinat Yisrael veha-Tziyonut (1974)*, op. cit.

35.   See: 'Al Normaliyut ...'. See also: N. Rotenstreich, 'Zionism as Ideology and Historical Force', *Zionism in Transition*.

36.   See note 33.

37.   Shlomo Avineri, *ha-Raayon ha-Tziyoni li-Gvanav*, Tel-Aviv, 1980, pp. 247–57.

38.   'Negating the Diaspora – A Symposium', *Jewish Frontier*, December 1979.

39.   Shlomo Avineri, 'Mikhtav le-Yedid Yehudi be-America', *Maariv* 17 March 1987. See also his remarks in 'Is America Exile?' *Forum*, Spring 1988.

40.   ha-Raayon ha-Tziyoni, op. cit., pp. 253–6.

41. Eliezer Schweid, 'Shlilat ha-Golah ke-Yesod ha-Musar ha-Tziyoni', *mi-Yahadut le-Tziyonut, mi-Tziyonut le-Yahadut*, Jerusalem, 1984, pp. 162–8.
42. Eliezer Schweid, 'Ken Shlilat ha-Golah', ibid., p. 208.
43. Eliezer Schweid, 'Elements of Zionist Ideology and Practice', *Zionism in Transition*, p. 245.
44. Eliezer Schweid, 'Ken Shlilat ha-Golah', *mi-Yahadut le-Ziyonut ...*, pp. 201–2.
45. Eliezer Schweid, 'Israel as a Spiritual Center for the Diaspora'. *After Four Decades – The Responsibilities of Israel and the Diaspora to Jewish Life and Culture*, Memorial Foundation for Jewish Culture, 1988.
46. 'Kesem ha-Galut u-Veayat ha-Normalizatzia', *mi-Yahadut le-Tziyonut ...*, pp. 153–4.
47. Shmuel Ettinger, 'Zionism and its Significance Today', *Forum*, Winter 1978.

CHAPTER 11: RENEWED SEARCH FOR IDENTITY

1. See second part of interview conducted with him two years after the Six Day War, in Ehud Ben-Ezer, *Unease in Zion*, pp. 165–75.
2. Boaz Evron, *ha-Heshbon ha-Leumi*, Tel Aviv, 1988.
3. Ibid., pp. 410, 411, 424.
4. Boaz Evron, interview with Yediot Ahronot, 11 March 1988. See also his article, analysing the Canaanite outlook and its contemporary implications: Boaz Evron, 'Solutions and Problems'. *Jerusalem Quarterly*, 1987.
5. Boaz Evron, 'ha-Medina Adayin Lo Hukma', *Politika*, October 1987. See ibid., Yoram Kaniuk's emotional and forceful article 'Tzomet Akhzar', which expresses similar ideas. See also interview with the writer Binyamin Tamuz – 'Yesh Li Pehadim sheha-Tziyonut Tigrom le-Mapolet', *Yediot Ahronot*, 6 November 1987.
6. Joseph Agassi, *Bein Dat u-Leom: li-Krat Zehut Leumit Yisraelit*, (Religion and Nationality), Tel Aviv, 1984.
7. Joseph Agassi, 'Leumiyut Liberalit Kan ve-Akhshav', *Kivunim*, August 1985.
8. *Bein Dat u-Leom*, op. cit., pp. 198–204.
9. Ibid., pp. 220–1.
10. James S. Diamond, *Homeland or Holy Land? The Canaanite Critique of Israel*, Bloomington, Indiana 1986, p. 182.
11. See: *Israel: A Democratic Jewish Society Toward the 21st Century*, The Israel-Diaspora Institute, April 1986, p. 33. See also Bernard Avishai, 'To Praise Zionism and Bury It', *Moment*, October 1977. See also his book: *The Tragedy of Zionism*, New York, 1985, 373 pp.
12. 'Declaration of the Israeli Congress', *ha-Aretz*, 20 April 1988.
13. Three years previously the founders of the Israeli Congress, Yigal Elam and Zvi Kesseh, issued a manifesto entitled 'li-Krat Tziyonut Hevratit' (Towards Social Zionism), ha-Midrasha le-Tziyonut Hevratit, 1985. At the time they were still affiliated with the liberal-socialist wing of the Zionist consensus.
14. Yigal Elam to Shilo Gal, Head of the Etzion Bloc Regional Council.
15. Shulamit Aloni, 'mi-Leda ve-Ad Petira ve-Ad Bikhlal: Madua ha-Shem "Yisraeli" Ko Mekomem Otam?', *Politika*, October 1987.
16. Hillel Halkin, *Letters to an American Jewish Friend*, Philadelphia, 1977.
17. Ibid., pp. 238.
18. Ibid., p. 242.
19. Amos Oz, 'Sod ha-Kesem ha-Tziyoni', *be-Or ha-Tkhelet ha-Aza*, (Under this Blazing Light), Tel-Aviv, 1980.

20.   Amos Oz, *Po ve-Sham be-Eretz Yisrael*, Autumn 1982, (A Journey in Israel 1982),
      Tel-Aviv, 1983, p. 189.
21.   Ibid., p. 178.
22.   See A.B. Yehoshua, *bi-Zkhut ha-Normaliyut*, (Between Right and Right), Tel-Aviv,
      1980.
23.   A.B. Yehoshua, 'he-Hazon ha-Tziyoni shel ha-Normaliyut', *ha-Aretz*, 6 January
      1988.
24.   A.B. Yehoshua, *bi-Zkhut ...*, p. 21.
25.   Ibid., p. 45.
26.   *Mahu Yehudi (What is a Jew) – Symposium*, ed. A. Burg, World Jewish Congress,
      1987, p. 25.
27.   A.B. Yehoshua, Ani Yisraeli (I am an Israeli) – remarks at study day on 'Religious
      and Cultural Pluralism', held by the Spinoza Institute, Jerusalem – *Yediot Ahronot*,
      12 June 1987.
28.   See Chapter 6.
29.   Roy A. Rosenberg, 'Exile, Mysticism and Reality', in: *Diaspora*, ed. Etan Levine,
      New York, 1986, pp. 41–2.
30.   *Tikkun*, vol. 1, no. 1, September 1986.
31.   Leon Wieseltier, 'ha-Fantasia she-Nigzela', *Davar*, 25 March 1988.
32.   Leon Wieseltier, 'ha-Routinizatzia shel ha-Hagshama', *Nekuda*, October 1987.
33.   Arnold Eisen, *Galut – A Modern Jewish Reflection on Homelessness and Homecom-
      ing*, Bloomington: Indiana 1986.
34.   Arnold Eisen, *After Four Decades*, Memorial Foundation for Jewish Culture, 1988.
35.   Steven M. Cohen, 'The Self-Defeating Surplus', *Moment*, June 1987.
36.   Daniel Bell, 'Where are We?' *Moment*, 5 May 1986.
37.   David Sidorsky, 'Interpreting the Diaspora–Israel Relations', *Zionism Today, A
      Symposium*, The American-Jewish Committee, April 1986.
38.   See Fein's remarks in symposium on 'American Jews and Israel', *Commentary*,
      February 1988.
39.   Leonard Fein, *'Where are We?'* New York, 1988.
40.   See Fein, ibid., pp. 75, 79, 82, 86, 105, 110, 119, 127, 263, 284.
41.   Leonard Fein, 'No Need to Apologize', *Moment*. January–February 1980.
42.   It should be noted that at the 28th Zionist Congress in 1972, the venerable Kaplan
      (then aged 91) reiterated his idea of drawing up a constitution which would
      'strengthen and reformulate world Jewry as an organically-functioning society'.
      Congress Minutes, pp. 231–5.
43.   Jacob Neusner, *The Jewish War Against the Jews*, New York, 1984.
44.   'Can we be Zionists?' in *The Jewish War Against the Jews*, pp. 82, 85–6.
45.   Jacob Neusner, 'Zionism and Judaism', *World + 1*, January 1988, pp. 445–54.
46.   'Letters to the Editor', *Commentary*, 19 February 1988.
47.   This precis of Neusner's views is based on: Neusner, 'What has Israel Done for Us
      Lately?', *Interchange*, April 1976; Neusner, 'The Russian Jews Should go to Israel',
      National Jewish Post Opinion, 3 December 1986; and on his contribution to the sym-
      posium published by Maariv on the eve of Yom Kippur 1988, and a private letter to
      the author, August 1988.
48.   Jacob Neusner, 'The Spiritual Center', in: *A Stranger at Home*, Chicago 1981, p. 152.
49.   Neusner, *The Jewish War*, p. 1. See also *A Stranger at Home*, p. 101.
50.   Jacob Neusner, 'Understanding the Other: Israeli Views of Us, Our Views of Our-
      selves', *The Jewish War*, p. 114.
51.   Jacob Neusner, 'From Sentimentality to Ideology', *A Stranger ...*, p. 124.
52.   See: Neusner's speech at the central synagogue in São Paulo, 1988 (the text of which
      he kindly made available to the present author).

53. Jacob Neusner, 'Israel and Yavneh', *A Stranger ...* p. 164.
54. Jacob Neusner, *Death and Birth of Judaism*, New York, 1987, pp. 297, 335, 362–3.
55. Jacob Neusner, *Commentary*, Symposium, February 1988, p. 55.
56. *Washington Post*, 8 March 1987.
57. William Safire, *The Pollard Consequences*, *New York Times*, 3 September 1987.
58. Daniel J. Elazar 'Renewing the Zionist Vision', *Zionism in Transition*, Jerusalem, 1980, pp. 285–300. See also: Daniel J. Elazar (1) Toward a Jewish Definition of Statehood for Israel, (2) Zionism and the Future of Israel, (3) The State of World Jewry – A Contemporary Agenda, (4) Contemporary Jewry Between Two Revolutions: Center for Jewish Community Studies, Jerusalem.
59. Irving Greenberg, 'The Third Great Cycle of Jewish History', *Perspectives*, Clal, 1987, p. 14; 'The Third Era of Jewish History – Power and Politics', ibid, p. 46.
60. See Greenberg's article, 'In Praise of Dual Loyalty'.
61. The two-part article was written in the wake of the Pollard affair and was not published for various reasons. Greenberg was kind enough to make it available to me.
62. Howard Adelman, 'Land, Nation and State', *Israeli Democracy*, An Israel–Diaspora Institute Publication, Summer/Fall 1988.
63. In the first stage, Zionist seminaries were set up in seven cities: New York, Boston, Montreal, Toronto, Caracas, London, Paris and Capetown. In 1982 the members held an international meeting in Jerusalem, deliberations of which were published in *Zionist Ideas* (nos. 1–14), WZO, 1980–6.
64. 'Towards a Zionist Renaissance', *Zionist Ideas*, no. 5, December 1982, p. 52.
65. Ibid., p. 74.
66. Mervin F. Verbit, 'Zionism's Third stage', *Zionist Ideas*, no. 11, Summer 1985.
67. See Mervin Verbit, 'Jewish Identity and the Israel–Diaspora Dialogue', *Forum*, Spring 1983.
68. Ibid., p. 34. Similar views were voiced by Janice Stein of Canada in *Zionist Ideas*, no. 5, p. 79.
69. Sidney M. Schwartz, 'Redefining Zionism', ibid., pp. 36–45.
70. Henry Weinberg, 'The Status of Diaspora and Israel–Diaspora Relations', *Zionist Ideas*, no. 7, 1983, pp. 5–6.
71. Abraham Rothstein, 'A Post-Apocalyptic Diaspora', *Zionist Ideas*, no. 6, 1983, pp. 28–34.
72. See his statements in *Zionist Ideas*, no. 11, 1985, p. 62.
73. *Zionist Ideas*, no. 5 (Special Issue), December 1982, pp. 80–5.
74. Israel Finestein, 'An Approach to a New Emphasis', *Zionism in Transition*, pp. 301–6.
75. *Zionism in Transition*, pp. 67–70.
76. Stuart Eizenstat, 'We are Still One', *Moment*, January–February 1988. It is noteworthy that Eizenstat's remarks are highly reminiscent of the resolution of the 12th Dialogue of the American Jewish Congress of 1976. They too refer to the special place and status of Israel within the Jewish people; emphasize the mutual dependence of Jewish communities; note that immigration is the final stage of a process of involvement in national affairs; and assign to Zionism the task of consolidating the self-awareness and solidarity of the various diasporas. See: *Congress Monthly*, March–April 1977.
77. Henry Siegman, 'li-Krat Tziyonut Hadasha', *ha-Aretz*, 6 April 1988.
78. Ismar Schorsch, 'A Light unto the Nations', a speech delivered in a debate on Zionism held by the Conservative Movement in New York, September 1988.
79. Reference is to Nathan Rotenstreich's definition, cited in this work, and to the resolution passed at the 12th Israel-American Dialogue, *Congress Monthly*, March–April, 1977.
80. On this see views of Jacob Neusner and Leonard Fein as elucidated in this chapter.

81.   *The pessimists*:
      'Irving Greenberg, 'Will there be one Jewish People by the Year 2000?' *Perspect-*
      ives, Clal, 1987; I.G., 'The One in 2000 Controversy', *Moment*, March 1987; B.A.
      Koskin, P. Ritterband and J. Schenker, 'Jewish Population in the USA 1986', North
      American Jewish Data Bank, Reprint no. 1 1987; See: Yeshayahu Liebman, 'Ekhut
      ha-Hayyim ha-Yehudiyim be-America', *Gesher*, Spring 1988, p. 47; S.M. Cohen and
      Ch. S. Liebman, 'The Quality of American Jewish Life – Two Views', AJC 1987.
      The optimists:
      Charles E. Silberman, *A Certain People – American Jews and their Lives Today*,
      New York, 1985. Also interview with the author in *Moment*, September 1985;
      S.M. Cohen and C. Goldscheider, 'Jews More or Less', *Moment*, September 1984;
      S.M. Cohen, 'The One in 2000 Controversy', *Moment*, March 1987; Calvin
      Goldscheider, *The American Jewish Community*, Brown Studies, 1986.

82.   See Shlomo Avineri, 'Mikhtav le-Yedid Yehudi be-America', *Maariv*, 17 March
      1987; Annette Dulzin, 'The Spy and the American Jew', *New York Times*, 7 Septem-
      ber 1986. In this article she discusses the illogical sense of exile of American Jews
      whom she met during a tour of various communities during the Pollard affair. The
      present author can attest to conversations with Jewish intellectuals and public figures
      in the United States at the time, who confessed voluntarily to a shortlived sense of
      '*galut*' anxiety when the existence of an American Jewish spy for Israel was
      revealed.

83.   Steven M. Cohen: 'Israel in the Jewish Identity of American Jews', in: *Jewish*
      Identity in America. ed. David M. Gordis and Yoav Ben-Horin. Los Angeles, 1991,
      p. 121. See also: S.M. Cohen, *American Modernity and Jewish Identity*, New York,
      1983.

84.   See: Stuart E. Eizenstat: 'American Jews and Israel', in: *American Modernity and*
      Jewish Identity, p. 139.

85.   Michael A. Meyer: *Jewish Identity in the Modern World*, Seattle, 1990, p. 81.

86.   Ibid., p. 82.

87.   Eizenstat, p. 155.

88.   David Vital: *The Future of the Jews; A People at the Crossroads?* Cambridge, Mass.
      1990, p. 148.

Index